"I constantly encourage students and pastors to [...] in the early church from the pulpit, in classes [...] The common response, which opens a window [...] knowledge and in the church's history with w[...] can I find those stories?' *Christian Women in the Patristic World* is now the answer, as it populates that bleak landscape with dynamic women. This is a book for every pastor's and teacher's bookshelf because it not only tells stories about women but also shows how the early church, which has often been maligned for its reputation when it comes to women, was more formed by women than many know."

—**Scot McKnight**, Northern Seminary

"Poet Mourid Al Barghouti has famously said, 'If you want to dispossess a people, the simplest way to do it is to tell their story and to start with, "secondly."' If we start with Basil of Caesarea and Gregory of Nyssa and not with Macrina, their sister, who influenced and guided them, we end up with a truncated understanding of Cappadocian theology. If we start with Augustine the bishop and not with Monica's influence on her son, we will scarcely understand the Theologian of the Heart. In this book, Cohick and Hughes begin where good history ought to begin: with 'firstly.' They bring to the fore the often overlooked protomartyrs, theologians, teachers, ascetics, and politicians of the early church—the dispossessed women whose stories animated the imagination of Christians for centuries and whose influence, authority, and legacy has been preserved in the literary and material record. This is an exceptional book."

—**George Kalantzis**, Wheaton Center for Early Christian Studies, Wheaton College

"Lynn Cohick and Amy Brown Hughes bring a welcome gift to patristic scholarship and to the classroom with this volume. Skillfully weaving together the most recent and cogent scholarship on women in early Christianity, they successfully show the critical and integrative contributions of early Christian women to the complex development of Christian theology, literature, liturgy, and monasticism. Theologically nuanced, historically informed, contextually careful, and delightfully written, this book will both enlighten and challenge readers, scholars, and students alike."

—**Helen Rhee**, Westmont College

"This sophisticated and wide-ranging study will be of great interest to anyone concerned with the status and roles of women in the early Christian world. Abundantly illustrated and sensitive to the many problems of interpretation posed by sources, it takes us on an exhilarating ride from the second to the fifth century. Cohick and Hughes model the practice of 'responsible remembrance' that they encourage in their readers."

—**David G. Hunter**, University of Kentucky

# CHRISTIAN WOMEN
## in the
# PATRISTIC WORLD

### Their Influence, Authority, and Legacy
### in the Second through Fifth Centuries

## Lynn H. Cohick
## and Amy Brown Hughes

**Baker Academic**

*a division of Baker Publishing Group*
Grand Rapids, Michigan

Published by Baker Academic
a division of Baker Publishing Group
P.O. Box 6287, Grand Rapids, MI 49516-6287
www.bakeracademic.com

Printed in the United States of America

Library of Congress Cataloging-in-Publication Data
Names: Cohick, Lynn H., author. | Hughes, Amy Brown, author.
Title: Christian women in the patristic world : their influence, authority, and legacy in the second through fifth centuries / Lynn H. Cohick and Amy Brown Hughes.
Description: Grand Rapids, MI : Baker Academic, 2017. | Includes bibliographical references and index.
Identifiers: LCCN 2017018733 | ISBN 9780801039553 (pbk. : alk. paper)
Subjects: LCSH: Women in Christianity—History—Early church, ca. 30–600.
Classification: LCC BR195.W6 C625 2017 | DDC 270.1082—dc23
LC record available at https://lccn.loc.gov/2017018733

17  18  19  20  21  22  23        7  6  5  4  3  2  1

*To Scott and Sally Harrison,*
*parents of Lynn H. Cohick*


*To Yvonne Brown,*
*grandmother of Amy Brown Hughes,*
*memory eternal!*

# Contents

# Illustrations

# Acknowledgments

A casual conversation, sharing a similar vision about research into early Christian women, grew over three years into this book. We are indebted to family, friends, and colleagues who encouraged and supported our efforts over the last few years as the dream became a reality. We are grateful to James Ernest, then executive editor at Baker Academic, who supported and guided this project through its initial stages. His encouragement and wise counsel helped shape its content and scope. James handed over the reins of the project to the capable hands of Bryan Dyer, acquisitions editor at Baker Academic. We deeply appreciate the energy and sound advice he provided in bringing this book to completion.

To the Wheaton College PhD students Jeremy Otten and Caleb Friedeman, many thanks for your painstaking editing and double-checking footnotes and bibliography. We express gratitude to Emrie Smith, a Christian Ministries major at Gordon College, for her careful help indexing our volume.

Thanks also to the editors, Carrie Schroeder and Catherine Chin, and the other contributors to *Melania: Early Christianity through the Life of One Family* for granting us access to your marvelous book ahead of its release date (University of California Press, 2016).

I (Lynn) am thankful for Wheaton College providing me a yearlong sabbatical to get to know the characters that animate these ancient stories and explore the lives of these ancient women. And I am grateful to the women in my family who shaped me: my mother, Sally, my sister, Ann Louise, and my grandmother, Elise Louise Garden Duncan Harrison, whose stories of life in the early 1900s fascinated me and planted the love of history deep within me.

I (Amy) am thankful for Gordon College granting me some space in my first-year teaching schedule to bring this book to fruition and for my husband, Benjie, who listened to all my stories about Thecla and Macrina and empresses. I am also grateful to George Kalantzis, my *Doktorvater* and friend who helped me to learn how not to hedge or hesitate and to speak boldly and take risks. Many women have shepherded, mentored, and taught me over the years. I am grateful for my mom and my sister, my dear friends and colleagues from my graduate work at Wheaton, and those who have pastored me from their kitchen tables and from the pulpit.

# Abbreviations

## General

| | | | |
|---|---|---|---|
| AM | *anno mundi* (in the year of the world) | esp. | especially |
| | | ET | English translation |
| b. | born | et al. | *et alii*, and others |
| BCE | before the Common Era | i.e. | *id est*, that is |
| ca. | *circa*, approximately | NASB | New American Standard Version |
| CE | Common Era | repr. | reprint(ed) |
| cf. | *confer*, compare | rev. | revised (by) |
| chap(s). | chapter(s) | sing. | singular |
| d. | died | trans. | translator(s), translated by |
| ed(s). | editor(s), edited by, edition | | |

## Ancient Sources

| | |
|---|---|
| *Aen.* | Virgil, *Aeneid* |
| *An.* | Gregory of Nyssa, *De anima et resurrectione cum sorore sua Macrina dialogus* (*Dialogue on the Soul and the Resurrection with His Sister Macrina*) |
| *An.* | Tertullian, *De anima* (*On the Soul*) |
| *Ann.* | Tacitus, *Annales* (*Annals*) |
| APTh | Acts of Paul and Thecla |
| Barn. | Epistle of Barnabas |
| *Beat.* | Augustine, *De vita beata* (*On the Happy Life*) |
| *Cels.* | Origen, *Contra Celsum* (*Against Celsus*) |
| *Chron.* | John Malalas, *Chronicon* (*Chronicle*) |
| Chron. Pasch. | [anonymous], Chronicon Paschale (Paschal Chronicle) |
| *Conf.* | Augustine, *Confessiones* (*Confessions*) |
| 1 Cor. | 1 Corinthians |

| | |
|---|---|
| *Dial.* | Justin Martyr, *Dialogus cum Tryphone* (*Dialogue with Trypho*) |
| Did. | Didache (Teaching of the Twelve Apostles) |
| *Ep.* | [various authors], *Epistulae* (*Epistles/Letters*) |
| Eph. | Ephesians |
| Exod. | Exodus |
| Ezek. | Ezekiel |
| Gal. | Galatians |
| Gen. | Genesis |
| *Haer.* | Hippolytus, *Refutatio omnium haeresium* (*Refutation of All Heresies*) |
| *Haer.* | Irenaeus, *Adversus haereses* (*Against Heresies*) |
| Heb. | Hebrews |
| *Hist.* | Livy, *Ab urbe condita libri* (*Books from the Foundation of the City = History of Rome [and the Roman People]*) |
| *Hist.* | Rufinus, *Eusebii Historia ecclesiastica a Rufino translata et continuata* (*Eusebius's "Ecclesiastical History" Translated and Continued by Rufinus*) |
| *Hist. eccl.* | Eusebius, *Historia ecclesiastica* (*Ecclesiastical History*) |
| *Hist. eccl.* | Evagrius Scholasticus, *Historia ecclesiastica* (*Ecclesiastical History*) |
| *Hist. eccl.* | Socrates Scholasticus, *Historia ecclesiastica* (*Ecclesiastical History*) |
| *Hist. eccl.* | Sozomen, *Historia ecclesiastica* (*Ecclesiastical History*) |
| *Hist. eccl.* | Theodoret of Cyrrhus, *Historia ecclesiastica* (*Ecclesiastical History*) |
| *Hist. Laus.* | Palladius, *Historia Lausiaca* (*Lausiac History*) |
| Ign. *Smyrn.* | Ignatius, *To the Smyrnaeans* |
| *It. Eg.* | Egeria, *Itinerarium Egeriae* (*Itinerary of Egeria*) |
| 1–2 Macc. | 1–2 Maccabees |
| Matt. | Matthew |
| *Mor.* | Plutarch, *Moralia* (*Morals = Customs and Mores*) |
| Num. | Numbers |
| *Ob. Theo.* | Ambrose, *De obitu Theodosii* (*On the Obituary of Theodosius*) |
| *Or.* | Gregory of Nazianzus, *Oratio* (*Oration*) |
| *Ord.* | Augustine, *De ordine* (*On Order*) |
| *Paed.* | Clement of Alexandria, *Paedagogus* (*Christ the Educator*) |
| *Pan.* | Epiphanius, *Panarion* (*Adversus haereses*) (*Refutation of All Heresies*) |
| Pass. | Passion of Perpetua and Felicitas |
| Phil. | Philippians |
| Pol. *Phil.* | Polycarp, *To the Philippians* |
| Ps(s). | Psalm(s) |
| *Pud.* | Tertullian, *De pudicitia* (*On Modesty*) |
| Rev. | Revelation |
| Rom. | Romans |
| 1 Sam. | 1 Samuel |
| *Serm.* | Augustine of Hippo, *Sermones* (*Sermons*) |
| Song | Song of Songs |
| *Stat.* | John Chrysostom, *Ad populum Antiochenum de statuis* (*To the People of Antioch, about the Statues*) |
| *Symp.* | Methodius of Olympus, *Symposium sive Convivium decem virginum* (*Symposium, or Banquet of the Ten Virgins*) |
| 2 Tim. | 2 Timothy |

| Vit. Const. | Eusebius, *Vita Constantini* (*Life of Constantine*) |
| Vit. Macr. | Gregory of Nyssa, *Vita s. Macrinae* (*Life of St. Macrina*) |
| Vit. Mel. | Gerontius, *Vita Sanctae Melaniae Iunioris* (*Life of the Holy Melania the Younger*) |

## Journals, Series, and Collections

| AARTTS | American Academy of Religion Texts and Translations Series |
| ACO | *Acta Conciliorum Oecumenicorum*. Edited by Eduard Schwartz et al. Berlin: de Gruyter, 1914–84. |
| ACW | Ancient Christian Writers |
| AThR | *Anglican Theological Review* |
| AYBRL | Anchor Yale Bible Reference Library |
| BibInt | Biblical Interpretation Series |
| BRev | *Bible Review* |
| CAGN | Reardon, Bryan P. *Collected Ancient Greek Novels*. Berkeley: University of California Press, 1989. New ed., 2008. |
| CCEL | Christian Classics Ethereal Library. https://www.ccel.org/. |
| CCR | Columbia Classics in Religion |
| CCSL | Corpus Christianorum: Series Latina. Turnhout: Brepols, 1953–. |
| CH | *Church History* |
| CIL | *Corpus Inscriptionum Latinarum*. Berlin, 1862–. |
| ClQ | *Classical Quarterly* |
| CSHJ | Chicago Studies in the History of Judaism |
| ECF | Early Church Fathers |
| ExpTim | *Expository Times* |
| FC | Fathers of the Church |
| FCNTECW | Feminist Companion to the New Testament and Early Christian Writings |
| GCS | Die griechischen christlichen Schriftsteller der ersten [drei] Jahrhunderte |
| GNO | Gregorii Nyssenni Opera |
| GTR | Gender, Theory, and Religion |
| Historia | *Historia: Zeitschrift für alte Geschichte* (University of Erfurt) |
| HTR | *Harvard Theological Review* |
| Hug | *Hugoye: Journal of Syriac Studies* |
| JBL | *Journal of Biblical Literature* |
| JECS | *Journal of Early Christian Studies* |
| JFSR | *Journal of Feminist Studies in Religion* |
| JLA | *Journal of Late Antiquity* |
| JRS | *Journal of Roman Studies* |
| JTS | *Journal of Theological Studies* |
| LCL | Loeb Classical Library |
| MAMA | *Monumenta Asiae Minoris Antiqua*. Manchester and London, 1928–93. |
| NovTSup | Supplements to Novum Testamentum |
| NPNF[1] | *The Nicene and Post-Nicene Fathers*, Series 1. Edited by P. Schaff. Repr., Peabody, MA: Hendrickson, 1994. |

| | |
|---|---|
| *NPNF*² | *The Nicene and Post-Nicene Fathers*, Series 2. Edited by P. Schaff and H. Wace. Repr., Peabody, MA: Hendrickson, 2004. |
| OECS | Oxford Early Christian Studies |
| OECT | Oxford Early Christian Texts |
| PG | Patrologia Graeca [= Patrologiae cursus completus: Series graeca]. Edited by J.-P. Migne. 162 vols. Paris, 1857–86. |
| PO | Patrologia Orientalis |
| SC | Sources chrétiennes |
| SCH | Studies in Church History |
| SHR | Studies in the History of Religions (supplements to Numen) |
| *SJRS* | *Scottish Journal of Religious Studies* |
| StPatr | Studia Patristica |
| SWR | Studies in Women and Religion |
| *TJT* | *Toronto Journal of Theology* |
| *VC* | *Vigiliae Christianae* |
| VCSup | Supplements to Vigiliae Christianae |
| WUNT | Wissenschaftliche Untersuchungen zum Neuen Testament |
| YCS | Yale Classical Studies |
| ZAC | *Zeitschrift für Antikes Christentum / Journal of Ancient Christianity* |

# Time Line of Major Persons and Events

Acts of Paul and Thecla, mid-second century (ca. 150)?

Passion of Perpetua and Felicitas, 203

Diocletian, emperor 284–305

Helena, ca. 284–ca. 329

Great Persecution, 303–13

Constantine, emperor 306–37, sole emperor 324–37

Methodius of Olympus, author of the *Symposium*, dies ca. 311

Edict of Milan, 313

Council of Nicaea, 325

Melania the Elder, ca. 341–ca. 410

Monica, ca. 332–87

Marcella, ca. 325–410

Gregory of Nyssa, ca. 335–ca. 395

Macrina, ca. 327–79

Paula, 347–404

Jerome, ca. 347–420

Augustine of Hippo, 354–430

Theodosius I, emperor 379–95

Council of Constantinople, 381

Melania the Younger, ca. 385–ca. 439

Egeria, late fourth–early fifth century

Sack of Rome by the Visigoths, 410

Theodosius II, emperor 408–50

Cyril, bishop of Alexandria, 412–44

Pulcheria, 399–453

Eudocia, ca. 400–460

Council of Chalcedon, 451

Robber Synod, 449

Council of Ephesus, 431

Nestorius, bishop of Constantinople, 428–31

Leo, pope of Rome, 440–61

# Introduction

After sitting for three days listening to his message, she made a fateful decision that would change the course of her life and the lives of countless others for centuries to come. Her choice established a norm for faithful conduct and inspired generations of men and women to forgo their ordinary life for one of celibacy and asceticism. Her life was used as a meme for theological and philosophical reflection and ethical direction. Her name was Thecla, the protomartyr whose story in the Acts of Paul and Thecla reverberated from the mid-second century well into the Middle Ages. A member of a leading family in her city, Thecla was engaged to wed a young man from another wealthy household. Then she heard Paul's gospel message, and she changed the direction of her life.[1] Thecla's story sprouted in the second century, and her influence mushroomed as a myriad of others modeled their life on hers, visited shrines dedicated to her, and bought clay votive lamps with her image and symbols stamped upon them.

This book explores stories of women like Thecla, women who helped construct the growing Christian movement and left their legacy in devotional practices, written texts, and glittering mosaics. We look at Perpetua, an early martyr whose testimony, "I am a Christian," sealed her fate and was memorialized in the yearly liturgical cycle of the church. We examine the visual witness to Christian beliefs preserved in Rome's catacombs in the late second to fourth centuries. Overlapping this underground activity,

---

1. For an English translation, see Wilhelm Schneemelcher, ed., *New Testament Apocrypha*, trans. R. McL. Wilson, rev. ed. (Louisville: Westminster John Knox, 1992), 2:239–46. See also Jeremy W. Barrier, *The Acts of Paul and Thecla*, WUNT 2/270 (Tübingen: Mohr Siebeck, 2009).

Helena, mother of Constantine the Great, declared her Christian identity by opening the imperial coffers to build imposing basilicas in Jerusalem and Bethlehem. Both Helena and Egeria, a wealthy woman from the western edges of the empire, set out on pilgrimages; and we discover that these journeys were much more than personal quests for spiritual renewal. We study another influential mother, Monica, the mother of Augustine, who is remembered by her son for her tireless commitment to prayer for his salvation, her bright mind for philosophical dialogue, and her maturity in faith that drew them both into communion with God. We meet Macrina, who embraced the monastic life and guided her brothers, Gregory of Nyssa and Basil of Caesarea, in spiritual and philosophical teachings. Melania the Elder and her granddaughter, Melania the Younger, along with Paula and Marcella, give us examples of aristocrats-turned-ascetics who abdicated their wealth and powerful societal positions in order to establish monasteries, promote scholarship, and participate in key doctrinal discussions of their day, such as the protracted controversy over Origen's teachings. We also examine two empresses of the Theodosian court, Pulcheria and Eudocia. Pulcheria was the powerful sister of the Christian emperor Theodosius II and a dedicated virgin who influenced two of the most important councils in church history; Eudocia became Theodosius's wife, as well as a poet and pilgrim who was often at odds with the imperial house.

The perceptive reader will have picked up the recurring themes of virginity and asceticism woven within these women's lives. These were more than lifestyle commitments; they reflect deep theological convictions shared by male theologians of the early church. The women in our book also contributed to the lively contemporary philosophical discussions surrounding human nature, the human body, and the future of humanity. Women like Paula and Melania the Elder participated in these debates and helped shape early Christianity with their intellectual acuity, their desire to live lives marked by devotion to God, and the authority that accompanied a chaste lifestyle.

The early church historian Peter Brown coined the phrase "men use women to think with," drawing on the anthropologist Claude Lévi-Strauss.[2] This is certainly true, but perhaps not the whole truth. Our study reveals men and women thinking together about the nature of the Christian church and its teachings. The women considered in our book captured the imagination of average Christian pilgrims, learned male authors, and government officials. Indeed, some of the women we discuss exercised authority in the imperial

2. Peter Brown, *The Body and Society: Men, Women, and Sexual Renunciation in Early Christianity*, new ed., CCR (New York: Columbia University Press, 2008), 153.

government, wrote influential prose and poetry, and traveled on pilgrimage and established basilicas and martyr shrines and relics. This book celebrates their legacy.

## Why We Wrote This Book

Sometimes it happens in a single moment, a chance comment, a juxtaposition of text and circumstance. You sense you have glimpsed the tip of the iceberg and feel compelled to explore. This book grew out of such experiences. In graduate school in the 1980s, I (Lynn) read Julian of Norwich's *Showings*; I was pregnant with my first child. The juxtaposition is important, for Julian's vision includes a rich reflection on Christ as our Mother. This fourteenth-century anchorite gave me my first glimpse of women's influence and authority in the life of the church. I wanted to investigate more and plunged into the church fathers' work. If reading Julian's *Showings* was like a walk in a gentle summer rain, then Tertullian's hateful comment, "Woman is the devil's gateway,"[3] stung like hail in a thunderstorm. I decided to abandon the exploration for a time, for lack of a suitable guide to help navigate the unfamiliar terrain. Recent scholarship, however, has provided important methodological insights that allow today's readers to navigate the early Christian texts' rhetoric concerning women and the category of female. Greater attention is now paid to the role and influence of women in theological conversations and controversies. It seemed a good time to resume my journey into the world of Christian women in the early church.

I (Amy) am often asked why I became a historical theologian of early Christianity, what it was that gripped my imagination and pricked my desire to contribute to the two-thousand-year-old conversation by Christians speaking about God. For me it was sitting in an undergraduate class and hearing about the controversial second-century prophetesses Priscilla and Maximilla. All of a sudden my charismatic tradition, which before had seemed to me to be a novel force for mobilizing the church, had a history beyond the New Testament. Almost fifteen years later and on the cusp of doctoral work, I was approached by Sarah, a twenty-year-old pastor's daughter, after a service at my small urban church in Aurora, Illinois. She asked, "What is my role now in the church as a single, young adult woman? Where do I fit?" I knew Sarah well, and her earnest question confirmed that part of my journey as a theologian was to answer her question. This book gave me the opportunity to tell some stories about women in early Christianity and

3. Tertullian, *On the Apparel of Women* (*De cultu feminarum*) 1.1.1–3 (CCSL 1.343–44).

how they were instrumental in constructing the church and its teachings in various ways.

## How We Wrote This Book

This book emerged as a joint effort to explore Christian women's lives and thought in the early church through the Late Antique period, roughly the second through the fifth centuries. It attempts to fill out the reader's knowledge of the historical periods and provide helpful strategies for interpreting the documents and archaeological evidence in their theological and historical settings. For example, this historical period saw the establishment of creeds and doctrines as church councils, made up of male clerics and scholars, defined Christian doctrine. But this is only part of what happened—and if this half is told as though it is the entire story, a false impression is created that women were ancillary to the development of the church's doctrines and practices. As our study shows, however, women made numerous contributions to theological discussions and religious practices.

### Advocating Agency: Negotiating Virtues in the Ancient World

Our approach stands over against both those works of modern scholarship that simply lament and dismiss the church fathers as hopelessly misogynistic, as well as those that take a naive, pious perspective on the evidence, for both approaches fail to deal analytically with the sources. Within these early Christian writings, we find disparaging comments about women or the female sex as well as active engagement and genuine conversation with learned women. We do not read the church fathers' statements about women as direct windows into church doctrine and practice; rather, we nuance these texts by considering the ways women themselves shaped their lives and their social worlds. As Susan Hylen observes with reference to the Acts of Paul and Thecla, the text does "give insight into what the author wanted to persuade the audience of, and what he assumed they would take for granted."[4] She makes the important observation that a society's key values and dispositions are negotiated by the individuals within it; and they decide how to convey civic virtues by choosing among multiple options in expressing those values. For example, she notices that key virtues incumbent upon women included showing loyalty to family; exhibiting modesty in dress, speech, and interaction with men; and working

---

4. Susan E. Hylen, *A Modest Apostle: Thecla and the History of Women in the Early Church* (Oxford: Oxford University Press, 2015), 7.

industriously. Showing loyalty to family might necessitate a public statement; however, a public statement might be viewed as immodest. Individuals dealt with these multiple social norms in creative and integrative ways,[5] such that a modest matron might offer a public statement or gesture on behalf of her city—and be considered entirely modest.

Hylen perceptively points out the problems with dividing the ancient social world into two diametrically opposite spheres: the private/female sphere and the public/male sphere. And she rejects the assumption that female agency can be seen only in countercultural resistant postures. This older form of argument often concluded that women primarily chose celibacy to resist patriarchy within marriage. Hylen suggests instead that women chose celibacy as an expression of their society's expectations of modesty. She points to Thecla and states, "Early readers would have likely understood Thecla's modesty and leadership as a coherent part of a single picture."[6] Ancient women could express their agency by conforming to their society's values even as their act of performing these values also shaped these very values. Modern readers might see a contradiction in the text that the ancient reader would accept as appropriate for the given occasion. For example, the second-century reader might have seen as natural "the appearance of women in leadership roles because domestic virtues took on added importance as evidence of civic responsibility."[7]

Nevertheless, women often faced an uphill march in pursuing their goals. We examine the many obstacles (ideological, cultural, theological, and political) that prevented women, in general and within Christianity, from living their lives to the same full extent that was available for men of comparable rank and station. We pay close attention to the rhetorical and historical contexts of these men's reports in order to bring early Christian women into greater focus. Our book seeks to paint a general landscape of possibilities for women based on public records, physical evidence such as inscriptions or catacomb art, and texts. We understand that the visual and textual representation of a woman may be grounded in the events of her life, and also that such representation informed the religious identity of the community that embraced the figure. The evidence shows that these women carried theological influence, as we will see with Gregory of Nyssa's remembrance of his sister Macrina as an authority on christological imitation and on the nature of the resurrection (chap. 7) and with Melania the Elder's involvement with the Origenist

5. Ibid., 17.
6. Ibid., 74.
7. Ibid., 11.

controversy, a wide-ranging debate on the reception of some of the more speculative teachings of Origen, including the nature of the resurrected body and the preexistence of souls (see chap. 8). Our hope is that this book will attract readers who are exploring the patristic period and educate them about the lives of the most important women from this period, so that their influence can be better integrated into the history of the church. To accomplish this, we must explain our approach in greater detail as it relates to the study of women more generally.

## Advocating Contextual Reading: Paying Attention to Historical Context

A historical subject is necessarily contextualized, having lived, thought, and acted in a past age. This contextualization is the basis of her authority to speak informatively about her historical period, but she is also very much a part of that age, not living in a historical vacuum. She grew up with a set of values, had specific understandings of how the world works, how things should and should not be. These views, beliefs, and observations are not necessarily reflective of what we might today consider "true." Again, these beliefs were not static but were shaped and reshaped by people of that time as they negotiated their culture's virtues and values. What it means is that historical subjects, such as Christian men and women, are constituted by their experience; however, experience is not the sole property of the subjects: they are in fact formed through experience. Experience is not the base from which "true" history springs; it is "at once always already an interpretation *and* is in need of interpretation."[8] Experiences as reflected in ancient texts cannot be taken as read without seeing their rhetorical and political nature. Said another way, we reject the idea that historians can simply read and understand a text and then turn around to present their findings to the world, free of any agenda or binding theoretical system. Experience needs explanation. Experience will not grant the historian unmediated access for the reconstitution of women in history.

## Advocating "Responsible Remembrance": Feminism and Christian History

Poor Pandora! According to Greek mythology, not only was she created as a punishing "gift" after man had stolen fire from Prometheus, but also she, the first of womankind, opened a jar out of curiosity and released all kinds of

---

8. Joan Wallach Scott, *Gender and the Politics of History*, rev. ed. (New York: Columbia University Press, 1999), 37.

evil. This story not only denigrates the creation of woman but also blames her for the ills of the world. Pandora introduces difference into a homogeneous world by her very presence, her femininity a dangerous enigma that brings catastrophe.[9] Pandora serves as the archetype for the dangerous female, and women have been trying to shake or reconstruct (or at times embrace) this myth ever since. Broadly speaking, the effort to stamp out Pandora's reputation reflects the aim of feminist interpretation: to shake off the misconceptions of women as dangerous other and to reconstruct history in order to include women's contributions and those of other marginalized groups.

Feminists have shone the spotlight on history and literature, demonstrating how the oppression of women is deeply entrenched, systemically permeating political structures, domestic life, and religious devotion. Of course, Christianity is not immune to the charge of denigrating women and in fact has often been the appropriated force behind the subjugation of women and even the instigator of atrocities against various groups of women. Because of this oppressive norm, feminists read texts with a hermeneutics of suspicion, assuming that the author is reflecting a patriarchal bias. Yet even in the most oppressive of societies and situations, we have examples of women living their lives with creative energy and mobility, taking opportunities as they arise, owning agency and demonstrating religious conviction in ways that surprise modern sensibilities, and contributing to the variegated story of early Christianity.

We are fortunate enough to have accounts of some of these ancient and modern women. Sometimes their presence is redacted or reconstrued by a male writer for various reasons (not all nefarious), and sometimes we have the prospect of entering the world of such a one directly through diaries or other writings. We do not have nearly enough of these accounts, but what we do find is that Christian women often had to navigate the tricky congress between their femaleness and the faith, tradition, and Scriptures that they held so dear.

In this book we will be looking at women of various regions, backgrounds, situations, and temperaments from the earliest centuries of Christianity and remembering the many ways they assumed authority, exercised power, and shaped not only their legacy but also the legacy of Christianity. This remembrance is self-aware. Perhaps controversially, this remembrance is not a neutral reading; rather, this reading is functionally an "admission of advocacy," a speaking for the participation of the other, those who have been relegated

---

9. Vered Lev Kenaan renders Pandora as introducing "difference" into the world of interpreting classical texts in *Pandora's Senses: The Feminine Character of the Ancient Text*, Wisconsin Studies in Classics (Madison: University of Wisconsin Press, 2008).

and silenced.[10] For our sake and for the sake of others, we need to commit to advocacy and practice what Justo González calls "responsible remembrance."[11]

Advocacy is a necessary position when it comes to the activity of remembering the contributions of early Christian women. Because for the most part their personages are recorded only through the pens of male writers, it is not always clear as to where women fit into that new culture of Christianity. Unfortunately, this pattern continues for centuries, leaving women to ask, "Where is my place between Eve and Mary, heroine and servant, saint and whore?"[12] Part of the role for advocates for early Christian women is to bear the responsibility to critique the patriarchal norm and the vitriolic language used by some of the church fathers, such as Tertullian. And the responsibility extends to considering positive views of women found in these texts as well. As Susanne Heine observes, "There is no doubt that a history of Christian hostility to women can be written, but so too can a history of Christian friendliness towards women."[13]

Furthermore, we should not be surprised to find early Christian writers' interpretations of the biblical texts laced with contextual gender ideologies. It is all the more important, then, to read these texts with a keen eye toward the cultural, interpretive, and theological assumptions present at that time. As modern readers we will bring our own assumptions to bear on the biblical text and its interpretation; this is unavoidable. As a result, we might be put off by how these biblical women are portrayed by the church fathers. Our reading should be one of advocacy for a more inclusive gender framework in reading the biblical text; yet our reading of these ancient interpreters should also be marked by charity. We must take into account that a writer cannot excuse himself from his context and the information available at the time. But this charity does not mean we excuse the author's silencing or oppression of women because "that's just how it was back then."

### Early Christian Women and Theology

A fundamental presupposition of this project is that women were instrumental in the construction of Christian identity and theology in the

10. Mary Ann Tolbert, "Defining the Problem: The Bible and Feminist Hermeneutics," in *The Bible and Feminist Hermeneutics*, ed. Mary Ann Tolbert, Semeia 28 (Chico, CA: Scholars Press, 1983), 118.
11. Justo González, *Mañana: Christian Theology from a Hispanic Perspective* (Nashville: Abingdon 1990), 79.
12. Susanne Heine, *Women and Early Christianity: Are the Feminist Scholars Right?*, trans. John Bowden (London: SCM, 1987), 26.
13. Ibid., 5.

first five centuries of Christian history. The theology piece is often missing in explorations of women in early Christianity, and for understandable reasons. First, the theology of early Christian women is not immediately accessible since we have so few sources written by women. At several points in this book we address the scarcity of sources and thus how to read texts about women written by men. We rely on the efforts of many fine scholars who have worked through the theoretical and methodological issues that come to the forefront when reading early Christian texts. Second, our exploration of theology in general tends to assume particular conceptions of what constitutes a theological work. In reading early Christian texts, there has been a tendency to expect that theology was primarily done and found in treatises on theological subjects, and therefore to limit exploration of a theological topic to those said treatises and those who wrote them. Fortunately, this approach to early Christian theology has been in the process of reexamination and revision. One example of this shifting and broadening of our understanding of early Christian theology is happening in scholarship on Gregory of Nyssa, whom we will meet in chapter 7. Like most early Christian writers, Gregory did not understand theology in the modern sense as a separate discipline from such things as biblical commentary or exhortations to asceticism.[14] A more synthetic reading of writers such as Gregory takes into account his broader conception of theology and by extension a broader understanding of theology in early Christianity. Freeing early Christian theology from a presumed dogmatism pigeonholed in the form of treatises allows for the rich texture of early Christian theology to emerge in its diverse instantiations.

Fundamental to our approach is the supposition that theology in the early church was a dynamic and organic project that included a myriad of voices and approaches. It is a significant error to limit constructive theological work to councils and specific kinds of texts because, as will become clear especially in regard to the central discussions of the Trinity and Christology in early Christianity, core work on these subjects was happening in imaginative rewritings of Plato, the construction of the Christian historical narrative, letters between friends, dialogues in the middle of the night, the establishing of monastic communities in homes and in the desert, pilgrimages to the Holy Land, the reception of the martyr tradition, and the ascetic negotiation with the body. Construction of early Christian theology is best viewed as through a prism

---

14. See Morwenna Ludlow, *Gregory of Nyssa: Ancient and (Post)modern* (Oxford: Oxford University Press, 2007); and Sarah Coakley, *Re-thinking Gregory of Nyssa* (Oxford: Blackwell, 2003).

that captures the nuance, the fluctuation between rigidity and flexibility, the creative invention and the emphasis on embodiment.

In this prismatic paradigm for interpreting early Christian theology, women's theologizing is fundamental to the development of Christian thought and should not be relegated to the fringe or regarded as a concession prize at best. Women were key in the central discussions of trinitarian theology and Christology, for example. Teasing out their contributions becomes a more fruitful venture within the framework of theologizing that includes "performing" theologies (embodied participation, such as virginity, in a theological discourse) and performative theological acts, such as building and funding monasteries or other sites of devotion and utilizing network or familial relationships for the purposes of furthering a theological cause.[15]

## What Is in This Book

We situate Christian women in their historical context because we are interested in knowing what we can about their lives. Thus we have structured this book as a chronological sweep from the second to the fifth centuries. This enables us to walk with the generations of women who grow up in the community and pass along their faith to the next generation. And it allows us to highlight the tremendous shift that occurs within Christian history when Emperor Constantine establishes Christianity as a protected and even favored religion in the empire. Yet there are potential pitfalls to this chronological approach that we will attempt to avoid.

Most important, the chronological structure does not suggest that the church developed in some preordained fashion. We are not implying that the church moved from primitive to advanced or the reverse, from an early golden age to an age of political corruption. We are not charting progress. Rather, we are highlighting the remarkable changes in the participation of women throughout the development of early Christianity in the context of the volatile and shifting imperial landscape of the Roman Empire. As we move through the second century's age of apologists and missionaries, we find very little concerning women apart from the few prophetesses and teachers. The third century can be characterized by martyrdom and misery for many as sporadic assaults were made on Christian communities. This is also the age

15. See Kate Wilkinson, *Women and Modesty in Late Antiquity* (Cambridge: Cambridge University Press, 2015), esp. 1–27. On virginity as "performing" Christology, see Amy Brown Hughes, "The Legacy of the Feminine in the Christology of Origen of Alexandria, Methodius of Olympus, and Gregory of Nyssa," *VC* 69 (2015): 1–26.

of the catacombs in Rome, which testify to Roman Christian burial practices in artwork that bedazzles the eye and frustrates the interpreter. The fourth century marks the rise of the Christian emperor, and with him the beginning of public, political Christianity. Women in the imperial family wield great authority, while wealthy women use their patronage to influence and shape theological debates. In the fifth century, the invading Visigoths and Vandals overthrow much of the Roman Empire, and Rome itself falls (twice). The center of Christianity moves to Constantinople (modern Istanbul). Pilgrims and refugees shift from West to East, and the church wrestles with internal conflict. Women patrons build monasteries, support theologians such as Jerome and Rufinus, and write letters and texts engaging in the theological debates that whirled around the Mediterranean.

In the first chapter, we focus on the second-century text the Acts of Paul and Thecla. The story develops from the biblical references of the apostle Paul traveling to Asia Minor (modern Turkey). The leading character in this story is a young, wealthy woman, Thecla, who embraces Paul's message, leaves her fiancé, and pursues an ascetic life. This story remained influential throughout our period, with families in the fourth century naming their daughters "Thecla," and men in the sixth century embracing an ascetic lifestyle based on her example. The place of asceticism continues to grow within the Christian movement and will become a critical part of later theological discussions, as discussed in chapters 7 and 8.

The second chapter focuses on the Passion of Perpetua and Felicitas, most likely the earliest extant writing by a woman in Latin. The work places front and center the reality of martyrdom and its role in forming Christian identity. Shrines dedicated to male and female martyrs, as well as to their relics (often bones), became part of the pious landscape in the succeeding centuries. Additionally, this account highlights how these Christian women understood themselves as mothers and daughters. And we explore the impact of the Roman social world as female slaves serve as model martyrs.

The third chapter explores the visual world of the early Christians. Here we focus on the Roman catacomb frescoes, especially those depicting meal scenes and the *orans* figure—a human standing with arms outstretched to either side of the body and elbows slightly bent. These images invite reflection on the roles women played in the worship practices within the church and family.

Chapter 4 covers arguably the most dramatic period of social and political change experienced by the church in its history. The fourth century begins with the Great Persecution (303–13),[16] then sees the shift toward Christianity with

16. All dates are CE unless identified as BCE.

the rise of Constantine and the establishment of lasting creedal statements at the Council of Nicaea (325) and the Council of Constantinople (381), and finishes with the reign of Theodosius I, the father of Pulcheria the empress, whose life we trace in our final chapter. In chapter 4 we look at how martyr stories about women were preserved in the work of the fourth-century church historian Eusebius, from whom we gather so much of our knowledge of the church's first three centuries, and we meet a new version of the famous Thecla in the work of Methodius of Olympus.

In chapter 5, we remain in the early fourth century for a bit longer to focus on Helena, the mother of Constantine. Helena becomes the archetype of piety for the Christian empresses who follow. Legend has it that she is responsible for the recovery of the True Cross (the one on which Jesus was crucified) while on pilgrimage to the Holy Land. We will piece together what we know about Helena and consider how a legend is made.

In chapter 6, close attention is paid to another female writer, Egeria, and her description of her pilgrimage and year spent in the Jerusalem church. Egeria's *Itinerary* highlights the land and landscape of the Holy Land in the late fourth century or early fifth century and offers the earliest detailed description of Christian liturgical practices. The *Itinerary* allows us to explore questions of Christian worship practices and fits nicely with our exploration of the Roman catacombs in chapter 3.

Another famous mother takes center stage in chapter 7. Monica, mother of Augustine, famously prodded her son and prayed for him. For Augustine, her voice was often indistinguishable from the voice of God. We also explore the life of Macrina, a wealthy woman who founded a monastery on her estate and is remembered by her well-known brother Gregory of Nyssa as a philosopher and ascetic exemplar. Both these women are accessible to modern readers only through writings of their male family members. This chapter addresses the difficult interpretive process created by the lack of written materials from the women themselves; it concludes that the male authors were seemingly motivated by a desire to promote these women as examples for others to emulate—including the male authors themselves! Their writings testify to these women's capabilities and provide them a legacy through which their words and deeds continue to influence generations.

"Who would be able to give a worthy and clear account of the truly masculine acts of this blessed lady?" Chapter 8 pursues this question from the pen of Gerontius, who wrote a biography of Melania the Younger. Like her grandmother, Melania the Elder, she promotes the ascetic life that promises freedom through renunciation of their substantial wealth. The grandmother established a monastery in Jerusalem, supported the theologian Rufinus, and studied the Scriptures and earlier commentators deeply. Her granddaughter continued in her matriarch's footsteps by training and instructing virgins and engaging in theological conversations. On the other side of the Origenist controversy, we find Paula and Marcella. These aristocrats-turned-ascetics supported Jerome in his theological and monastic endeavors. Marcella remained in Rome, and Paula resided in Bethlehem near Jerome.

The final chapter moves us into the imperial household, but we do not leave the ascetic life behind. Pulcheria, the sister of Theodosius II, chooses the life of a virgin over producing a possible heir to the throne. Her opinions and ideas deeply influence her brother, and she wields a great deal of power. Eudocia, the wife of Theodosius II, did not share her sister-in-law's esteemed birth, and she found herself frequently at odds with Pulcheria. She was highly educated, she gave many speeches, and some of her poetry survives. These two imperial women greatly influence their times, albeit in different ways.

Taken together, these nine chapters highlight how important the female voice was to the early church. It is tempting to relegate a woman's voice to the margins, for she did not speak in the councils, nor do we have her letters debating a doctrine with her male peers. Yet the continuing work of the church in developing its identity and its presence in the community happened outside the channels of ecclesial pronouncements. We recognize these women's contributions to the development of Christianity, its doctrines, and its ethics.

### What Is Not in This Book

#### Gnosticism

The careful reader might assume that we would have included a chapter on women and gnosticism. Such an expectation might be based on evidence of previous scholarship, beginning with Elaine Pagels's groundbreaking book *The Gnostic Gospels*,[17] which was awarded the National Book Award. Pagels introduced to a broad audience the astonishing find of gnostic texts discovered near Nag Hammadi, Egypt, in 1945. The fifty-two works written in Coptic include titles such as the Gospel of Thomas, the Gospel of Philip, the Gospel of Truth, the Gospel to the Egyptians, and the Apocryphon of John. These primary source texts were probably copied between 350 and 400. They provide an autonomous and insider voice at the historians' table, a table whose seats until that time were occupied only by early church heresiologists who condemned gnostic ideas and activities. Pagels argues that

17. Elaine H. Pagels, *The Gnostic Gospels* (New York: Random House, 1979).

the Nag Hammadi texts provide a much-needed opportunity to reexamine gnosticism. She contends that the evidence "clearly indicates a correlation between religious theory and social practice. Among such gnostic groups as the Valentinians, women were considered equal to men; some were revered as prophets; others acted as teachers, traveling evangelists, healers, priests, perhaps even bishops."[18] Pagels sees different attitudes toward sexuality and gender within the gnostic and the orthodox groups. "In simplest form, many gnostic Christians correlate their description of God in both masculine and feminine terms with a complementary description of human nature."[19] Pagels asserts that the gnostic communities' social and political frameworks were grounded in their principle of gender equality. She contrasts that with the orthodox texts portraying God in masculine terms, which shape social practices where men have authority over women.

Nevertheless, Pagels's arguments did not go unchallenged.[20] Elisabeth Schüssler Fiorenza argued that, instead of having an egalitarian social structure, the gnostic communities held females to be subordinate and inferior to males.[21] Interestingly, both scholars believed a rather straight line could be drawn from the gnostic texts to the social world of the gnostics themselves. Anne McGuire represents a third option, arguing that the imagery of the texts provides very little material from which to sketch the members of the gnostic communities. She explains, "The relation between the mythic worlds of Sophia, Barbelo, Eve, and Norea and the social worlds of real 'Gnostic' women is not clear, and the task of reconstructing the social roles of women in 'Gnosticism' remains one of the most challenging in the study of ancient Mediterranean religions."[22]

Moreover, we do not have much in the way of specific, nonbiblical women known to us from their texts. Within the heresiologists' writings, we have four historical women mentioned: Helena, Marcellina, Philumena, and Flora. Helena is identified as the companion of Simon Magus, the originator of the

18. Ibid., 60.

19. Ibid., 66.

20. Daniel L. Hoffman, *The Status of Women and Gnosticism in Irenaeus and Tertullian*, SWR 36 (Lewiston, NY: Edwin Mellen, 1995), offers an extensive critique of Pagels's arguments and a theological interpretation of Irenaeus's and Tertullian's views on women.

21. Elisabeth Schüssler Fiorenza, *In Memory of Her: A Feminist Theological Reconstruction of Christian Origins* (New York: Crossroad, 1983), 274–79.

22. Anne McGuire, "Women, Gender, and Gnosis in Gnostic Texts and Traditions," in *Women and Christian Origins*, ed. Ross S. Kraemer and Mary Rose D'Angelo (Oxford: Oxford University Press, 1999), 257. See also Anne McGuire, "Gnosis and Nag Hammadi," in *The Routledge Companion to Early Christian Thought*, ed. D. Jeffrey Bingham (New York: Routledge, 2010), 204–26.

gnostic movement, according to Irenaeus. Pulling the bits of information together, McGuire suggests that Helena's relationship to Simon is portrayed as "earthly manifestations of a familiar mythic pattern."[23] Irenaeus describes Marcellina as a Carpocratian who taught in Rome in the mid-second century.[24] Philumena is linked with the follower of Marcion, Apelles, and is identified as a prophetess by Hippolytus.[25] The fourth-century antiheresy work by Epiphanius contains a copy of a letter by Ptolemaeus written to "my dear sister Flora."[26] Ptolemaeus took over from the founder of the Valentinian gnostic school, Valentinus, about 160. His letter to Flora is apparently a response to her questions about the Mosaic law. The letter assumes an erudite reader, but beyond that, we cannot form a picture of Flora.

From the third century, we have a Roman funerary inscription dedicated to Flavia Sophē that reads:

> You, who did yearn for the paternal Light,
> Sister, spouse, my Sophē,
> Anointed in the baths of Christ with everlasting, holy oil,
> Hasten to gaze at the divine features of the aeons,
> the great Angel of the great council (i.e., the Redeemer),
> the true Son;
> You entered the bridal chamber and deathless ascended
> To the bosom of the Father.[27]

McGuire evaluates the inscription, observing that masculine names of God are used and that the rituals of baptism and anointing are commended, as is the expectation of a visionary experience.[28] In an interesting and useful discussion, McGuire traces her own development in analyzing gnostic texts. She remarks that at one point she argued that Norea (the daughter of Eve) was a "powerful female model of redemptive subversion."[29] However, she has shifted her conclusions to argue that Norea "participates in just such a system

---

23. McGuire, "Women, Gender, and Gnosis," 260. See Justin Martyr, *First Apology* (*Apologia i*) 1.26.1–3; Irenaeus, *Against Heresies* (*Adversus Haereses*) 1.23.2–24.4; Tertullian, *On the Soul* (*De anima*) 34; Hippolytus, *Refutation of All Heresies* (*Refutatio omnium haeresium*) 6.19; Epiphanius, *Refutation of All Heresies* (*Panarion* [*Adversus haereses*]) 21–22; Origen claims Celsus talks about this, in *Against Celsus* (*Contra Celsum*) 5.62.

24. See Irenaeus, *Haer.* 1.25.6; Origen, *Cels.* 5.62; Epiphanius, *Pan.* 27.6.1, 8.

25. Hippolytus, *Haer.* 7.38.2 (GCS 26.224).

26. Epiphanius, *Pan.* 33.3.1–33.7.10. For an English translation, see Bentley Layton, *The Gnostic Scriptures: A New Translation with Annotations and Introductions* (Garden City, NY: Doubleday, 1987), 306–15.

27. McGuire, "Women, Gender, and Gnosis," 267.

28. Ibid.

29. Ibid., 272.

of power: an ideological system in which true identity and value reside only in the spiritual."[30] McGuire's scholarship highlights the dynamic situation current in gnostic studies. For our purposes in drawing sketches of historical Christian women in the early centuries, we cannot use the mythic discussions of archetype females and the feminine as indicative of the female gnostics and their social world.

In conclusion, the myths embraced by gnostics are not linked in the texts to specific practices that would help us today flesh out their cultural, communal, and liturgical spaces. Given our goals of describing women's lives within the limitations of historical research, the Nag Hammadi collection offers us little to work with. If this book focused on the nature of "female" and "male" in discussions in the second and third centuries from those who claimed the label "Christian," then gnosticism would factor heavily in the discussion. Or, if this book dealt with the give-and-take of theological development within the early centuries of the church, gnostic texts would play a major role. Instead, our book focuses on the women who participated in the communities holding to the *regula fidei*, the confessions that are claimed by what will be called the orthodox church. Therefore, we have elected to set aside the Nag Hammadi material and the hotly debated questions surrounding the definition of gnosticism.

### Mary, the Mother of Jesus Christ

The astute reader might also ask why we do not discuss Mary, Jesus's mother, in this book. The reasons include that she is a biblical character, and we chose to begin our survey with Christian women who lived after the apostolic period. Additionally, the historical development of the cult of Mary requires a separate book of its own.[31] Moreover, this history shows that in

30. Ibid.
31. For more information from historical and various theological positions, see Beverly Roberts Gaventa and Cynthia L. Rigby, eds., *Blessed One: Protestant Perspectives on Mary* (Louisville: Westminster John Knox, 2002); Scot McKnight, *The Real Mary: Why Evangelical Christians Can Embrace the Mother of Jesus* (Brewster, MA: Paraclete, 2007); Tim S. Perry, *Mary for Evangelicals: Toward an Understanding of the Mother of Our Lord* (Downers Grove, IL: IVP Academic, 2006); Nicholas Constas, *Proclus of Constantinople and the Cult of the Virgin in Late Antiquity: Homilies 1–5, Texts and Translations*, VCSup 66 (Leiden: Brill, 2003); Leslie Brubaker and Mary B. Cunningham, eds., *The Cult of the Mother of God in Byzantium: Texts and Images*, Birmingham Byzantine and Ottoman Studies (Farnham: Ashgate, 2011); Vasiliki Limberis, *Divine Heiress: The Virgin Mary and the Creation of Christian Constantinople* (London: Routledge, 1994); Stephen Benko, *The Virgin Goddess: Studies in the Pagan and Christian Roots of Mariology*, SHR 59 (Leiden: Brill, 2004); Amy-Jill Levine and Maria Mayo Robbins, eds., *A Feminist Companion to Mariology*, FCNTECW 10 (London: T&T Clark, 2005).

the period covered by this book, and especially in the third and fourth centuries, when Christian art and iconography begins to flourish, we find, "in surviving frescoes in the catacombs and on other media such as gold glass in the catacombs, Mary is more noticeable by her absence than her presence."[32] Finally, she will make brief appearances in the later chapters as we discuss important events and church councils. For example, imperial women were deeply involved in the Council of Ephesus (431), a council determining that Mary should be known as Theotokos, "bearer of God."

### *Olympias, Gorgonia, the Desert Mothers, and Others*

This book is certainly not an exhaustive treatment of women in Late Antiquity, and the reader familiar with early Christian women will notice that some important women do not feature prominently (or at all). We have aimed to identify some broad themes of women's contributions to the development of Christianity and have constructed each chapter not only to profile these women but also to identify how they participated in wider developments. For example, martyrdom, linked to christological imitation, transitions to living a life of death in asceticism. Again, pilgrimage revealed exegetical exploration, theology developed through dialogue, and the empresses shaped the pious Christian ideal.

Thus the women we selected have a connection in some way to another woman (or several women) in the rest of the book so as to show the interdependence of piety we find throughout these early centuries. The point of highlighting these connections is not to show direct cause and effect or to identify some line of "orthodox" women that preserved a "pure" Christianity. Instead, we demonstrate how women were right in the thick of everything, how their participation and contributions were vital to the construction and maturation of the early church, and how men and women depended on one another for the sake of their love for Christ.

To this end, we have identified a series of lines of "succession" that are not necessarily as starkly delineated as the episcopal or imperial succession but that nonetheless are threads that draw women (and men) together across the passing centuries. One of those major seams holding together that interdependence is the continuing importance of Thecla for the theological and devotional lives of many Christians, including for Macrina, as well as for Gregory of Nazianzus (a longtime friend of Macrina's brother, Basil of Caesarea), who

---

32. Eileen Rubery, "From Catacomb to Sanctuary: The Orant Figure and the Cults of the Mother of God and S. Agnes in Early Christian Rome, with Special Reference to Gold Glass," in *Papers Presented at the Conference on Early Christian Iconography, Held in Pècs, Hungary*, ed. Allen Brent and Markus Vinzent, StPatr 73 (Leuven: Peeters, 2014), 135.

spent considerable time at Thecla's shrine in the fourth century. Another is the carefully treasured narrative of Christic imitation that almost seamlessly shifted from martyr to virgin ascetic. We also see the dramatic sweep that was the interdependence of piety between empress and bishop, empress and the desert fathers, and empress and the Roman aristocrat-turned-ascetic. In order to highlight these connections and draw women into the core of the development of Christianity in the second through fifth centuries, we have spent time on the broader historical and theological context. This means that women like the Constantinopolitan heiress and ally to John Chrysostom, Olympias, the fascinating lives and sayings of the Desert Mothers like Amma Sarah, Amma Theodora, and Amma Syncletica, other important family members, like Gregory of Nazianzus's mother, Nonna, and his sister Gorgonia, the famous hermit Pelagia from Antioch, and so many others are not included.[33] That there are too many women to fit into one book is not a bad problem to have! And yet, as we will see, overall our information about women's lives falls far short of the level of data we have on men at this time.

### Tolle Lege: "Take Up and Read"

Most of the historical literary evidence during this period that we have to work with comes from and is about those from the upper class. Of course Late Antiquity boasts some exemplary writers, but widespread literacy is a modern Western phenomenon. Those who wrote and could read were, generally speaking, members of a class who could afford the time and the education. Thus we are working with a comparably small set of potential writers and works that have the possibility of being preserved. Even then, preservation in and of itself is not a given. Centuries before the printing press, bookmaking was time-consuming, laborious, and costly.[34] Yet some substantial advances

33. For texts about Gorgonia, Pelagia, the Desert Mothers, and many others, see Patricia Cox Miller, ed., *Women in Early Christianity: Translations from Greek Texts* (Washington, DC: Catholic University of America Press, 2005); for translations of a collection of Syriac hagiographies of women, see Sebastian P. Brock and Susan Ashbrook Harvey, *Holy Women of the Syrian Orient*, Transformation of the Classical Heritage 13 (Berkeley: University of California Press, 1998); for a text of the anonymous fifth-century Life of Olympias, see Elizabeth A. Clark, *Jerome, Chrysostom, and Friends: Essays and Translations*, SWR 2 (New York: Edwin Mellen, 1979); for a translation of the *Life of Syncletica*, see Elizabeth A. Castelli, "Pseudo-Athanasius: *The Life and Activity of the Holy and Blessed Teacher Syncletica*," in *Ascetic Behavior in Greco-Roman Antiquity: A Sourcebook*, ed. Vincent Wimbush (Minneapolis: Fortress, 1990), 265–311.

34. See Anthony Grafton and Megan Williams, *Christianity and the Transformation of the Book: Origen, Eusebius, and the Library of Caesarea* (Cambridge, MA: Harvard University Press, 2006).

mitigated these problems. Christians were fond of the codex, a significant shift in format that allowed for more versatility, portability, and preservation of written texts. In contrast to papyrus scrolls, the codex looks more like a modern book. This advancement brought about new utility in the composition and copying of texts and new accessibility in the engagement with texts. When he overhears a child in a neighboring house chanting, "*Tolle lege* [pick up and read]," Augustine reaches for the accessible, codified Letters of Paul that he had with him. The portability and ease of reference of codices changed how readers and writers engaged with texts.

Still, writing and reading were the provinces of the upper class. Interestingly, although Christianity continued the trend of primarily upper-class writers reflecting on and engaging with primarily upper-class subjects, we also find some of those same upper-class writers pursuing nonconventional subjects and content. As we will deal with in more detail in chapter 9, educated Christians had a complicated relationship with the literary composition of biblical works. This created some difficulty for those Christians who were especially keen to go toe-to-toe with their pagan ideological rivals. It was no small task, though; the Gospel of Mark just could not compete with Homer on any kind of rhetorical or literary level. The power of the narrative of Christ and the early Christian church, however, was understood by Christians to transcend those established literary forms and challenge social structures. Christianity contested and even overturned what were considered fundamental ways of understanding the world. One example of this was the biblical and christological concept of strength in weakness. It was understood by Christians that imitation of Christ was central to the corporate and individual's self-understanding; no one's status or gender or age or physicality or background could negate their modeling Christlike behavior. Thus we have cherished narratives of the slave-girl Blandina, aged Desert Fathers and Mothers, young female virgins, old widows, and many others who are held up as exemplars of the Christic-shaped devotion of confession, suffering, and death.

Our research is limited by our sources, for the vast majority of women's lives in the ancient church are inaccessible simply because no literary record of their lives exists or ever existed. Therefore we must be careful not to imprint the experience of one woman onto the multitude. In this book we are dealing with women of status more often than not; while we can draw some conclusions about their lives and the lives of other women by extension, we must be circumspect about the reach of those observations. One thing that we can do, however, is to be mindful as we work through a text to note when others are involved and to engage our imagination beyond the saint who dominates a text. For example, when we imagine Melania the Elder in her convent, we should imagine her with a cadre of women around her and draw attention especially to those who are named in the text so as to not allow their presence to pass by unnoticed. When we hear of Augustine's congregation clamoring for Melania the Younger's husband to be ordained, we should imagine this crowd and work to understand their resorting to extreme measures and the array of possible reasons for it. Aristocratic saints wielded great power in early Christianity, but we must not allow them to cast such a shadow as to obscure those who supported, those who learned, and those who served around them.

We hope that readers of this book will develop a fuller understanding of women in the patristic period as they seek to bring this important period of the church's history to bear on the present. We recognize that women have always played important roles in many aspects of church and Christian society, and it is no innovation to suggest that this is how things should be. At the same time, we will show how the women we discuss had to work around various impediments in order to speak their thoughts and act on their convictions. It is worthwhile to think theologically about the causes of gender inequity in the patristic period. We hope that Christians today engage with the many significant ideas raised and discussed in the church fathers, while at the same time not uncritically reproducing those elements that were unhelpful for the lives of Christian women. We trust that, by telling the stories of Christian women in the patristic period—and taking seriously their Christian beliefs (doctrine, worship, Scripture, and community)—our book will help readers today to remember a fuller and richer Christian history and engage in their own communities with a stronger, sharper, and sophisticated appreciation for the Christian women of the second through fifth centuries. Reading texts about and by early Christian women helps us expand our understanding of what the Christian story is. Join us as we follow Augustine's example and *tolle lege*.

# 1

# Thecla: Christian Female Protomartyr and Virgin of the Church

A young woman smitten by a man's presence—this is the stuff of romance. A woman striving to chart her own path, undaunted by obstacles—this is inspiring. A woman rejecting a life of respectable stability and marital love and choosing an existence of want and possible danger—this is puzzling. A story that combines all this and more is bound to captivate, and indeed the story of Thecla has challenged and inspired Christians, especially in the second through fifth centuries. Yet Thecla is a shadowy figure, which may explain the resilience of her memory and influence, for subsequent generations viewed her as an exemplar for their own times, whether for martyrdom, asceticism, or virginity. Her story is told on the pages of the Acts of Paul and Thecla (APTh), or simply Acts of Thecla, although her narrative probably circulated separately in some cases.[1] It seems likely that some form of this text was written in the mid-second century (if not earlier) and was incorporated into the Acts of Paul as various traditions of Paul were collected. We set the stage for her story below in a brief overview of the church in the second century.

1. For an English translation, see Schneemelcher, *New Testament Apocrypha*, 2:239–46. See also Barrier, *Acts of Paul and Thecla*; Barrier's numbering system will be used in what follows.

## Introduction to Christian Women in the Second Century

Christian women in the second century traveled with their male counterparts in uncharted waters as the fledging church of the New Testament stretched beyond its Jewish boundaries and reached into the gentile pagan world. This century sees the separation, by and large, of Jewish and gentile followers of Jesus, as well as the rise of rabbinic Judaism. Second-century Christians were also testing the waters on orthodoxy, or right belief, asking questions about the nature of Jesus Christ and of God the Father. But much of the second century is taken up with questions of practice—when and how to baptize, take communion, and fast. As gentiles turned from paganism to Christianity, questions arose on proper "Christian" behavior over against pagan lifestyles. Perhaps nowhere is this clearer than in the area of sexual ethics. Second-century Christians debated the role of sex in marriage and the worthiness of a continent life. Celibacy and virginity were promoted, as well as marriage to a fellow believer, while second marriages—that is, remarrying after one's spouse died—were criticized. In line with the wider philosophical teachings of the day, Christians valued self-control and self-restraint, but in ways that expressed their Christian beliefs. Asceticism, which included extensive fasting and refraining from sex within marriage, or from marriage entirely, will frame conversations about proper Christian lifestyle for centuries to come.

Alongside conversations about asceticism, we find a growing interest in institutional issues and leadership as a developing "orthodox," or mainstream, Christianity began to take shape. Churches discussed issues at the boundaries, such as prophecy, visions, and who speaks as a genuine prophet. And the churches focused on organization at the center, promoting offices such as deacon, presbyter, and bishop. Questions surrounding the proper expression of Christian faith in daily life and in liturgy animated the second century. And all this happened on the world stage, where the wider culture was hostile toward and suspicious of the emerging Christian groups. Moreover, plagues and earthquakes unnerved the population of the Roman Empire, and political unrest, including civil war, disquieted the city and countryside. These were unsettling times, and the portrait of Christian women highlights the uneasy, apprehensive mood. After a brief sketch of her story, we will discuss how best to interpret Thecla's narrative.

## Introduction to Thecla

"Written by the hand of Thecla." So penned the patriarch of Constantinople, Cyril Lucaris, in his note to Charles I, king of England, when in 1627, the patriarch handed the king the ancient biblical manuscript known as Alexandrinus. Cyril's note explains that Thecla, an honorable Egyptian woman who lived about the time of the Council of Nicaea (325), wrote this copy of the Bible. She was a daughter of the founder of a monastery in Egypt, was persecuted for her faith, and died just after the Council of Nicaea. Originally, her name was attached to the end of the manuscript, but the document was later damaged. About one thousand years later, an Arabic hand noted in the margin of the manuscript's second page, "They say that this book was written by the hand of Thecla, the martyr."[2] It is historically unlikely that this manuscript was penned by the Thecla of APTh, because she lived at least a century before it was copied. Nevertheless, it is appropriate that her name be immortalized in this way, and it echoes down through the centuries, as witnessed by its presence for over thirteen hundred years in the Alexandrinus manuscript's history.

Thecla's story reflects the topic of Christian asceticism and highlights the links between that and women's writing, reading, and teaching. The ancient world connected the disciplines of study—writing and reading—with eating and drinking. Thus the one might be seen as a substitute for the other in the ascetic lifestyle. In Thecla's story, she neither eats nor drinks for three days and three nights but only listens to Paul's words.[3] Thecla, the learned ascetic, inspired countless Christians, and her story influenced generations.

### Who Is Thecla?

The narrative begins not with Thecla but with the apostle Paul. Indeed, one of the complicating factors in interpreting Thecla's story is that it stands within the wider Acts of Paul literature, and this collection of stories has its own convoluted textual history. Paul arrives in Thecla's hometown of Iconium (modern Konya, Turkey) and begins to preach his gospel from a neighbor's house. Thecla is mesmerized by his teachings, and embraces them with great fervor. She remains at her window, listening for three days, and determines to follow Paul's ascetic message. This creates a family crisis that propels the rest of Thecla's life, for she refuses to marry her fiancé. Her mother, Theocleia, is furious, and her fiancé, Thamyrus, is devastated. Thecla is undeterred.

2. Kim Haines-Eitzen, *The Gendered Palimpsest: Women, Writing, and Representation in Early Christianity* (Oxford: Oxford University Press, 2012), 6.

3. Such connection continued through the centuries, as in the case of Macrina, Gregory of Nyssa's sister, whose secret family name was Thecla. See Gregory of Nyssa, *Life of Macrina (Vita s. Macrinae)* 3, in *Macrina the Younger, Philosopher of God*, trans. Anna M. Silvas, Medieval Women: Texts and Contexts 22 (Turnhout: Brepols, 2008), 112. Macrina is discussed in chap. 7.

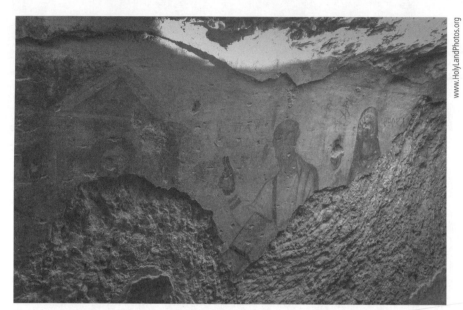

Figure 1.1. A cave outside Ephesus with a fifth- or sixth-century fresco depicting St. Thecla sitting at her window listening to Paul's gospel.

Due to the treachery of Paul's two companions, Demas and Hermogenes, who conspire with Thamyrus, Paul is arrested. The crowd shouts that he is a magician, for he turns wives against their husbands. The governor asks Paul to speak to these charges, and Paul gives a brief account, after which the governor has him committed to prison until a later time when he can talk with Paul more directly. Thecla leaves her house at night to visit Paul in his prison cell and reaffirms her commitment to follow Paul and his teaching. She sits at his feet and kisses his chains. When Paul is taken back to see the governor, she remains in the cell, rolling about in the spot where he sat.

Shortly thereafter, Thecla is called to stand before the governor, which she does with much joy. However, when he asks her why she has refused to marry her fiancé, she remains silent but gazes at Paul. Her obstinacy enrages her mother, who calls for her death. In the first of two appearances in the arena, Thecla faces being burned alive, while Paul is beaten and driven out of the city. As she enters the theater, she looks about for Paul, and sees "the Lord sitting as Paul," who then disappears into the heavens (APTh 3.21). She walks naked to the pyre, and the governor is amazed at her "power." The fire burns, but Thecla is preserved by a violent storm with hail that kills others in the theater.

Then the narrative jumps to Paul, who with his host family has fled the city and is staying in a nearby cave. They are praying and fasting, and then one of the children goes to the market to buy some bread. There he meets Thecla, who has been searching for Paul. They are reunited, and she begs to go with Paul as he continues his ministry, stating that she will cut her hair to follow him. He refuses, saying that she is young and beautiful and thus might yet succumb to temptations. Even so, she asks to be baptized, and he indicates that it is not yet time for that, but if she is patient, she will receive the water.

In the very next scene, the host family returns to Iconium, and she and Paul arrive in Antioch, where her beauty arouses the desire of Alexander, a leading figure in the city. When Alexander tries to embrace her, Thecla tears his cloak and knocks his crown from his head. At such provocation, he has her taken to the governor, who condemns her to the wild beasts. As she waits her fate, she is given to the care of a leading woman of the city, Tryphaena. This wealthy mother has a vision of her deceased daughter, who declares that Thecla will take her place, and that she, the daughter, will be moved to a righteous place because of Thecla's prayers.

Before the spectacle, Alexander goes to Tryphaena's house and asks for Thecla. The woman adamantly refuses, even though she knows that such a refusal means that Thecla will face a horrific death in the arena. Tryphaena understands Thecla to be a divine mediator whose prayers can save her daughter. As Thecla enters the arena, some in the crowd are appalled at what they see as a miscarriage of justice, but their voice does not carry the day. The beasts attack, but a lioness protects her from a charging bear, and then dies while killing a lion. More beasts are sent into the arena. Thecla raises her hands in prayer, and then she plunges into a pool populated by ferocious seals, thereby experiencing baptism. A lightning strike kills all the seals, and Thecla emerges whole, with a cloud of fire covering her nakedness. Even more beasts are set out, but many women in the crowd have had enough. They throw herbs and spices into the arena to calm the animals. Next bulls are brought in and Thecla is to be drawn and quartered, but her ropes burn and she is freed from the raging beasts.

This proves to be too much for Tryphaena, who faints away as though dead. The city magistrate and Alexander grow terrified because Tryphaena is related to the emperor, and her death at their sponsored spectacle could land them afoul of the ruler. The governor stops everything and asks Thecla who she is that such miracles have happened. Unlike earlier in the story where she remained silent, now she speaks: "I am a slave of the living God" (APTh 4.12). She is released, to the great joy of the women in the crowd. Thecla is restored to Tryphaena, who recovers and confesses her own belief in the resurrection and in her daughter's resurrected life. Tryphaena welcomes Thecla into her home and gives all her wealth to Thecla, who remains eight days while teaching Tryphaena and her

Figure 1.2. In a fifth-century relief, Thecla stands triumphant with lions at her side.

household. Then, seeking Paul, Thecla travels to Myra. For the journey, she dresses as a man and is joined by a group of young men and women. Upon greeting Paul, she tells him of her baptism. He receives the news with joy and blesses her with the words "Go and teach the word of God" (4.16). After this, Thecla returns to her home city of Iconium. She goes to the house of Onesiphorus, the family who hosted Paul at the beginning of our story.[4] There she falls on the very spot where Paul has taught, and she too then begins to teach the word. Her former fiancé having died, she visits her mother, who seems unconvinced by her daughter's testimony. Yet others are persuaded as Thecla teaches. Next she travels to nearby Seleucia, and then dies a peaceful death.

Several additional endings of our story exist in the manuscripts. They add to her experiences in Seleucia, reporting that she lived outside the town and on a mountain, where she endured the devil's temptations. Women travel to her to be taught, and some stay with her to live a monastic life. Those overcome with illness are healed, and unclean spirits are cast out by God's power in her. Yet the physicians of Seleucia are jealous and decide to destroy her power. They determine that she has such power because she is a virgin, falsely concluding that she is a priestess for the goddess Diana, and so they send some local riffraff to rape her. This gang of young men are identified as lions in the text, likely a reference back to the beasts she faced in the arena in Antioch. When they arrive at her door, she reasons with them about the power of God to save her yet again, and then miraculously the side of her cave opens and she walks through, whereupon it closes upon her. The young

4. A believer named Onesiphorus is mentioned in 2 Tim. 1:16; 4:19.

ruffians are left holding only a bit of her veil. The narrator reports that this is how the first female martyr and apostle of God, the virgin Thecla, died.

## How Should We Interpret the Material?

### Reading Thecla: The Historical Figure

As we engage Thecla's story in the twenty-first century, we are perhaps first of all aware of a profound distance between our frames of reference and Thecla's world. The intense physical violence of the arena, the strong asceticism, and the fantastical miracles—these are disorienting to modern readers. Yet the ancient Roman arena was a reality, where criminals were tossed to the beasts, made to fight to the death, or burned alive. As we will see in the next chapter, Christian martyrs faced a similar fate. We might have a sneaking admiration for Thecla's gumption in following her own path, however torturous it might be, but the ancient Roman traditionalist would be shocked at Thecla's rejection of wealth and social stability. And while we might puzzle over all the miracles mentioned, the pagan, Jew, and Christian of the second century lived in a world filled with the supernatural; indeed, the sharp divisions between natural and supernatural that we take for granted in a post-Enlightenment world did not exist. Their question was not "Can miracles happen?" but rather "By what power did such an event occur?"

This cultural and intellectual distance, however, can work in our favor because it allows us to experience and engage the *text* from a variety of perspectives, even if the *world* that produced the text varies profoundly from our own. We might ask whether only the uneducated lower classes relished such stories. Were these stories the fantasies of the downtrodden, fairy tales created by those who had no hope? And what were the author's intentions in writing this story? We can ask how and why Thecla's story excited the imagination of Christians for several hundred years. Throughout this book we will explore several key topics and themes sown in this story, motifs that germinate in the third century and blossom in the fourth and fifth centuries.

We get to know Thecla and her story through the narrative. We know that later Christians spoke of her as a model to imitate. But that raises the question: Is she a historical figure? Does her narrative draw on a historical figure? There are several ways to address this question. If one means, is there a first-century Thecla who worked alongside the apostle Paul in Asia Minor?, then we must recognize that we have no other first-century evidence of such a person. Is it possible for there to be a woman named Thecla who, like Euodia and Syntyche (Phil. 4:2), Lydia (Acts 16:14), Priscilla

(Acts 18:2; Rom. 16:3), and Junia (Rom. 16:7), served as Paul's coworker? Moreover, the text gives several historical details that tantalize. These include the historical person of Thecla's patron Tryphaena, who lived in the middle of the first century and was a queen of Pontus and a relative of Emperor Claudius.[5] Her kingdom was on the border between the Roman and Persian Empires, and for that reason Rome courted her favor, at least until Nero's reign. We know of her dynasty only through coins and inscriptions, which suggests to some that the person who wrote APTh lived in a period of close proximity to this kingdom's existence, for memory of the queen quickly faded. Such historical details lead some to suggest that behind the current APTh is a first-century work "by some person not far removed from the events, able to compose a history, or at least a poetical idealisation of history."[6] However, the historical Queen Tryphaena was a priestess of Livia who lived in Cyzicus and not Syrian or Pisidian Antioch.[7] The geographical details about Iconium and the royal road system within the story are accurate for the time, as are the basic descriptions of the legal procedures and treatment of criminals.

Ultimately, these historical details do not add up to the conclusion that the text reveals solid historical events about a real figure, Thecla, the faithful disciple of Paul and of Christ. If she existed as a historical figure, the account of her life has been enhanced, changed, and remixed such that only the barest outline of historicity can be discerned. More plausible is the theory that Thecla's narrative builds on a charismatic late first-century or early second-century female disciple whose persona invited reflection. Like a grain of sand captured by an oyster is overlaid with rich layers of protein and crystals to become a pearl, so too it may be that a first-century female teacher caught the attention of a pious writer who sketched her testimony, to which a later witness added layers and interpretations, producing a lasting pearl of remembrance in the current figure of St. Thecla.

If the historical details of a historical Thecla are lost in the mists of the past, would we do better to describe her as a myth? Not necessarily, since "myth" carries the sense of ancient past and cosmic forces, as in the story of Prometheus, who stole fire from the gods and delivered it to humanity. Others suggest the term "legend," which has the value of suggesting at least a figure rooted in history; however, in ancient Greece a legend was told in verse, not

5. William M. Ramsey, *The Church in the Roman Empire before A.D. 170* (New York: Putnam's Sons, 1892), 385–87.
6. Ibid., 388.
7. Esther Yue L. Ng, "*Acts of Paul and Thecla*: Women's Stories and Precedent?," *JTS 55* (2004): 19.

prose.[8] Thecla is first and foremost a literary character. We access her from a narrative, not from a personal diary (as we have from the martyr Perpetua), a court transcript, or a historian's notes (as for Helena, mother of Constantine, described by Eusebius in his *Ecclesiastical History*), but that does not make her story a fairy tale. Gillian Clark helpfully sorts out aspects of truth in her comment concerning the martyr-acts: "They are presented as an expression of truth, even if that truth is (in Aristotle's terms) poetic rather than historical, an account of what could happen rather than what did happen."[9]

### Reading Thecla: Methodological Considerations

Our reasonable cautiousness concerning the figure of Thecla should not blind us to the historical information embedded in the narrative's assumptions about second-century life among Christians. As Susan Hylen observes, the text does "give insight into what the author wanted to persuade the audience of, and what he assumed they would take for granted."[10] Readers must be alert to the difference between descriptive and prescriptive, and to the rhetoric that encourages a way of life rather than disinterestedly describes a lifestyle. We can discover something about how early Christians understood themselves and their world by focusing on decisions women made. Kate Wilkinson notes that women's agency is itself a means to access real women's lives, for although men have appropriated women's voices, nevertheless women's own agency was at work in the social construction of gender in the society.[11]

Ancient Greco-Roman culture is the broad canvas on which Christian women painted their world. Hylen suggests that we analyze how ancient women creatively expressed the cultural virtues of self-control, modesty, and civic engagement. She challenges previous scholars' arguments that empha- sized an internal consistency to culture and promoted a dichotomy between private and public spaces, relegating women to private areas and men to public settings. This sort of analysis leads to the conclusion that women public leaders were an anomaly. Hylen rightly contends, and we agree: "The demands for traditional feminine behavior did not cancel out women's ac- tive roles."[12] Her conclusion is based on reconsideration of the way cultural

---

8. Bryan P. Reardon, ed., *Collected Ancient Greek Novels* [CAGN] (Berkeley: University of California Press, 1989, 2008), 1.

9. Gillian Clark, "Bodies and Blood: Late Antique Debate on Martyrdom, Virginity and Resurrection," in *Changing Bodies, Changing Meanings: Studies on the Human Body in Antiquity*, ed. Dominic Montserrat (London: Routledge, 1998), 103.

10. Hylen, *Modest Apostle*, 7.

11. Wilkinson, *Women and Modesty*, 13.

12. Hylen, *Modest Apostle*, 4.

values are expressed, for at any given time, two cultural virtues might seem to be at odds (modesty and civic engagement), but the ancient woman would negotiate her expression of these values. Hylen continues, "The dispositions of culture shape human action, but they allow for multiple expressions of the same values, and even, to some extent, choice between the values expressed."[13] In the story of Thecla, and in other ancient stories, we should not be surprised to find seemingly competing values. Instead, we should recognize the complicated cultural context that encouraged women (and men) to act according to their culture's values in ways that also reflected their own understanding and commitment to those values.

This means that women, including Christian women, might choose conservative expressions of modesty as they demonstrate their agency. Kate Wilkinson argues that modesty is "an opportunity for active self-formation and self-representation in a community."[14] As such, modesty is not a private matter, for it is performed among others. Nor is modesty an outcome of self-restraint but is itself a process pursuing self-control. Wilkinson continues, "As a performance, however, modesty belongs to the subject of the action; she is accountable for its content and efficacy."[15] This interpretation of women's agency is an important corrective to earlier scholarship's thesis that agency is synonymous with autonomy and can only be seen in countercultural moves and poses of resistance. Its importance lies in part in revealing the honor culture of the ancient world, which stressed community over against individuality. And in part, this interpretation calls into question the equation of authenticity with resistance to the status quo, for it undermines the notion that culture is static and imposed as a set of rules onto the individual. Instead, individuals are constantly deciding how to manage and express competing and even at times contradictory cultural values.

### Reading Thecla: The Plot Thickens

If decisions reveal agency, then within Thecla's narrative we should attend to her choices, and those made by other women. Thecla's rejection of the status quo demonstrated by her refusal to marry is not her only expression of agency. Her insistence on public modesty, so important to the Roman world, also reveals her agency and self-expression. The story's plot is one window through which to view women's agency in the narrative, for it highlights the essential pieces of the narrative and thus the key themes that drive the

13. Ibid., 10.
14. Wilkinson, *Women and Modesty*, 17.
15. Ibid., 24.

narrative. A serendipitous meeting launches the narrative: Thecla hears Paul preach and embraces his message. This new relationship drives the action as these two meet, separate, rejoin, separate again, reunite, and then have a final separation. Their relationship has been interpreted in various ways, usually in conjunction with a decision on the story's genre. We will look at genre options below; at this point we return to the plot and notice that during these times of separation Thecla is severely tested. These tests warrant a closer look. What exactly is being tested? Thecla's resolve to remain a virgin is challenged by her family and by a leading man in Antioch, Alexander. Thus we might say that the plot reveals the supreme importance of virginity. However, a minor character, Onesiphorus, is married and models faithful ascetic living with his family. He is not asked to leave his wife and children; rather, they extend hospitality to itinerant preachers such as Paul and worthy celibates such as Thecla. Again, one might argue that marriage is rejected, but the same caveat concerning Onesiphorus would apply. Thus the plot turns on the issues of marriage and virginity. Supporting both claims is the foundational assertion that the ascetic life, governed by self-control and denial, is essential, for only those made pure by such means will inherit the resurrection.

A second fundamental part of the plot is Thecla's baptism.[16] In her second encounter with Paul, after he is driven from Iconium and she is miraculously saved from the pyre, she asks that he baptize her. He refuses, saying that she might yet fall into temptation. When they meet again, it is after she declares herself to have been baptized (she plunged into a pool filled with killer seals during her ordeal in the arena in Antioch). Paul accepts this baptism and blesses her to continue her teaching. He sees the baptism as evidence of Thecla's faithfulness in the face of martyrdom, a fate brought about not particularly because she confesses to being a Christian, but because she rejects a leading suitor (Thamyris, then Alexander) and humiliates him by her rebuff.

A third force behind the narrative is the figure and support of Tryphaena, whose own daughter's death and uncertain afterlife provides the opportunity for Thecla to demonstrate her powers of prayer and intercession. The deep bond between Thecla and Tryphaena will be explored below. Here we stress that Tryphaena's protection ensures that Thecla retains her virginity before her ordeal in the arena. She also supports Thecla financially so that the latter may travel back to Iconium and then on to Seleucia, living a life of relative solitude. Tryphaena serves as the model pupil of Thecla and sees the truth of the resurrection that Thecla teaches. In some longer endings

16. Ng, "Acts of Paul and Thecla," 11.

of the story, Thecla's powers continue during her long life as she teaches the word of God and heals many from her abode outside of Seleucia. It is her healing powers, seen in connection with her virginity, that ultimately bring about her end as she is swallowed by the cave wall before the eyes of her would-be rapists.

Why should questions of marriage and virginity drive the plot? The answer to these questions points back to the beginning of the story, to a description of what Thecla heard that day from her window. In his beatitudes, Paul preached about continence, about undefiled flesh, and about virgins. Those who keep to these practices will have their reward in their salvation; they will be the temple of God and angels of God. Thecla clings to her virginity because of the promised heavenly reward: resurrection from the dead.[17] Death as experienced by Tryphaena's daughter, Falconilla, is seemingly unpleasant, although no details are given; thus, Thecla's message of resurrection to a life of rest and peace was compelling. Virginity was not only related to the afterlife, but it also spoke volumes in the current age. Peter Brown describes the virgin body as "intact" and thus possibly representing "a condensed image of the individual, always threatened with annihilation, poised from birth above the menacing pressures of the world."[18] Additionally, virginity exemplified the self-restraint and self-control that the story as a whole encourages. Thecla's concern to remain chaste before being thrown to the beasts in Antioch would have resonated with her Roman audience, whose own founding myth celebrated a modest matron who valued her chastity over her very life.

This well-known myth, recounted by the ancient historian Livy, emphasizes the importance of female chastity in Roman society. Lucretia, the industrious and virtuous wife of a fifth-century BCE Roman, was raped by Sextus Tarquinius, prince of the Etruscan tyrant ruling Rome. Her virtue was never doubted by her husband and father, yet she drove a dagger through her heart so that no woman after her might ever doubt her commitment to her chaste devotion to marriage.[19] For the married and unmarried woman, her chaste life was of paramount importance for the public good. Lucretia's example of chaste virtue stands with Thecla's determination to remain a virgin. And the virtue of self-restraint demonstrated was equally valued by men who likewise (but perhaps in different ways) expressed self-control. In this way, Thecla served as a role model for both Christian men and women. In other

17. Ibid., 10.
18. Brown, *Body and Society*, 159.
19. Livy, *Hist.* 1.57–58.

words, the Acts of Paul and Thecla is not simply or primarily a story about a pious early Christian; it is a rhetorical masterpiece that draws readers in, compels them to view the world through the eyes of Thecla, and urges them to live in light of that new vision.

### Reading Thecla: The Upside-Down Story

One particular rhetorical device deserves special mention: Thecla's story turns upside down some common Roman virtues and values by redefining what is honorable and what is shameful. Since honor and shame were coded to gender, that means that our story uses typical feminine virtues such as silence and passivity and presents them as of the highest honor, superior to the masculine traits of dominance and physical power: "Constructing themselves as female, seemingly powerless to stop their suffering at the hands of Roman male authorities, Christians in fact challenged and defied Roman claims to power."[20]

Within the story itself, we find the rhetorical strategy that Ross Kraemer calls "gender inversion"—that is, the promotion of typically feminine virtues as higher and better than masculine virtues, and the presentation of females as exemplifying masculine traits of self-control or courage better than the males in the story. The story elevates typical feminine qualities to be normative for all and challenges typical masculine virtues such as courage to include submission to force or power, as Thecla does in the arena. Kraemer writes, "The fundamental associations of femininity with weakness, powerlessness, passivity, limited intellect, and numerous other deficiencies were effectively exploited to demonstrate the ultimate power of the Christian God."[21]

The gender-inversion theory invites reflection on the vivid images of Thecla's body, naked in the narrative and to the reader's imagination, and subjected to horrific tortures. Scholars are divided on how to understand the remarks concerning Thecla's nakedness. Is this a voyeuristic look at a young beautiful female? Or is the nakedness symbolic of her purity? Or perhaps this picture simply reflects the reality of any person, male or female, in the arena? While the symbolism of nakedness must be considered, we should not forget, assuming this text was written in the second century, that it accurately reflects the torture that criminals and slaves underwent in the arena. A story of a martyr involves violence, including humiliation through nakedness that accompanies

20. Ross Shepard Kraemer, *Unreliable Witnesses: Religion, Gender, and History in the Greco-Roman Mediterranean* (Oxford: Oxford University Press, 2011), 135.
    21. Ibid.

such punishment. Thecla's response to the governor, that God has clothed her with salvation, might provide the key to interpreting her nakedness. She appears naked to the audience, but she believes herself to be clothed, perhaps implying that the audience is naked. She writes her own reality; she reconfigures what is shame and who has power. She endures all they can think to do to her body and emerges victorious—a victory fully realized in the resurrection. Brown states, "To the Christian reader, Thecla at her most exposed was the privileged vehicle of the indestructible power of Christ."[22]

While Roman virtues might be resisted or redefined, they can also be embraced by women, who enact them with their own agency. Kate Wilkinson argues that "ancient women had intentions, desires, hopes, and thoughts that they enacted on their own behalf."[23] Decisions that support the status quo, such as modest silence for women, are seen as a demonstration of the woman's agency. Alongside inverting or resisting a social norm or cultural virtue, a woman's conforming actions are owned by her. Whether she resists cultural norms or pursues conservative values such as modesty, the woman is a true subject who chooses actions that reflect her thoughts.

In our story, we find both gender inversion and conformity to existing norms woven in the narrative's fabric. Recall that Thecla is silent for much of the introduction; this may be a signal that Thecla is a highborn woman who is a protected virgin and not a sexually available slave. Later, once her modesty is established, she speaks privately to Paul, and then publicly in the arena to the governor of Antioch. Additional examples of women's voices breaking the silence occur in Antioch, pushing against the feminine virtues of silence and passivity. For example, just before Tryphaena is introduced, a chorus of women speaks out against Antioch's governor and his condemnation of Thecla. Again, these women cry out against the judgment while they and their children watch in horror as Thecla is paraded through the city on the day before her ordeal. A third time, the women shout as Thecla enters the arena to face the beasts, declaring a miscarriage of justice. During the spectacle, women mourn when the lioness that protected Thecla dies, they cry out when Thecla is about to dive into the pool of killer seals, and they toss perfume, spices, and flowers onto the arena floor to dull the beasts. Finally, when Thecla is exonerated and released, the women thank God and cry out, "One is God [or: there is one God] who has saved Thecla" (APTh 4.13). The women's public, truth-speaking voices enact the civic virtue of demanding

22. Brown, *Body and Society*, 157. See also Helen Rhee, *Early Christian Literature: Christ and Culture in the Second and Third Centuries* (New York: Routledge, 2005), 137.
23. Wilkinson, *Women and Modesty*, 21.

justice and reinforce the value of modesty in seeking to protect a wellborn virgin and defend the honor of a leading lady of the city.

### Reading Thecla: Alongside Other Women in the Story

Strong bonds between women, especially between mother or surrogate mother and daughter, take center stage in Thecla's story and serve to promote the Christian remapping of family that minimized natal relationships and elevated believers as "brothers and sisters" in the Lord.[24] The emphasis on women's relationships is quite pronounced in Thecla and Tryphaena's bonding. Tryphaena does more than simply keep Thecla secure until her appearance in the arena. The bereaved mother finds consolation in her relationship with Thecla, who becomes her "child." Even more, Thecla is drawn into Tryphaena and Falconilla's relationship, which continues although the daughter has died. Falconilla visits her mother in a dream, announcing that Thecla can take the daughter's place with her mother. Thecla prays for Falconilla (now in some way her "sister"), who finds rest and eternal life. Tryphaena accepts Thecla's calling and ascetic desire, at great cost to herself. When Alexander comes to her home asking one last time to make Thecla his wife, Tryphaena drives him away, even while she knows that such action will send Thecla to the beasts, and she will once again be mourning a daughter. Indeed, her grief overwhelms her, and she faints after seeing Thecla tied to bulls. This is not seen as evidence of female weakness, but rather the governor and Alexander both stop the spectacle immediately and release Thecla back to Tryphaena. Thecla's survival is seen as a return from the dead, as confirmation that the dead are raised. Tryphaena exclaims that now she knows that "my child" lives; the reference is most immediately to Thecla, but perhaps it also implies her confidence that Falconilla is indeed now in a place of rest and peace. Tryphaena is mother to Thecla in that she transfers her property to Thecla, and she is patron to her by welcoming her to her home and learning the word of God from Thecla. In the blending of the two roles, we see here a developing picture of the church's understanding of family as fictive kinships that allow strangers to become mother and daughter, as well as pupil and teacher.

This reading of Thecla's story reveals historical data in its narrative and also creates a literary world with upside-down values and a thick plot. Weaving these threads together requires a closer look at the possible genre of the Acts of Paul and Thecla and the likely expectations an ancient reader would bring to such a text.

24. Kate Cooper, *Band of Angels: The Forgotten World of Early Christian Women* (New York: Overlook, 2013), 77–91, offers an accessible discussion of Thecla and her mother, Theocleia.

## The Genre of the Acts of Paul and Thecla

We meet Thecla in a narrative, and thus we must explore how the ancient world understood narratives. The Acts of Paul and Thecla incorporates similarities with ancient romance novels and with developing Christian hagiography. As with so many things, where we start will largely determine where we end up. If we start with the notion that the Acts of Paul and Thecla is best read as a type of romance novel, with traits similar to contemporary Greco-Roman romance novels, then we tend to focus on the political dynamics of the story, the exchanges between traditional family structures (marriage, honoring parents), and ascetic Christian goals that reshape the kinship structures to privilege other believers over one's biological family. If we begin with the assessment that the Acts of Paul and Thecla is hagiographic, then the accounts of miracles and the miraculous take center stage as the saint is developed for the church's encouragement. If we lead with the gendered expectations and reversals of the story, we pay close attention to rhetoric in the characters' development and interactions, and perhaps we draw conclusions about social conventions. If we begin with the expectation that this work influenced the piety of Christians for several centuries, our ear becomes attuned to the theological nuances present in the story. A narrative as rich and influential as the Acts of Paul and Thecla deserves a close reading from a cultural, theological, and literary perspective.

What follows is a summary of the ways in which the Acts of Paul and Thecla's composition is understood—that is, what might be its genre. The task of establishing genre is not an idle exercise, because genre gives the reader a clue as to how the text should be read. If someone begins a tale with "Once upon a time," you might settle into your chair in delighted anticipation of an exciting story that will end happily ever after. Not all genres are as fixed as our fairy tale, and certainly in the ancient world, we should not imagine an ideal, abstract "Romance Novel Template" or "Hagiography Model" from which all authors drew. Yet we should expect clues within the text, like our "once upon a time," that guide readers' expectations as to the nature of the material.[25]

### *The Acts of Paul and Thecla and the Ancient Romance Novel*

We might think that the romance novel was a Victorian invention, but the first few centuries of the Roman Empire produced several such tales. These works "are narrative fiction in prose—imaginative, creative literature" that was

---

25. Edith M. Humphrey, *Joseph and Aseneth* (Sheffield: Sheffield Academic, 2000), 38–40.

Figure 1.3. Thecla's initial encounter with the apostle Paul is depicted on this ivory panel of a fifth-century chest.

most popular in the second century.[26] It is not clear how this genre started, but its impulse seems to stem from the romantic poetry developed toward the end of the Roman Republic and the rise of the Roman Empire. This was combined with the existing genre of historiography and with the rising interest in the relationship between marriage and the city or wider social and cultural environment. Yet it should not be forgotten that this genre was about entertainment.

Five romances form the core of the evidence, but about twenty texts have been identified in fragments or as references. About fifty to one hundred pages in length in their English translations, they generally follow a typical plotline wherein a young, handsome, and wealthy couple fall deeply in love, then find themselves separated. Enduring terrible misfortunes and trials as well as experiencing exciting adventures, they are at last reunited, and they marry and, we might say, live happily ever after. The young couple remains steadfastly devoted during their time of separation. Ancient novels share an interest in travel and include erotic details and miraculous deeds. The story reaffirms the wider social goals of social stability through promoting elite marriages. Interestingly, the romance novel fades from view with the chaos brought about by the invasions of Rome. Ancient Roman literary historians speak very little, and then not positively, about this genre.

Scholars have noticed the similarities to the romance genre in Thecla's plot, which includes meeting Paul, then being separated from him and enduring horrible tribulations, only to be reunited at the end. Beyond this structural similarity, however, can we find deeper connections that help us understand the message of Thecla's story?

26. *CAGN*, 1.

One broad theory suggests that the Acts of Paul and Thecla seeks to over-turn the prevailing cultural norms espoused in the romance novels. In this theory, the plotline of both the romance novel and the Acts of Paul and Thecla is not so much about romance as it is about civic life and politics. While the romance novels end with marriage and reinforce the elite Roman social codes for social and civic life, Thecla's story begins with eschewing her own betrothed and ends with her firm commitment to remain a virgin, thus challenging the prevailing norms that center civic life in the elite family. For example, Kate Cooper suggests that the romance novel carries a second plotline wherein two rival male political forces vie for supremacy.[27] The Acts of Paul and Thecla is read as the words of the emerging Christian male leaders, who seek to usurp the traditional control of the city from the wealthy elite. Thecla becomes a vehicle to establish a new order based on a Christian vision of society, but this vision also retains the old order's insistence on male elite dominance. Cooper's view is provocative but ultimately inadequate to explain the early church's understandings.[28]

A second position builds on the idea of comparing the Acts of Paul and Thecla to a romance novel but suggests that the Thecla story does more than replace one pagan male rival with a Christian interlocutor seeking a similar sort of civic power. Instead, this second view suggests that the Acts of Paul and Thecla calls into question the very nature of Roman marriage as representative of proper civic life.[29] That is, the Acts of Paul and Thecla seeks to overthrow the elites' vision of marriage that had developed during the Roman Empire. In Augustus's time, the understanding of marriage as a private affair between elite Roman citizens was reshaped into a public institution legislated by the state. This meant, first, that marriage was a source of honor for men, because the public realm bestowed (or rescinded) honor. Second, there grew a belief that a happy marriage was one filled with harmony, or *concordia*, between husband and wife. Such harmony was viewed as symbolic of the elite families' relationship with their city, as its cultural and political leaders: "In the second century the married couple was employed as the image for the type of devotion and harmony holding between all members of a society."[30] Third, the

27. Kate Cooper, *The Virgin and the Bride: Idealized Womanhood in Late Antiquity* (Cambridge, MA: Harvard University Press, 1996), 51–56.

28. Shelly Matthews, "Thinking of Thecla: Issues in Feminist Historiography," *JFSR* 17 (2001): 47–50.

29. Andrew S. Jacobs, "'Her Own Proper Kinship': Marriage, Class and Women in the Apocryphal Acts of the Apostles," in *A Feminist Companion to the New Testament Apocrypha*, ed. Amy-Jill Levine with Maria Mayo Robbins, FCNTECW 11 (New York: T&T Clark, 2006), 19.

30. Judith Perkins, *The Suffering Self: Pain and Narrative Representation in the Early Christian Era* (New York: Routledge, 1995), 48.

continence promised between the novel's lovers included both the woman *and the man*. The romance novels allow for a few sexual encounters by the male, but these are carefully coded to reinforce the overarching concern of fidelity to the marriage and thus the city.[31] The elite marriage was public, representing civic loyalty, and the public virtue of *concordia* was internalized within the marriage relationship.

If the romance novel pulls a bit at the hem of this story line from time to time by referencing lower-class experiences of love alongside the elite couple's story, the Acts of Paul and Thecla yanks on the thread, unraveling the whole by challenging the elite's vision of the goals of life. In the Thecla story, the notion of marriage as civic duty and moral responsibility of the elite is upheld by her mother but critiqued by Paul's gospel. Thecla embraces the Christian model of kinship, which devalues familial ties and loyalty to clan. Thus the call of continence for Thecla comes not as a call to reject sex, or even embodiment; it comes as a call to reject her social class. The insight here is that marriage represented different things to the various social classes. For the elite Thecla, her renunciation of the marriage package includes rejecting the moral and civic underpinnings that gave meaning to the conjugal union.

### The Acts of Paul and Thecla and Ancient Hagiography

The romance novel genre as backdrop for understanding the Acts of Paul and Thecla has garnered wide support among scholars. Yet some point to hagiography as a helpful lens through which to read Thecla's story. Hagiography is a biography of a saint or holy person. The term can be defined as "ideologically directed biography."[32] Hagiography has also been placed alongside fictional history, which contains embroidered events, and the line between hagiography and fiction is not always clear. Even more, hagiography is well described not so much as a genre, but as *"a manner of narration."*[33] That is, the hagiographer is interested in venerating the saint's life for the edification of the reader.

Why does this category seem appropriate to some scholars? The reasons relate to their dissatisfaction with the explanatory powers of the romance novel lens to answer questions about Thecla's ascetic, devotional choices. For example, the romance novel includes erotic scenes of both heterosexual and homosexual desire. Some see a similar emphasis on erotic desire in Thecla's

31. Perkins, *Suffering Self*, 71.
32. *CAGN*, 3.
33. Glenn E. Snyder, *Acts of Paul: The Formation of a Pauline Corpus*, WUNT 2/352 (Tübingen: Mohr Siebeck, 2013), 121, emphasis original.

behavior toward Paul. They point to her kissing his chains and rolling on the floor where he has previously sat. They notice her steady gaze toward Paul when she initially hears his message from her window seat, and her fervent glances at the crowd to see Paul when she is first brought into the arena in Iconium. Yet others are not persuaded, suggesting instead that her actions represent the devotion of a disciple to her teacher, and by extension to her God. Thecla represents the model disciple's response to the imprisoned martyr, and her actions bespeak "cultic piety."[34] By this reading, Thecla's kissing his chains or rolling where he sat in prison reflects her conviction that his body is holy. The author hints as much in the opening description of Paul given to Onesiphorus as one who has the face of an angel. Paul later states that those who fear God are blessed, as they shall become angels of God. Thecla is said to "love" Paul (APTh 3.19), but the Greek term used (*storgē*) primarily refers to love between parent and child, or love as an abstraction. Rarely does the term carry sexual connotations.[35] Finally, when she enters the arena and her confidence stumbles, she looks into the crowd and sees "the Lord as Paul"; thus this vision enables her to endure. Glenn Snyder suggests that this episode calls to mind "the cultic practice [of] gazing on an image of the apostle and thus seeing the Lord."[36] Along these same lines, Susan A. Calef suggests that the trials faced by Thecla are best seen in relation to the biblical emphasis on trials producing perseverance, coupled with the romance novel's emphasis on fidelity.[37] Thus the separation of Thecla and Paul serves to test her commitment to the faith and message of the gospel. The tribulations form character and demonstrate steadfast devotion to God.[38]

Answering the genre question is an important piece of the interpretive puzzle, because genre guides the reader in discerning central themes of the work. The Acts of Paul and Thecla draws on the romance novel as a structural framework and also the hagiographical approach to encourage pious behavior in imitation of the saint. The hybrid nature of the narrative's genre

34. Ibid., 125.
35. Ibid., 125n93.
36. Ibid., 129.
37. Susan A. Calef, "Thecla 'Tried and True' and the Inversion of Romance," in Levine and Robbins, *Feminist Companion to the New Testament Apocrypha*, 180.
38. Snyder, *Acts of Paul*, 129–37, suggests that our narrative might also draw intertextually from the biblical stories of Abraham and Sarah. Snyder draws intriguing parallels, including that Genesis and the APTh tell a story of the woman's capture twice. In both stories (1) foreign males find Sarah/Thecla so beautiful as to be driven to distraction, and (2) familial males deny a relationship with the female, such that (3) the female is taken captive. During the second captivity incident, (4) both Sarah and Thecla's chastity is preserved, and upon release (5) both Abraham/Sarah and Paul/Thecla are given material goods. Isaac and Rebekah used a similar ruse, informing strangers that they are brother and sister (Gen. 26:6–11).

Figure 1.4. Thecla's influence continues today, as witnessed by the St. Thecla monastery near Damascus, Syria.

highlights the complexity of the Acts of Paul and Thecla and perhaps reveals why Thecla's story influenced subsequent centuries of Christian men and women. Its complexity allows flexibility and nimbleness as each generation of readers faced its own challenges. Perhaps Thecla's politically charged resistance to Roman social norms of marriage helped second- and third-century disenfranchised Christian men and women counter their dominant and dominating culture. Here the roles of both Thecla's mother, Theocleia, and the patron/mother figure of Tryphaena come into focus. The former represents the Roman status quo, while the latter serves as Thecla's new mother, her new "kin" who offers protection and financial support. Yet the same action of rejecting marriage could be interpreted by wealthy Christian women in the fourth and fifth centuries as advocating virginity and renunciation of wealth.

## Conclusion

In the second and third centuries, Thecla's story was used to think about ascetic lifestyle, the doctrines and practices of baptism and public teaching, and the configuration of kinship or family ties. In the fourth century, her story was shared on her martyr feast day, and pilgrims flocked to her shrines, perhaps for healing, perhaps for a glimpse of divine power. A large church marking her martyr's shrine was built near Seleucia, Asia Minor, her alleged last abode. Current excavations have uncovered three fifth-century churches, including one measuring eighty meters in length, as well as a large Roman bath and numerous water cisterns.[39] A late fourth- or early fifth-century visitor, Egeria, writes about her journey there; we will meet her in chapter 6.[40] A century later, two women from Syria travel north to Thecla's shrine, forgoing food throughout the journey.[41] Key theologians visited this site; in 374, Gregory of Nazianzus traveled there, in part to escape an unpleasant job post.[42] He included Thecla as the only woman in a list of early apostolic martyrs that included Peter and Paul, James, Stephen, John, Luke, and Andrew.[43]

Thecla's reputation continued to influence Christians. In the fourth century, the bishop of Olympus, Methodius (d. 311/312), presents Thecla as a philosopher and a great teacher of the church. As any good philosopher would do, Thecla models right living. For Methodius, Thecla imitates Christ and thus can serve as a philosopher to the church. She served, as well, as a model for Olympias, a fifth-century deaconess in the cathedral of Constantinople. In the Life of Olympias, the author includes an extensive description of Thecla: "a citizen of heaven, a martyr who conquered in many contests, the holy one among women, who despised wealth, hated the sharp and transitory pleasures of this world, refused a pecunious marriage and confessed that she would present herself a chaste virgin to her true Bridegroom." And the author continues, "Olympias walked in the footsteps of this saint, Thecla, in every virtue of the divinely-inspired way of life."[44] Olympias was a wealthy woman whose first marriage lasted two years; she refused a second marriage even though Emperor Theodosius insisted that she marry one of his kinsmen. She was a close associate of John Chrysostom, who exchanged many letters with her, seventeen of which are extant. Another fourth-century figure, Gregory of Nyssa, reveals that his sister, Macrina, has a secret family name given her by

39. Stephen J. Davis, *The Cult of Saint Thecla: A Tradition of Women's Piety in Late Antiquity*, OECS (Oxford: Oxford University Press, 2001), 6, citing Ernst Herzfeld and Samuel Guyer, *Meriamlik und Korykos: Zwei christliche Ruinenstätten des rauhen Kilikiens*, MAMA 2 (Manchester: Manchester University Press, 1930), 1–89.
40. Davis, *Cult of Saint Thecla*, 5; Egeria, *Itinerary of Egeria (Itinerarium Egeriae)* 22.2, in *Egeria: Diary of a Pilgrimage*, trans. George E. Gingras, ACW 38 (Westminster, MD: Newman, 1970), 22–23.
41. Theodoret of Cyrrhus, *A History of the Monks of Syria* 29; English translation in *Women's Religions in the Greco-Roman World: A Sourcebook*, ed. Ross Shepard Kraemer (Oxford: Oxford University Press, 2004), 404–5.
42. Gregory of Nazianzus, *Concerning His Own Life (De vita sua)* 548–49 (PG 37:1067).
43. Gregory of Nazianzus, *Oratio (Oration)* 4.69 (*First Invective against Julian the Emperor* [*Contra Julianum*]).
44. Life of Olympias 1.1, in Kraemer, *Women's Religions in the Greco-Roman World*, 228. For a full text of the anonymous fifth-century Life of Olympias, see Clark, *Jerome, Chrysostom, and Friends*, 127–42.

her mother at birth: Thecla.[45] And Jerome promises Eustochium, a young virgin and a daughter of his patron Paula, that Thecla, Mary the mother of Jesus, and Miriam will greet her in heaven.[46] Stephen Davis notes that Thecla was a "female saint whose popularity rivalled that of Mary in the early church."[47]

Her story continued to inspire into the fifth and sixth centuries. One example is the story of Eugenia, the daughter of the Roman eparch Philip in Alexandria, set in the late second century.[48] One day while traveling from the city to a village, she reads the story of Thecla and chooses to follow her example. In *the Life of Eugenia*, the author recounts how Eugenia embraces Thecla's model. She declares herself free from her family by cutting her hair, dressing in men's clothing, and going on pilgrimage. Eventually she resides in a male monastery, concealing her female identity under her short hair and male clothing. Eugenia grows in her piety such that she performs miracles and becomes head abbot. In an ironic twist, a woman healed by Eugenia accuses her of making sexual advances. To prove her innocence and the propriety of her monastery, she reveals that she too is a woman.

Several points should be noticed. First, Thecla's example encourages women to pursue the ascetic life with great determination. Second, women read Thecla's story, which highlights the rising educational level among Christians in the later centuries.[49] Archaeologists have discovered two pocket-sized books of the Acts of Thecla in Egypt, dating from the fourth and fifth centuries.[50] The picture of Eugenia reading Thecla while traveling matches the evidence. Third, in her defense in court against charges of sexual misconduct, Eugenia specifically states she has imitated Thecla, and to show that she is female, she tears her garment to reveal her breasts. Interestingly, her pose presents a picture similar to those stamped on votive clay containers, as Thecla stands naked to the waist.[51]

In Syria, the Syrian Orthodox patriarch in 512–18, Severus of Antioch, writes about the miracles and healings that continue to happen at Thecla's shrine. In his homily given on her feast day (September 24) he makes this clear.[52] Again, in a letter exchanged with Solon, metropolitan bishop of Seleucia, in

45. Gregory of Nyssa, *Vit. Macr.* 3 (Silvas, *Macrina the Younger*, 112).

46. Jerome, *Epistles* (*Epistulae*) 22.41.

47. Davis, *Cult of Saint Thecla*, 4.

48. Ibid., 143–48.

49. John Chrysostom, a fourth-century bishop of Antioch, speaks of wealthy women who wore miniature Gospel books on chains as necklaces; *Homilies on Matthew* (*Homiliae in Matthaeum*) 72 (PG 58:669).

50. For details, see Davis, *Cult of Saint Thecla*, 146.

51. Ibid., 147.

52. Severus of Antioch, *Cathedral Homilies* (*Homiliae cathedrales*) 97.

about 511, Severus encourages Solon to be confident in his faith, declaring that "assuredly the honorable in virginity and first of female martyrs, and skilled maker of these things, I mean the holy Thecla, will clothe you in such raiment to do honor to her vote concerning you."[53] The wider context is important: at this time in history, the church has divided between those who adopted the decisions of the council at Chalcedon and those who reject them. These men are part of the non-Chalcedon group. Notice that Thecla is called upon as providing strength in a doctrinal dispute, adding her pious weight to these men's position.

Thecla's story was not only for women; men also were inspired to follow her example. John, bishop of Tella in Syria, was drawn into the ascetic life after reading her book. His biographer describes a well-to-do family and a childhood in which John's father passed away and his mother and a local priest raised him. He was nurtured in the Christian faith. After reading Thecla's story, John withdrew to a small upper room in his home and established himself as an ascetic. Thecla captured the imagination of the poor, the pilgrims, and the bishops. Her story was celebrated on her feast day, and votive lamps were stamped with her seal. This sixth-century anonymous Syrian hymn nicely encapsulates the power Thecla held among the pious followers of Christ during the early centuries of the church.

> "The king shall delight in thy beauty" (Ps. 45:12)
> Christ who speaks in Paul
> —He who said: "I have come to put fire on the earth" [cf. Luke 12:49–53]
> by inflaming with his love the soul of the holy virgin Thecla,
> He burned from her the bonds of fleshly brotherhood,
> He preserved her virginity in purity,
> He supported her in the combat of martyrdom,
> He quenched the fire,
> And placed a muzzle and a bit in the mouth of carnivorous beasts,
> He rendered the idolatrous bondmaid an evangelist and apostolic,
> preaching and proclaiming the word of life everywhere amid all dangers.
> By her prayers bestow, our Savior, upon men and women alike
> Thoughts of chastity and thy great mercy.[54]

53. Catherine Burris and Lucas van Rompay, "Some Further Notes on Thecla in Syriac Christianity," *Hug* 6.2 (2009): 338, citing E. W. Brooks, *The Sixth Book of the Select Letters of Severus Patriarch of Antioch in the Syriac Version of Athanasius of Nisibis*, vol. 1, *Text*, part 1 (London: Williams & Norgate, 1902), 12–13; ET from Brooks, *Sixth Book*, vol. 2, *Translation*, part 1 (1903), 12.

54. Burris and Rompay, "Some Further Notes," 339; ET from E. W. Brooks, *James of Edessa: The Hymns of Severus of Antioch and Others*, PO 6–7 (Paris: Firmin-Didot, 1911), 2:620–21 (208–9).

In sum, the brilliance of Thecla's story depends not on proving she was in some way a historical figure but on the story's flexibility to meet the new demands of each generation. The blurry historical outline allows her to take new shapes and contours as the church adapts to new circumstances, most notably from being a persecuted minority to providing the religion of the empire. Thecla is a malleable figure that bends to the immediate needs, while still retaining a strong connection to the past. And Thecla is a venerable character, one that is revered by subsequent generations as a figure who inspires, who teaches, who models. Part of the genius of Thecla is that she is a character in a cosmic drama: she is every person or "the church," vulnerable to the terrifying forces of "the world" and yet victorious. Her story tells the church's story and models the church's proper posture toward the world. Thecla becomes what any specific generation of the church needs her to be. In a limited sense, perhaps Thecla is the ancient church's avatar,[55] for she makes a new appearance in successive generations. She presents a "self" to the world that the church upholds and aspires to imitate.

55. There appears to be no easy analogue to Thecla in our own day, but we offer this analogy: Thecla is like a comic book character, who is reappropriated in successive generations. Batman and Superman first fought the Nazis, then the Communists, then perhaps big business. Superheroes are not "real" in a historical sense, but they have their "mild-mannered" side (Bruce Wayne, Clark Kent) that fronts a "normal-guy" facade. Their powers are portrayed as for good, against evil, and stand for American values like freedom and justice and capitalism and rooting for the little guy. In that sense, these heroes inspire each generation, even as in each generation the hero addresses specific cultural values such as the civil rights movement, women's rights, and environmentalism.

# 2

# Perpetua and Felicitas: Mothers and Martyrs

Augustine (354–430), bishop of Hippo in North Africa, exclaimed that "God's holy servants Perpetua and Felicity, adorned with the garlands of martyrdom, burst into bloom in perpetual felicity, holding onto the name of Christ in the war, and at the same time also finding their own names in the reward."[1] His audience knew these women's stories well, for every year they commemorated their "birthday"—that is, the day of their martyrdom, when they were born in heaven (*natalicium*).[2] These two women, along with four men, were martyred on March 7, 203, during the reign of Septimius Severus (Passion of Perpetua and Felicitas 7.8). The spectacle that included their deaths celebrated the birthday of Septimius's younger son, Emperor Geta.[3] Such festivals were

1. Augustine, *Sermons* (*Sermones*) 280.1; trans. Edmund Hill in *Sermons III/8 (273–305A) on the Saints*, The Works of Saint Augustine: A Translation for the 21st Century, ed. John E. Rotelle (Hyde Park, NY: New City, 1994), 72.

2. Also well known is Blandina, a slave woman from the city of Lyons (in modern-day central France) whose example of courage and fortitude astonished the crowds. See Eusebius, *Ecclesiastical History* (*Historia ecclesiastica*) 5.1.3–63.

3. In 195 Septimius Severus granted the title of Caesar to his older son, Caracalla; he followed with the same action in 198 for his younger son, Geta; and he gave the title Augustus to Caracalla. In 209, Severus granted Geta the title Augustus. Septimius Severus died in February 211, and Caracalla murdered his brother, Geta, in December of that year. The following year, he banned any celebration of Geta's birthday. This information helps us date the martyrdom of Perpetua, as well as the writing of this story, for the Latin retains Geta's name.

common across the empire; *munera* (sing. *munus*) focused on gladiatorial games and athletic contests as public entertainment; in this case, the brutal cabaret resulted in six martyrs' deaths. These witnesses help shape Christian identity and establish liturgical and devotional practices, such as veneration of saints and relics, for centuries to come, indeed to this present day. Although the age of the early Christian martyrs ends with the rise of Constantine and his Edict of Milan (in 313; see chap. 4), their testimony unto death embodies the Christian ideal of suffering and sacrifice.

The early martyrs' witness and the church's reflection on suffering relative to their martyrdom continue to shape and inform churches now. It may be tempting for Christians to use the sufferings of today's martyrs to further a contemporary cause, even promote vengeance against those perpetrating the violence. An antidote to this approach is a nuanced examination of the ancient narrative, paying close attention to the theological importance given to confident nonretaliation in the face of oppressive violence.

## Introduction to Female Christian Martyrs

As the church entered the second century, questions about doctrine and identity were forged in the crucible of persecution. Although very few Christians died a martyr's death in this century, the image of martyr became a key figure around which Christians explained their worldview and its opposition to aspects of the Roman culture. It is possible that as many women were martyred as men; at least we could say that the torture and savagery were meted out in equal measure to men and women—the martyr's death was not a respecter of gender.

What is perhaps less recognized is the place of motherhood alongside martyrdom in the stories of female martyrs. As we saw in chapter 1, Thecla, the beast fighter, is also known as the church's first female martyr.[4] She defies her mother, gains a surrogate mother, and refuses the promise of motherhood with her rejection of marriage. In the Passion of Perpetua and Felicitas, we find Perpetua, a young mother nursing her son. Based on her acceptance of

---

4. Thecla is known as the first *female* martyr of the church. The church's first martyr is Stephen; his death is described in Acts 7. Church tradition memorializes the apostles Peter and Paul as martyrs. The earliest martyr after the apostolic age is Ignatius, bishop of Antioch, who writes seven letters to churches in Asia Minor and Rome and to Polycarp, bishop of Smyrna, as he travels from his home city to Rome to face his death. About fifty years after Ignatius, Polycarp, bishop of Smyrna, a city on the coast of Asia Minor, is martyred. Polycarp was the teacher of Irenaeus, bishop of Lyons in central Gaul (modern-day France). Irenaeus takes the reins of this bishopric after the previous elderly bishop and many congregants are martyred in 177. Their story is told in the "Letter of the Churches of Vienne and Lyons," in Eusebius, *Hist. eccl.* 5.1.3–63.

the Christian gospel, and in a stance quite unbecoming for a Roman matron, she defies her father. We read about Felicitas, a young slave who gives birth to a daughter directly before dying a martyr's death in the arena with her fellow martyrs. Their defiance of conventional expectations for familial *pietas*, or faithful rendering of family obligations, is especially evident in the female martyrs' stories. Through the martyrs' actions and words, the early church forged a new model of community and familial responsibilities, which rightly shocked the ancient world, and still today, though perhaps for different reasons, raises scholars' eyebrows.

In this chapter we examine the stories of these two important martyrs, Perpetua and Felicitas. Our investigation operates at two levels. First, we pay attention to historical questions and present a plausible reconstruction of the life of the martyr and the church that preserved her memory. Second, we address the catechetical and rhetorical emphases promoted in the passion stories of these martyrs. In this latter regard, Robin Darling Young offers a theologically rich definition of Christian martyrdom as "a public liturgical sacrifice in which the word of Jesus and his kingdom was confessed and acted out, and an offering made that repeated his own."[5] In this explanation, Young draws on the third-century theologian Origen, who declared that martyrdom is going "in procession before the world."[6] The historical reality of persecution (and the threat of persecution) generated the need to speak about its meaning within the purposes of God as the Christians understood it. A developing theology of suffering, as well as the critique of elite Roman social values, especially duties to one's family (*pietas*), reinforced the significance of the martyr's testimony. The female martyr's witness sharpened the church's critique of Roman family values, even as it also may have affirmed the Roman culture's assumptions about the inherent weakness of the female. The gospel was so strong, the church could argue, that by its power even a weak female was made stronger than the strongest warrior.

## Definition of Martyrdom

At first glance, it may seem that the definition of a martyr is obvious, but a closer look reveals more complexity. The key issues revolve around the agency of the one killed, the authority of the one who executes, and the community

---

5. Robin Darling Young, *In Procession before the World: Martyrdom as Public Liturgy in Early Christianity* (Milwaukee: Marquette University Press, 2001), 11.

6. Origen, *Exhortation to Martyrdom (Exhortatio ad martyrium)* 42; see Young, *In Procession before the World*, 14.

who remembers the death. Questions emerge as to the role of the martyrs in their own deaths. Did they provoke authorities into arresting them?[7] Could a martyr's death be labeled suicide?[8] The government's involvement distinguishes a martyr's death from suicide. One school of thought argues that martyrdom grew out of a Christian appropriation of the Roman idea of the noble death.[9] While the ideal of dying with honor factors into a martyr's death, fundamentally different values support the "noble death" promoted by the Romans. Additionally, by beginning with the assumption that martyrdom is a Christian phenomenon, this theory neglects Jewish history of the second century BCE. At this time, a pagan king, Antiochus IV, outlawed practices of Judaism, including circumcision, Sabbath, and food laws such as abstaining from pork. Jews who did not renounce their ancestral religious customs were under threat of torture and even put to death. Ultimately, a resistance movement known as the Maccabean Revolt vindicates these witnesses and overthrows the Seleucid government, establishing the Hasmonean dynasty. Their triumph is celebrated each year at Hanukkah.

Thus a second perspective suggests that martyrdom began with these Maccabean martyrs and continued within the early church.[10] This perspective argues that a martyr is one who accepts a violent death at the hands of pagan authorities rather than submit to a decree or demand contrary to their convictions, which are shared by a community (and thus are not idiosyncratic beliefs).[11] Jewish martyrdom at this time can be characterized by the defense of the Jewish law against "a tyrannical oppressor, a threat to the nation, [as well as] heroic endurance by the ostensibly weak . . . and a victory which is inherent in the death itself."[12] While both Jewish and Christian martyrs served

7. For a discussion on voluntary martyrdom, see Candida R. Moss, "The Discourse of Voluntary Martyrdom: Ancient and Modern," *CH* 81.3 (2012): 531–51.

8. Kathleen Gallagher Elkins, "Mother, Martyr: Reading Self-Sacrifice and Family in Early Christianity" (PhD diss., Drew University, 2013), 99n9. She cites Émile Durkheim, who classified martyrdom as suicide, but his definition has not influenced many who study the martyrdom of the early church.

9. G. W. Bowersock, *Martyrdom and Rome* (Cambridge: Cambridge University Press, 1995).

10. W. H. C. Frend, *Martyrdom and Persecution in the Early Church: A Study of the Conflict from the Maccabees to Donatus* (New York: New York University Press, 1965).

11. Jan Willem van Henten, "Jewish and Christian Martyrs," in *Saints and Role Models in Judaism and Christianity*, ed. Marcel Poorthuis and Joshua Schwartz (Leiden: Brill, 2004), 163–81.

12. Tessa Rajak, "Dying for the Law: The Martyr's Portrait in Jewish-Greek Literature," in *Portraits: Biographical Representation in the Greek and Latin Literature of the Roman Empire*, ed. M. J. Edwards and Simon Swain (Oxford: Clarendon, 1997), 40. She argues that immortal life is not necessarily part of the victory, and that the martyrs desired God to drive the evil king out of the land. This chapter is also republished in Rajak, *The Jewish Dialogue with Greece and Rome: Studies in Cultural and Social Interaction* (Leiden: Brill, 2002); see esp. 100.

to inspire their respective communities, Christians also promoted martyrdom as a way to propagate their religion.

A third position suggests that martyrdoms should be viewed as a discourse emphasizing ideological convictions. Candida Moss defines martyrdom as "a set of discursive practices that shaped early Christian identities, mediated ecclesiastical and dogmatic claims, and provided meaning to the experience described by Christians as persecution, and in doing so produced a new economy of action."[13] She advises caution in aggregating martyrdom accounts, instead promoting a close reading of individual texts to highlight the diversity of genres and ideologies among this ancient collection. Moss wisely warns historians against imposing a linear and cohesive progression of martyr ideology and theology. And she points out that ancient martyrdom and the discourse surrounding martyrdom are not the sole purview of the ancient orthodoxy, for various groups identifying as Christian held positions on martyrdom.[14]

A final position stresses the social, cultural, and political ramifications of martyrdom. It sees Christian martyrdom as "a public witness . . . of a private belief in opposition to that of the majority."[15] Martyrdom was a political act that reached into both the public and private spaces of society. By embracing martyrdom, Christians challenged the status quo, the fundamental principles upon which Roman culture was based.

### Early Christian Views of Martyrdom

How did the early Christians talk about martyrdom? The second-century Christian writer Tertullian declared that "the blood of Christian [martyrs] is seed [of the church]."[16] Tertullian viewed martyrdom as something that could attract pagans to the church, and some historians today argue that onlookers were impressed and even attracted to the martyrs' witness.[17] For example, Tacitus the historian, writing in the early second century, speaks of the emperor Nero's punishment of Christians sixty years earlier. Blaming the

13. Candida R. Moss, *Ancient Christian Martyrdom: Diverse Practices, Theologies, and Traditions*, AYBRL (New Haven: Yale University Press, 2012), 16.

14. For a review of Moss's *Ancient Christian Martyrdom* and *The Myth of Persecution: How Early Christians Invented a Story of Martyrdom* (New York: HarperOne, 2013), see Amy Brown Hughes, "Responsible Remembrance: Rethinking Persecution and Martyrdom in the Early Church," *Books & Culture* (November/December 2014): 8–9.

15. Thomas J. Heffernan, *The Passion of Perpetua and Felicity* (Oxford: Oxford University Press, 2012), 18.

16. Tertullian, *Apology* (*Apologeticus*) 50.13.

17. Rodney Stark, *The Rise of Christianity: A Sociologist Reconsiders History* (Princeton: Princeton University Press, 1996).

Christians for the great fire that burned about two-thirds of Rome, Nero put Christians up on poles and then set them ablaze as torches to light the streets. Tacitus states that the people of Rome were sympathetic to the Christians' fate and believed that Nero acted with excessive cruelty.[18] Other scholars, however, contend that most pagans were repulsed at martyrs' religious and social behaviors. A third possibility is that the pagans lumped the Christians in with other prisoners executed in spectacles. Daniel Boyarin argues that pagans did not distinguish a Christian's death in the arena from that of a criminal.[19] It is only the memory of their deaths preserved by the martyrs' communities that makes their deaths worthy of the label martyrdom. His observation highlights a key aspect of our texts and the stories within them: Christians preserved them and incorporated them into Christian liturgies, pilgrimages, and catechetical ideals.

## Ancient Views of Christians and the Games

Jakob Engberg looked at all pagan works written between 110 and 210 that refer to Christians, and in every case but one they mention the execution of Christians. Most pagan sources remark on the Christian's readiness to die.[20] They assume that their readers would have seen or heard of Christians dying in the arena. The second-century physician Galen dismisses Christian ideas but admires their ethic of ascetic restraint.[21] Arrian (ca. 87–160), a pupil of the philosopher Epictetus, is less enamored. While he admits that Christians share his disdain of the material things of this world, including their own lives, he warns his readers that the Christians do not come to this place through reason.[22] Celsus, a famous second-century antagonist to Christianity, knows of the martyrs' resurrection beliefs, but he thinks such ideas ridiculous and perhaps evidence of madness.[23] In sum, most of these authors sympathized with the Christian martyrs' contempt for death but thought it absurd or ignorant to endure a torturous death willingly.

18. Tacitus, *Annals* (*Annales*) 15.44.
19. Daniel Boyarin, *Dying for God: Martyrdom and the Making of Christianity and Judaism* (Stanford, CA: Stanford University Press, 1999), 94.
20. Jakob Engberg, "Martyrdom and Persecution: Pagan Perspectives on the Prosecution and Execution of Christians, c. 110–210 AD," in *Contextualising Early Christian Martyrdom*, ed. Jakob Engberg, Uffe Homsgaard Eriksen, and Anders Klostergaard Petersen (Frankfurt: Peter Lang, 2011), 96–97.
21. Galen, *Commentary on Plato's "Republic,"* cited in Engberg, "Martyrdom and Persecution," 105.
22. Arrian, in Epictetus, *Discourses* (*Diatribai*) 4.7; cited in Engberg, "Martyrdom and Persecution," 109–10.
23. Origen, *Cels.* 8.55–56.

One must remember that gladiatorial games were common within the Roman Empire. What started in the third century BCE as funerary celebrations then grew by the imperial period to focus on military victories and promote the imperial cult: "The gladiatorial contests became ritualized entertainment with strong political motives."[24] Today we tend to think of these spectacles as involving only Christians, but the vast majority included criminals, prisoners of war, and slaves, although some were professional gladiators with celebrity status among the crowds. A gladiator trainer, known as a *lanista*, could charge twenty denarii for a healthy gladiator per fight, but might ask a one-thousand-denarii recompense for one who dies or is maimed in an event. Slaves would bring honor to their owners, and by extension to themselves, if they bravely took the painful blows and offered their necks when losing the fight. Even a criminal might gain honor if he fought bravely.[25] Most who were killed in the arena were slaves or criminals, for as the first-century philosopher Seneca wryly commented, these games might reform the guilty, might deter others, and certainly could rid society of miscreants.[26]

### Women in the Arena

What should be clear to the reader from this brief description is that very few women were gladiators. This fact becomes important as we read the martyrdom accounts, for women are frequently mentioned.[27] The average pagan attending a spectacle would not expect to see women in the arena. As described in the Passion, even the bloodthirsty crowds pause when two young women, Perpetua and Felicitas, enter the arena. For us today, these women we meet in this chapter might seem to be, on the one hand, very familiar to us in their concern for their infants, their delight in caring for their babies, and their worry about childbirth. On the other hand, their willingness to hand over their newborn or infant children to caregivers and then march to their death—this is hard for us to wrap our minds around.

24. Jesper Carlsen, "Exemplary Deaths in the Arena: Gladiatorial Fights and the Execution of Criminals," in Engberg, Eriksen, and Petersen, *Contextualising Early Christian Martyrdom*, 78.
25. Cicero, *Tusculan Disputations* (*Tusculanae disputationes*) 2.41.
26. Seneca, *On Clemency* (*De clementia*) 1.22.1; and Carlsen, "Exemplary Deaths," 85.
27. Antti Marjanen, "Male Women Martyrs: The Function of Gender-Transformation Language in Early Christian Martyrdom Accounts," in *Metamorphoses: Resurrection, Body and Transformative Practices in Early Christianity*, ed. Turid Karlsen Seim and Jorunn Økland, Ekstasis 1 (Berlin: de Gruyter, 2009), 247. Marjanen argues that Perpetua's becoming a male in her vision communicates her courage and stamina in the arena as a gladiator.

## Female Jewish Martyrs and the Church

Who were these female martyrs of the early church? Ironically, they precede the church, for they include Jewish women who lived under the rule of the infamous Antiochus IV Epiphanes, a Seleucid ruler of the early second century BCE (mentioned above). He outlawed circumcision, Sabbath observance, and food laws, and he confiscated and burned Torah scrolls (1 Macc. 1). In 2 Maccabees and 4 Maccabees, we read the story of two mothers who circumcised their infant sons; they were later arrested and then, with their sons hung at their breasts, were paraded through the streets and flung to their deaths from the Jerusalem city wall (2 Macc. 6:10). In a second episode, a mother watches her seven sons tortured and killed as she encourages them to stand fast against the tyrant's demands to break their ancestral law. "Last of all, the mother died, after her sons" (2 Macc. 7:41). The church commemorated the martyrdoms, for as Augustine claimed, "they were Christians" (*Serm.* 300.2); they "died for the name of Christ veiled in the law" (300.5).

## Passion of Perpetua and Felicitas: Authorship

Perpetua and Felicitas's story has come down to us in two different Latin versions, the Passion of Perpetua and Felicitas[28] and the *Acta Brevia Perpetuae et Felicitatis*.[29] One Greek text of the Passion survives.[30] The Passion's structure includes two introductory chapters written by an editor, followed by chapters 3–10 allegedly from Perpetua, which form the core of the Passion. These chapters include four visions, as well as descriptions of her encounters with her father, her nursing son, and fellow prisoners. Chapters 11–13 recount the vision of Saturus, a male martyr. The work closes with the final chapters (14–21) describing Felicitas's childbirth and the martyrs in the arena. The *Acta* is preserved in two slightly varied accounts, both of which are different

28. Latin: *Passio Sanctarum Perpetuae et Felicitatis*. The Greek version, (ET as) *Passion of Perpetua and Those Put to Death with Her in Africa*, as well as the Latin, is available in *Passion de Perpétue et de Félicité suivi des Actes*, edited with French translation by Jacqueline Amat, SC 417 (Paris: Cerf, 1996).

29. The identification of this Latin work as "Acta" was done by van Beek, in an effort to distinguish this composition about Perpetua from the text known to scholars as the Passion of Perpetua. Within the manuscripts themselves, the "Acta" is identified as the *passio* of these martyrs. See Cornelius I. M. I. van Beek, ed., *Passio sanctarum Perpetuae et Felicitatis*, vol. 1, *Textum Graecum et Latinum ad fidem codicum mss.* (Nijmegen: Dekker & Van de Vegt, 1936), 58.

30. Thomas J. Heffernan offers a detailed discussion of the manuscript evidence in "The Language of Composition," in *Passion of Perpetua and Felicity*; see Oxford Scholarship Online, 2015, doi:10.1093/acprof:osobl/9780199777570.003.0003.

again from the Passion in their detailed account of the trial, presented as a transcription of the event. Because the *Acta* does not include all four of Perpetua's visions, and because the Passion is most likely the earliest accounting of the events, we will focus on this text. The Passion circulated in both Latin and Greek very early in its history.

The editor notes at the beginning of the text that Perpetua wrote much of the work, *manu sua et suo sensu* (Pass. 2.3), "in her own hand and in accordance with her own understanding."[31] If this claim is true, Perpetua's work is the earliest known piece of prose written by a woman in Latin. A simple claim that Perpetua wrote chapters 3–10, however, goes beyond the evidence. Ross Kraemer and Shira Lander argue that reconstructing Perpetua's martyrdom is hampered by the variety of literary evidence and the "conflicting and indeterminate historical references."[32] They rightly recognize the difficulty in determining a distinctive female voice and "gendered stylistic grounds,"[33] for there is no way to establish what counts as evidence for women authors. Suggesting that the hagiographic nature of the text erects a high barrier to discovering historical events, Kraemer and Lander prefer to regard the Passion as generally representing these women's experiences and events, without claiming historical certainty or female authorship.[34]

Other scholars maintain that Perpetua is behind this text, but exactly how her narrative was used remains an open discussion.[35] Sara Parvis proposes a Latin original for the entire work, evidenced by the "differences of Latin prose rhythm of the different sections of the *Passio*, which make no sense in a translation."[36] Such distinct writing styles, Parvis concludes, are best explained as representing distinct "first-person narratives by Perpetua and Saturus."[37] Erin Ronsse translates the editor's description in 2.3: "This very

31. Translation by Heffernan, *Passion of Perpetua and Felicity*, 126; see 5–17 for an argument that Perpetua wrote the work.

32. Ross S. Kraemer and Shira L. Lander, "Perpetua and Felicitas," in *The Early Christian World*, ed. Philip F. Esler (London: Routledge, 2000), 2:1051.

33. Ibid., 1056.

34. Ibid., 1058.

35. Walter Ameling, "*Femina Liberaliter Instituta*—Some Thoughts on a Martyr's Liberal Education," in *Perpetua's Passions: Multidisciplinary Approaches to the "Passio Perpetuae et Felicitatis,"* ed. Jan N. Bremmer and Marco Formisano (Oxford: Oxford University Press, 2012), 92–98, argues that the level of skill exhibited in the text is consistent with educational opportunities for wealthy women in North Africa in the late second century. Cooper, *Band of Angels*, 103, states that "the surviving records from the early third century preserve the voice of a single ordinary woman [Perpetua] who found herself in circumstances in which the heroism of a Thecla . . . was precisely what was needed."

36. Sara Parvis, "Perpetua," *ExpTim* 120.8 (2009): 366.

37. Ibid.

woman has already thus recounted the entire sequence of her testimony in the same way it was diligently recorded by hand and remains a memento of her sensibility."[38] She argues that the current Passion shows a skilled editor's hand, concluding that Perpetua's oral words are behind the text, but the written text is not from her pen. Ronsse's contention is not based on skepticism about female literacy or abilities, but rather on the text's overall structure and rhetorical integrity. Perpetua's exhortation was authoritative, Ronsse maintains, and served as a model for subsequent generations of men and women who aspired to such faithfulness or desired the martyrs' intercession before God.

The editor's own identity is hidden from us, but some speculate that Tertullian wrote these chapters. This supposition is based on alleged stylistic similarities and his attraction to the New Prophecy, a likely affiliation of this editor, given the comments about the "New Prophecy."[39] Yet others suggest that literary similarities are tenuous at best. Not much is gained or lost by remaining agnostic regarding the editor's identity, for his opinions on key theological debates are clear, and his admiration for the martyrs is beyond question.

## Summary of the Passion of Perpetua and Felicitas

Briefly put, the Passion tells the martyrs' story beginning with the charges leveled against them and their subsequent arrest. It focuses on Vibia Perpetua, age twenty-two years, a "well born, liberally educated, and honorably married" woman (Pass. 2.1).[40] Her husband is not mentioned in the text, but her father, mother, brothers, and infant son all play a role in the unfolding drama. Her family's description helps place her socially. Most likely Perpetua's family traveled from Rome to Carthage around 36 BCE with the resettling

38. Erin Ronsse, "Rhetoric of Martyrs: Listening to Saints Perpetua and Felicitas," *JECS* 14 (2006): 300.

39. The New Prophecy began in Asia Minor in the 160s. The movement stressed prophecy and was led by three key figures—a man named Montanus and two women, Priscilla and Maximilla—seen as inspired by the Holy Spirit. Asceticism was a prominent feature, as was an apocalyptic focus on the end of days. In time the New Prophecy (later known as Montanism) came to be regarded as heretical; its churches were desecrated, its shrines destroyed, and its writings burned. But in the early stages, from about the middle of the second to the early decades of the third century, its views fit within the broad definition of orthodoxy. Church writers such as Hippolytus and Tertullian confirmed that the New Prophecy was trinitarian and held to the saving work of Christ. Tertullian himself appears to have joined the New Prophecy in his hometown of Carthage, likely no later than 207.

40. Translation from Heffernan, *Passion of Perpetua and Felicity*, 126.

Figure 2.1. The *Menologion* or *Service Book* of Basil II includes this depiction of Perpetua, Felicitas, and the other martyrs at their deaths.

of the Eighth Legion. Her family was not of the elite senatorial rank or the equestrian order, but was likely a well-known member of the decurion rank.

The bulk of the narrative features four of Perpetua's visions, as well as poignant scenes with her father, who seeks to dissuade her from her confession. Perpetua offers details about prison life, her care for her infant son, and the attitudes of her fellow martyrs. Another martyr, Saturus, presents his vision, which promises heaven as the martyrs' sure reward. Felicitas, a pregnant slave woman, endures a dramatic childbirth of a premature baby girl, which allows her to join her fellow martyrs the following day in the arena. The editor describes their gruesome deaths, celebrating their faithful testimony to the very end. This same editor shapes the reader's expectations with the opening two chapters, stressing the martyrs' visions and actions as evidence of the work of the Holy Spirit in granting new prophecies and visions to the church. These new deeds are as praiseworthy as the old, because the same "Holy Spirit is always working among us even now" (Pass. 22.11).[41]

## Introduction to Perpetua's Visions

The Passion includes four visions of Perpetua, and these serve as explanations to Perpetua and other martyrs of their current plight and coming martyrdom.

41. Translation from Heffernan, *Passion of Perpetua and Felicity*, 135.

As such, they provide the theological scaffolding for the narrative, even as the encounters with her father propel the plot. The visions revolve around two major questions: What will happen to her and the other prisoners? Will she be able to stop the suffering of her deceased brother? The visions shape the editor's description of her final hours.

We intentionally speak of these as visions, not dreams, because the latter term suggests a passive experience that is entirely personal and serendipitous. In the Latin texts, it is clear that at the vision's conclusion, Perpetua "understands," rather than "awakens." A further distinction is made between her visions and her experience in the arena, when the editor tells us that Perpetua was in a trancelike state during the attack by the mad heifer: "She awakened, as if from a sleep—she was so deep in the spirit and in ecstasy—and looked about her, and said, to the amazement of all: 'When are we to be thrown to the mad cow, or whatever it is?'" (Pass. 20.8).[42] This deep spiritual trance that shielded physical suffering from her consciousness is of a different nature than her four visions. The editor does not judge her trance in the arena negatively; rather, it is another indication, along with her visions, of her spiritual power and depth. Her final charge of encouragement to her fellow martyrs is made all the more powerful because of her episode of rapturous joy.

The text indicates that Perpetua could ask for visions, expect to receive them because she was facing martyrdom, and instruct the community based on their authoritative message. A close examination of Perpetua's visions sets the stage for understanding her martyrdom. They show us how Perpetua understood her faith. Even more, the church affirmed her understanding and promoted it annually in its celebrations of her martyrdom and its public reading of her visions. To appreciate fully her rich interpretation and her self-understanding reflected therein, we will examine each vision in turn before drawing some general conclusions from the four visions.

### Visions 1 and 4: The Battle in the Arena

Perpetua's first and fourth visions focus on her upcoming battle in the arena. In the first vision, she learns that she, along with the rest of the prisoners, will be condemned to death. And in the fourth vision, she discovers more about the identity of her antagonist and the ultimate outcome of the contest. In both visions, she fights faithfully against the devil and is given a reward by Christ, but this bare statement fails to capture the rich allegorical and intertextual content of each vision.

42. Translation from Heffernan, *Passion of Perpetua and Felicity*, 134.

In the story line, Perpetua and the others have been arrested, placed under house arrest, baptized, and then moved into prison—all in the space of several days. After a little time in prison, one of her fellow incipient martyrs, identified as "my brother," asks that Perpetua might request from God a vision. He thinks she will receive what she asks for because she is steadfastly making her confession. And he wants her to ask God whether "there will be suffering or freedom" (Pass. 4.1).[43] It is not entirely clear what he is asking. On the one hand, it may be that he questions whether they will go to their deaths in the arena or be released. At issue is whether the governor will follow through on his threat of punishment. It seems unlikely that he could back down since they have been convicted of capital charges. On the other hand, perhaps the fellow martyr wonders whether any in their group will recant. At her baptism, Perpetua remarks that it was shown to her by the Spirit that nothing should be asked of this water "other than the endurance of the body" (3.5).[44] Most likely this word means that she will face the ultimate test of courage—namely, sharing in the sufferings of Christ. Therefore, the "brother" might wonder whether anyone in the group will recant and thus not endure suffering.[45]

### Perpetua's First Vision

In her first vision, Perpetua sees a ladder reaching to heaven, made of bronze and having weapons of all sorts attached to its sides. At the bottom waits a serpent, while at the top is a garden with a multitude in white dress and a white-haired shepherd milking sheep. Her instructor, who might also be her husband (see discussion below), has mounted the ladder before her and waits for her at the pinnacle. She steps on the serpent's head and then is at the ladder's top and draws near to the shepherd. She receives from him a bit of cheese/milk, and when she has eaten it, the crowd calls out, "Amen!" The sweet taste of the cheese remains in her mouth as the vision ends. When she relays her vision to the brother, they both agree that it portends their suffering.

43. Translation from Heffernan, *Passion of Perpetua and Felicity*, 127.
44. Translation from Heffernan, *Passion of Perpetua and Felicity*, 126.
45. In the story about Blandina and her fellow martyrs, we learn that some recanted, for they had not been prepared to withstand torture (Eusebius, *Hist. eccl.* 5.1.11), and they were imprisoned anyway and horribly tortured (5.1.33). Others recanted and then reaffirmed their Christian faith (5.1.46). One of these martyrs, a woman named Biblias, first recanted and told falsehoods about Christians. Eusebius indicates that she was brought in for further torture, so as to wring from her more impious lies. Ironically, rather than crumble, she stood tall as a Christian (5.1.25–26).

This vision includes allusions to several biblical texts and images, including the ladder, the serpent, the garden, and the shepherd. The ladder immediately calls to mind Jacob's ladder (Gen. 28:12), although here figures only travel up the ladder and must take care not to impale themselves on the metal weapons attached to its sides. The serpent who waits at the bottom is most likely the devil, who led Eve to sin in Genesis 3:1–5. Perpetua steps on his head before safely traversing the ladder. In so doing, she executes, if you will, the foretold punishment that the serpent would strike at the heel of Eve's offspring, but the offspring would tread on the serpent's head (Gen. 3:15). It is no accident that she defeats the Egyptian (the devil) in her fourth vision in this same way, crushing his head (Pass. 10.10–11).

The white-haired shepherd is the Christ figure, whose white hair (Rev. 1:14) and shepherding role (John 10:11; Heb. 13:20; Ps. 23:1) were well known in the church. In the next chapter we will look more closely at the art of the early church; Christ as the Good Shepherd is one of the earliest images depicting Christ. Those around Christ are the faithful martyrs, dressed in white (Rev. 6:9–11), and the lush garden suggests the garden of Eden before the fall. The cheese/milk, sweet to the taste, draws an "Amen!" from the watching martyrs in the garden.

The scene suggests the Eucharist celebration. The ancient world believed that the mother's breast milk was blood redirected from her womb to her breasts and in the process was heated and thus became white.[46] Such an understanding facilitates connecting the milk that makes children grow with the blood of Christ remembered in the wine of the Eucharist. First Peter 2:2–3 speaks of "the pure, spiritual milk" that new Christians should crave, so that they grow strong (see also John 6:53). Tertullian explains that those ready to be baptized are to disown the devil and his angels and be immersed three times in the water, after which, as newborn children, they take the Eucharist for the first time. In this case, it is a mixture of milk and honey,[47] followed by the typical bread and wine.[48] We can imagine, then, that Perpetua and her fellow martyrs were baptized and then took milk and honey before partaking of the Eucharist for the first time (since catechumens did not take the Eucharist). The gathered church would have said "Amen!" at the conclusion of the Eucharist or at some point in the liturgy.[49] Perpetua's vision reinforces her own baptismal experience, even as it points her to her second baptism.

46. Plutarch, *Morals (Moralia)* 495D–496A = *On Affection for Offspring* 3.
47. The "land flowing with milk and honey," drawn from the Hebrew Bible (see Exod. 3:8), also plays a role in the early church's imagination.
48. Tertullian, *On the Military Garland/Crown (De corona militis)* 3.
49. See the Teaching of the Twelve Apostles (Didache) 10.6.

The verb "take" (*accepi*), describing her acceptance of the cheese, is used in one other place, in her fourth vision when Perpetua takes the victory branch from the hand of the gladiator trainer, the Christ figure (Pass. 4.9; 10.12). The visions are linked not only by this verb, but also by the identity of the antagonist as the devil.

### Perpetua's Fourth Vision

We turn now to look more closely at her fourth vision, noticing both its similarities to her first vision and also its significant differences. This vision is a culmination of her teachings and is the boldest statement of her victory in the Lord. She does not ask for this vision, but it serves to clarify what she will face in the arena.

The vision began, she says, with Pomponius, the deacon who cared for the incipient martyrs, banging on her prison door. She unlocked it and followed him on an arduous walk to the amphitheater. Standing in the arena, she is quite surprised that no beasts were loosed; instead, she sees a huge Egyptian man, a gladiator or wrestler, preparing to fight her. Then she too is prepared to fight. She comments, "I was stripped naked, and I became a man" (Pass. 10.7).[50] Then her helpers rubbed her body with oil, while the Egyptian rolled in the dust. At this point, as the match is ready to commence, a towering figure emerged in the center of the arena, the gladiator trainer, who will award the victory to the winner. The punching and kicking began, with the Egyptian trying to grab her heel and Perpetua kicking his face. She landed the final blow to his head, and he fell on his face, whereupon she stepped on his head. With the crowd cheering, she walked to the trainer, who kissed her and granted her peace, and she took the proffered branch. She walked to the exit, the Gate of Life. At this point, the vision ends, and Perpetua understands that she will face not beasts but the devil. Even more, she is convinced that she will win.

As with her first vision, so too here we see the biblical allusions to defeating the devil or serpent by striking his head (Gen. 3:15). Identifying the enemy as the Egyptian likely draws on the archenemy of the Israelites, Pharaoh (see also Ezek. 29:3). If readers have questioned the cosmic nature of the martyr's battle so far in the story, after this vision they are certain that the martyrs face not "flesh and blood" but the devil himself (see Eph. 6:12 for a possible biblical allusion).

Unlike her other visions, in this case much of what she sees corresponds with typical wrestling or gladiatorial matches in games throughout the empire.

---

50. Translation from Heffernan, *Passion of Perpetua and Felicity*, 129.

It is likely that she visited some or at least heard of the events when she was a pagan. For example, each competitor had a team that prepared him with oil, after which he rolled in the dust. Each arena had at least two gates, the Gate of Life and the Gate of Death. Yet not all of the details reflect actual practices, which should not worry the reader, for the vision is not intent on describing a gladiatorial game, or a *pankration*, but depicts a cosmic duel in which Perpetua is a combatant.

Perhaps the most studied aspect of her vision is the statement "I became a man." The Latin reads, *facta sum masculus*, citing the feminine form of the participle (*facta*) when stating she became male. Notice that the text does not use the term *vir* or *mas* but *masculus*, with the diminutive ending.[51] Moreover, the female pronoun is used throughout the chapter to refer to Perpetua, and the trainer speaks of her as "this woman" who if victorious will receive the branch. These syntactical details suggest that the text is not interested in describing a physical change to her female body; nevertheless, Perpetua's statement is important for the current research interests on the construction of gender, of femininity and masculinity, in the ancient world. The phrase "becoming a man" is another way of saying, "I am courageous." Interestingly, Polycarp, bishop of Smyrna, who was martyred in the 160s, is enjoined by a voice from heaven to "be a man" as he heads to his death (Martyrdom of Polycarp 9.1, *andrizou*; cf. 2 Macc. 7:27–29). There is no question that he is male, but as a very old man, he has lost the virility of his youth; he must show courage in the martyr's test. Perpetua's statement also serves an immediate narrative purpose, which is to explain why the handsome young men begin rubbing oil on her naked body.[52] She is now a gladiator, fit to fight the Egyptian.

In sum, the text does not encourage readers to imagine that Perpetua herself physically changed from female to male or considers herself as male. Rather, the text claims for Perpetua the masculine quality of courage that her culture gender-types as masculine. As Barbara K. Gold explains, "The terms came to describe less a static state or a sexual category than a moral category: to 'become female' was to become morally weak or degenerate; to 'become male' was to attain 'a higher state or moral and spiritual perfection.'"[53] A few generations after Perpetua, Palladius will express a similar sentiment

51. Barbara K. Gold, "Gender Fluidity and Closure in Perpetua's Prison Diary," *Eugesta* 1 (2011): 245, notes, "This word . . . might indicate by its very form an ambiguity in the text about the strength and duration of the transformation."

52. Some suggest that the image is erotic; if so, it is similar to the typical eroticism of descriptions of gladiators being prepared for their matches. If she was not a "man," then the erotic nature of the image would leap off the page.

53. Gold, "Gender Fluidity," 244, citing Kari Vogt, "'Becoming Male': One Aspect of an Early Christian Anthropology," *Concilium: International Journal for Theology* 182 (1985): 72–80.

concerning Macrina, Olympias, and Melania, that they were "more like men than nature would seem to allow."[54]

## Perpetua's Visions of Her Deceased Brother

While her first and fourth visions focus on her trials and ultimate victory, in the second and third visions Perpetua wrestles with the fate of her deceased brother, Dinocrates. The narrative presents Perpetua with the other martyrs in deep prayer, during which time she is told by a voice to consider her brother's fate.

Figure 2.2. Perpetua is memorialized in this mosaic in the sixth-century Archiepiscopal Chapel, Ravenna, Italy.

Public domain

She obeys this prompting and begins to pray earnestly for him. That night she has her first vision concerning his situation, in which she sees him suffering. Equipped with this knowledge, she begins to pray all the more vigorously, and with a confidence that her testimony for God will be rewarded by her brother's release from suffering. In an ironic twist, on the day she is put in stocks she receives a vision affirming her brother's freedom from his suffering and his new, happy existence.

### Perpetua's Healing Prayers

Woven within the narrative are the specifics of her visions. She is in a state of deep prayer, groaning before the Lord (Pass. 7.2). In this moment, she sees her little brother in a hot, dirty place with an intense thirst and the visually appalling disfigurement of his facial cancer. He is out of her reach, separated by a deep chasm. On his side there is water, but it is tantalizingly out of his reach. Several points are worthy of notice here. First, her brother is in a state of intense physical suffering, compounded by the psychological pain of seeing water but being unable to quench his thirst. This image is in direct contrast to Perpetua's own prison situation. She indicates that prison is not unpleasant, for though her father has her infant son, she is not worried about him, and her breast milk has miraculously dried up. Second, the image likely alludes to Jesus's parable of the rich man and Lazarus (Luke 16:19–31). In Luke's story,

54. Gold, "Gender Fluidity," 238, cites Palladius of Galatia's *Lausiac History* (*Historia Lausiaca*) (420 CE).

the rich man at his death undergoes severe physical pain, including thirst.[55] Moreover, he is separated from paradise by an immense abyss. Finally, the rich man can see across the chasm and speak to those on the other side. It is difficult to say whether the text invites this direct allusion to a Gospel story, or whether the story was embedded in Perpetua's or the church's catechism of the afterlife. In any case, we find Perpetua's vision conveying images and information about theological concerns—namely, the fate of the dead.

### Perpetua's Efficacious Prayers for the Dead

Perpetua's prayers for her deceased brother fit a growing belief in the efficacy of a martyr's prayers. About fifty years later, Cyprian, bishop of Carthage, and his church faced a serious onslaught from Emperor Decius. Many Christians disowned their faith and made the imperial sacrifice. Then they turned to the incipient martyrs, those who confessed their faith and were awaiting death, and begged for their prayers for forgiveness. The lapsed Christians might be given a certificate of forgiveness, which may have restored them to fellowship in the church, although this is not entirely clear.[56] These martyrs, "confessors," were believed to have a special closeness to God, not only because they were steadfast in the face of torture, but also because they would soon be in heaven, standing before God.

Augustine, writing 150 years after Cyprian, lamented the growing practice of invoking the saints' and martyrs' intercession, and references this episode from Perpetua's visions. The context of his remarks is a rebuttal to Vincentius Victor, who advocates for the special powers and merit that martyrs or incipient martyrs have to grant prayers, even saving the dead, apparently.[57] Augustine reminds Vincentius that Perpetua's story is not part of the biblical canon, that she might not have written the text, and finally that we cannot assume that Dinocrates is unbaptized at his death. It is difficult to know how to interpret Augustine's opening salvo that the Passion is not canonical. Does this imply that Vincentius or others are promoting such a status? Or is Augustine speaking hyperbolically to reinforce its secondary rank relative to the biblical canon? Again, does Augustine question Perpetua's authorship as a way to reduce and limit her authority overall as primarily a martyr? Augustine

55. It is possible that she is also drawing on the common polytheistic assumption that thirst is a common experience in Hades; see Homer, *Odyssey* 11; Virgil, *Aeneid* 6.
56. Shira L. Lander, "Ritual Power in Society: Ritualizing Late Antique North African Martyr Cult Activities and Social Changes in Gender and Status" (PhD diss., University of Pennsylvania, 2002), 218.
57. Augustine, *The Nature and Origin of the Soul* (*De natura et origine animae*) 12, http://www.ccel.org/ccel/schaff/npnf105.xvii.iv.xii.html.

cannot write off Perpetua as heretical, for her memory is celebrated in the church. Therefore, "he must acknowledge Perpetua's authority while seeking to define and limit it as well."[58]

It seems clear enough that Augustine hopes to show both that Perpetua's prayers were not salvific for Dinocrates and that only Christ can redeem. To make his case, he argues that Dinocrates was baptized and then lapsed. Thus Perpetua's prayers are on behalf of another Christian to Christ, who himself provides the way to salvation. But was Dinocrates baptized? His father was a staunch pagan, which suggests that the boy was not baptized.[59] However, his mother was a Christian, and the boy was desperately sick. It may be that his mother took him to the church for healing, with or without her husband's permission. If her husband did know, perhaps the church's failure to cure the boy's cancer contributed to the father's animosity toward his daughter's decision to join the church.

For our purposes, the discussion about Perpetua's actions, relative to the fate of the dead, highlights the martyr's enormous power and authority wielded over the wider Christian public. Female confessors dispensed assurance of forgiveness and interceded before God with great effectiveness for the eternal rest of loved ones. We noticed in the last chapter that Thecla assured Tryphaena of the eternal peacefulness of her deceased daughter, Falconilla. Perpetua's prayers, confirmed in visions, reflect similar assumptions. Neither woman wore a bishop's robe, but their authority in prayer and intercession stood on par with, and perhaps at times exceeded, that of male ordained clergy. Indeed, the clergy also prayed to the martyred saints for aid, visited their shrines, and celebrated their commemoration "birthdays" in the church.

Interestingly, Perpetua rarely cites Scripture, in contrast to the citations and allusions found in the editor's opening chapter. This might simply be a result of her recent conversion: she probably was a Christian for only a year or two before her martyrdom. Alternatively, this may indicate that she did not read the Scriptures, or at least did not read them with an effort toward memorization. Finally, the lack of citations may reflect the resources available to her, or perhaps the catechetical approach of the Carthage church, or even her educational level. Her biblical understanding, if you will, is conveyed by narrative and image, not direct citations of biblical texts. Her information and understanding of the Christian story were based on liturgy and the teachings of her catechetical instructor.[60]

58. Joseph Farrell, "The Canonization of Perpetua," in Bremmer and Formisano, *Perpetua's Passions*, 310.
59. Ibid.
60. Ameling, "Martyr's Liberal Education," 98.

Perpetua's visions express her theological views and structure the events in prison. But the Passion's drama is not limited to fighting the devil in visions; Perpetua faces another, equally intense battle with her father. It is a fight they both lose, for their relationship fractures beyond repair. Parvis suggests that Perpetua is intent on building a different sort of family: "In her notion of the family of God, which she both fervently believed in and passionately tried to build, I think we do find a genuine and characteristic theology."[61] An important component of this new family is a reidentification of her "father" as Christ or God the Father. In her first vision, she is the shepherd's daughter (Pass. 4.9), and in the fourth, the trainer's daughter (10.13).

### Perpetua and Her Father: Roman Family Structure

Perpetua defied her father in a series of encounters that she recalls as painful, but ultimately necessary if she is to achieve her goal of faithful witness. She rejects her father's pleas to desist from her Christian convictions and is strongly supported in that decision by her fellow Christians. To our ears, this situation sounds unfortunate, for we too like to see harmony among family members. To the ancient world, however, her behavior was unthinkable, deplorable. The Roman familial system regarded the highest form of piety as that which honored the paterfamilias, the father of the family. A son or daughter's greatest responsibility lay with supporting their parents, especially the father. The pagan Roman expectations for family, under which Perpetua would have been raised, included the father's responsibility to care for his children, with the expectation that when he was old, they would care for him. At this time, women married *sine manu* (without hand), which meant that their fathers did not give absolute authority over their daughters to their husbands at marriage. The daughter remained connected financially with her birth family. This set of convictions was perhaps the strongest cord tying together the moral fabric of ancient society. We cannot overemphasize its centrality and thus the Christians' audacity in flouting it. As Hanne Sigismund-Nielsen notes, "It is no exaggeration to say that pagan Roman society was built on the notion of *pietas*."[62] The traditional structure ensured continuation of the family line, retention of family wealth, propitiation of ancestral cult and gods, and continued political and economic influence in the city.

61. Parvis, "Perpetua," 371.
62. Hanne Sigismund-Nielsen, "Vibia Perpetua—an Indecent Woman," in Bremmer and Formisano, *Perpetua's Passions*, 112.

That is why Celsus, a second-century critic of Christianity, reviles the new religion. He writes that Christian teachers claim to hold the truth and denounce fathers and schoolteachers as speaking nonsense. These Christian teachers say to unsuspecting potential converts that "if they like, they should leave father and their schoolmasters, and go along with the women and little children . . . that they may learn perfection. And by saying this they persuade them."[63] Celsus recognizes that in teaching disobedience to the father, Christianity drives a stake into the heart of the family structure of the Roman family.

Not only did Christians promote a new "family" structure that relegated father and mother to a status of outsider or worse, but also the martyrs further reinforced this paradigm. Keith Bradley observes that this rhetorical and historical move was not merely unconventional, but was also revolutionary.[64] Bradley asks important questions of this martyr tradition, illustrating his thesis that "through the vehicle of martyrdom Christianity promoted familial discord in a way that was new, and not at all part of the Roman family experience in the pre-Christian epoch."[65] Thus Bradley states, "If, consequently, Christians were assaulting the bond between father and child, they were in a sense threatening the very foundations of society."[66] And the most egregious of "sinners" in this regard would be the socially elite female martyr, whose defiance of these fundamental piety responsibilities shamed her family and cast her as immoral and without pity. Modern readers should therefore recognize that, in Perpetua's day, most people would have felt sympathy for Perpetua's father, who is indignant and amazed at his daughter's total rejection of morality, as he sees it. The Roman authorities understandably pushed back against this threat to their family structure by executing a few Christians in public spectacles.

In truth, Perpetua's choice leaves her father without aid in his elderly years, and to that physical pain is added the shame of a daughter's abandonment. Even more, her father calls attention to the fact that she is abandoning her nursing son to her father's care. Such a decision on her part could be evaluated as selfish, arrogant, and hurtful. Bradley argues that Christianity's teaching on family is unnatural, irresponsibly individualistic, and deeply subversive to the Roman moral fabric. Even more, he claims that Christianity overall,

---

63. Origen, *Cels.* 3.55, in *Origen: Contra Celsum*, ed. and trans. Henry Chadwick (Cambridge: Cambridge University Press, 1953), 165–66.

64. Keith Bradley, "Sacrificing the Family: Christian Martyrs and their Kin," in *Apuleius and Antonine Rome: Historical Essays* (Toronto: University of Toronto Press, 2012), 107.

65. Ibid.

66. Ibid., 106.

including expressions such as martyrdom, was damaging to the Roman society because it promoted the self above the community.

Hence the church sought to justify or at least explain Perpetua's actions. Approximately two hundred years later, Augustine remarks that the devil used Perpetua's father to undermine her faith, because the bond between father and daughter and the expectations of familial piety were stronger in that relationship than between husband and wife. A generation after Augustine, in nearby Carthage, Quodvultdeus[67] explains in a sermon that Perpetua was given supernatural strength to combat and overcome her father's entreaties. Arguably, these fourth- and fifth-century church leaders viewed this social expectation as the highest hindrance to Perpetua accepting martyrdom.

These observations help us see the radical nature of martyrdom, as well as the Christian teachings that undermined traditional family structures and the central power configurations in the Roman imperial period. Christian eschatology taught that wealth and land were to be distrusted and that political and religious systems, intertwined as they were with the imperial cult, were anathema or cursed by their God. Instead, Christians created new families based on confession, not kinship. This new structure gave unprecedented influence to noble women within the church community, evidenced by Perpetua's continuing legacy as one who faced death and social shame, thus receiving her sure reward, according to the text.

## Perpetua and Her Father: Encounters in the Narrative

Perpetua's description of her father and her accounts of her four encounters with him after she is arrested have been variously interpreted, although all agree that it is very clear her father is not a Christian. Bradley sees in her portrait evidence of a loving father who is deeply sorrowful at his daughter's plight and yearns for her return to the family fold.[68] On the other end of the spectrum, M. A. Tilley suggests that Perpetua frees herself from patriarchal rule as she rejects her father's control.[69] To better understand the wide range of opinion, we will look at the specific incidents between Perpetua and her father in turn.

---

67. Quodvultdeus was bishop of Carthage in the 430s. See Luke 14:26 for New Testament language that speaks of "hating" father and mother, this on the lips of Jesus; cf. Matt. 10:37.
68. Bradley, "Sacrificing the Family," 118–19.
69. M. A. Tilley, "One Woman's Body: Repression and Expression in the *Passio Perpetuae*," in *Ethnicity, Nationality and Religious Experience*, ed. P. C. Phan, Annual Publication of the College Theology Society 37 (Lanham, MD: University Press of America, 1995), 58.

### Perpetua's First Encounter with Her Father

When Perpetua is initially arrested, before she is taken to prison, her father seeks to dissuade her. Perpetua describes him as *pro sua affectione* (Pass. 3.1), which is often understood to indicate that her father had affection for her. However, the phrase can also be understood to refer to his affection in the sense of strong emotion of a negative sort. Ronsse suggests that a better translation would be that her father was in "his state of frenzied agitation."[70] Therefore, Ronsse argues, from the beginning of Perpetua's account she paints her father as the enemy, sophisticated in his persuasion and relentless in his desire to see her recant. Perpetua matches her father with equal rhetorical skill. For example, in this same encounter, Perpetua asks her father to regard a "vase lying here, . . . this small water pitcher or whatever."[71] First she asks her father to make a picture in his mind; next she links that image with herself, and in so doing she superimposes her own self-description onto an image he has formed in his mind. His violent response—attacking her eyes—makes sense because she has forced him to see an image that he resents and resists.[72]

### Perpetua's Second Encounter with Her Father

The second visit with her father occurs at a public hearing. Perpetua has been baptized and has received a vision cementing her conviction that she will be martyred. In front of the magistrate, her father pleads with her, his daughter, reminding her of her mother, aunt, brothers, and young son who will mourn her prideful decision, to say nothing about his own pitiful state. Her father kisses her hands, prostrates himself at her feet, and calls her not "daughter" but *domina*, or "lady" (Pass. 5.1–5). In this he mirrors her brother's honorific title in the previous chapter. Some suggest that here we see his acknowledgment of her special status before God, in line with her brother's confession (14.1).[73] Therefore, the father might not be simply humbling himself before his daughter, but acknowledging her ability to intercede with God. If so, it seems not to have changed his resolve against her actions nor caused him to convert. Perpetua records another visit, at another hearing, separated by an unspecified number of days. Clutching her young son, her father comes to the forum and drags her from the platform, begging her to make the sacrifice

70. Ronsse, "Rhetoric of Martyrs," 320. She translates *sua* as possessive pronominal reference and feminine because it is linked with the ablative feminine "affection" (ablative indicates separation, or source, or even cause or instrument).
71. Heffernan, *Passion of Perpetua and Felicity*, 126.
72. Ronsse, "Rhetoric of Martyrs," 320.
73. Sigismund-Nielsen, "Vibia Perpetua," 109–10.

for the emperor's health. At this point the procurator, Hilarianus, points to her father and asks her to spare her father and son by offering the sacrifice. Perpetua declines, declaring that she is a Christian, but her father persists in his pleas.

Hilarianus then does something quite shocking: he has the father publicly beaten with a rod. This action is so unusual that some scholars suggest it to be historically unreliable.[74] The basis for this conclusion rests in part with the father's likely social class and with the lack of evidence of daughters publicly dismissing their fathers' wishes.[75] Most believe the father is from the class known as *honestiores*, of the decurion rank, eligible to serve in the local city council and honored with choice seats in the city's theater. Important for our purposes, this group was exempt from torture in a trial, and if convicted of a capital crime, was beheaded, not cast to the beasts. It seems unlikely that Hilarianus would subject a highborn Roman citizen to a beating with rods, yet as Thomas J. Heffernan astutely observes, "This Roman father . . . does not behave like an elite Roman male."[76] The reason for Hilarianus's order is not clear. Perhaps he hopes not only to condemn the daughter's flouting of her father's wishes, but also to punish her father for his humiliating pleading, which shames the entire *honestiores* class. Perhaps he hopes to persuade Perpetua to change her mind, but if so, his tactic utterly fails. It may be that his frustration, and his desire to set an example, leads Hilarianus to condemn Perpetua to the beasts (*ad bestias*). This horrible punishment was typically reserved for criminals and slaves, not for wellborn Roman matrons. His decision would further humiliate her family.

### Perpetua's Third Encounter with Her Father

Her father plays his final card when he refuses to bring her child to her in prison. Does he imagine that with this refusal he will convince her to recant? Does he think that her love for her son will win over her (obstinate) resolve to remain in this foreign cult? If so, he is to be disappointed yet again. Miraculously, she says, her milk has dried up, and her child no longer needs her (Pass. 6.7–8). The break with her family is complete.

Interestingly, throughout the narrative no one questions Perpetua's father's claim on her son. Yet in the ancient world, Perpetua's husband or his family had rights over the child. This raises a question: Why did the son go to the house of his maternal grandfather? Perhaps her husband disowned Perpetua

74. Heffernan, *Passion of Perpetua and Felicity*, 26.
75. Ibid.
76. Ibid.

and her child due to her conversion to Christianity, and thus his family could not claim the son either.[77] Because Perpetua is under her father's *potestas* (power), he can claim the son. Carolyn Osiek offers a persuasive argument that Perpetua's husband is Saturus, identified in the narrative as her teacher and fellow martyr. If he was her husband, and his family rejected him for converting to Christianity, then they might also have disowned his son.[78]

Osiek offers several reasons for identifying Saturus as Perpetua's husband. First, it explains why Perpetua is not labeled as a widow, or divorced, for her husband is still living at the time she writes. Second, Saturus plays a key role in her first vision: it is he who proceeds up the ladder before her and reassures her that she too can climb it successfully. Additionally, she is central to his vision (Pass. 11.4), and at the end of the narrative, the editor reports that he was the first to die, even as he was the first to climb the ladder, a reference to Perpetua's first vision (21.8). Third, he is not introduced to the reader, suggesting that he is well known to them. Osiek concludes, "This examination of literary features shows that the strongest relationship in the narrative is surely not that of Perpetua and Felicitas, nor that of Perpetua and her father, but of Perpetua and Saturus."[79]

### Perpetua's Fourth Encounter with Her Father

Her final visit with her father occurs shortly before her martyrdom. He takes himself to the prison and then abases himself before her—truly an unthinkable posture for a man in his social position. Perpetua states that her father's language could "move creation itself" (Pass. 9.2),[80] but it does no more than cause her to grieve his unhappiness. Throughout these meetings, her father's old age is emphasized, a detail that reinforces his horrible shame. Firmly embedded cultural norms dictate that the father should receive his daughter's unquestioned filial loyalty, that he might finish his days with honor. His own pleadings that she not disgrace him permeate the encounters. "Give up your pride," he cries. "Do not destroy us all. For, if you are punished, none of us will be able to speak freely again" (5.4).[81] The reader wonders why Perpetua records these encounters with her father and presents him as increasingly effeminate.[82]

77. Ibid., 27–28. See also Brent D. Shaw, "The Passion of Perpetua," *Past and Present* 139 (1993): 25.
78. Carolyn Osiek, "Perpetua's Husband," *JECS* 10 (2002): 287–90.
79. Ibid., 290.
80. Translation from Heffernan, *Passion of Perpetua and Felicity*, 129.
81. Translation from Heffernan, *Passion of Perpetua and Felicity*, 127.
82. Gold, "Gender Fluidity," 240.

Perhaps Augustine's comments noted earlier give us a clue; he states that ties to one's parents are stronger than to one's spouse. Within the Passion narrative, Perpetua's fiercest enemy is her father, and his lack of manly authority proves his vanquished state. Augustine, perhaps with unintended irony, continues that critique and goes further by emphasizing how the daughter is changed into a man, a reference to her fourth vision, when she sees herself as a wrestler in the arena set to fight the Egyptian. Augustine argues on two levels, interweaving the identities of Perpetua as daughter and as a man. He claims that Perpetua was already so resistant to the siren calls of lust that the devil did not use her husband to tempt her away from her martyrdom. Instead, he used her father, recognizing that Perpetua valued family duty. He suggests that in fact Perpetua was a loyal daughter, but more loyal to her Lord. She never shirks her familial duty, for she grieves her father's mistreatment. What this Christian daughter resisted, Augustine declares, is the devil, who used her father to promote his tricks with beguiling words. In a subtle shift of argument, Augustine says Perpetua is really a man in terms of courage. And her father is revealed to be controlled by the devil, the one who also contrived to have him beaten and humiliated. Thus by making the father a puppet of God's archenemy, Augustine arguably emasculates him more than does the Passion.

Augustine pulls back from the immediate relationship between daughter and father, to speak in general terms about family and about the folly of unbelief, which must be rejected regardless of who exhibits it. With this stroke, Perpetua's father becomes a generic unbeliever and thus one whose words must be disregarded and resisted. The scenes morph in Augustine's hands to suggest a disembodied battle between the "man" Perpetua and the devil, who takes the shape of her father. In this way, with a straight face Augustine can sermonize that Perpetua did not violate "the commandment by which honor is owed to parents, . . . and . . . she kept her affection for him undiminished."[83]

Another point to consider here is that Perpetua gave aid to her biological family, albeit in a manner that might not have been appreciated or recognized by her father. The text explains her actions as a redirection of concern for kin. Instead of focusing on sustaining the family's wealth, land, and progeny, Perpetua concerns herself with the eternal fate of her family members. Her father may have counted that of little worth since he had buried his young son and hoped his living sons and daughter would fulfill their obligations to him. But her actions demonstrate that within her reconfigured set of values,

83. Augustine, *Serm.* 281.2, in *Sermons (273–305A) on the Saints*, 79.

she offered her young brother the most precious gift as she sees it: entrance to everlasting joy.

## Perpetua and Motherhood

Perpetua's love for her young son is perhaps the most unusual aspect of Perpetua's narrative, at once touchingly sentimental and yet disconcertingly out of sync with the single-mindedness of the martyr. Her feelings ring true in depicting a Roman mother's concern for her nursing child, and yet she relinquishes the boy to her father, a man with whom she has grave differences. What a strange expression of love—certainly her father claimed as much! Yet she believes she acts with consistency relative to her Christian convictions. Her story of motherhood warrants closer inspection. We will find a woman offering protective love for her child yet also captivated by a prize beyond motherhood.[84]

### Motherhood and Nursing in the Roman World

In his introduction the editor indicates that Perpetua is a young mother of twenty-two years who has a young son still at her breast. At this time, children were nursed until age two or three. It was a sign of great devotion for a wealthy woman to nurse her own child, for most used wet nurses. For example, the philosopher and ethicist Plutarch, writing the century before Perpetua, encourages women to nurse their children, fearing that using a wet nurse creates an emotional chasm between mother and child.[85] Even more, breast-feeding shows that the mother is concerned for the character of her child. With her pure milk, the mother also teaches her child pure morals and pure (Latin or Greek) speech. Inscriptions and art alike celebrate a nursing mother. For example, a sarcophagus of the second century CE shows a mother nursing her child, with her husband looking tenderly upon them.[86]

84. Joyce E. Salisbury, *Perpetua's Passion: The Death and Memory of a Young Roman Woman* (New York: Routledge, 1997), 87, makes an interesting suggestion that Perpetua held an "ambivalent position regarding her son [that] reveals some potential ambiguity regarding the roles of mother and martyr." This conclusion likely overreads Perpetua's comments that she was anxious for her son, and may overstate the distinction between Christian female martyrs and the Maccabean mother martyr.

85. Plutarch, *Mor.* 1 = *De liberis educandis* 1.1.5; for a general discussion, see Lynn H. Cohick, *Women in the World of the Earliest Christians: Illuminating Ancient Ways of Life* (Grand Rapids: Baker Academic, 2009), 146.

86. Sarcophagus of M. Cornelius Statius, in the Louvre Museum, Paris. See Cohick, *Women in the World of the Earliest Christians*, 145.

Again, a Latin inscription contemporary with Perpetua's time reads, "Of Graxia Alexandria, distinguished for her virtue and fidelity. She nursed her children with her own breasts. Her husband, Pudens the emperor's freedman [dedicated this monument] as a reward to her. She lived 24 years, 3 months, 16 days."[87]

A wealthy matron who refused to nurse could be excoriated as selfish, vain, and lazy. She was obsessed with preserving the shape of her breasts and the flatness of her stomach. Additionally, she opened the door to foreign influence within her home, for a foreign wet-nurse brought her barbarian ways and tongue into the household. With this backdrop, we better understand Perpetua's concerns for breast-feeding her son, as well as its rhetorical significance in the story. With the details about nursing, Perpetua tells the reader that she has done the utmost for her child, sacrificing her looks and her social leisure time for his sake. She convinces us that she is a good mother by these actions, which makes her eventual surrender of the child to face martyrdom all the more poignant and compelling.

### Motherhood and Nursing in the Roman Prison

Perpetua experiences the darkness and heat of the prison in part as a mother overwhelmed for the safety and comfort of her child. Within the terror of closed space, filled with a mob jostling about, Perpetua does her best to physically protect him. She rejoices when two deacons bribe prison guards to allow her and the other Christians to move out of the dungeon and into a more open section of the prison facility. Her first action is to nurse her weakened child. Then she passes him to her mother and brother but is unable to rest without her son. After "many" days, she requests that the child be returned to her, and with that, her worry ceases: "Suddenly the prison became my palace, so that I wanted to be there rather than anywhere else" (Pass. 3.9).[88]

This is an interesting section, for it could indicate that she does not nurse the child for many days. Practically speaking, in this situation her milk would dry up for lack of use. Yet as the story continues, it is clear that she has milk; indeed, later in the story she cites her milk drying up without pain in her breasts as a miracle from God (Pass. 6.8). The story lacks verisimilitude if it suggests that a young mother can go "many days" without nursing (and with no adverse symptoms), only to pick it up again at full strength. One might

87. *CIL* VI.19128.L; translation in Mary R. Lefkowitz and Maureen B. Fant, *Women's Life in Greece and Rome: A Source Book in Translation* (Baltimore: Johns Hopkins University Press, 1982), 188.
88. Translation from Heffernan, *Passion of Perpetua and Felicity*, 126.

suggest that in these details about nursing, we have a male author's clumsy attempt to portray Perpetua as a devoted mother. However, it is possible that Perpetua nurses the baby each day, when her mother and brother visit her for a few hours. In this scenario, she would continue to produce milk and would be able to produce more when her son returns to stay with her in prison. This reconstruction makes the reasonable assumption that Perpetua grew more accustomed to the rigors and hardships of prison, and so grew less fearful of her son's safety. Additionally, this reconciles her later comment about her father having her son with the statement that she continued to nurse her son (6.2, 7). It may be that the boy was taken and returned to her regularly, sometimes remaining days at a time with her. If these words about nursing her son reflect Perpetua's historical experience in some measure, then we must assume that her son regularly, even daily, was with her until her condemnation to the beasts by Hilarianus. At that point, contact with her son ceased, and a miracle occurred, according to Perpetua. Instead of the expected pain from a broken heart and swollen breasts (and possible mastitis), she was freed from any worry on her son's behalf (6.8).

### Motherhood and Nursing in Theological Reflection

Yet the picture of milk and nursing might also be theologically significant to Perpetua and to the editor.[89] Her visions pick up themes of thirst, drinking, and nourishment that comes from milk, which link her physical situation with her intellectual or spiritual contemplation. Her first vision ends in a garden, where a shepherd milks sheep and gives her a mouthful of the cheese, and the chorus around her says, "Amen!" (Pass. 4.8–9). Her vision ends with the sweet taste of the milk/cheese still in her mouth. We suggest that Perpetua builds a correspondence between her experience as one who produces life-giving milk for her son, and the shepherd who offers life-granting milk. Along with a likely allusion to the Eucharist, we propose that Perpetua might be building a complicated connection between literal and spiritual milk, wherein the former fades away as the latter becomes more definitive. Her vision portends her martyrdom, and two subsequent encounters with her father reaffirm its pronouncement. The sweet, spiritual cheese/milk of her vision replaces her own milk and thus her identity as a nursing mother.

The themes of thirst and satiation continue, but now in a different realm. Whereas she began her prison experience overwhelmed with concern for her

---

89. The editor draws on the physical experience of Felicitas's childbirth, including the commencement of lactation, as significant embodied events that resonate with spiritual realities.

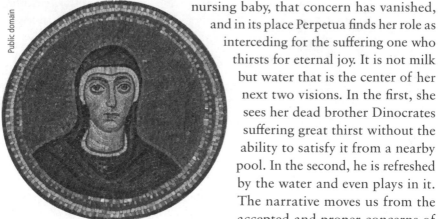

Figure 2.3. Felicitas is memorialized in this mosaic in the sixth-century Archiepiscopal Chapel, Ravenna, Italy.

nursing baby, that concern has vanished, and in its place Perpetua finds her role as interceding for the suffering one who thirsts for eternal joy. It is not milk but water that is the center of her next two visions. In the first, she sees her dead brother Dinocrates suffering great thirst without the ability to satisfy it from a nearby pool. In the second, he is refreshed by the water and even plays in it. The narrative moves us from the accepted and proper concerns of a Roman mother for her nursing infant, to the Christian ideal of a martyr confessor focused on life-giving intercession.

## Felicitas the Slave Woman and Her Daughter

Perpetua is not the only mother in this story. Felicitas, the slave woman also martyred with Perpetua, is pregnant at the time of the arrest and gives birth only two days before the spectacle. The editor reports that her appearance in the arena shocks the crowd. She clearly shows signs of her recent childbirth experience as she stands naked before them. Specifically the editor mentions that her breasts drip milk.[90] Perhaps if this were an isolated note, we might be tempted to relegate it to minimal importance. However, because the previous twenty chapters encourage reflection on nursing, milk, and thirst, the reader is alert to this detail about Felicitas. Yet the reader also might notice a significant difference between Felicitas's experience and Perpetua's nursing: Felicitas does not actually nurse her daughter. Her milk spills to the ground without nourishing her infant, while Perpetua's milk dries up before the day of martyrdom. Breast-feeding and milk are not the central images used to explain Felicitas's motherhood experience; rather, it is her labor and delivery that catches the attention of the editor.

90. The editor does not mention blood; one would assume that if her milk has let down, her uterus would also be contracting, and thus blood would flow down her legs. That this is not mentioned might be due to modesty, but we also wonder if it is not mentioned so as to focus the reader's attention on milk and its theological meaning.

### Felicitas: Labor and Delivery

Felicitas's labor is intense because, as the editor tells us, she is delivering a preterm fetus. Rather than this premature labor being bad news, however, it is actually an answer to the prayers of the martyrs. Roman law forbade the execution of a pregnant woman, for the child belonged to the husband or, in this case, the slave owner. Thus, two days before the spectacle, the group entreats the Lord that she might deliver her baby and thus join them in the arena. Felicitas knows that, if her pregnancy goes to term, she will face execution alongside common criminals; to avoid that fate, she desires a premature labor. The editor reminds the reader of the commonly held assumption that labor in the eighth month is more painful, and this information puts the group's prayer in an interesting light. Indeed, it was widely thought that labor in the eighth month usually leads to the death of both the mother and her fetus.[91] The group, including Felicitas, knows that the prayer, if answered, will bring great physical distress to their "sister," if not death in childbirth. Yet ironically their prayer, if answered, will bring about her death two days hence. The prayer's power is recognized in her safe delivery of a baby girl, but the content of the prayer reveals the strangeness of Christian values concerning mothers and children. Within the narrative, then, all characters recognize this slave woman's willingness to undergo great physical pain in two different ways that are yet linked through agony and, as we will see, the image and reality of milk and blood.

Felicitas compares labor pain with the expected pain she will face in the arena. It may be that no midwife attends her, although later the editor waxes poetic, saying that Felicitas went from the midwife to the gladiator, from blood to blood (Pass. 18.3).[92] During the labor, however, she hears only the taunts of a male guard. Men are not generally present at a woman's labor and delivery, so his presence dishonors Felicitas and likely reinforces her slave status. Felicitas retorts to her tormentor that when she is in the arena, there will be one in her who suffers for her (15.6). When a wealthy woman, such as Perpetua, went into labor, she likely had three women attending, if she and her family followed typical medical advice. It is possible that Perpetua helped Felicitas in her labor; however, the text promotes the view that Felicitas alone endures the labor, her fellow Christians having done their part by praying for labor to commence. Whether or not she does labor alone, the text presents this

---

91. Jan N. Bremmer, "Felicitas: The Martyrdom of a Young African Woman," in Bremmer and Formisano, *Perpetua's Passions*, 44. See also Anna Rebecca Solevåg, *Birthing Salvation: Gender and Class in Early Christian Childbearing Discourse*, BibInt 121 (Leiden: Brill, 2013), 73.
92. Solevåg, *Birthing Salvation*, 207.

picture to emphasize that Felicitas will not be alone when she faces another agony, the beasts in the arena.

### Felicitas: Labor and Suffering

While she is in the throes of labor, her prison guard mocks her. He acknowledges her present agony and then taunts her that her sufferings will only get worse because she has refused to honor the emperor with a sacrifice. Her sharp retort is neither ladylike nor suitable for a slave, yet the editor presents her words as a key interpretive lens for understanding the work of Christ in the testimony of the martyr. Felicitas concedes that she suffers now alone in labor, but adds, "Then there will be another inside me, who will suffer for me, because I am going to suffer for him" (Pass. 15.6).[93] Felicitas's words (remembered by the community or invented by the editor) link her suffering as a new mother giving birth with the suffering she will undergo as a witness to the "one who will suffer for me," meaning Christ. In a fascinating mixing of images, she births a girl who has been inside her and confidently asserts that she will have another life in her when she endures a second suffering in the arena. Even as she has given life to a female, yet it will be she who is birthed to eternal bliss if she is faithful in the final test. Each of these points deserves a closer look.

### Felicitas: Labor and Her Daughter

Felicitas gives birth to a female child. This could be a historically reliable detail, for the editor notes that a "sister" or fellow believer raised the girl (Pass. 15.7). The past tense of the verb probably signals that the Christian community knew this girl. Again, the verb "brought up" (Latin *educavit*) can be translated as "educated," which further supports the idea that the churches in Carthage knew Felicitas's daughter. While most readers would naturally be interested in the fate of Felicitas's child, the note that she grew up in the church might also serve a didactic purpose. Each year on the anniversary of her mother's death, this daughter would have listened to the story of her own "miraculous" birth, and the daughter's presence in the midst of the congregation would provide immediacy to the story. According to Ronsse, even if one concludes that the daughter is but a rhetorical invention of the editor, nevertheless she models for the reader the correct response to her mother's story: "She [the daughter] is the hope and possibility that their message will continue to be embodied in future generations."[94]

93. Translation from Heffernan, *Passion of Perpetua and Felicity*, 132.
94. Ronsse, "Rhetoric of Martyrs," 325.

Not only that, but the daughter also serves Felicitas's reflections on her own second birth, as it were, upcoming in the arena. Ronsse explains that this "nameless daughter is the hermeneutical figure her mother uses to explain her faith and the promise that future generations will continue to incarnate, and thereby model and teach, Christian practices."[95] Would it have been different if she had delivered a son? Perhaps not in terms of the birthing experience itself, for her labor pains would have been the same for a male or female child. But Felicitas connects her female child just born with her own new birth, her upcoming "baptism by blood" in the arena. Felicitas as a mother can reflect Christ, the one who gives life and who births his followers. Felicitas as a martyr resembles her female child, who receives life from her "mother" Christ.

## Felicitas in the Arena

Felicitas's statement "Now I alone suffer what I am suffering, but then there will be another inside me, who will suffer for me, because I am going to suffer for him" (Pass. 15.6)[96] creates an intriguing visual picture: Christ is somehow within her, as her child was inside her. And yet also this same Christ will suffer for her in the arena, in a manner analogous to her labor. These three strands are woven together—a woman's labor in childbirth, Christ's suffering (his passion), and a Christian's agony in the arena—to make a fabric of martyrdom.

### *Felicitas and* Imitatio Christi

Christians at this time stressed *imitatio Christi*, a reference to Jesus's words that those who follow him should take up their crosses (Matt. 16:24; Luke 9:23). Felicitas's statement echoes this general sentiment but, according to Ronsse, also "emphasizes her imminent incarnation of Christ and, therefore, the mutual identification of Christ as martyr."[97] Ronsse taps into the power of Felicitas's claim. The young mother imagines herself embodying Christ's sufferings in two related occasions, in her labor and delivery and then in her suffering in the arena. While the guard sees only a suffering slave who will endure greater pain a few days hence, Felicitas sees her childbirth experience as representative of Christ's passion. Her successful delivery of a baby girl is a metaphor for her own "born-again" salvation in the arena. While Perpetua was granted visions to support her and encourage her and the group before

95. Ibid., 324.
96. Translation from Heffernan, *Passion of Perpetua and Felicity*, 132.
97. Ronsse, "Rhetoric of Martyrs," 324.

the spectacle, Felicitas alone is given a physical test, which she successfully passes. She then serves as a personification of the hope of resurrection; she is, by analogy, Christ giving birth to a child. With her single assertion, "Now I alone suffer what I am suffering, but then there will be another inside me, who will suffer for me, because I am going to suffer for him" (Pass. 15.6),[98] she sums up the message of the entire narrative. From the mouth of a slave woman, this is radical indeed.

Perhaps too radical! For in the early fifth century, Augustine realigns her bold confidence by reemphasizing female frailty and thus the greater distance that female martyrs must travel in their journey to a "manly spirit." He demotes the magnitude of her suffering in labor by explaining that it was simply her debt paid, her just punishment for Eve's sin in the garden of Eden (Gen. 3). And not just Felicitas, for Augustine links Eve and Perpetua as well in speaking of the devil, who through Eve "knocked out man." These female martyrs' victory was due to "the one" (Christ) who filled them with courage, enabling "these women to die faithfully like men."[99]

### Felicitas and Second Baptism

As the incipient martyrs enter the arena, both women are described by the editor in keeping with their social class and recent experience. Perpetua is calm, dignified, yet bold in her direct gaze at the crowd. This matches the authority given her by the visions. Felicitas is described by her recent "miraculous" labor and delivery. She is joyful to be with her fellow martyrs as they face the beasts together. The editor adds that she is "advancing from blood to blood, from the midwife to a net-bearing gladiator—now to be washed after childbirth in a second baptism" (Pass. 18.3). Blood from her delivery is matched by her blood shed as she is mauled by the beasts and then slashed with a sword. In both cases, the mother martyr endures the pain, enduring voluntarily and actively for a greater reward. Yet the midwife's work could not be more opposite to that of the gladiator. The midwife guides and helps the parturient to live through her labor and deliver a healthy baby, while the gladiator tries to inflict as much pain as possible before administering the coup de grâce.

The phrase "washed after childbirth in a second baptism" creates a startling image. The editor pulls together several ideas from the narrative, developing theology, and the wider culture. With respect to the narrative, we recall that soon after their arrest, all of the incipient martyrs were baptized with water

98. Translation from Heffernan, *Passion of Perpetua and Felicity*, 132.
99. Augustine, *Serm.* 281.1, in *Sermons (273–305A) on the Saints*, 78.

(3.5). The verb "washed" hints at the purity ensured by the faithful completion of the martyr's test. The editor connects the blood of childbirth with the blood of the martyr, who at her death will be born in heaven. He invites the reader to imagine Felicitas's labor and delivery, which includes suffering and blood, and then overlays that image with events in the arena, where her blood again will flow, drawn by torture and the sword. The primary focus in this description seems to be that of new birth, linked with her daughter's actual birth. Childbirth provides a fecund metaphor to explore the range of meaning within the idea of martyrdom as second baptism.

Theologically speaking, the concept of martyrdom as a second baptism can be traced to the Gospel of Luke, where we read: "But I [Jesus] have a baptism with which to be baptized, and what stress I am under until it is completed!" (12:50; see also Mark 10:38). Jesus refers to his passion, and Tertullian picks up this idea as he reflects on martyrdom and the benefit obtained by the martyr, including immediate access to paradise upon death.[100] Implied with this conviction is the idea that all of a martyr's sins are forgiven. Water baptism washes a person of their sins and brings them into a new family, the church. Martyrdom imitates Christ's own bloody end and was seen as a second washing that secures salvation. The editor of the Passion dwells not on the idea of forgiveness of sins, but on new birth and washing.

Not only Felicitas but also Saturus is washed in blood. With a single vicious bite from a leopard, blood gushes from Saturus, so much so that, as the editor explains, the crowd acknowledges his second baptism (unwittingly). The crowd sees the blood from Saturus and mockingly shouts, "A saving bath, a saving bath" (Pass. 21.2), a parody of a typical greeting exchanged outside the Roman baths that wishes the person good health.[101] The editor grabs hold of the irony and declares that indeed Saturus is safe, saved, because this second washing proves his salvation.

To Pudens, the attending soldier and new convert, Saturus has prophesied that he will be killed with a single bite of a leopard. That his prediction comes true confirms for Pudens the truth of his new faith and the certainty of Saturus's salvation as a martyr. The idea of Saturus's new birth in heaven is secondary to Pudens's new birth/faith in Christ (Pass. 21.3).

Felicitas's embodied female experience of childbirth is a worthy type for the theologically rich concept of second baptism. Without that emphasis, the reader would not appreciate the importance of second birth within second

100. Tertullian, *On Baptism* (*De baptismo*) 16.1; *Antidote for the Scorpion's Sting* (*Scorpiace*) 6.9–11; *An.* 55.5.
101. Heffernan, *Passion of Perpetua and Felicity*, 359.

baptism. The editor is most likely male, so we have a man's reflection on childbirth experienced by a martyr who undergoes a second baptism shortly after her labor and delivery.

### Felicitas: Slave and Martyr

The editor of the Passion shapes Felicitas's childbirth experience to draw out theological and catechetical points. Yet he is also clear that she is a slave. The editor introduces her as a household slave, but we are not told to which house she belongs. One possibility is that she comes from Perpetua's household. This would account for the fact that she and Perpetua, a woman of high social status, are under house arrest together. It would also explain why a fellow Christian woman takes her daughter and cares for her, for the slave's owner is the person in charge of any house-born slaves. In this case, perhaps Perpetua herself owns Felicitas, or perhaps Saturus owns her, whether or not he and Perpetua are married. It is improbable that Perpetua's father owns Felicitas because he seems unlikely to relinquish his property to the care of a Christian surrogate mother.

### Felicitas and Perpetua: A Comparison

Perpetua and Felicitas share a faithful witness to their Lord, but the descriptions of their deaths draw on different metaphors and images of bravery and courage, as well as the converse, submission and endurance. Perpetua faces the challenges of the arena as a man ready to wrestle his opponent; the meeting is an agonistic contest of strength and skill. Felicitas passively endures painful labor, and in the arena she is tossed by the cow and becomes unconscious, and Perpetua helps her to her feet. She remains silent, and her death by sword is not remarked upon specifically. And yet both are seen as adequate, even true, representations of Christ's passion, to which their own passion attests. The distinctions might be accounted for by the fact that they come from contrasting social classes. Perpetua represents nobility, albeit of a middling rank. Her actions compare to those of one freeborn and thus reflect free choice, authority, and a command of the situation. Felicitas remains a slave throughout the entire narrative; she gives birth as a slave, then suffers and dies a torturous death as a slave. That is what makes her words (or the words given her by the editor) so shocking and powerful. She declares that her death will demonstrate a man's power—namely, Christ in his suffering. Hers is the most eloquent speech act of the martyrs' testimonies.

In sum, the central theme throughout the martyr narratives is the martyr's imitation of Christ's passion. His resurrection, so strongly declared by his followers, shows him a victor over death, the most relentless enemy. In our narratives, Felicitas models the suffering Christ of the cross, while Perpetua highlights the image of Christ victorious in his battle with death. In every case, the female body is the place where Christ shows his victory. And female martyrs such as Perpetua reflect theologically on their visions and experiences. In these actions, women perform their theological convictions that challenge Roman familial virtues and piety of their day. Christ's suffering unto death on a cross was viewed as passive and thus effeminate, based on the gendered virtues of his day. These female martyrs reject such definitions of passivity by courageously enduring martyrdom, thus acting out the sacrifice of Christ.

## Remembering Perpetua and Felicitas in the Church: An Example from Augustine

Augustine, however, reasserts the maleness of courage in *Sermon* 281, given at one of the anniversary celebrations of the martyrs' deaths.[102] With a few rhetorical sleights of hand, he renders Perpetua and Felicitas as "male" even as he admits their female frailty. He is not only concerned to reestablish the virtue of courage as masculine; he also wishes to reinforce the superiority of Christ, known through the church and the bishops, over against a growing veneration of saints and martyrs that existed in part outside the control and supervision of the church's hierarchy.[103] Augustine paints Perpetua and Felicitas as "everyman" with a pun based on their names. Felicitas's name means "happiness, felicity." And Perpetua's name is related to the adjective "perpetual"; Augustine concludes that all the martyrs desire the "perpetual felicity" that is gained in their martyrdom (*Serm.* 281.3; 282.1). He declares that the martyrdom of Perpetua and Felicitas, therefore, is actually named for all the martyrs, including the four male martyrs who died with the women.

102. The dating of these three sermons is debated; one estimate is that *Serm.* 280 was given ca. 400 CE; *Serm.* 281 perhaps in 405–10 CE; and *Serm.* 282 between 415 and 420 CE. See Augustine, *Sermons III/8 (273–305A) on the Saints*, 76, 80, 85–86.

103. Paul F. Bradshaw and Maxwell E. Johnson, *The Origins of Feasts, Fasts, and Seasons in Early Christianity*, Alcuin Club Collections 86 (Collegeville, MN: Liturgical Press, 2011). The authors point out that both elite church leaders and average Christians participated in the *sanctorale* calendar and venerated the saints. It is not the case that bishops held to an intellectually rational faith while the uneducated laity believed in the miracles and fantastic stories of the martyrs. That scene perhaps resembles our modern world but does not represent the ancient landscape. Augustine believed in miracles, in the merits of the saints, and in the festivals celebrating their feats. He disliked when the church did not have a controlling hand in the process.

Therefore, Augustine intimates, we should not celebrate these women's specific martyrdoms, but rather the general example of martyrs within the story, especially the contrast between the weakness of women and the strength of Christ, a man.

Not only their names but also their femaleness is taken up by maleness in Augustine's argument. He claims that the female martyrs had a more difficult time of it because they are frail, and then pulls back from that conclusion to notice that their courage comes from "the one man," meaning Christ. Does Augustine imply that the male martyrs did not need that extra boost of courage from "the one man" (*Serm.* 281.1)? In *Sermon* 282, he suggests as much, for in explaining the reasons why the Passion recognizes two women, he contrasts the greater miracle of strength shown by naturally weak women with the natural strength of the men who "engaged in the contest for the sake of perpetual felicity" (282.3). Augustine's point, that men died as well as women on this day long ago, is valid, but the Passion takes its rhetorical force not from men's voices, but from a woman's visions and a slave's safe labor and delivery.

## Conclusion

Felicitas's bold courage in facing the labor of childbirth and the tortures of the arena belies her slave status. Perpetua's visions and intercession mark her as a powerful saint, one on whom generations of Christians have called for aid. In the stories we read, slave women are given voice, a matron becomes a man, and Christian identity is forged in the heat of martyrdom. Few Christians actually faced the wild beasts or other tortures; nevertheless, those who did became a central factor in Christianity's developing identity. Because both men and women could earn the martyr's crown, women modeled faithfulness and courage as much as did their male counterparts. In chapters 3, 5, and 6, through a study of catacomb art, developing church liturgy, and pilgrimages in the Holy Lands, we will see further examples of Christian women's expressions of their religious faith.

# 3

# Christian Women
# in Catacomb Art

Pablo Picasso is credited with the statement, "Every now and then one paints a picture that seems to have opened a door and serves as a stepping stone to other things."[1] The sentiment holds for uncovering ancient art. In 1894, Giovanni DeRossi (1822–94) and his protégé, Josef Wilpert, made a remarkable discovery. In the Catacomb of Priscilla in Rome, in a large room known as the Greek Chapel (*Capella Greca*),[2] they discovered a third-century fresco depicting a meal with seven figures, each approximately ten inches tall, aligned along a curved table on which were two platters and a cup, with baskets of bread placed along both sides of the table. Wilpert christened the fresco *Fractio Panis*, "The Breaking of Bread," indicating his belief that the painting represented an early celebration of the Eucharist.[3] He identified as male the figure on the far left, breaking the bread, acting as the priest, and distributing it to the remaining seated male figures, with the lone female figure in their midst, distinguished by her veil. The "priest" seems to be either sitting on the table

1. Susan Van Sleet, *Mary and Me beyond the Canvas: An Extraordinary Story of Adoption, Loss, and Reunion* (Denver: Outskirts Press, 2013), 138.
2. In the Greek Chapel, we find many frescoes, including the *Adoration of the Magi*, the oldest rendering of the Virgin with Child; the *Three Hebrews in the Fiery Furnace*; *Moses Striking the Rock*; and the *Story of Susanna*.
3. In this chapter we use the label *Fractio Panis* for convenience, not to suggest that we agree with his conclusions.

Figure 3.1. The *Fractio Panis* fresco in the Greek Chapel of the Catacomb of Priscilla has generated much discussion about who and what the scene depicts.

or with feet on the table, and stretching out hands to the person seated on the left, who is accepting whatever is in the outstretched hands. The remaining five figures are talking among themselves, not focusing on the individual with the bread in hand. The *Fractio Panis* is one of several frescoes in this long rectangular room; the room itself is able to hold approximately twelve people, and along one wall is a stone bench.

For about one hundred years, this interpretation of the *Fractio Panis* went unchallenged. Then in the 1990s a series of arguments contesting the majority opinion emerged. For example, in 1993, Karen Jo Torjesen suggested that the fresco presents one woman breaking bread in a Eucharist service for six other women.[4] Fourteen years later, Nicola Denzey argued that the "priest" is more likely a slave, on the basis of both the small size of the figure relative to the other figures and the pose, which seems "curiously perched alongside or even *on top of* the table. . . . No priest—not even an ancient one—would put his feet on the same level as the body of Christ."[5] She postulates that all the participants

4. Karen Jo Torjesen, *When Women Were Priests: Women's Leadership in the Early Church and the Scandal of Their Subordination in the Rise of Christianity* (San Francisco: Harper-SanFrancisco, 1993), 52.

5. Nicola Denzey, *The Bone Gatherers: The Lost Worlds of Early Christian Women* (Boston: Beacon, 2007), 99.

of the meal are women, and that the veil worn by one figure might indicate status, such as being in mourning; it need not be indicative of distinguishing the female figure from male figures: "In other words, there are many reasons why only one woman in a group would be veiled; the veil is a marker of *status*, not of *gender*."[6] Battle lines were drawn, and on one side were those who saw this fresco as evidence for the ancient practice of a male priesthood administering the Eucharist. On the other side were those who claimed the fresco witnessed to a time in the early church when women served the Eucharist.

At issue were two enigmas not necessarily related to each other. First, were the figures male or female? Second, was the meal a Eucharist celebration or a funerary meal? Because much of the argument concerning women's participation as pastors, ministers, and priests today relies on a reconstruction of historical precedence, the stakes are quite high in interpreting ancient texts and paintings. Our concern here is not to weigh in on current discussions of church order, but to probe the possibilities open to Christian women in the early church. Indeed, the issues are broader still, raising questions about how to "read" catacomb art. After briefly surveying textual evidence for women's offices in the early church, we turn our attention underground, to the art of the catacombs—evocative and enigmatic, inviting us to imagine women in the church in new ways.

## Women's Offices in the Church

In the early second century, Pliny the Younger, a governor in the region of Bithynia (modern-day northern Turkey, along the southern shores of the Black Sea), interrogates two leaders of the fledgling sect known as Christians. He speaks of these two slave women as ministers or deaconesses (Latin *ministrae*).[7] About this same time Ignatius, the bishop of Antioch who died a martyr in Rome, writes to a congregation in Smyrna about "the virgins who are called widows."[8] The bishop of Smyrna, Polycarp, who was martyred around 167, writes to the Philippian church about "our widows [who] must be sober-minded as touching the faith of the Lord, making intercession without ceasing for all men, abstaining from . . . every evil thing, knowing that they are God's altar, and that all sacrifices are carefully inspected, and nothing escapes Him."[9] Writing at the end of the second century and into the third,

6. Ibid., 98.
7. Pliny the Younger, *Ep.* 10.96.
8. Ignatius, *To the Smyrnaeans* (Ign. *Smyrn.*) 13.
9. Polycarp, *To the Philippians* (Pol. *Phil.*) 4.3, trans. J. B. Lightfoot, on the Early Christian Writings website, http://www.earlychristianwritings.com/text/polycarp-lightfoot.html.

Tertullian likewise emphasizes the role of widows in the church, stating that
a penitent sinner might repent "before the widows, before the presbyters [*ante
uiduas, ante presbyteros*], imploring the tears of all, kissing the footprints of
all, clutching the knees of all."[10] In a letter sent to his wife, Tertullian praises
the *univera* (once-married) woman who embraces widowhood rather than
a second marriage. He speaks of the order (*ordo*) of widows, who can be
compared to the altar of God.[11]

Kevin Madigan and Carolyn Osiek provide an invaluable resource that
summarizes the literature, focusing on terms such as "widow," "female
deacon," and "presbyter." The evidence reveals a range of practices, and
the presence of women deacons in the early church varied, based on local
traditions. For example, Madigan and Osiek report that "the office of the
diaconate for women definitely existed in the West by the fifth century, but
was not widely accepted."[12] However, female deacons in the East appear
to be a common and familiar sight. They "appear in all kinds of contexts:
funerary, dedicatory, as recipients of letters and subjects of letters, guardians
of shrines, heroines of ecclesiastical conflicts, monastic superiors and followers, choir leaders, those who take care of others' concerns and those who
cause concern to others—and more."[13] A key text in ascertaining women's
functions in liturgy is *Letter* (*Epistula*) 14 by Pope Gelasius I, written on
March 11, 494, wherein he laments the news he received about certain church
practices being done by women. The text's interpretation is contested because
the wording is rather vague and imprecise to our eyes, but the issue seems
to revolve around women serving at the sacred altars in some churches. It is
unclear specifically what he was promoting and what he was criticizing about
the practices of the recipients. Scholars are divided about whether this letter
reveals the practice of ordaining women to serve as priests at the altar and
perform the liturgy of the Eucharist.

Because of the ambiguity within the literature and the apparent differences among local practices, scholars are reluctant to state categorically
that women did or did not serve as priests. But even if a definitive statement
cannot be made about whether women participated in the Eucharist liturgy
(indeed, it is difficult to be definitive about any historical practice within a

10. Tertullian, *On Modesty* (*De pudicitia*) 13.7, translation in Kevin Madigan and Carolyn
Osiek, eds. and trans., *Ordained Women in the Early Church: A Documentary History* (Balti-
more: Johns Hopkins University Press, 2005), 180.
    11. Tertullian, *To His Wife* (*Ad uxorem*) 1.7. See http://www.newadvent.org/fathers/0404.htm.
    12. Madigan and Osiek, *Ordained Women*, 148. See also John Wijngaards, *No Women in
Holy Orders? The Women Deacons of the Early Church* (Norwich: Canterbury, 2002).
    13. Madigan and Osiek, *Ordained Women*, 96.

movement as widespread as Christianity in the second and third centuries), there is evidence of broad participation of women in the church's life as virgins, widows, deacons, and presbyters. The survey of literature at the very least indicates that the early church debated the proper responsibilities of various offices, as well as the range of functions performed by men and women in the ordained and appointed positions. Said simply, the environment is fluid, messy, and changing. It invites us to be imaginative and creative as we interpret catacomb art, open to the dynamic character of the early church.

## Overview of the Catacombs

The catacombs of Rome developed as burial sites for those who resided in Rome: pagan, Jew, and Christian. Bodies of the deceased were interred in these underground tunnels. Estimates suggest that there are about sixty catacombs, with forty-two having been excavated.[14] The catacombs were dug in stone known as tuff, which is soft, making it both easy to dig into and useless for construction. They were built outside the city because the law did not allow bodies to be buried within the city limits. The poorer members of society often participated in funerary clubs, contributing a small amount each month so that one's remains would be suitably interred. They might meet regularly for meals and often buried members in communal columbaria (rooms to hold burial urns). Romans enjoyed a funerary banquet, known as *refrigerium*, celebrating the anniversaries of the person's birth (*dies natalis*) and death, as well as festivals such as the *dies Parentales* (February 13–21), the *Lemuria* (May 9, 11, 13), and the *Rosaria*, or Feast of Roses (May and June).[15] Often the grave included a metal tube up to the ground's surface, allowing relatives to drop food and wine down to the deceased's remains. Additionally, catacombs included special rooms equipped with benches and tables for memorial meals. "Numerous representations of the funerary banquet carved on gravestones or painted on the walls of mausolea and hypogea [underground vaults or burial chambers] bear witness to the special importance of the ceremonial meal eaten at the tomb."[16] Roman women were actively involved in these meals and the rites for the dead, and some were official mourners who sang and chanted songs of mourning. As Torjesen

14. Reita J. Sutherland, "Prayer and Piety: The *Orans*-Figure in the Christian Catacombs of Rome" (MA thesis, University of Ottawa, 2013), 55.

15. J. M. C. Toynbee, *Death and Burial in the Roman World* (Baltimore: Johns Hopkins University Press, 1971), 51–72, includes excellent photos of burial sites.

16. Ibid., 62.

reminds us, we should not be surprised, therefore, to see women depicted in funerary art.[17]

Christians honored their deceased family members in the *cubiculum*, a room "carved out of the wall of a catacomb used for interment of remains and as a mortuary chapel."[18] The *cubiculum* might hold several remains. Roman Christians continued to celebrate the *refrigerium*, as well as meals for the martyrs; Augustine writes about such practices done by his Christian mother, Monica.[19] We should not be surprised, then, at the several meal scenes depicted in the catacombs, although, as we noted briefly above, scholars offer several possible interpretations of how these banquet scenes should be understood.

Several misconceptions have grown up around the catacombs. For example, it has been said that Christians hid in the catacombs to avoid persecution.[20] The truth is that the catacombs were known by Roman authorities, as Jews, Christians, and pagans all used the underground burial sites. Moreover, the efforts to excavate and decorate the tombs could not have been hidden, as workers and artisans trekked in and out of the tunnels. Some falsely assume that catacomb art was produced for the uneducated laity to help their faith, while literary treatises provided the theology for the educated. Yet although the catacombs reveal a socioeconomic range among Christians, the art was not a "Christianity-lite" sort of production geared for the lower classes. Another misconception is that the catacomb art was personal and private. While it is likely that families paid for the specific piece of work, the art was produced by a general group of artisans, who drew on a standard set of iconographic images. Robin M. Jensen states, "On the one hand, Christians relied on the standard repertoires of the (mostly pagan) artisans and workshops that executed the work. On the other, the art's content reflected the faith and values of the whole Christian community."[21] A related misapprehension is that the art was private, in the sense of being beyond the oversight of church officials, who allegedly

17. Karen Jo Torjesen, "The Early Christian *Orans*: An Artistic Representation of Women's Liturgical Prayer and Prophecy," in *Women Preachers and Prophets through Two Millennia of Christianity*, ed. Beverly Mayne Kienzle and Pamela J. Valker (Berkeley: University of California Press, 1998), 46.

18. Sutherland, "Prayer and Piety," 55.

19. Augustine, *Confessions* (*Confessiones*) 6.2.2, in *The Confessions*, The Works of Saint Augustine: A Translation for the 21st Century, vol. I/1, ed. John E. Rotelle, trans. Maria Boulding (Hyde Park, NY: New City, 1997), 135–36.

20. It is true that Christians faced persecution, at different times and with differing intensities, but the catacombs were not secret places of refuge.

21. Robin M. Jensen, *Understanding Early Christian Art* (New York: Routledge, 2000; repr., 2007), 22.

disapproved of visual representation. The data, however, does not support this conclusion. For example, Tertullian speaks of cups that include a figure of Christ the Good Shepherd.[22] Additionally, the well-decorated Callixtus Catacomb (honoring Pope Callixtus, 217–22), was the church's property, and all third-century popes are buried here (except Callixtus). Catacomb art was not produced as popular art by otherwise silenced minorities, but expressed the "gradually emerging public 'face' of a religion that was developing its identity—and making it visible."[23]

A final misconception is based on an argument from silence, in this case, a visual silence. Christian catacomb art can be dated as early as the late second century, and because of this, some suggest that for the first two centuries of the church, the faithful renounced all images. That is, they were aniconic (no icons or images). This assumption was based in part on the misconception that Jews did not have any artwork in their synagogues. But this latter view has been challenged in large part through a study of the extraordinary artwork of the third-century synagogue located in the ancient city of Dura Europos, located in what is now modern Syria. Although this synagogue is later than the second century, scholars suggest that it reflects earlier Jewish sentiments.[24] Moreover, the earliest Christians had no particular aversion to art per se, only to idols and depictions of gods and goddesses and their cults. For example, in the late second century Clement of Alexandria declares that it is permissible for Christians to use seals or finger rings with images because one needs them to do business. But he cautions against using pagan gods' images, instead suggesting a "dove, the fish, a sailing ship, a lyre, an anchor, or a fisherman."[25] Therefore, catacomb art should not be seen as a Christian capitulation to polytheistic impulses, but as a vehicle to express Christian ideas in ways that were meaningful and meaning-creating for the faithful.

22. Tertullian, *Pud.* 7.1–4, describes cups with sheep and a shepherd painted on them; see also Clement of Alexandria, *Christ the Educator (Paedagogus)* 3.11, who suggests a dove, fish, ship, lyre, or ship anchor as a possible ring seal. Seals to avoid include drinking cups, a sword, or a bow, the latter two being weapons of war.

23. Jensen, *Understanding Early Christian Art*, 22.

24. Rachel Hachlili, *Ancient Synagogues—Archaeology and Art: New Discoveries and Current Research*, Handbuch der Orientalistik 105 (Leiden: Brill, 2013), 223. She explains that while first-century CE synagogue art did not include "figurative designs," by the end of the second century "representational art began to flourish and figurative art played an extensive and essential part."

25. Clement of Alexandria, *Paed.* 3.11. See Sutherland's discussion in "Prayer and Piety," 10. Within Christianity, the dove signified the Holy Spirit; the fish represented an acrostic of the Greek word *ichthys: Iēsous Christos Theou Yios Sōtēr* (Jesus Christ Son of God Savior); the sailing ship represented the church; the lyre could be symbolic of Christ rescuing souls from death; the anchor symbolized hope; and the fisherman represented the apostles, especially Peter.

Figure 3.2. The Catacomb of Callixtus honeycombs beneath the earth.

## Tour of the Christian Catacombs

Many of the catacombs are open to the public today. A knowledgeable guide takes tourists through several tunnels dimly lit by electric light. Catacomb passageways with niches that held the bodies of the poor lead to rooms (*cubicula*) where those with a bit of money decorated the walls and ceiling with images of biblical scenes or nature. These frescoes would have been painted onto wet stucco, which had been plastered, perhaps in three coats, over the stone or brick.[26] Typical images included anchors, ships, and birds. Humans might be drawn in the *orans* position, which depicts a figure standing with arms outstretched to either side, often with a bit of a bend in the elbows. This is a classic pose indicating prayer or a pious demeanor. The figure is primarily presented as female in the visual record by both pagans and Christians, and for that reason, we will pay close attention to it below.

Along with typical Roman art figures, the Christian catacombs and sarcophagi (stone coffins) depict biblical scenes, including Jesus as a shepherd

---

26. Sutherland, "Prayer and Piety," 57. A *buon fresco* refers to paint applied onto wet stucco. If paint was applied after the stucco dried, then a binding agent such as oil or tempera (egg) was applied; this was known as *a secco*.

or at his baptism, and from the Old Testament (Jewish Scriptures) figures such as Adam and Eve, Abraham offering Isaac, Noah in the ark, and the three youths in the fire from the book of Daniel; surprisingly, the most popular figure depicted by far is Jonah—thrown from the boat, swallowed by the fish, sitting under the vine.[27] In fact, about 75 percent of the biblical scenes are from the Old Testament. While this may surprise readers today, on further reflection, the evidence is easily explained by pointing to the Septuagint (LXX), which is the Greek translation of the Hebrew Bible. Early church apologists and preachers promoted a unity between old and new covenants within the arc of sacred history, and through allegory they interpreted events and persons in the former as foreshadowing the latter. The LXX was the church's Bible, its teachings interpreted christologically, in light of the gospel.

Early in the fourth century, Christians decorated sarcophagi and the catacomb walls with scenes depicting Jesus healing or performing miracles. He is drawn simply, with no beard, no halo, no royal dress; indeed, he is dressed in much the same way as were the apostles and other disciples.[28] In the mid-fourth century, after Constantine, different scenes and themes of Jesus's life receive attention, such as the adoration of the magi and Jesus's triumphal entry into Jerusalem, leading Robin M. Jensen to suggest that such art focuses on stories in which his divinity is acclaimed.[29] Jesus the Good Shepherd, or stories of Noah and Jonah—these become less prevalent and then pass from view. In the fifth century we begin to see key events in Jesus's life story depicted, such as the annunciation, transfiguration, Last Supper, passion, and ascension.[30] We also see portraits of Jesus, the saints, and the apostles emphasized, without any story or event connected to the image.[31] Mosaics (art made by assembling small pieces of glass or stone and applying them to a surface) take the place of frescoes, and the catacombs fall out of use.

## Interpreting Christian Catacomb Art

Not only is it important to view the Christian catacomb art in correct relationship to the first two centuries of this movement, but also it is critical to

27. As Jensen, *Understanding Early Christian Art*, 72, rightly observes, the reclining Jonah shares similarities with the story of Endymion, to whom Zeus granted an eternal peaceful sleep.
28. Robin M. Jensen, "Early Christian Art and Divine Epiphany," *TJT* 28 (2012): 129.
29. Ibid., 137.
30. Ibid., 130.
31. Ibid., 141.

avoid interpreting the art anachronistically. We must resist the temptation to read back into the second and third centuries the liturgical and organizational structure of the fifth-century church, and then inappropriately label frescoes and images on sarcophagi based on later church practices. As we examine catacomb art, better approaches include understanding the wider Roman social practices, as well as paying attention to the power and flexibility of symbol. Do we see the art as one example among many of how the Romans treated their deceased?[32] Or should the vantage point privilege Christian identity first as one looks at the Roman Christians' burial art? Jensen takes this second tack, with the proviso that the earliest Christian artwork certainly drew on standard images of shepherd in the pagan material, and that the figure of Daniel was portrayed in ways quite like the figure of Hercules. Nevertheless, she sees a peculiar aesthetic that relates to typology, which results in differences in "form, content and purpose" in Christian art.[33] Jensen argues that "visual art often serves as a highly sophisticated, literate, and even eloquent mode of theological expression."[34] She contends that catacomb art conveys rich theological reflection and demands of the viewer a solid and extensive knowledge of the biblical text. Each biblical scene is meant to bring to mind the entire biblical narrative. And even as text helps interpret image, so too image shapes interpretation of text as meaning is produced.

A careful comparison of Roman art and Christian catacomb art (which is Roman Christian) yields the following findings, according to Jensen. First, Christian art is episodic and thus should be viewed as representing the entire narrative from which it serves as a snapshot. Second, catacomb art images and scenes are seemingly haphazardly juxtaposed into a somewhat muddled presentation (from our modern perspective). Finally, the art is presented in a crude manner, which may indicate either a lack of resources or a decision to move toward "abstract expressionism."[35] Underneath this argument is a foundational claim in a metanarrative that holds together the various depictions and figures: "These images also interact with one another to create a cumulative message that was intertextual and typological."[36]

32. E.g., Jaś Elsner, "Archaeologies and Agendas: Reflections on Late Ancient Jewish Art and Early Christian Art," *JRS* 93 (2003): 114–28; Leonard V. Rutgers, *The Jews in Late Ancient Rome: Evidence of Cultural Interaction in the Roman Diaspora* (Leiden: Brill, 2000). See the discussion in Robin M. Jensen, "Compiling Narratives: The Visual Strategies of Early Christian Visual Art," *JECS* 23.1 (2015): 1–3.
33. Jensen, "Compiling Narratives," 3.
34. Jensen, *Understanding Early Christian Art*, 3.
35. Jensen, "Compiling Narratives," 23.
36. Ibid., 25.

## Interpreting Female Figures in Catacomb Art

Answers to and assumptions about the problems of interpreting catacomb art outlined above play a big role in the analysis of the female figures. For example, if one holds that the artwork represents an expression of Christianity that is alternative or even contrary to the literary works' presentations, then one might conclude that the female figures in the frescoes present a substitute liturgy wherein women served Eucharist or baptized congregants. And of course the converse applies, and in the past scholars simplified the *orans* image and labeled all ambiguous occurrences as symbolic, representing "piety" or "faith" or "the church," rather than allow for the possibility that some might represent historical women, even as they allowed that some male *orans* figures were likely representing historical men.[37] Yet we have seen the power of the martyrs—including Thecla, Perpetua, and Felicitas—in shaping Christian piety and theology. In the following chapters, we will examine the continuing literary output by women and their contribution to developing theology, as well as explore the political authority employed by imperial women such as Helena, Constantine's mother. Thus, while we cannot assume that a given example of catacomb artwork is a historical window into the event depicted (such as a literal meal), we should keep uppermost in mind the art's power in presenting and shaping the ideas and identity of the Christians who produced it.

## The *Orans* Figure

We begin our examination of the catacomb art with a study of the *orans* figure in the frescoes. First we will sketch its use in the wider culture, and then we will explore what early Christians intended to convey with this figure. Following this, we will examine meal scenes. Yet the reader should always keep in mind the plethora of colorful images of plants, animals, birds, biblical

37. Janet H. Tulloch, "Image as Artifact: A Social-Historical Analysis of Female Figures with Cups in the Banquet Scenes from the Catacomb of SS. Marcellino e Pietro, Rome" (PhD diss., University of Ottawa, 2001), 10–11, points to four interpretations by well-known scholars: (1) Henri Leclercq (Roman School), who argues that the *orans* figure is the spirit of the dead now at peace and praying for their loved ones still alive; (2) G. B. de Rossi, who argues that the *orans* figure is a symbol of the church, especially when connected with the Good Shepherd figure; (3) André Grabar, who calls the *orans* figures "image-signs," signaling piety, specifically the piety of the deceased; (4) Lucien de Bruyne, who sees the *orans* figure as a symbol of faith for the church, including its baptism and Eucharist rites as initiation concerns. Tulloch suggests that scholars have not always appreciated the significance of the female *orans* figure (standing figure with arms outstretched). This figure might stand alone, alongside other figures, or within a biblical scene, making her gesture's meaning difficult to establish.

Figure 3.3. This woman's outstretched arms represent the classic *orans* pose (Catacomb of Priscilla).

stories, and decorative garlands that brightened these underground caves. The ancient visitor would experience each *orans* figure or meal scene not by itself but within a context of many visual stimuli as they walked cautiously along the narrow, hewed pathways by lamplight.

### The Orans *Pose in the Ancient World*

The *orans* was part of the Roman pagan world; it is found on coins, presented in statues, and represented on paintings and on gold discs layered within glass vessels such as bowls and cups. As mentioned above, this image is of a standing human figure with arms outstretched on either side, often bent at the elbow and presented as facing the viewer. Most typically the figure is presented as female, but in the Egyptian funerary stelae, we find a male *orans* with either the gods Anubis and Horis flanking him, or a falcon and jackal (or two jackals).[38] The stylized Roman *orans* pose could signify a praying figure, or more typically the virtue of *pietas*, which stresses family loyalty, devotion, and duty to one's kinfolk. As Cicero explains, it is *pietas* "which admonishes us to do our duty to our country or our parents or other

38. Torjesen, "Early Christian *Orans*," 44.

blood relations."[39] Centuries later, Augustine declares that the chief goal of a Christian is the supreme good of being united to God: "This is the worship of God, this is true religion, this right piety, this the service due to God only."[40] In those intervening centuries, Christians continued to engage the wider Roman imperial culture while forging their own identities as Roman Christians.[41] As we explore the catacombs of Rome, "we find the richest collection of *orant* figures, and their distribution makes it clear that this image was a key part of the burial iconography for both pagans and Christians at this period."[42]

The *orans* pose was closely associated with the female imperial family members, as seen in the rather common presentation of the empress Livia, Augustus's wife, in the *orans* position either on coins or as a statue. In this rhetorical expression, the imperial court stressed their commitment to family values and the virtue of *pietas*. About one hundred years after Livia, in the reign of Trajan, imperial coins show the goddess Pietas on the reverse and an imperial woman on the obverse. Additionally, we find the *orans* statue in public spaces in Rome, including the *atrium Vestae* in the Forum. The *orans* figure might be shown standing next to an altar fire, perhaps putting incense on the flames. It seems that Pietas "became depicted as an *orans* and the *orans* became associated with Pietas."[43] Thus by presenting Livia or another historical woman in the *orans* pose, the artist signaled the woman's virtuous life. And by showing the bust of *Pietas* on coins, the Roman Empire was promoting the female personification of the virtue. We should remember that Roman Christians would handle such coins regularly and thus be familiar with their cultural and political implications.

### The Orans *Pose in the Christian Catacombs*

Examining the Christian catacombs, we find 158 *orans* figures in 16 different catacombs, including 36 males (about 22 percent), and among the 107 female figures, 85 are unveiled. Approximately 10 percent could not be firmly determined to be female or male.[44] Several Old Testament figures are presented in

39. Cicero, *Invention of Rhetoric* (*De inventione rhetorica*) 2.22. Cicero lived in the final decades of the Roman Republic. He references the *orans* pose in *Letters to Friends* (*Epistulae ad familiares*) 7.5; see also Virgil, *Aen.* 2.688; Apuleius, *On the World* (*De mundo*) 33.

40. Augustine, *City of God* (*De civitate Dei*) 10.3. See http://www.ccel.org/ccel/schaff/npnf 102.iv.X.3.html.

41. Space limits prevent us from exploring Christian experiences beyond the Roman Empire, such as those of Christians in the Persian and African contexts.

42. Rubery, "From Catacomb to Sanctuary," 143.

43. Sutherland, "Prayer and Piety," 32.

44. Sutherland, "Prayer and Piety," 59–60, citing Aldo Nestori, *Repertorio topografico delle pitture delle catacombe romane*, 2nd ed. (Rome: Pontificio Istituto di Archeologia Cristiana,

an *orans* pose, including Susanna, Daniel, Noah, the three youths in the fire, Jonah, Abraham, and Isaac. Some female *orantes* have names attached to the figure, including Grata, Dionysia, and Veneranda; the last is paired with her patron saint, Petronilla, in the Callixtus Catacomb.[45] The *orans* image was polyvalent but also included consistent themes. For example, in every case the female *orans* was fully clothed, often with rich attire, and she faced the viewer, stretching out her arms on either side of her body. Often she is in the center of the painting; in some cases the *orans* image is repeated or placed at the apex in a painted pendent.

The backdrop varies widely: alongside biblical scenes one might find the *orans* in a pastoral setting, with birds, or standing next to *capsae*, boxes or baskets that hold scrolls or books. In some cases, we see groups of two or three female *orantes*; at other times both male and female *orantes* might be named. This variety of backdrops suggests that context is crucial for determining whether the figure is typological, represents a historical person (the deceased), or is allegorical (such as representing the church).

### *The* Orans *and Christian Prayer*

Torjesen focuses on the *orans* figure's presentation of prayer, observing that prayer in the ancient world represented a powerful link between human and divine. The widow and virgin were understood to be especially powerful in their prayers due to their ascetic lifestyle. As we noticed above, the office of widow was an ordained position, and widows sat in the front of the church with the other clergy. In his letter *To the Philippians*, Polycarp declares that a widow's prayer is like serving at the altar.[46] Virgins were known to sing or recite psalms at funerals and later at the martyrs' shrines. In making these links, Torjesen suggests that the catacomb art reflects in a stylized and symbolic way women's involvement in liturgical practices of the congregation. Reviewing the available evidence, Torjesen concludes that the *orans* image is effective because viewers could connect the symbolic meaning with a concrete expression of that intention. "The symbolic or

---

1993). See also Sharon Marie Salvadori, "*Per Feminam Mors, Per Feminam Vita*: Images of Women in the Early Christian Funerary Art of Rome" (PhD diss., New York University, 2002), 355n6, who finds 279 images of the *orans* position in "paleochristian sarcophagi and hypogeal paintings."

45. Salvadori, "*Per Feminam Mors*," 361.

46. Pol. *Phil*. 4.3. The second-century work known as the Didache (Teaching of the Twelve Apostles) describes the celebration of the Eucharist as including simple, prescribed prayers but adds that a presiding prophet who feels so inspired by the Spirit should pray freely as led by the Spirit. See Did. 9–10.

allegorical meaning of the figure must have some relationship to its literal meaning."[47]

To illustrate her contention, Torjesen points to one of the earliest depictions of a Christian female *orans*. In the Catacomb of Callixtus, we find three vignettes painted across the middle panel separating the upper and lower burial niches. In the first scene, we have the figures of Abraham and Isaac, both drawn in the *orans* pose, representing the sacrifice (or binding) of Isaac (see Gen. 22). The center picture is a meal scene showing seven figures (discussed below). Next to this scene is another that presents a small tripod table with fish and bread upon it, flanked by a female *orans* and a male figure reaching to touch the food on the table. Many scholars suggest that this last scene represents celebration of the Eucharist.[48] Torjesen suggests that this *orans* figure assists the eucharistic minister and offers liturgical prayers for the congregation.[49]

### The Orans *Pose and Christian Piety*

Christian literary evidence aids our interpretation of this enigmatic scene, but we may also profit by connecting the scene to the Roman virtue of *pietas*, also often depicted in the *orans* pose. Christians took advantage of the visual image to present a new or modified understanding of familial and civic duties and loyalties. Christians went a step further and connected the pose with the position Christ assumed on the cross. Tertullian declares that Christians pray with hands lifted and outstretched in imitation of Christ's death on a cross.[50] Earlier in the second century, the Epistle of Barnabas recalls the story of Moses and the Israelites battling the Amalekites. In this story from Exodus 17, Moses stands with his arms extended from his sides, held by Aaron and Hur. The Epistle of Barnabas declares that this action was a type of the cross upon which Jesus suffered.[51] Writing at the end of the second century, Irenaeus likewise sees a prefiguring of Christ's crucifixion in this Exodus 17 story.[52]

47. Torjesen, "Early Christian *Orans*," 45.
48. Part of the difficulty in interpreting the *orans* figure with the tripod table is its appearance only once in the catacombs explored thus far. Moreover, the depiction of Isaac and Abraham *orantes* that is paired with this scene is likewise unrepeated and should be factored into the interpretation of the female *orans*. The late second-century church father Irenaeus suggests that the binding or sacrificing of Isaac points to the crucifixion of Jesus (*Haer.* 4.21).
49. Torjesen, "Early Christian *Orans*," 51.
50. Tertullian, *On Prayer (De oratione)* 14.
51. Barn. 12.2; see also Justin Martyr, *Dialogue with Trypho (Dialogus cum Tryphone)* 91, 112, 131.
52. Irenaeus, *Demonstration of Apostolic Preaching (Epideixis tou apostolikou kērygmatos)* 46.

As we weave these threads together, we may discern the dim outline of Christ on the cross, casting shadows in the form of Moses battling the Amalekites, and perceive the Roman *orans* as expressing the highest virtue, with echoes of altars and sacrifices connected with the figure.[53] Perhaps the use of the female *orans* in a Christian catacomb scene prodded viewers to savor a theologically or religiously rich image. Sharon Marie Salvadori contends, "*Pietas* in *orans* was not chosen for its 'neutrality.' It was a semantically loaded image turned to Christian advantage."[54] Perhaps, as Eric Smith suggests, the *orans* figure is "a hidden transcript of the subordinate."[55] As insiders within the Christian community, the viewers mentally reworked a classic Roman pose to disrupt the dominating imperial rhetoric. The *orans* speaks subversively to the power of the cross and portrays the claims of the minority Christian communities.

### The Orans *Figure of Susanna: A Case Study*

Salvadori moves in this direction in her analysis of the figure of Susanna depicted twice in the *orans* pose in the Greek Chapel of the Catacomb of Priscilla. Susanna's story is told in the additions to Daniel included in the Septuagint. In this story, Susanna is a chaste daughter wrongly accused by two evil elders of sexual misdeeds.[56] In fact, they attempt to seduce her, and she escapes their clutches. A young Daniel exonerates Susanna by his clever decision to interrogate each elder separately. When their stories do not match, he concludes that they are lying, and Susanna is vindicated. Analyzing the fresco, Denzey calls attention to the large size of the figures; at over two feet tall, they dwarf the figures in the nearby *Fractio Panis*, which are about ten inches in height. Salvadori suggests that the Susanna *orans* figure represents God, who hears the prayers of the faithful and delivers. She adds that the *orans* pose would call to the viewers' minds the crucified Christ. Additionally,

---

53. Salvadori, "*Per Feminam Mors*," 401, suggests that perhaps Christians took up this connection to sacrifice and altered the sacrificial image to focus on Christian piety as *imitatio Christi*.

54. Ibid., 409.

55. Eric C. Smith, "Mimicry, Mirroring, Subversion, and Critique: Reading Heterotopia in the Cubicula of the Sacraments" (PhD diss., University of Denver and the Iliff School of Theology, 2013), 140.

56. Janet Huskinson, "Women and Learning: Gender and Identity in Scenes of Intellectual Life on Late Roman Sarcophagi," in *Constructing Identities in Late Antiquity*, ed. Richard Miles, Routledge Classical Monographs (New York: Routledge, 1999), 205, in her examination of sarcophagi art, points out that Susanna is one of few biblical women who are presented as learned in Scripture and has been shown holding a scroll. Huskinson analyzes sarcophagi made in the third and early fourth centuries in Rome.

the viewers might recall another story of Daniel, when he is in the lions' den. Salvadori observes that Daniel too is presented in the *orans* pose. For Salvadori, the figures of Daniel and Susanna prefigure Christ, and as such, should be experienced as prefiguring the "soteriological power of Christ's death on the cross."[57]

As persuasive as this analysis may be for the figure of Susanna, Salvadori rightly cautions that each female *orans* must be appreciated in her own context, and not all *orans* figures carry a soteriological or christological reverberation. We saw above that Christian art can be polyvalent, so we need not find the single or only message. Indeed, the choice to present thoughts in frescoes, with common yet malleable images, perhaps invites each viewer to allow the mind to wander across several possible stories. As we will see below, Denzey follows this approach in suggesting new interpretations of the Susanna figure with the *Fractio Panis* and the other artwork of this room, with fruitful results.

## Meal Scenes in the Catacombs

As we shift to discuss meal scenes, we will remain for the moment in the Greek Chapel and resume our discussion of the *Fractio Panis*. The reader will recall that this artwork opened our discussion. This scene was originally understood to be a Eucharist meal, attended by the presiding priest, with six additional people present, including one woman. The difficulty in analyzing the fresco is due in no small part to its deteriorated condition, but also to modern assumptions about how the church would have functioned in the third century. Concerning the *Fractio Panis*, Denzey points out that the fresco does not have "obvious visual referents to a funerary meal . . . such as tripod stands, beverage heaters, or amphorae of wine."[58] Yet she also rightly observes that "the lively casualness of their poses seems to militate against reading this painting as sacramental or Eucharistic."[59] Additionally, she postulates that all the figures are female, and the veiled woman's head covering signifies social status of some sort. Denzey wonders whether the veiled woman might be offering a toast, since her gaze travels beyond the table and her right arm is raised.[60] These comments illustrate the difficulties in interpreting the meal scenes, as

57. Salvadori, "*Per Feminam Mors*," 389.
58. Denzey, *Bone Gatherers*, 96. She is, overall, sympathetic to the assessment of the fresco as a funerary meal.
59. Ibid., 97.
60. Ibid., 98.

one discerns the connections made with the wider Roman customs and the developing liturgical practices.

Determining whether a Christian commissioned a catacomb fresco, consequently, is not simple. Moreover, even if a Christian authorized the work, it is an additional step to determine whether the fresco should be understood as a specifically Christian moment, such as a historical Eucharist or a symbolic heavenly banquet, or as a reflection on that believer's Roman cultural practices, or even a combination of the two. Therefore, before addressing these concerns, a brief description of meal scenes is in order.

## Characteristics of the Banquet or Meal Scene in the Catacombs

We have a total of twenty-two banquet or meal scenes in the Christian catacombs. These scenes usually feature five to seven figures on one side of a half-circle table, known as a sigma table, shaped like an uncial sigma: C. Often seven tall baskets of bread flank to the right and left of the table. The table might have a plate of bread and/or of fish on it, as well as a cup. The figures might be sitting, standing, or reclining. A slave, distinguished as such by the short tunic, may be presented as standing or sitting. Differentiating male and female figures might be accomplished by examining hairstyles; for example, women often parted their hair in the center, while men generally wore their hair without a part. Veils, ribbons, and elaborate hairstyles also can distinguish a female figure.[61]

In the Catacomb of Marcellinus and Peter, eight banquet scenes are identified in frescoes dating from the late third and early fourth centuries. Women and men sit along one side of the sigma, as we have come to expect. In these paintings we never find men alone holding the cup; either we find a man and a woman holding cups, or two women clasping cups. Only in this catacomb do we find a standing female figure holding a raised cup. There are no reclining females drinking from a cup, and if a male is shown drinking, he is reclining at the center of the sigma table. In two frescoes, a woman wears a diadem, and in another fresco, a veil. The latter is quite rare in the Christian catacombs.

Interestingly, in this catacomb we also find twelve Greek-Latin inscriptions on the walls above the diners. Phrases similar to AGAPE MISCE MI (Love, mix/give me to drink) and IRENE PORGE CALDA (Peace, offer wine mixed with hot water) often occur, although these terms appear in different

---

61. Madeleine Emanuel, "The Utility of the Fractio Panis as Evidence in the Case for Women's Ordination" (MA thesis, Claremont Graduate University, 2014), 35–36.

Photo PCSA Archives

Figure 3.4. Fresco of a banquet in the Catacomb of Marcellinus and Peter.

combinations.[62] Janet H. Tulloch analyzes the evidence and postulates that PORGE CALDA references wine mixed with hot water. She reminds readers that "wine . . . was an integral part of Greek and Roman culture and religions. Gods expected it, the dead needed it, and oaths were sworn with it."[63] Christians also celebrated with diluted wine. Augustine describes his mother's custom to take cakes, bread, and wine to the shrines of saints on festival days. Monica partook of wine diluted with hot water from a cup, taking only sips of the liquid so as to avoid any hint of impropriety. When she was in Milan, Italy, she stopped such practice based on the prohibition laid out by Bishop Ambrose, who urged Christians to avoid superstitions about the dead and also the drunkenness that was part of such revelry.[64]

62. The Latin MISCE is the second-person singular present imperative active of the verb *misceo*, which usually means "to mix two liquids" and often refers to wine mixed with water. The Latin PORGE is the second-person singular present imperative active of the verb *porrigo*, which can mean "to stretch out in sleep or death" or "to offer." CALDA is an accusative plural term meaning "hot," perhaps referring to wine mixed with hot water. The Greek AGAPE means "love" or "goodwill," and IRENE means "peace and rest." See Tulloch, "Image as Artifact," 235–38.

63. Ibid., 251.

64. Augustine, *Conf.* 6.2.2 (Boulding, 135–36). See Augustine's *Ep.* 54, *To Januarius*, in which Augustine relays Monica's adaptation regarding new fasting practices at Ambrose's church in

### Time Represented in the Catacomb Banquet Scenes

According to Tulloch, the best way to understand these phrases that accompany the banquet scene is to appreciate how the fresco presents time. She suggests that within the paintings, we have both ordinary time, which involves all the figures doing things at the same time, and ritual or mythical time, which is nonlogical and nonsequential. Thus one could have a mythical (dead) figure speak to a living or historical figure. The banquet could reflect historical activities as well as connect to eschatological hopes and link the deceased with living relatives. Tulloch's theory moves us away from the binary options of historical reality or allegory as the two interpretative options for the meal scenes. Moreover, Tulloch's theory allows for present reference to be tied to eternal relevance. The frescoes represent Christian ritual that allows one to move from ordinary to ritual time, thus making the underground room a ritual space: "The effects of the Christian ritual activity represented in these frescoes also allow for the implied image-action and speech to function eternally."[65]

Pulling together the inscriptions with the drawings, Tulloch argues that the frescoes represent a family meal honoring the deceased in a rather typical Roman fashion, but with an eye to Christian teachings on proper decorum and resurrection life. She resists identifying the meal as a Eucharist, primarily because this can raise anachronistic expectations or shut down further exploration of the painting. Moreover, she rightly observes that whatever the action signifies, it is never done solely by a male, which means it cannot be a gender-specific act. She suggests that the female figures co-led a "cup-offering rite (or libation ritual) to honor the deceased."[66]

### Theology Represented in the Catacomb Banquet Scenes

Not everyone agrees with Tulloch's conclusions, but most admit that the banquet scene frescoes invite a deeper engagement with the historical, cultural, and liturgical practices of the early church. Jensen goes further to stress the theological dimensions informing the banquet frescoes found throughout the catacombs. She reminds us that catacomb art is funerary art, displayed next to the resting place of the deceased. She holds that the meal scenes present the viewer with a vision of a heavenly banquet, promised by Jesus in Matthew 26:29: "I tell you, I will never again drink of this fruit of the vine until

---

Milan (*Saint Augustine: Letters*, vol. 1, trans. Wilfrid Parsons, FC 12 [New York: Fathers of the Church, 1951], 253–54).

65. Tulloch, "Image as Artifact," 329.

66. Ibid., 25.

that day when I drink it new with you in my Father's kingdom."[67] Those who commemorate their loved one's passing testify with this fresco to their confidence that the dead will be resurrected to enjoy heaven together with Jesus.

Denzey takes a similar focus as she examines frescoes in the Greek Chapel. She suggests two themes that connect the various paintings: God's deliverance and the role of women in salvation history.[68] Denzey supports this second theme by tracing how women feature prominently in the various frescoes, including the visit of the Magi to Mary and her child, Jesus, and the common scene of Jesus raising Lazarus, with the unique inclusion of Mary and Martha. Additionally, a portrait of an unnamed woman is painted above the doorway. Finally, Denzey speculates that two of the frescoes have been misidentified. She suggests that a badly preserved figure formerly identified as Daniel with a lion is better understood as a representation of Thecla.[69] She also argues that the image thought to portray the Susanna cycle is better understood as representing either the life of the deceased person or the biblical figure Mary Magdalene.[70] She lays out her argument for identifying the character as Mary Magdalene by reminding readers of Mary's story. In John's Gospel, Mary Magdalene arrives at Jesus's tomb first, sees the stone rolled back from the entrance, informs Peter and the beloved disciple, and then remains weeping at the tomb. At this point, Jesus appears to her, and when she reaches out to touch his feet in worship, he cautions her not to hold him. This gospel scene is repeated frequently in later Christian art (John 20:17). Perhaps we have the first example of it here in the Greek Chapel.[71]

Denzey reaches forward to the sixth century in imagining pilgrims who visited the catacombs. Specifically, she builds on the itineraries of Christians visiting martyr shrines in Rome and wonders whether they came to the Catacomb of Priscilla, to its Greek Chapel, to venerate the martyr Prisca/Priscilla, Paul's coworker and the wife of Aquila (see Acts 18:1–3; Rom. 16:3–4). Denzey paints the scene: devoted women descend into the catacomb with oil lamps

67. Robin M. Jensen, "Dining in Heaven: The Earliest Christian Visions of Paradise," *BRev* 14.5 (1998): 37–38.

68. Denzey, *Bone Gatherers*, 105.

69. Ibid., 107, notes that the early medieval work *Commendatio animae* (Commendation of the Soul, in Western ritual) includes prayers for the dead but names only Thecla, the Virgin Mary, and Susanna among the women. Both Mary and Susanna are clearly present in the Greek Chapel. For an extensive discussion of the figure of Susanna in this chapel, see ibid., 108–12.

70. Denzey, *Bone Gatherers*, 112. Denzey states that even if this chapel art reflects a historical female deacon, and the meal represents a Eucharist, this does not mean that the female leading the meal was a priest; she could be a consecrated virgin. Additionally, this fresco may represent a group rivaling the orthodox Christian communities. She concludes that "women may have been early Christian priests, but they would not have been Catholic priests" (116).

71. Ibid., 110–11.

for an all-night vigil in the chapel, surrounded by frescoes of female saints and exemplars of the holy life.[72]

These sixth-century pilgrims follow the tradition of their coreligionist Egeria, who visited holy sites and venerated the martyrs. We will meet Egeria in chapter 6 and join her pilgrimage. The text of her journey breaks off in the midst of her description of the Christian Feast of Dedication commemorating the dedication of the Basilica of the Holy Sepulchre on the day (in September) when the cross of Jesus was "discovered" by Helena, Constantine's mother, the subject of chapter 5. Egeria writes of the vast number of pilgrims who flood the city to participate in the rituals, laity and clergy alike from the four points of the compass. Egeria's voice ends in midsentence as she describes a vigil at the church on the Mount of Olives, the place commemorating the Lord's ascension. There in a grotto (cave) outside Jerusalem, Jesus taught his apostles; now pilgrims gather at the site in worship and remembrance. So too, in the catacombs in Rome, men and women gather and remember, surrounded by paintings that testify to their faith.

## Conclusion

The reexamination of the *Fractio Panis* and other meal scenes in the catacombs has reinvigorated discussions about the roles played by men and women in the early church. Revisiting past conclusions has raised questions about meal scenes' relationship to historical events in the past or present or hoped-for future, and these concerns stand alongside related questions as to whether the meal is best understood literally, symbolically, liturgically, or theologically. Moreover, investigations of history, social status, religious teachings on the afterlife, and cultural practices honoring the dead—all of these concerns are at play when analyzing catacomb and funerary art. The frescoes engage the viewer emotionally and cognitively, inviting a shared experience. The exact nature of such experience is now beyond our grasp, but in the echoes left in these ancient underground chambers, we can discern the voices of women who were active participants in Christian rituals and practices.

Familiar visual images such as the *orans* pose continued to be used into the post-Constantine period, but now representing the Christian imperial family. For example, Eusebius tells us that Constantine, the first Christian emperor, is portrayed in the *orans* position over entrances in his palaces across the empire.[73] Saints and martyrs are also represented in this way.

72. Ibid., 123.
73. Eusebius, *Life of Constantine* (*Vita Constantini*) 4.16.

Gold glass vessels found in large numbers within the catacombs offer interesting evidence of this transition. Gold discs, sandwiched between two glass layers, often show anonymous figures or personifications of the soul in the *orans* pose; yet among the over four hundred vessels or fragments we also find named figures in this pose, including St. Peter, St. Paul, and St. Agnes.[74] These vessels, created primarily in the fourth century, were cemented with the tiles that surrounded the *loculi*, or burial niches, serving as identification markers and decoration. The gold glass vessels ranged from

Public domain

Figure 3.5. A gold glass vessel with St. Agnes in the *orans* pose from the Catacomb of Pamphylus.

five to ten centimeters in diameter and were produced by relatively unskilled craftsmen. One of these gold glass vessels of St. Agnes in the *orans* pose survives today in situ in the Catacomb of Novaziano.

The figure of St. Agnes, martyr under Emperor Diocletian (245–311), becomes an important imperial saint of the Constantinian dynasty. Ambrose, bishop of Milan (339–97) and instructor of Augustine, wrote a treatise on virginity in honor of his sister, Marcellina, in which he extolled Agnes, who died bravely by the sword for her confession.[75] She rejected marriage to the son of the Roman prefect Sempronius, embracing Christ as her bridegroom, Ambrose declares. Another version of her story places her in a brothel as punishment for her rejection. When a young man dares to gaze upon her, he is thrown to the ground, convulsing and blind, and her virginity is preserved. She was a favorite saint of Constantina Augusta, the daughter of Constantine the Great and sister of the Arian Emperor Constantius II (337–61). It was she who encouraged her father to build the Basilica of St. Agnes, thus linking the imperial family to this martyred saint. The period was marked by intense theological debate surrounding the Arian controversy, and Eileen Rubery wonders if the relatively high number of gold glass discs dedicated to St. Agnes signals the doctrinal discussions and policy shifts underway. She asks if "the image of S. Agnes [could] even have acted as a covert symbol of support for the embattled Pope and the anti-Arian doctrine?"[76] In the next chapter we take up Rubery's question more broadly as we begin a new era in the church's history. The seismic shifts in politics, great doctrinal debates, and liturgical developments offer new contexts for Christian women to express their faith.

74. Rubery, "From Catacomb to Sanctuary," 147.
75. Ambrose, *On Virgins* (*De virginibus*) 1.2.
76. Rubery, "From Catacomb to Sanctuary," 169.

# 4

# From Pagan to Christian, Martyr to Ascetic

## The Early Fourth Century

Discussions of the early fourth century are generally dominated by the monumental shifting of political power and the larger-than-life personages of Constantine, Arius, and Athanasius, resulting in relatively little attention paid to women during this time. In the mid- to late fourth century, however, women seemingly burst onto the scene, founding monasteries, patronizing scholars, participating in doctrinal controversies, and gaining reputations as exemplars of Christian devotion. The important work of this chapter, then, is to focus on what happened before these "abrupt" changes and pay attention to the stories of women that were passed around during the late third and early fourth centuries. We will map the transition from the church as a minority voice that gained strength from times of trial and suffering to a protected church that cherished its martyr history and used it as fuel for its future. Unfortunately, there are very few sources from which to draw our understanding of Christian women at this time. What we do have, though, demonstrates that women were instrumental in the construction of Christian identity and theology in the midst of a shifting empire.

First, we will set the scene with the Great Persecution and Constantine's rise to and consolidation of power. Then we will turn to Eusebius of Caesarea, the historian who inaugurated an entirely new form of understanding the past, set the tone for centuries of Christian historians, and witnessed Christianity's important shift from persecuted *superstitio* (nonprotected, nonrecognized religious faction) to protected (and even favored) religion in the Roman Empire under Constantine. We will focus on how Eusebius received and understood the martyr tradition and how the martyrdom of women in particular helped shape the faith of the persecuted church. These stories substantively fashioned and fueled the burgeoning ascetic movement later in the fourth century. Since Eusebius is one of our key witnesses to this shift in Christian history, it is vital to consider how he conceived of the Christian tradition and its role in passing the baton of the Christian witness. We will also look at one of the earliest literary incarnations of Thecla, from the late third or early fourth century, in Methodius of Olympus's *Symposium*. His combination of the victorious virgin and ascending philosopher was foundational for Christian practice in the Greek East. Thecla's influence extended to the Latin West, helping to sow the seeds of Western monasticism and medieval mysticism. Some of the central theological themes we will find in these texts directly influenced women of the later fourth century.

### The Great Persecution

At the end of the third century, trouble had been brewing for some time between the Romans and Christians. The Christians had proved themselves irritating by refusing pagan worship and its intimate ties to the perceived flourishing of the empire. The Romans were suspicious of anything new or "trendy" because it threatened the important and delicate balance between the Romans and their gods. Christians were a new and therefore unknown and potentially dangerous entity.

Before Emperor Diocletian's set of edicts beginning in January 303, which set off the infamous imperially sanctioned persecution of Christianity, the shape and magnitude of Christian suffering varied from region to region and even city to city. During the second and third centuries some were subjected to heinous tortures, such as those outlined in the Passion of Perpetua and Felicitas and the Martyrs of Lyons and Vienne,[1] while others lived relatively unscathed, at least with regard to their physical well-being. Generally speaking, Christians were intensely disliked. They were easy targets for blame when an economic, military, or political venture went awry. In the second and third centuries, Christians were often hated and cast as scapegoats, but they were not consistently targeted because of their Christianity per se.[2] They were, however, viewed as troublesome or seditious because they threatened the way

---

1. For the letter from Vienne and Lyons, in Gaul, see Eusebius, *Hist. eccl.* 5.1.
2. See Moss, *Ancient Christian Martyrdom*.

Romans gauged the health of the empire. When Diocletian became emperor in 284, he was immediately faced with a fractured empire that was strained economically because of previous mismanagement and a series of assassinations of emperors. A gifted administrator, Diocletian set out to pull the empire from the brink of ruin by appealing to the core of Roman identity; and he succeeded. Returning to the glory of Rome involved a heavy investment in the infrastructure of Roman culture, bound as it was with pagan practice. Diocletian's reforms did not initially include the systematic persecution of Christians; that would come almost twenty years later.

The series of edicts beginning in 303 was of a different order than the scattered crackdowns and general discrimination against Christians. To gain control of the empire again and delimit threats to that program, the regime officially targeted Christians.[3] Their gatherings were curtailed, their churches were destroyed and property confiscated, and their leaders were imprisoned. Moreover, Christians were executed if they did not perform the official sacrifice ordered by the emperor. From the Romans' perspective, anyone's refusal to do so meant that they stood apart from the core of what it meant to be Roman and support the success of the empire. Christians fell into this category. Hostility that had been churning under the surface and erupting only sporadically was now officially sanctioned. Any hope to regain even the previous state of uneasy rapprochement was weakened as each edict was issued. No longer were provincial governors like Pliny writing to emperors like Trajan, asking what to do about this little fledgling group in the absence of official policy. The empire had taken a definitive step and made into policy what had previously been circumscribed in localized situations. The future of Christian flourishing in the Roman Empire seemed quite bleak.

### Constantine (Ruled 306–37, Sole Emperor 324–37)

Constantine must have indeed been a surprise, then, especially so soon after the empire had exercised its muscle in compelling conformity. By melding Christianity with his military reclamation of Rome, Constantine overturned the expectation that the empire was irreversibly and thoroughly pagan. Now military might was not determined by the Roman pantheon but by the one God of a sectarian group heretofore branded as a threat by the empire. After Constantine's defeat of Maxentius at the Battle of the Milvian Bridge on October 28, 312, Constantine and Licinius (emperor of the West, 308–13,

---

3. Eusebius recounts the rollout of the edicts beginning in *Hist. eccl.* 8.2, in *Eusebius: Ecclesiastical History, Books 6–10*, trans. J. E. L. Oulton, LCL 265 (Cambridge, MA: Harvard University Press, 1932), 259.

and of the East, 313–24) issued the Edict of Milan in 313, which ended the persecution of Christians across the empire. Little more than a decade would pass before a Roman emperor was sitting among a group of bishops at Nicaea, participating in doctrinal discussions and brokering peace in the church. This was an astounding shift.

Around 318, as Constantine busied himself in solidifying his position as emperor, increasing numbers of Christians were getting involved in what began as a local disagreement between an unsuspecting bishop and a presbyter named Arius. Arius was troubled by Bishop Alexander of Alexandria's teaching concerning the Son of God that, to Arius, threatened the transcendence of God. He argued that this did not square with Scripture and thus kicked off a decades-long debate about the nature of the Trinity. Alongside this intra-church disagreement, the still nascent Christianizing Roman Empire was going through a sea change itself, with Constantine consolidating his power once and for all with his defeat of Licinius in 324. The long path to sole emperor had finally been consummated, only for Constantine to be faced with a church in an uproar. He convened a council at Nicaea, where around three hundred bishops gathered in the summer of 325 to make decisions about a whole host of issues affecting Christian practice, including what to do about Arius.

This story is familiar: much has been written about the hinge of history that was Constantine and Christianity's precarious and unlikely journey toward domination in the fourth century. The empire would not be officially declared Christian until Theodosius I in 380, but the Edict of Milan (313) was the genesis. By declaring Christianity a protected religion under Roman law, Constantine and Licinius were not only granting previously unavailable rights and securities to Christians but also exposing Roman identity to a way of thinking that previously had been perceived as incompatible with Roman ideals. The legacy of Roman success rested upon adherence to a structured societal rhythm that was attuned to appease the gods. If the rhythm was interrupted, crops might not grow and wars would be lost. To be Roman was to be pagan and to consider any alternative threatened destruction upon society.

Christianity's shift from a minority voice to a flourishing and dominant perspective, however, took more than military campaigns and a hands-on emperor who would make it his mission to unite the empire, quell the bickering Christian factions, and change the pagan face of the Roman skylines. Constantine constructed an atmosphere that allowed Christianity to take root in a way it had not been able to do before. And take root it did. Christians clung to the heritage of the apostles and martyrs even as they crossed that metaphorical border from *superstitio* to practicing a legal religion in the Roman Empire. Female martyrs and legends would be among those to gain even more renown as the Christians prioritized the preservation of their lives and stories of their deaths. This work to preserve pious heritage bled over into the search for how to be Christian in this new favorable but precarious environment.

## Eusebius and the Framing of Remembrance

### Making Empire by Making History

Eusebius of Caesarea (263–339) is an important witness to the late third and early fourth centuries. As a Christian bishop during the Diocletianic persecution, he saw firsthand the effects of the increasingly severe edicts before he experienced a period of extraordinary change under Constantine. Eusebius's *Ecclesiastical History* is one of the most important early Christian texts, not only because of its narrative approach, which recounts Christianity as one big story, but also because it inaugurates an entire tradition of ecclesiastical history writing that is informed by a particular theological understanding of history. Eusebius was not simply interested in "what happened," but also in what Christianity was and its place in the general history of humankind.[4] His rendering of Constantine was likely equal parts fueled, on the one hand, by the kinetic, joyful disbelief of one who had just survived the great ordeal of the Diocletianic persecution, and, on the other hand, by the sober realization that a new world was at his fingertips, which he would write into being so as to ensure its success.

Eusebius's *Ecclesiastical History* appears to have had two aims: to construct a narrative that validated Christianity's existence in the first place and then to secure Christianity's place as central to the future of the empire. One element in the work that accomplishes these twin objectives is the remembrance of martyrological history as the cornerstone upon which the foundation of Christianity's survival and theological integrity is built and secured. Eusebius not only knew many stories of the women discussed earlier in this book but also, as the head of the library at Caesarea, spent his life collecting their stories and the stories of other martyrs, even adding to their number with oral accounts from his own time.[5] Eusebius constructed a narrative of Christianity where suffering Christians were the root system that grounded and nourished the tree of Christianity. Martyrs were central to this approach, as were bishops who "suffered" because of "heretics." The unbroken succession of those who were tasked with preserving the Christian tradition overshadowed the

---

4. Arthur J. Droge, "The Apologetic Dimensions of the *Ecclesiastical History*," in *Eusebius, Christianity, and Judaism*, ed. Harold W. Attridge and Gohei Hata (Detroit: Wayne State University Press, 1992), 492.

5. See Grafton and Williams, *Christianity and the Transformation of the Book.*

imperial succession, repackaged as it was into a narrative of the rise and fall of emperors based on their orientation to the plight of Christians.

In early Christianity, apostolic succession referred specifically to the transference of authority and entrusting of doctrinal integrity to legitimate bishops. But the principle functioned in less official ways as well. The baton was passed between martyrs and later between ascetics: from Monica to her son Augustine, from Melania the Elder to her granddaughter Melania the Younger, from the slave Blandina to the young man who died with her in the arena, from Thecla to Macrina, from local martyrs to the pilgrims who sought out their shrines, and from Jesus (in a vision) to Helena Augusta. Yet this brand of succession was not of a lesser, informal nature. Formal or authoritative succession is often singularly associated with the transition from orthodox bishop to orthodox bishop. Sources such as Eusebius make it clear that the succession of bishops was indeed paramount for doctrinal integrity. However, it is a categorical mistake to designate this brand of succession as the only conduit through which power flowed effectively, erecting a single-layered preservation of doctrinal integrity and authority.

The sources do not display a breezy comfort with such a narrow rendering of authority; instead, alongside one branch of the family tree of early Christianity that marks the "official" genealogy of bishop succession, we find various other branches tracing other lines of succession that also represent the transmission of authority and the preservation of the apostolic and, more specifically in some cases, the martyrological traditions. Moving forward, it is necessary to recognize that the church did not uniformly think of authority as exclusively the purview of bishops; in fact, there was an opening up of the ability to have power in the late third and early fourth centuries that made possible the blossoming of ascetic devotion, which was largely though not exclusively dominated by women. Thus power, authority, and legacy during this transitional period of empire and Christianity were not limited to bishops and councils but were much more nuanced and expansive in scope. Certainly, some other ways to exercise power are more properly characterized as informal, but labeling such things as patronage, leading a community of women, or even the influence of posthumous literary representation as "informal" are misnomers. The ever-evolving distinctions made in early Christianity served to mark these lives and legacies as unquestionably part of the tradition of authoritative and effective power and authority.

### Writing Martyrs: The Ecclesiastical History

While writing the *Ecclesiastical History*, Eusebius witnessed monumental shifts in the empire. To put it into perspective, when Eusebius began writing this work,[6] Christianity was barely tolerated in the empire and was about to be subjected to an official persecution; by its last edition, Constantine had issued the Edict of Milan (313) making Christianity a protected religion in the empire, had become sole emperor, and had joined a group of bishops at Nicaea to work through some doctrinal issues that were causing division. It is no wonder that Eusebius kept editing his work![7] What specifically concerns us here is how Eusebius responds to the persecution and the framework he puts in motion for Christianity to receive the martyrs into the great tradition of the church. His method laid the groundwork for the legitimate succession of the apostolic tradition both to remain firmly within the purview of bishops and to expand into new arenas of authority, such as those who suffered but were not executed for whatever reason (confessors), the legacy of the martyrs, and eventually ascetics.

At the beginning of book 5, Eusebius includes the famous account of the Martyrs of Lyons and Vienne. He received the letter concerning the events that happened in the Roman province of Gaul via the churches in Asia and Phrygia. The letter depicts a localized persecution of Christians who, accused of Thyestean feasts (cannibalism) and Oedipodean intercourse—a typical charge that displays a mischaracterization of Christianity—suffered "every kind of abuse and punishment" and still remained zealous in their devotion to Christ.[8] The governor, the soldiers, and the mob finally reached their limit and became furious with a specific group of Christians. One of those listed was a slave girl named Blandina, "through whom Christ showed that things which are mean and obscure and contemptible among men are vouchsafed great glory with God because of the love towards him shown in the power and not boasted of in appearance."[9] This depiction of Blandina is stunning in and of itself, considering that in Roman society she lacked the status of a

---

6. Timothy D. Barnes convincingly locates books 1–7 to a date in the 290s based on a simultaneous publication of the *Chronicon* and the *Ecclesiastical History* in 295–97, with a terminus ad quem of 303, when the Diocletianic persecution began; see his *Constantine and Eusebius* (Cambridge, MA: Harvard University Press, 2006). Robert M. Grant, on the other hand, posits that Eusebius began the work later, writing the first edition during the Diocletianic persecutions (303–11); see his *Eusebius as Church Historian* (Eugene, OR: Wipf & Stock, 2006).

7. In total, Eusebius's original history had five editions; some editions involved large changes like the addition of entire new books, while others included relatively small changes. These more "minor" edits illustrate just how fickle and precarious this transitional empire really was. In one of the later editions Eusebius scrubbed anything positive about Licinius after Constantine defeated him in battle and became sole emperor. The final edition quietly removed any reference to Crispus after Constantine had him killed for reasons unknown.

8. Eusebius, *Hist. eccl.* 5.1, in *Eusebius: Ecclesiastical History, Books 1–5*, trans. Kirsopp Lake, LCL 153 (Cambridge, MA: Harvard University Press, 1926), 407–37.

9. Eusebius, *Hist. eccl.* 5.1 (Lake, 415).

human being; she was a *res*, a possessed "thing." Legally she lacked any claim to integrity of body and had no standing in court.[10] We turn to Blandina's story here to highlight Eusebius's reception of it and the theological work of this martyrological account.

## BLANDINA, SLAVE GIRL AND AGENT OF CHRIST

While Blandina's mistress is portrayed as a hand-wringing wreck, Blandina is filled with such immense power that her torturers cannot break her even after an entire day of exhausting their expansive repertoire of cruelties. According to her torturers, her body is broken and she should die. Blandina does not give them the satisfaction of seeing her will broken or her death. Instead, she is compared to a "noble athlete" who is strengthened in the conflict. She clings fast to her identity—"I am a Christian woman, and nothing wicked happens among us"—which affords her freedom from pain amid the brutality. The recounting of her tortured body resisting death so as to die on her own terms serves as a purposeful parallel to Jesus's approach to his own death. In John 10:18, Jesus speaks of how he chose to lay his life down: "No one takes it from me, but I lay it down of my own accord. I have power to lay it down, and I have power to take it up again. I have received this command from my Father."

The martyrs showed their mettle by remaining alive against all expectations. They were made "a spectacle to the world."[11] Blandina stood out among the group for her very particular posture as she hung on a stake to be picked apart by birds. The author of the letter interprets this image as follows:

> She seemed to be hanging in the shape of a cross, and by her continuous prayer gave great zeal to the combatants, while they looked on during the contest, and with their outward eyes saw in the form of their sister him who was crucified for them, so that she persuaded those who believe on him that all who suffer for the glory of Christ have for ever fellowship with the living God.[12]

10. See Jennifer A. Glancy, *Slavery in Early Christianity* (Oxford: Oxford University Press, 2002).

11. Eusebius, *Hist. eccl.* 5.1 (Lake, 427).

12. Eusebius, *Hist. eccl.* 5.1 (Lake, 427). Translators have disagreed over who does the persuading in this section—that is, whether the verb's subject is Christ or Blandina. Elizabeth A. Goodine and Matthew W. Mitchell argue convincingly that to remove Blandina as the subject is an error in translation; see their essay "The Persuasiveness of a Woman: The Mistranslation and Misinterpretation of Eusebius' *Historia Ecclesiastica* 5.1.41," *JECS* 13 (2005): 1–19. Generally, translators have emphasized Christ acting *through* Blandina. Goodine and Mitchell state that making Blandina the subject does not negate the theological point that Christ works *through* Blandina; they declare that Blandina herself cannot be ignored: "To deny Blandina her place

The birds and beasts gave Blandina a wide berth; so again, Blandina was taken back to jail to await another attempt to kill her. The author of the letter interprets her endurance through trials as mounting proof of her defeat of the devil and encouragement for fellow Christians: "for small and weak and despised as she was, she had put on the great and invincible athlete, Christ; she had overcome the adversary in many contests, and through the struggle had gained the crown of immortality."[13] Blandina makes it all the way to the end of the gladiatorial contests and is brought into the arena with a young man of fifteen named Ponticus. He suffers right alongside Blandina, encouraged by her and mothered by her into martyrdom.[14] This relational engagement occurring amid spectacle and its denial of participants' "claim to membership in human society" is notable.[15] About those who suffered in the arena, whether criminals, prisoners of war, Christians, or slaves, Elizabeth A. Castelli observes: "All of them were marginal people marked by *infamia*, a status that attached to their person and rendered them legally, socially, and symbolically out of bounds, beyond the pale."[16] According to Moss,

> Blandina's exemplarity functions not only to invite the audience to join the cohort of martyrs in battle, but also to invite them into her Christian family. The audience can become children of Blandina through martyrdom and also through participation in the broader Christian community. In this respect, Blandina's conduct does not model familial abandonment but, rather, creates a Christian family within the world of the text.[17]

---

as the subject of this clause disrupts the process by which this text suggests Christ works in the world, that is, with and through a human being, even a lowly human being" (4). This textual issue is no minor point, considering that the theological ramifications and the legacy of Blandina differ significantly depending on the translation. For example, Moss reads Blandina as one who "disappears" and whose "imitation elides identity" (*Ancient Christian Martyrdom*, 112–13). According to Moss, this results in Blandina receding and being "supplanted by Christ." A shift in translation that preserves her agency and identity in this still transformative imitation does not necessitate these conclusions.

We have made use of Kirsopp Lake's translation for Eusebius's *Ecclesiastical History* but adapted this particular section to reflect the changes that result from Goodine and Mitchell's argument. Lake's translation avoids making Christ the direct subject by translating the verb as an infinitive. This move, however, does not get at a crucial point made in the text: that Blandina is not merely a stand-in for Christ, like a stunt double, but is acting on behalf of Christ as his empowered agent.

13. Eusebius, *Hist. eccl.* 5.1 (Lake, 427).

14. Eusebius, *Hist. eccl.* 5.1 (Lake, 433).

15. For a discussion about the spectacle of the Roman arena and martyrdom, see Elizabeth A. Castelli, *Martyrdom and Memory: Early Christian Culture Making*, GTR (New York: Columbia University Press, 2004), 104–33.

16. Ibid., 108.

17. Moss, *Ancient Christian Martyrdom*, 112.

Blandina's mothering in the arena subverts the destruction of status and humanity associated with the arena. Her hope held her fast as a bull flung her broken body around the arena. Blandina was finally "sacrificed" and garnered the admiration of the spectators for her long-suffering conduct.[18]

### PRESERVING THE PEDAGOGY OF THE MARTYRS

Eusebius is not the author of this letter, but neither is he a mere copyist or anthologist. While the *Ecclesiastical History* is not a short work, very little extraneous information is included. As in book 8 with the Martyrs of Palestine, Eusebius often abridges documents he includes. Figuring large in his decision-making process is a determination of what content best serves his theological purpose in writing an edifying history of the church. Eusebius includes his edited version of the narrative of the Martyrs of Lyons and Vienne because, in his determination, these particular Christians needed to be part of the fabric of the making of Christian memory. That means the slave girl's sufferings and the theological reflection upon them are important to Eusebius's understanding of how the church should receive the martyr tradition. The dying of the martyrs is a theological act that mediates Christ to those who witnessed it firsthand and those who hear the story later. In a very real way, martyrs build the church; the distinct christological shape of their sufferings is a catalyst and mooring point for the faith of others.[19]

With the first seven books capping his account of the succession of the apostles, he moves into the events of his own day. He starts book 8 with some context: the destruction of churches, organized book burnings in the public square, and the gamut of pastoral leadership, from those who hid in fear to those imprisoned who mocked their captors. Eusebius then outlines exactly the kind of content about the persecution he is going to include, which boils down to "only such things as may be profitable, first to ourselves, and then to those that come after us."[20] Eusebius's narrative is instructive in an exhortative sense, meaning that he fully intends for Christians to be encouraged in the faith and strengthened in their resolve to endure and remember. The pedagogical nature of recounting about the martyrs feeds into the constructive aspect; in a very real way, Eusebius reconstructs the church of the past and

---

18. Eusebius prefers the term "sacrificed" because it indicates a consecration through death. To describe the "crown" the martyrs will receive after enduring the contest, he uses the term *aphtharsia* ("incorruption," not merely immortality), emphasizing the contrast with the corruption of their physical bodies through the torture they suffered. Being a martyr is to "depart manifesting [Christ's] glory" (*Hist. eccl.* 5.1.27), an athlete of piety and a soldier of God.

19. See Castelli, *Martyrdom and Memory*.

20. Eusebius, *Hist. eccl.* 8.2 (Oulton, 257).

present, building for the future by rooting the growth of the glorious tree of the church in the martyrs.

In reading Eusebius's account of the persecutions, it is important to remember that he is witnessing the suffering and the dying firsthand.[21] Christians will be obsessed with martyr stories for centuries to come, but Eusebius does not linger on the tortures or shy away from a kind of journalistic reporting of the details he sees and hears. The directness of his portrayal extends to his theological interpretation of the events. What Eusebius sees is obvious to him: "the present, divine power of our Savior, Jesus Christ himself, the object of their witness, and the clear manifestation of that power to the martyrs."[22] This passage says a great deal about the link between martyrs and Christ, yet it also says something important about what it was like to be there and see these events for oneself. That Christ witnessed to the witnesses proved the Christian hope: man-eating beasts were quelled, naked bodies brought glory instead of the shame intended by the persecutors, and bold joy erupted when a Christian was faced with a death sentence. For Eusebius, Christ was *there*.

## Martyrs and Future Ascetics

By grounding Christianity in the sufferings of the martyrs as concomitant with the preservation of the apostolic tradition, Eusebius directly associated the success of the Christian project with martyrological remembrance and theological integrity, linking the two together almost indistinguishably. Eusebius understood the martyrs to be fundamental to Christianity's core; and Christians to come would take him seriously. But what happened when Christianization became an imperial policy and martyrs were no longer expected? Christianity expanded the martyrological tradition and succession to include those who lived lives of death, or ascetics. But how did this transition happen? Eusebius's *Ecclesiastical History* and Methodius of Olympus's dramatic revision of Plato's *Symposium*—a revision that puts Christian virgins front and center—give us some possible avenues to trace how Christianity navigated this transition literarily and theologically.

Neither Eusebius nor Methodius was solely responsible for creating an enduring affinity for martyrs in Christianity. Taking a cue from the New Testament, earlier Christians than they understood their sufferings and even their deaths as part of the heritage of Jesus and the apostles. For the earliest

---

21. Eusebius recounts having seen firsthand the steadfastness of those who suffered numerous lashes, fought multiple rounds with various man-eating beasts, were decapitated, and were burned with fire.

22. Eusebius, *Hist. eccl.* 8.7 (Oulton, 271).

Christians, theirs was a story of a church entrusted with something they knew to be precious; it was a gift from those who had seen and experienced God in the flesh. It was a treasure they had to preserve and pass on to new generations and to diverse cultures. It was a gift that was undeniably personal and corporate. It was also a gift baptized in the blood of their grandmothers, parents, and friends. Martyr stories and their circulation were the early Christians' way of connecting to and constructing their legacy. It was paramount to have post-Constantine preservation of the apostolic heritage and the martyr legacy considered to be continuous with it. The powerful legacy of martyr devotion was seen not only as a connection to the past but also as a foundation for the identity of a new Christianized Roman Empire.

## Methodius and the Virgin-Philosopher

Methodius of Olympus (d. 311/312) might not be the most well-known early Christian writer, but he inhabits an important space in Christian history and theology. Aside from Eusebius of Caesarea, Methodius is the only writer to fill the void in extant ancient Eastern literature from the death of Origen (ca. 254–318) to the Arian controversy.[23] We do not know much about Methodius; we are not even completely certain of where he was situated as a bishop.[24] Yet his work played a significant role in later doctrinal developments and controversies. Therefore, Methodius is in a unique position to grant access to a vibrant combination of ascetic tendencies, theology, and exegesis in Asia Minor before the Nicene Creed was adopted (in 325). He is perhaps the only writer to whom we can refer for a window into the fermenting of ascetic theology in the decades before the results were widespread.

Methodius's only work that survives in its entirety in Greek, the *Symposium*, gives us a new spin on Thecla as one among many fictive female philosophers, each of whom gives a speech that normalizes virginity as the Christian way of life.[25] Probably written during the last three or four decades of the third century or possibly very early in the fourth, the *Symposium* is

23. Katharina Bracht, *Vollkommenheit und Vollendung: Zur Anthropologie des Methodius von Olympus*, Studien und Texte zu Antike und Christentum 2 (Tübingen: Mohr Siebeck, 1999), 1.
24. Methodius's works reveal little about their author and leave much to conjecture. See Lloyd George Patterson, *Methodius of Olympus: Divine Sovereignty, Human Freedom, and Life in Christ* (Washington, DC: Catholic University of America Press, 1997), 19–21.
25. All translations are mine (Amy's) unless otherwise indicated. For the critical editions, see Methodius of Olympus, *Symposium sive Convivium decem virginum* (*Symposium*, or *Banquet of the Ten Virgins*), in *Méthode d'Olympe: Le Banquet*, ed. Herbert Musurillo, trans. Victor-Henry Debidour, SC 95 (Paris: Cerf, 1963); GCS 27:1–141; PG 18:28–220; an English

more concerned with delving into the theological debates of the time than with practical instruction on how to live as a virgin, a topic that would dominate later discussions.[26] In addition to the historical literary gap the work inhabits and its unconventional rendering of virgins and virginity, the *Symposium* has another remarkable oddity: Methodius writes himself into the dialogue as a woman (using the pseudonym Eubolion, the feminine form of Eubolius) and presents himself as an observer and reporter of events, but not as a participant in the philosophical dialogue.

### A Philosophical Picnic

Methodius of Olympus's *Symposium* is a reimagining of Plato's famous dialogue of the same name. Instead of Plato's ten Athenian men giving speeches in praise of erotic love, Methodius's ten virgins give speeches on virginity. In the *Symposium* the victorious virgin Thecla and several other virgins who are gathered on the grounds of a paradisal estate are imagined as eminent philosophers of Christianity. As in Plato's version of a symposium, the virgins hold a friendly competition for the best speech. The virgins' presence and speech in the dialogue point to an expanded vision of the Christian life that has at its core the christologically shaped virginal life, which Thecla, Thalia, and the other women consider to be synonymous with philosophy. Thecla is declared the winner of the contest; her reception of this honor wins her the role of leading the choir of virgins as they make their eschatological ascent to Christ. In this section, we will focus on some of the central themes that arise in Thecla's speech and speak to the developing theological and philosophical conception of virginity and its link to its martyrological past.

### Thecla the Philosopher and Champion

The virgins are presumably Methodius's creations, except for Thecla, who, as we learned in chapter 1, has at least a literary existence beyond and undergirding the *Symposium*. Her story of unflagging devotion to Paul and her miraculous perseverance in trials had, by Methodius's time, been practically canonized and would continue to grow in influence into the fourth and fifth centuries.[27] The host of the banquet, Arete—whose name means "virtue"—

---

translation by Herbert Musurillo is available under the title *St. Methodius: The Symposium; A Treatise on Chastity*, ACW 27 (Westminster, MD: Newman, 1958).

26. Jason König, *Saints and Symposiasts: The Literature of Food and the Symposium in Greco-Roman and Early Christian Culture*, Greek Culture in the Roman World (Cambridge: Cambridge University Press, 2012), 151–54.

27. See Davis, *Cult of Saint Thecla*.

introduces a new Thecla, who directly links the difficult-to-categorize virginal protomartyr from the Acts of Paul and Thecla to a perfect role model for virgins embarking on the philosophical life in the *Symposium*. Arete says to Thecla: "I have faith in your ability to offer me fitting discourse. For you lag behind no one in your grasp of philosophy and universal culture, not to mention that you were instructed by Paul regarding the gospel and the divine."[28] Thecla is therefore accorded a kind of authority of succession as one who receives the gospel and preserves it. She offers the eighth speech at the banquet, which can be divided into two main parts: a discussion about virginity (*parthenia*) and a theological interpretation of Revelation 12.[29]

Virginity might seem to be an odd subject matter for a theological treatise, but for Methodius, the chaste or virginal life *is* the Christian life. This is a broader and more theological read of virginity than one who merely abstains from sexual activity.[30] For Methodius, the virgin perfectly exemplifies transformation and participation in Christ unto eschatological union in the resurrection.

For Thecla, Christ is the "Archvirgin" (*archiparthenos*)—a title Methodius created to illustrate how Christ inaugurated a new way of living by first living it himself. Christ is truly the way of virtue, the one in whom all of the virtues coalesce and find their perfect expression. As Methodius knew, everything changed with Christ, and that change was so radical that it threw a wrench into the monotonous cycle of birth and death. With Christ, a new humanity with a new social order and relational goal emerged. A new way was open to all, a way that did not need to cave in to perpetuating society but instead heralded a new order, a new kingdom. Christ was the first to live this new way that allowed for the perfect expression of all of the virtues, the way of chastity—a way that for Methodius was the true archetype for philosophy. The chaste or virginal life, as Methodius understood it, was dedicated to loving and following Wisdom—that is, Christ—himself.

One of the most poignant images that we find in Plato and in some of the writers of the early church is that of "pedagogical pregnancy." Basically, this means that there is a relational aspect and a productive result to encountering truth. In Platonic terms, after one is liberated from the cave, it is their

28. Methodius, *Symp.* 8.6–10 (SC 95:200–201); "of universal culture," ἐγκυκλίου παιδείας—Greek university studies prior to professional studies.

29. Methodius, *Symp.* 8.1.1–5 (SC 95:200–201); Musurillo, *Methodius*, 105. Bracht, *Vollkommenheit und Vollendung*, 195–96.

30. Methodius is clear that sexual renunciation is not an imperative for all Christians: the meadow of the church is beautiful in its diversity, including the flowers of chastity (ἁγνεία) as well as the flowers of those who rear children (τεκνογονία) and who choose the continent life (ἐγκράτεια) after marriage (Methodius, *Symp.* 2.7.37–44 [SC 95:86–88]).

responsibility to help others do the same.[31] Thus, Plato describes Socrates as a "midwife," one who brings forth virtues in others.[32] The early Christians had not only Plato to work with but also Paul, who uses similar imagery (e.g., Gal. 4:19). The chaste and virginal are able to see the reality of true wisdom and, as the church, are "travailing and begetting anew natural men as spiritual men."[33]

With this in mind, we turn to Thecla's exegesis of Revelation 12, where she warns that the road to immortality is not easy; the evil one lies in wait to destroy the chaste. In this passage, the virgins find a biblical heroine to whom they can look for strength: the woman (the "Mother") who is situated in the heavens and clothed in light. In pain she gives birth to a man-child in the face of a dragon who would seek to destroy the child.[34] Thecla describes the vision of the woman, who is their Mother the Church, and how she crushed the dragon and was renewed by virginity.[35] Thecla interprets this Mother as the presence of God manifested in God's people. Using this ecclesial image, Thecla proposes that the woman represents the virgins prepared for eternal marriage who are not only unsullied in their persons but also, collectively, pregnant with those who will be birthed in baptism as spiritual children of the church. The procreative vision of virginity depicts a nurturing mother who travails in the face of evil to bring forth children in the "likeness and form of Christ" and who will thus attain incorruptibility.[36] The parallel with Plato's portrayal of the one pregnant with virtue giving birth to beautiful ideas is striking and obviously not accidental.[37] For both Plato and Methodius, pedagogical pregnancy is central to the philosophical formation and the process of encountering truth. But Methodius takes this concept one step further. The perception of the mystery of grace in one's encounter with truth as the person of Christ provokes wisdom and understanding to conceive in the soul so as to bring about the birth of Christ.

31. Plato, *Republic* (*De re publica*) 514a–520a.
32. Plato, *Theaetetus* 148e–151d.
33. Methodius, *Symp.* 8.6.5–8 (SC 95:216–17).
34. Methodius, *Symp.* 8.4.25–47 (SC 95:210–13).
35. Methodius, *Symp.* 8.10.1–7 (SC 95:224–25).
36. Methodius, *Symp.* 8.6.9–14 (SC 95:216–17). It might seem obvious to interpret the "man-child" in Rev. 12 as Christ, yet Thecla does not interpret the man-child to be Christ exclusively; she generalizes the "child" to include all those who are formed in Christ's image: "For I think that the church is here said to bring forth a masculine child because the spiritually enlightened purely receive the features [χαρακτῆρας] and likeness [ἐκτύπωσιν] and manliness [ἀρσενωπίαν] of Christ, the form according to the likeness of the Word is formed in them and is begotten in them according to genuine knowledge and faith, and thus Christ is noetically begotten in each one" (*Symp.* 8.8.4–10 [SC 95:220–21]).
37. For a comparison of the speeches of the philosopher Socrates and Thecla, see Bracht, *Vollkommenheit und Vollendung,* 186–91.

Beyond what we see in Plato's *Symposium*, pregnancy and birth in Thecla's rendering are given added specificity to coincide with Christian theology—the "beautiful ideas" birthed are collectively personified to be Christ himself. The Christ who is born in the soul is the man-child, and the pregnancy described here mirrors the physical pregnancy of Mary. The incarnate Christ is not an idea or a form but a person. The pregnancy and birth that Thecla propounds subsumes and generalizes the physical pregnancy and birthing process experienced by Mary so that it says something true about the church bringing forth Christians in baptism. The eschatological restoration of humanity's original likeness to God is contingent upon the process of pedagogical pregnancy that perpetuates the encounter with Christ and brings about this restoration and re-creation through the birthing of Christ in others.[38]

Thecla is not the only one who speaks of pedagogical pregnancy in the *Symposium*. In her speech Thalia offers Paul's story as an example of how this birthing process works. Paul was "birthed" and "nursed" by Ananias (Acts 9:1–19).[39] Once he was a grown man who was made anew and fully developed in spiritual perfection, he was made the bride of the Word. Then "receiving the seed of life and conceiving, he who had previously been called a child now became Church and Mother, himself bearing in travail those who believed in the Lord through him until Christ was likewise formed and born in them."[40] The example of Paul establishes pedagogical pregnancy as a primary function of every Christian's life. Once Christ has been begotten in one's soul, the enlightened one, according to Thecla, receives the features, image, and manliness of Christ; in other words, they become a "Christ." In this way, men share in the "feminine" acts of pregnancy and birth, and women share in the "manliness" of Christ.

Returning to Thecla's exegesis of Revelation 12, we find Thecla calling upon the virgin-mother(s) to imitate her as victor and bride by standing up

38. Ibid., 138. Bracht notes how seriously Methodius takes the concept of "new creation." The creative activity of God functions so that the effects of sin and the fall—loss of the likeness, immortality, and perfection, all characteristics that make a human a creature of God—are repealed in baptism (157). The indwelling of Christ has effectively altered the interior of the Christian and makes that person a Christ. According to Bracht, "He sees man as a creature whose interior is not his own but filled by another. This other who dwells in man defines his nature: if it is sin then the human is sinful; if it is the Logos, then the man becomes a Christ" (144).

39. Methodius, *Symp.* 3.9.1–14 (SC 95:110–13).

40. Methodius, *Symp.* 3.9.5–11 (SC 95:110–13). Note the feminine language ascribed to Paul: Ὅτε δὲ ἠνδρώθη καὶ ᾠκοδομήθη ἤδη εἰς τελειότητα πνευματικὴν ἀναπλασθεὶς καὶ "βοηθὸς" ἀπειργάσθη καὶ "νύμφη" τοῦ λόγου τὰ σπέρματα τῆς ζωῆς ὑποδεξάμενος καὶ συλλαβών, τὸ τηνικαῦτα ὁ πρότερον χρηματίσας παιδίον ἐκκλησία γίνεται καὶ μήτηρ ὠδίνων καὶ αὐτὸς τοὺς δι' αὐτοῦ τῷ κυρίῳ πεπιστευκότας, ἔστ' ἂν καὶ ἐν τούτοις ὁ Χριστὸς μορφωθεὶς ἀποτεχθῇ.

to the beast and the onslaught of heresies.[41] Thecla rallies the virgins by using the words of Paul from Ephesians 6: "Equip yourselves strongly for battle, arming yourselves. . . . You will cause incalculable terror to him if you strike with great resolve and courage, and certainly he will not stand his ground upon seeing you prepared for battle by him who is more valiant."[42] Christ has already defeated the beast, making it defenseless to those virgins who will deal the final blow. As a kind of general charging her soldiers to do battle, Thecla commands: "With sober and virile heart, take up arms in opposition to the swollen beast; do not give him any ground and do not be shaken by his boldness. For infinite glory will be yours if you conquer him and carry off his seven crowns, for this is the prize of our contest according to what our teacher Paul has laid out for us."[43] The virile virgin is one who has begotten Christ and is herself a Christ united together with other virgins who have the power to overcome the devil, destroy him, and win "the seven crowns of virtue" after having engaged in seven contests of chastity.[44] The virgin is also on the winning side of the battle against heresy and should understand that she is to fight and to win. A virgin as a victorious mother is an example of a performing theology that is christologically based and, on that foundation, stands against the onslaught of heresy. These images conjure up the obvious parallels of Thecla's legendary story: leaving marriage behind, muting her dress, cutting her hair, and withstanding the beasts. In a sense, Thecla delivers two discourses at the same time. Her speech at the banquet runs alongside the discourse of the received tradition of her life. No doubt Methodius assumes that the reader would and should associate this philosophical virgin with the legendary Christian heroine.

To be the virile virgin who wins in the arena, did Thecla herself embrace "manliness" in such a way as to leave her femininity behind? Perhaps part of the answer lies in the second interlude of the *Symposium*, where we return to the two women from the introduction to the dialogue. Eubolion (Methodius) affirms her heroic legacy and connects the banquet's Thecla with the Thecla of legend: "And so magnificent did she frequently show herself as she engaged in those first great contests of the martyrs, possessing a zeal equal to her willingness, and a strength of body equal to the superiority of her purposes."[45] This statement is more than a simple laudation of Thecla; it is an important statement of how Methodius views the Christian woman

41. Methodius, *Symp.* 8.12.1–6 (SC 95:232–33).
42. Methodius, *Symp.* 8.12.11–19 (SC 95:232–33).
43. Methodius, *Symp.* 8.13.1–6 (SC 95:234–35). Methodius is referring to Rev. 12:3.
44. Methodius, *Symp.* 8.13.6–9 (SC 95:234–35).
45. Methodius, *Symp.* Interlude II.30–34 (SC 95:260–61; adapted, ACW 27:130).

martyr and ascetic. For Methodius there is no requirement for a woman to set aside her "femininity" to become a champion.[46] Thecla's discourse shows her to be a woman of remarkable philosophic greatness, and Methodius states that her physical strength is "equal" in its greatness. And Thecla is not the exception to the rule, but, as is evident in her discourse, every devoted virgin has the capacity to be a champion like her. This is the power of the combination of Thecla's philosophical reimagining and the reception of her legendary life.

### Virginity Is the Christian Way of Life

What is particularly interesting about Methodius's reimagination of Plato's *Symposium,* in which ten virgins replace ten sexually active males, is that the subjects discussed are normative in some way for all Christians. The fact that Methodius chooses to set the discussion of chastity as necessary for Christians in general among a group of women does not mean that Methodius was some sort of protofeminist or, on the other side, a promoter of chastity as a requirement exclusively for obedient, Christian women. He sets up all of the women as philosophical paragons of Christ-initiated, virtue-binding chastity. Methodius does not portray the virginal life as exclusively for men or women, and he freely associates the chaste and virginal life with feminine *and* masculine attributes.[47] All men and women need to learn about chastity from these chaste, virginal, and philosophic women who are leading the church into eternal bliss with Christ.

Methodius's fluid use of gendered language illustrates that for him, masculine and feminine are not necessarily mutually exclusive but are nonoppositional principles that indicate participation in the image of God. The woman-specific nature of physical pregnancy is just that—woman specific; but all Christians, men and women, can be pregnant and give birth insofar as they are in Christ. While Methodius does not enter into an exhaustive explanation of the implications of such a view, Thecla's discourse also makes it clear that men do not have a corner on what would be considered "male"

46. Susan Hylen observes that "manliness" is assumed as the virtue to which both men and women should aspire in the *Symposium* but that "throughout the work Thecla remains both female and a leader. Presumably Thecla is an example of one who has acquired the stamp of Jesus' manliness. Yet Gregorion's description at the end of Thecla's speech also reinforces her femininity by describing her blush and declaring her 'entirely fair of body and soul' (8.17.26). Thecla's manliness does not erase her feminine beauty and modesty" (*Modest Apostle*, 107).

47. Patterson notes that Methodius's appearance as a woman in the text suggests that he does not expect what might be considered the "feminine qualities" of chastity to be embraced only by women (*Methodius of Olympus*, 67).

characteristics—that is, virility and courage—but that Thecla possesses these attributes insofar as she is in Christ. Back in chapter 1 we discussed Thecla and the virtue of endurance, a "feminine" virtue taken up by men and women as they emulate Christ. In the second century CE, endurance in martyrdom was essential, and by Methodius's time, we see courage and virility promoted in the philosophical sense, with women as exemplars. By defining the chaste and virginal life as the virtuous life, Methodius simultaneously opens up the chaste life to all Christians, grounding it in the community of the church; he also preserves the form of the virginal life that is exemplified by controlling one's passions, battling obstacles, and devotion to Christ.

## Conclusion

At the close of the third century the church was about to enter the most dramatic period of social and political change in its history. The story of Christianity in the first half of the fourth century tends to be dominated by the political and military exploits of Constantine and the first theological controversy that became an ecumenical (empire-wide) problem, but this only scratches the surface; the Christian narrative was not all about Constantine and councils. Christians keenly felt the need to be a part of the great tradition of the apostles and martyrs who went before them and blazed new pathways of devotion. Some left the safety of the walled Roman city behind and took up residence in the dangerous desert. Others kept close to home and became beacons of piety for their families and communities. Over the course of the fourth century, what for many began as a largely solitary life-choice developed into communities of Christians who, rather paradoxically, aided one another in their solitary adherence to a new kind of society. Communities of ascetics living outside of the typical Roman expectations for society popped up all over the empire and became in many ways the backbone of Christianity.

As Christianity's place in the Roman Empire solidified and traditional martyrdom became a memory, Christians sought new ways to pursue piety as heirs of the apostles and martyrs in this new world. The stories and legends of women like Thecla shaped generations of Christians through the many iterations of her story and through those who traveled to her shrine. Others, like Helena Augusta, Constantine's mother, whom we will meet in chapter 5, helped to build churches and shift the culture away from paganism's hold. It became common for Christians to latch onto the appropriate apostolic or martyr heritage in their own locales, and eventually the landscape was peppered with shrines and legends and relics of pious heroes that circulated with increasing popularity. Women were at the center of many other illustrious tales of devotion and piety in Christianity, their lives serving as guides on the path of Christian devotion and their deaths immortalizing them as exemplars of faith.

# 5

# Helena Augusta,
# "Mother of the Empire"

The late fourth-century historian, theologian, and translator Rufinus of Aquileia called Helena the "Mother of the Empire," owing not only to her parenting a son who becomes emperor but also to her parenting a fragile, newly born Christian empire.[1] Helena was not the first woman to exercise authority in the imperial court, but she became the standard of piety and power for the later Christian empresses. She was reputedly lowborn, a girl without status who had a mysterious but enduring relationship with a man who would become emperor. As Evelyn Waugh quips in his 1963 novelization of her life: "The life of St. Helen begins and ends in surmise and legend."[2] That being said, she was not some kind of ancient Cinderella. When she was a much older woman, Helena journeyed to Jerusalem on an official imperial visit that included lavish displays of piety and support for the church. Later accounts detail this venture as a daring tale of recovering a priceless artifact. In these reports Helena all but dons a hat and a whip to become the imperial forerunner of Indiana Jones.

1. Rufinus, *Eusebius's "Ecclesiastical History" Translated and Continued by Rufinus (Eusebii Historia ecclesiastica a Rufino translata et continuata)* 10.8, in *The* Church History *of Rufinus of Aquileia, Books 10 and 11*, trans. Philip R. Amidon (Oxford: Oxford University Press, 1997), 18.
2. Evelyn Waugh, *Helena* (New York: Penguin 1963), 9.

## From Stable to Court

Helena Augusta (Flavia Iulia Helena Augusta) was the mother of Constantine, but her claim to fame (which would be told and retold from the late fourth century through the medieval period) was her supposed discovery of the cross of Jesus Christ in Jerusalem. This is almost certainly a fiction; but the accounting of such an important find captured the imaginations of Christians throughout the Roman world. There are many reasons why the story of Helena intrigued Christians, some of which we will explore below, but one of the most obvious is that it was inspired by real people and events. Helena actually existed and visited Jerusalem on something like a pilgrimage, and the unearthing in Jerusalem of something billed as the True Cross happened around the same time. As we have seen, pilgrimages were an important aspect of piety at this time; moreover, Egeria's recounting of the liturgy in Jerusalem owes much to Helena's work in building the churches in the region. The existence and transmission of the story of Helena and the discovery of the True Cross offer us a glimpse into how the legacy of Christian women's devotion can affect the central stories that Christianity tells about itself and to itself.

Helena Augusta lived on the crest of the wave of a newly contextualized Christianity. Not only did she have a front-row seat to observe the shifting of the empire; as we will see, she helped to effect that shift. While the story of the discovery of the True Cross dominates Helena's legacy and effects its own pattern for Christian devotion for centuries to come, the events of her official trip to Jerusalem and the eastern provinces establish that Helena not only demonstrated great devotion but also exercised imperial authority to help stabilize a shaky section of the empire.

We do not know much about Helena, but what we do know makes what we do not know very frustrating. It is almost impossible to reconstruct even the most basic events of her life—such as her birth, marriage, and death—with certainty. Excepting some inscriptions and numismatic evidence, the only written evidence we have of Helena comes from after her death. The most important of these sources is the *Life of Constantine* by Eusebius, which he wrote shortly after Constantine's death in 337 and about ten years after Helena's death.[3] In the "uneasy mixture of panegyric and narrative history" that is the often garish *Life of Constantine*, Eusebius not only eulogizes an emperor; he also intends to inspire and even instruct Constantine's sons to

3. Eusebius, *Eusebius: Life of Constantine* (*Vita Constantini*), trans. Averil Cameron and Stuart G. Hall, Clarendon Ancient History Series (Oxford: Clarendon, 1999).

follow in their father's footsteps and stay the course.[4] Helena's story provides a legacy of devotion for Constantine's sons to embrace. Unfortunately, Eusebius does not include any information about the events prior to Helena's journey to Palestine and the eastern provinces.[5] But writing about Helena's journey to Palestine makes sense since he was the metropolitan bishop of Palestine and probably accompanied her on her travels throughout his province.[6] Eusebius was likely keen to share the exploits of the Augusta to the credit of the emperor and to indicate beneficence for Christianity on behalf of the empire in support of various building projects.

We are not sure where or when she was born, but some recent and fairly convincing studies place Helena's birth around 248.[7] One thing that the sources do agree on is that she was born into a humble station in life, not into an aristocratic—let alone imperial—family. Constantius (b. ca. 250, emperor 293–306, d. 306), Constantine's father, was a soldier who worked his way up through the ranks of the Roman army.[8] Sometime around 270 he stayed at an inn and met Helena the *stabularia*, a term scholars have rendered as meaning everything from the daughter of an imperial innkeeper to a prostitute.

Nailing down Helena's social status has proved to be quite difficult and indicates just how little we actually know about a person even as historically familiar as Constantine. The precise meaning of the term *stabularia* (literally, "a woman who comes from or works in the stables"), a term that only Ambrose of Milan uses in his oration on the death of Theodosius on February 25, 395,

4. Cameron and Hall, *Eusebius: Life of Constantine*, 1. The question of intended audience is contested. According to Cameron and Hall, the account is heavily stylized and likely was meant for a mixed group of Christians and pagans, particularly those with influence at court and the sons of Constantine (33).

5. Eusebius, *Vit. Const.* 3.41.2–47.3 (Cameron and Hall, 137–39).

6. Jan Willem Drijvers, *Helena Augusta: The Mother of Constantine the Great and the Legend of Her Finding of the True Cross*, Brill's Studies in Intellectual History 27 (Leiden: Brill, 1992), 3.

7. The only direct evidence for where Helena was born comes from Procopius (he claims it was Drepanum), but he is a relatively late source (sixth century). Drijvers notes that Procopius might have wanted to give an etymological explanation for the changing of Drepanum's name to Helenopolis (*Helena Augusta*, 11). Helena embarked on her journey toward the end of her life, probably in late 326 or early 327. Since after spring of 329 there are no new coins bearing her portrait, we can date her death to 328 or very early 329. If she was indeed eighty years old, as Eusebius records, then she may have been born around 248 (ibid., 13); see also Drijvers, "Helena Augusta, the Cross and the Myth: Some New Reflections," *Millennium-Jahrbuch* 8 (2011): 128.

8. Timothy D. Barnes outlines Constantius's career as beginning with his being a *protector* (attached to the "mobile central striking force of the Roman army"), then being promoted to rank of tribune ("either have continued to serve in the corps of *protectors* in the *comitatus* . . . or have been transferred to a provincial army"), and then serving as "governor of the Dalmatias" (*Constantine: Dynasty, Religion and Power in the Later Roman Empire*, Blackwell Ancient Lives [Oxford: Wiley-Blackwell, 2011], 27–28).

demands a complex consideration of etymology and what Ambrose possibly meant by the term.[9] Jan Willem Drijvers has argued that in this case *stabularia* is most appropriately rendered as "female innkeeper" or "a servant at an inn" and that Helena's life probably included sexual servitude.[10] While this may be the case, Barnes argues that there is no way to formulate a conclusion based on established linguistic usage.[11] Instead, he argues that if Helena were the daughter of a man who was in charge of an official lodging and rest stop for the imperial armies, then she would not have been as lowborn as is indicated by calling her a mere "stable-girl."[12] If Barnes is right, then Constantius's relationship with Helena makes more sense.

The general consensus in scholarship is that Constantius and Helena were not officially married because the difference in their assumed social statuses would not have allowed a lawful Roman marriage.[13] Barnes's conclusions about

9. Ambrose, *The Obituary of Theodosius* (*De obitu Theodosii*), in *Ambrose of Milan: Political Letters and Speeches*, trans. J. H. W. G. Liebeschuetz and Carole Hill, Translated Texts for Historians 43 (Liverpool: Liverpool University Press, 2010), 174–202. In Liebeschuetz's translation of the section on Helena in Ambrose's oration, he renders *stabularia* as "stable-girl" so as to retain its etymological meaning, as does Barnes in his translation of Ambrose's text:

It is claimed that she was originally a stable-girl [*stabulariam*], and that it was thus that she became acquainted with the elder Constantius, who afterwards obtained the position of emperor. Excellent stable-girl [*stabularia*] who so diligently searched for the manger of the Lord! Excellent stable-girl [*stabularia*], who was not unaware of that famous innkeeper who cared for the wounds of the man wounded by robbers (Luke 10.35)! Excellent stable-girl who preferred to be considered [Barnes adds: "as one who shoveled"] manure in order to gain Christ! For that reason Christ raised her from the manure to the position of an empress, as it is written, "He raised up the beggar from the earth, and lifted up the poor man from the dunghill" (Psalm 112[113].7). (Barnes, *Constantine: Dynasty*, 32)

10. Drijvers also draws from later writers—such as Philostorgius and Zosimus (second half of the fifth century), who intimate Helena's less-than-honorable upbringing—and claims that this likely refers to the sexual servitude of the *stabulariae*. Drijvers, like Barnes, cautions against too much reliance on a source like Zosimus, who was a strong opponent of Christianity and was fiercely hostile toward Constantine (*Helena Augusta*, 15–16). Drijvers reappraises some of his conclusions on other matters in a more recent article, but not his evaluation of Helena's social or marital status; see Drijvers, "Helena Augusta."

11. In response to Drijvers's claim about Helena as a lowborn woman who likely worked in a seedy inn, Barnes grants that it is possible for *stabularia* to be rendered this way but notes that "it fails to take account of the fact that the feminine noun *stabularia* not only does not appear to be attested before Ambrose (and hence is not registered in the *Oxford Latin Dictionary*), but also only occurs after Ambrose in authors who repeat, adapt, or allude to this passage. An appeal to established linguistic usage, therefore, provides nothing since the feminine noun *stabularia* is not documented before Ambrose." But, he notes, a male *stabularius* is (*Constantine: Dynasty*, 32).

12. For Barnes's argument regarding Helena's status, see *Constantine: Dynasty*, 30–33.

13. Based on a substantial gap in status, Drijvers makes the case that Constantius and Helena's relationship reflected that of concubinage, which was widely practiced at the time and allowed for partners of differing social statuses to legally cohabitate. If their statuses were as disparate as Drijvers and others claim, then it would indeed have been impossible for Constantius and Helena to have an *iustum matrimonium* (*Helena Augusta*, 17–18). Cooper grants that Helena

Helena's origins not being as "humble" as has been claimed and Constantius's origins not being aristocratic as assumed present a picture of a relationship that was possibly equal enough to merit marriage under Augustan law. It would make sense if this were the case since, while the invalidity of his parents' marriage is often assumed, Constantine's legitimacy is seldom questioned. If Constantine's parents were not legally married, as Drijvers claims, then Helena's son could not have had a legitimate claim in the imperial succession.[14] A time line consistent with Ambrose's telling of the story has Constantius and Helena meeting in the spring of 272, followed by Constantine's birth on February 27, 273.[15] Their relationship ended around two decades later when Constantius at some point married Theodora (a necessary career move), who was either the daughter or stepdaughter of Augustus Maximian and with whom he had six children.[16]

Then Helena fades from the notice of history for some thirty years. Both Drijvers and Barnes consider it plausible that she resided in Trier and then in Rome at a large estate between 306 and 326, after her son announced his conversion to Christianity.[17] Information about Helena surfaces on imperial coins in 318/319, and she was formally proclaimed Augusta perhaps on November 8, 324. In 326 Helena commands the historical spotlight again with an official pilgrimage to the Holy Land and visit to the eastern provinces not long after Emperor Constantine executes his son Crispus and Constantine's wife Fausta dies mysteriously. Helena returns to the imperial court, where she dies in the presence of Constantine, probably around the age of eighty.[18]

## Augusta: The Security of the Empire

What does it mean for Helena to be an "Augusta"? As will become clear in chapter 9, imperial women at times exercised great influence, especially during the reign of the Theodosian emperors. The official title of Augusta designated

---

might have been Constantius's wife but also considers it more likely that she was a concubine (*Band of Angels*, 131).

14. Barnes, *Constantine: Dynasty*, 34–35.

15. Drijvers locates Constantine's birth in 272/273, when Helena was around twenty-four years old. It is not known whether she had any other children (*Helena Augusta*, 15).

16. Barnes, *Constantine: Dynasty*, 38–41; Drijvers places Constantius and Theodora's marriage in 289 and outlines the problems that this might have caused for Constantine and hereditary rights (*Helena Augusta*, 19); see also Drijvers, "Helena Augusta," 131.

17. Barnes, *Constantine: Dynasty*, 33–34; Drijvers, *Helena Augusta*, 21.

18. Eusebius, *Vit. Const.* 3.46.1 (Cameron and Hall, 139); Barnes, *Constantine: Dynasty*, 42; see Drijvers for a discussion of the evidence and possibilities for dating Helena's death (*Helena Augusta*, 73–75).

the mother, wife, sister, or daughter of the emperor as a prominent member of the imperial court. This does not mean imperial women actually ruled as co-regents, but it did magnify their authority in court circles.[19] So what sort of power and influence did Helena Augusta have in the court of Constantine?

Aside from the official imperial trip to Palestine and the eastern provinces that will be discussed in detail below, there is not much we can know for certain about what it meant for Helena to be the Augusta. What we do know comes in the form of numismatic (coins) and epigraphical (e.g., inscriptions on statues) evidence. While coins are a limited source of information, we can still learn quite a bit from looking at a few of them. Before she gained the title of Augusta, Helena's status in the imperial court is not often depicted. However, from the autumn of 324, when Constantine bestowed the title of Augusta on his mother, until her death, the number of new coins minted with Helena's portrait increased, along with inscriptions dedicated to her.[20] Thus her presence became more pronounced as a representative of the empire to the populace, and that directly tied her to the economic system. The importance of someone's likeness on money should not escape us. If one mentions Franklin, Grant, or Jackson to average Americans, they likely will recognize the reference to money. Most will also assume that those pictured on coins were significant leaders of the nation. Portraits on money convey influence and legacy.

In Helena Augusta's case the coins were minted and put into circulation almost immediately following Constantine's defeat of Licinius. Drijvers explains why this is significant: "That all this was planned in advance is indicated by the fact that, immediately after the battle of Chrysopolis, Constantine consciously presented himself on his coins not only as a *Victor* but also as a divinely inspired emperor, ruling the empire explicitly with the support of his next of kin. From October 324 onward, Constantine involved members of his family in the government of the empire."[21] Constantine honored Helena and his wife, Fausta, with the title Augusta, broadcasting the symbolic way they shared power with him as part of a united and powerful imperial

19. Drijvers, *Helena Augusta*, 39.

20. According to Eusebius, Helena "was acclaimed in all nations and by the military ranks as *Augusta Imperatrix*, and her portrait was stamped on gold coinage" (*Vit. Const.* 3.47.2 [Cameron and Hall, 139]); Drijvers, *Helena Augusta*, 39. Constantine also bestowed the title on his wife Fausta.

21. Drijvers, *Helena Augusta*, 41. Immediately after Constantine's defeat of Licinius in the autumn of 324, coins were issued in honor of HELENA AUGUSTA. The most widely minted HELENA AUGUSTA coin is the SECVRITAS REIPVBLICE ("security of the republic"; final E instead of AE was either a mistake at the design and text level or was the local spelling in Antioch, where the first coins were minted), a small bronze coin.

Public domain

Figure 5.1. Left: FL HELENA-AVGVSTA, draped bust, wearing mantle and necklace. Right: SECVRITAS-REIPVBLICE, Securitas lowering branch with left hand, raising hem of robe with right hand.

family. Anyone who held an imperial coin with Helena or Fausta's likeness would think of Helena and Fausta as "protectors and pillars of the new Constantinian society."[22] "Augusta" was not just an honorific; it was a title that commanded a level of authority in the imperial court and in the empire in general. Eusebius ascribes significant—if vague—honor to the position, which had international and military weight as well as discretionary financial power over the imperial treasuries.[23] We do not know exactly how much power or influence this designation held, but we know from Eusebius and other sources that her power increased. Her coinage called her *Securitas*—that is, a foundation upon which the security of the empire stood: "These coins present Helena and Theodora as the ancestresses of the respective branches of the Constantinian family. The fact that the former *stabularia* Helena was considered the ancestress of an imperial dynasty proves her authority and prominence within the family of Constantine."[24]

## Pilgrimage or Not a Pilgrimage? Helena Augusta in the Holy Land

In 326 Helena Augusta made her way across to Palestine, the first leg of a journey that also took her to the eastern provinces. By this time Helena Augusta was quite advanced in years, around eighty years old. Undertaking such a trip at her age is astounding, and what she accomplishes while on her

22. Drijvers, *Helena Augusta*, 41–42.
23. Eusebius, *Vit. Const.* 3.47.2–3 (Cameron and Hall, 139).
24. Drijvers, *Helena Augusta*, 44.

journey proves her to be a compelling influence and eminently suited to represent imperial authority. Ancient and modern sources tend to cast her visit to Jerusalem as primarily a pious pilgrimage. While Helena's visit was infused with Christian purpose, there was much more to it than visiting sacred sites and displaying her piety. Helena demonstrates her Christian devotion to be inseparable from her role as a trusted agent of the empire in Constantine's designs to invest in the Christianization of the empire.

While so many characterize Helena Augusta's journey as a pilgrimage to the Holy Land, she "most probably undertook her travels in order to propagate Christianity and to appease dissatisfaction concerning Constantine's policy of Christianization."[25] Instead of traveling as a humble pilgrim, Helena traveled as an Augusta, with a full retinue and with state purposes in mind. For this reason, there is a strong case for interpreting Helena's journey as an *iter principis* (official imperial journey) rather than a *peregrinatio religiosa* (religious pilgrimage), such as that of Egeria, whom we will meet in chapter 6.[26] To solidify his imperial power, Constantine needed to "go big or go home." Therefore he called Nicaea to get the bishops on the same page, started building churches, and negated the afflictions brought upon Christians by Diocletian's series of edicts. Changing the literal architecture of the land was a central aspect of Constantine's policy of Christianization. His verve for constructing a new empire radiated out from his projects in Palestine, where he built the Church of the Holy Sepulchre over the traditional site of Christ's tomb and built a basilica on the Mount of Olives (the Church of the Eleona).

Helena Augusta was the face of Constantine's Christianization campaign in Palestine and the eastern provinces.[27] She oversaw the large church projects in Palestine and confirmed that the reparation aspects of Constantine's governance were put into effect. We know what these reparations were from a couple of letters Constantine sent to eastern provincial governors. Along with proscriptions for the governors and officials against pagan sacrifice, against the setting up of cult statues, and against the consultation of oracles, those who lost civil rights and were made slaves to work in the mines or in textile mills were to be released and have their rights restored. Those who lost military rank were to be given the choice to return to the military or to

25. Drijvers, *Helena Augusta*, 55. Helena was not the only one sent by Constantine to the East; his mother-in-law Eutropia also went. We do not know if they traveled together, but Eutropia's trip also aligned with Constantine's policy of Christianization, informing the emperor of the remnants of pagan sites that needed to be eradicated from what Constantine wanted to make sure would be the Christian Holy Land (71). See also Drijvers, "Helena Augusta,"125.

26. Drijvers, "Helena Augusta," 139.

27. Drijvers, *Helena Augusta*, 58. Helena spoke Greek, another quality that made her an eminent choice for this mission.

live as civilians, and any property or goods that had been confiscated from Christian citizens or churches was restored. Presence is important for such a monumental public relations campaign, and Constantine had not stayed in the eastern provinces long enough—in the spring of 326 he returned to Rome to celebrate his *Vicennalia* (marking his twentieth year as emperor)—to affect the policies to his satisfaction. Thus Helena Augusta's journey served a very important purpose: "After his return to the West, queries about Constantine's reforms must have arisen in the eastern provinces. It would have been Helena's task on her 'pilgrimage' to help to solve these problems."[28]

Constantine's actions after becoming sole emperor were laser-focused on uniting the empire. Such a task demanded not only the show of strength in battle but also a harmonious, unified front on behalf of the imperial family. Unfortunately, this harmony collapsed only a short time later when Constantine had his son Crispus executed, and his wife, Fausta, suspiciously died after being suffocated in an overheated bathroom. The rumor mill kicked into high gear and plagued Constantine's legacy with speculation of an incestuous relationship between the two or an attempt by Crispus to grab power. There is no way to determine what actually happened or why, but one thing is certain: it ruptured that very important show of familial harmony and endangered the fragile reunification and Christianization of the empire.[29]

Helena Augusta's journey to Palestine and the eastern provinces, then, comes at a crucial time.[30] The only contemporary author to have written about the journey, Eusebius (in his *Life of Constantine*), directly connects it to Constantine's building projects in Palestine, which were necessary for his policy of Christianization to succeed. Helena was involved in the construction of the Church on the Mount of Olives (the Eleona) in Jerusalem and the Church of the Nativity in Bethlehem, probably by inspecting and overseeing their progress.[31] She also dedicated both churches to God and endowed them with many gifts.[32] Eusebius leans heavily on Helena's journey to Palestine as

28. Ibid., 59.

29. Cooper gives an overview of the various rumors that surrounded the deaths of Constantine's son and wife (*Band of Angels*, 138–39).

30. Drijvers notes that there was significant opposition to Constantine's policy of Christianization and stance against Arianism ("Helena Augusta," 141).

31. While Cooper's designation of Helena's construction of the church in Bethlehem as a deliberate linking of the imperial family with the "heavenly family" helps to elucidate the blurring directionality of piety, her rendering of Helena's appropriation of the Mother of God (Theotokos) to be so clear and so strategic a claim in order to enhance her and Constantine's authority is overstated (*Band of Angels*, 139).

32. Eusebius, *Vit. Const.* 3.43.1–3 (Cameron and Hall, 137–38); Drijvers notes that, according to Eusebius, the churches were built or founded by Helena; but, according to Drijvers, founding

being motivated by faith; she wanted to pray where Christ had walked and demonstrated laudable piety, humility, good deeds, generosity, and charity.[33] The impression Eusebius gives of Helena's display of pilgrim's piety overshadows the overarching secular impact of her journey. Of course his interest lies with showing a convincing portrayal of the long Christian arm of the empire, yet she traveled primarily as an Augusta.

Eusebius's picture of the pious Augusta does not necessarily contradict the official nature of her journey but places it in the context of the imperial business of promoting and enforcing Christianization in an area where the pagan presence did not take kindly to pro-Christian policies.[34] The Augusta was sent into a region that needed equal amounts of diplomacy and pressure to conform. Equipped with the free use of the imperial treasury, Helena doled out money to military units, possibly to ensure their loyalty; commanded the release of prisoners, exiles, and those enslaved in the mines; and brokered goodwill by works of charity to the poor.[35] She not only checked in on Constantine's larger building projects in Jerusalem and Bethlehem, but, according to Eusebius, also visited every church in the area and openly displayed her Christian devotion.[36] These actions indicated an official imperial visit: they imitated the general practice of emperors who visited cities in their empire, giving gifts, assessing the status of imperial projects, and showing beneficence and goodwill.[37] In his novelization Waugh muses that "she moved in a golden haze of benefaction, welcomed, it seemed, and dearly beloved by all."[38]

## Legend Makes Legacy: Helena and the True Cross

The story that is told about Helena's journey to Palestine does not owe much to the events mentioned above, even though at the time her presence probably had a significant impact for Constantine's policy of Christianization. Instead, the

---

of churches was a key part of Constantine's policy of Christianization, and he would have been the responsible party in their founding (*Helena Augusta*, 63–64).

33. Eusebius, *Vit. Const.* 3.42.1–2 (Cameron and Hall, 137).

34. Drijvers, *Helena Augusta*, 65–67.

35. Eusebius, *Vit. Const.* 3.44 (Cameron and Hall, 138).

36. Eusebius, *Vit. Const.* 3.45 (Cameron and Hall, 138).

37. Drijvers, "Helena Augusta," 139–40; Kenneth G. Holum notes that, beginning with Constantine, the chief imperial virtue *philanthrōpia* (love of humankind) began to look more like Christian *agapē*. Eusebius praises Helena for her generosity to the poor and states that she had Constantine's blessing to do with the imperial treasuries as she pleased (*Theodosian Empresses: Women and Imperial Dominion in Late Antiquity*, Transformation of the Classical Heritage 3 [Berkeley: University of California Press, 1982], 26–27).

38. Waugh, *Helena*, 129.

Public domain / Wikimedia Commons

Figure 5.2. Helena's discovery of the True Cross memorialized by sculptor Andrea Bolgi, 1629–39.

story that shapes the transmission of her memory is dominated by the fictive ascription to her of the discovery of the True Cross. The story is first told in a funeral oration that Ambrose gives in honor of Emperor Theodosius I almost seventy years after her death. By the mid-fifth century the story had rapidly spread, and three versions of the tale had exposed Christians throughout the empire to the legendary devotion of Helena Augusta and the miracle that would make her a saint. The tale had an extraordinary amount of staying power and remained popular well into the medieval period in Greek, Latin, Syriac, Coptic, Georgian, and several other languages.[39]

Fragments of wood purported to be from the True Cross rapidly dispersed beyond Palestine in the fourth century, and the story of its discovery traveled far and wide. If Helena had indeed found the cross, it would make sense for Eusebius to have made this connection. Eusebius does indeed narrate the discovery of the wood, but it is Macarius, the bishop of Jerusalem, who unearths it during the clearing of a temple of Aphrodite to make way for a new church. Eusebius includes this finding entirely separately from Helena's

39. Drijvers, *Helena Augusta*, 79. Drijvers identifies the three versions of the legend that were transmitted from the end of the fourth century and the mid-fifth century: the Helena legend, the Protonike legend, and the Judas Cyriacus legend. Drijvers divides the texts containing the Helena legend (the oldest of the three) into two groups: (1) texts of the legend in Eusebius's *Historia ecclesiastica* as extended by Rufinus (published in 402 or 403), Socrates Scholasticus (written between 438 and 443), Sozomen (the longest Greek version, written in the 440s), and Theodoret (also composed in the 440s); and (2) texts of the legend by Ambrose, Paulinus of Nola, and Sulpicius Severus. Of these seven, Rufinus's comes the closest to the original version of the Helena legend. The later Byzantine chroniclers John Malalas and Theophanes follow the version found in Sozomen, who knows the Judas Cyriacus version and explicitly rejects it. See Drijvers, "Helena Augusta," 125–74, for his more recent treatment of three pieces of evidence regarding legendary traditions of the cross's discovery.

pilgrimage to the Holy Land.[40] The linking of Helena with the discovery and
Macarius first occurred about fifty years later, in the continuation of Eusebius's *Ecclesiastical History* by Rufinus of Aquileia (400/401) and in a letter
by Paulinus of Nola written in 403, which Sulpicius Severus then included in
his chronicle ending in the year 400.[41]

It may seem obvious why such a discovery, even as a fiction, would be a
popular story to tell. The cross of Christ has historical significance, of course,
but for Christians it is tied to the very substance of belief. Prior to Constantine,
however, the cross was a symbol of relatively minor importance. It was only
after his reign that it greatly increased in popularity. By the time the legend
came into being in the latter half of the fourth century, the True Cross had
already been venerated for some time, especially in Jerusalem, and its relics
were widely distributed throughout the empire.[42] In Ambrose's oration about
Emperor Theodosius I, he relays the story that it was Helena who discovered
the True Cross among the three crosses found in Jerusalem.[43] Ambrose got
this story from a little-known *Church History* written sometime after 390
by Gelasius of Caesarea (no longer extant).[44] Later writers received the elements of the story found in Gelasius (probably gleaned from oral sources) in
roughly the same order with a few variations. Gelasius's recounting of the
tale was the source for all of the fifth-century church historians either directly
or indirectly, including Rufinus of Aquileia, Socrates Scholasticus, Sozomen,
Theodoret, and Gelasius of Cyzicus.[45] Each followed Gelasius of Caesarea's

40. Eusebius, *Vit. Const.* 3.29–40 (Cameron and Hall, 138); Barnes, *Constantine: Dynasty*, 44.
41. Barnes, *Constantine: Dynasty*, 31.
42. According to Drijvers, "From the fourth century on, the sign of the Cross appeared
nearly everywhere: engraved on coins, houses, sarcophagi and weapons, sewn on clothes, and
even used as a tattoo. Reverence for the Cross as a symbol was undoubtedly greatly stimulated
by the 'discovery' of what was considered to be the True Cross" (*Helena Augusta*, 81). See
chap. 2 in part 2 of Drijvers's *Helena Augusta* for a look at the growing popularity of the
cross as a symbol in Christianity and a discussion about why Eusebius might not otherwise
have mentioned its discovery.
43. Ambrose, *Ob. Theo.* 40–51 (Liebeschuetz and Hill, 197–201). At about the same time a
similar narrative is presented by John Chrysostom in his *Homilies on John* (*Homiliae in Joan-
nem*) 85. He does not mention that the cross was found by Helena; this indicates that there
might have been a more rudimentary version of the legend that did not include the Augusta
(Drijvers, *Helena Augusta*, 95).
44. Drijvers, *Helena Augusta*, 96–98. The history overlaps somewhat with Eusebius's *Ecclesiastical History* and then continues where he left off, beginning in 302/303 with the Diocletian
persecution, and finishes with the reign of Valens (364–78).
45. Drijvers, *Helena Augusta*, 99. See chap. 3 of part 2 of *Helena Augusta* for Drijvers's
comparing and contrasting the forms that Helena's discovery takes in each writer who includes
the story. The story was also transmitted by Socrates Scholasticus from Constantinople, who,
between 438 and 443, also wrote a continuation of Eusebius's *Historia ecclesiastica* covering
the years 304–439. See Socrates, *Hist. eccl.* 1.17, 21–22, in *Socrates: Church History from AD*

version, although sometimes they brought something original to the retelling of Helena's propitious discovery. Generally speaking, each writer includes four main themes: (1) Helena journeying to Jerusalem to search for the True Cross; (2) the identification of the True Cross; (3) the construction of the church, the sending of the nails and part of the True Cross to Constantine, and the preservation of the True Cross in Jerusalem; and (4) other activities and information about Helena, including charitable activities and eating a banquet with a group of virgins.

Like Eusebius, Rufinus emphasizes the Augusta's piety in his continuation of Eusebius's *Ecclesiastical History*. According to Rufinus, Helena was "a woman matchless in faith, devotion, and singular generosity, the sort of person whose son Constantine would be, and be considered to be"; she had a series of visions that prompted her to travel to Jerusalem.[46] Upon arriving, she inquired as to the location of the True Cross. Finding it was not an easy task because pagan emperors ("persecutors") had erected an image to Venus on the site, effectively shutting down any Christian worship or remembrance, but Helena was again led by divine direction. In an act reminiscent of the Israelite kings demolishing the high places, Helena tears down the image of Venus and finds three crosses in a heap. Joy at the discovery is dampened when there appears to be no way to distinguish the crosses from one another. Accidentally venerating a thief's cross would not do. Even Pilate's inscription found with the crosses could not give a clue as to which was which. For the third time in this compact telling, a divine intervention is needed, and one is supplied.

At this point Macarius, bishop of Jerusalem, enters the story with a plan to remedy the situation. Assuming that one cross's link to Christ would become evident through a healing, Macarius prays for God to reveal the True Cross as the linchpin of salvation that it is, and in succession he touches each of the three crosses to a terminally ill woman of high status.[47] The touch of

---

305–439, trans. A. C. Zenos, in *Socrates, Sozomenus: Church Histories*, vol. 2 of NPNF². The longest Greek version is found in Sozomen's *Church History* (*Historia ecclesiastica*), written in the 440s and covering the period between 324 and 439 in nine books. See Sozomen, *Hist. eccl.* 2.1–2, 258–59, in *Sozomenus: Church History from AD 323–425*, trans. Chester D. Hartranft, in *Socrates, Sozomenus: Church Histories*, vol. 2 of NPNF². The Greek writer Theodoret of Cyrrhus (393–ca. 466) also includes the legend in his *Ecclesiastical History* (*Historia ecclesiastica*), composed in the 440s and covering the period from the beginning of Constantine's reign until 428. His version is basically the same as those of the historians mentioned, albeit more condensed and organized differently. See Theodoret, *Hist. eccl.* 1.17, trans. Blomfield Jackson, in *Theodoret, Jerome, Gennadius, Rufinus: Historical Writings*, NPNF² 3:54–55.

46. Rufinus, *Hist.* 10.7 (Amidon, 16).
47. Rufinus, *Hist.* 10.8 (Amidon, 17).

Angela Christman

Figure 5.3. *Discovery of the True Cross* by Piero della Francesca. Helena Augusta and the queen of Sheba witness the True Cross raising a man from the dead.

the third cross evinces an immediate reaction from the dying woman, who opens her eyes, regains her vitality, and then takes laps around the house, praising God. This miracle confirms Helena's mission to reclaim the site for Christianity, and she pours all of her "royal ambition" into building a church. She presents part of the True Cross to her son after leaving the rest in a silver casket in Jerusalem. In addition to the True Cross, Helena found the nails and gave them to Constantine, who fashioned them into his helmet and a bridle for his warhorse.

The Augusta's activities in Jerusalem expand beyond the monumental discovery and the subsequent building projects. She is said to have had lunch with a group of consecrated virgins and treated them with such deference that she eagerly took on the role of a servant. Helena Augusta, "empress of the world and mother of the empire," appointed herself "servant of the servants of Christ," waited on them with food and drink, and poured water over their hands for them to wash.[48] For Rufinus, the Augusta's piety was displayed not only in evidence of divine leading but also in the shape of her service. We have encountered other women, such as Blandina, who clearly manifested Christ in suffering; here, in Helena, we have a transitional kind

48. Rufinus, *Hist.* 10.8 (Amidon, 18).

of imitation. The Augusta sloughing off all the benefits of imperial status to serve a group of virgins has parallels with Jesus's washing the feet of his disciples (John 13:1–16). It seems that the events of this lunch indicate a new social and ecclesiastical order: the imperial court in service to those who will be the new authoritative "martyrs" of the Christianized empire.

Many others were fascinated by the story of Helena's discovery. As previously mentioned, Ambrose, bishop of Milan, includes it in his funeral oration for Theodosius; Paulinus, bishop of Nola, mentions it in a letter; and imperial historian Sulpicius Severus puts it in his *Chronicle*, written around 403.[49] Ambrose's version reverberates with theological significance since it is in the context of magnifying the succession and legacy of Constantine.[50] Helena worships God, who is symbolized by the cross; she touches the sacred wood, and as a result the Holy Spirit becomes part of her and her gift of the nails, one for the bridle of Constantine and one for his diadem, which are passed down to his successors. Ambrose shows that the empire and emperor were saved as a result of having them. This combination of marking divine authority and protection forms a narrative for the empire and emperors to follow. Ambrose's version differs considerably from other versions because of his principal theme: the *hereditas fidei* (inheritance of faith).[51]

Helena holds a central role in Ambrose's narrative of the Christianization of the empire. While of comparatively minor importance to the other authors who include the story of the discovery, the nails from the True Cross are crucial for Ambrose. He credits the Augusta with a weightier role than even Constantine because she is the one who, under the direction of the Holy Spirit, recovers and passes on the nails from the cross, thereby claiming the heritage for the emperors to come: "In Ambrose's view, by finding the Cross and the nails Helena has rescued the emperors and has made them adherents and preachers of the Christian faith instead of persecutors."[52] Thus Helena establishes imperial Christian reign not only by giving birth to Constantine

49. Paulinus of Nola's version of the story is found in a letter he wrote in 403 to his friend Sulpicius Severus in reply to Sulpicius's request for a relic of a saint for the dedication of a newly built basilica. Paulinus relays that he only has a relic of the cross to offer, which he received from Melania the Elder, who got it from John, bishop of Jerusalem (385–417). Melania the Elder (see chap. 8), then, is a likely oral source for Paulinus. See Paulinus of Nola, *Ep.* 31, *To Severus*, in *Letters of St. Paulinus of Nola*, trans. P. G. Walsh, ACW 36 (New York: Newman, 1967), 2:125–33; Drijvers demonstrates that Paulinus did not get his version from Ambrose but either from Rufinus's *Historia ecclesiastica* or, more likely, from Melania the Elder. See Drijvers, *Helena Augusta*, chap. 4 of part 2, for an examination of the sources.

50. Drijvers, *Helena Augusta*, 111–12.

51. Ibid., 110.

52. Ibid., 112.

but also by actively instituting an imperial *hereditas fidei*. For Ambrose, Helena had a central theological role to play. The hiddenness of the True Cross was perpetrated by Satan and correlated directly to the persecution of Christians in the empire. Thus, when the True Cross is retrieved, Helena foils Satan's plan and ends the suppression of Christianity. It makes sense, then, that Ambrose deemed Helena to be a second Mary: "While Mary defeated Satan by giving birth to Christ, Helena defeats him a second time by finding and identifying the Cross. Through Helena's discovery of the Cross Christ is reborn, as a result of which the Christian empire is established."[53] With Helena a new kind of imperial succession is established that expands the purview of apostolic authority and succession beyond the margins of bishops and martyrs by accessing and appropriating an imperially shaped christological heritage.

From Ambrose, Paulinus, and others, the legend expands, taking on various forms, adding characters, minimizing or maximizing Helena's role, and spreading across the empire.[54] Helena's legacy is inseparable from the legacy ascribed to her in a spate of holy association for the sake of the empire. While not all of the elements are included by the church historians, main elements derived from the *Life of Constantine* ground the historians' accounts in something closer to plausible events: Helena's visit to Jerusalem, the statue/temple of Venus/Aphrodite erected on the site of Christ's tomb, the demolition of that statue/temple and the digging up of the ground, the building of the basilica on the site of the tomb, the building of churches by Helena in Bethlehem and on the Mount of Olives, and Helena's charitable works and her death at around eighty years of age.[55]

## Conclusion

How did Helena and her legacy become entwined with the fictive discovery? As Drijvers explains, it has very little to do with Helena or the True Cross and everything to do with political and doctrinal rivalry between Caesarea and Jerusalem at the end of the 340s and in the early 350s. Caesarea was the imperial center of power in Palestine and home to the ranking metropolitan bishop; its leadership also tended to be more favorable toward Arianism, while Jerusalem, the ancient and increasingly important center for Christian

53. Ibid., 112–13.
54. See chaps. 7–8 of part 2 in Drijvers, *Helena Augusta*, for an exploration of the content and transmission history of the fifth-century legends of Protonike, which is of Syrian origin, and of Judas Cyriacus, also likely of Syrian origin.
55. Ibid., 126–27.

devotion, tended toward Nicene formulations.[56] Since the earliest accounts
of the discovery likely did not attribute the discovering of the True Cross to
anyone in particular, how did Helena become attached to it? Drijvers posits
that it was because she was a prominent member of Constantine's family, and
it was known from Eusebius that the Augusta was a pious woman who had
visited the holy sites in Palestine and was linked to the building of the churches
and the policy of Christianization on behalf of Constantine.[57] Helena's proximity and position made her the ideal candidate to recover the True Cross.
The combination of the piety and imperial stature of Helena with Macarius,
the bishop of Jerusalem, worked in Jerusalem's favor as signaling the shift
of imperial attention and favor to Jerusalem. It made sense if Constantine's
strategy of Christianization of the empire was to radiate out from Jerusalem
as the epicenter of Christian devotion.

The linking of Helena with the story of the discovery of the True Cross is
important because it symbolizes the establishment of a secular Christian reign
and the continuity of its rule; she becomes a "foundress of the new Christian
empire" along with Constantine.[58] She sends her son part of the True Cross
to bestow God's favor and protection upon the emperor and leaves the rest
in Jerusalem, housed in the church that is part of the building program that
is quickly transforming the city into a reflection of its eschatological figura-
tion as the "New Jerusalem."[59] Helena will become the model for empresses
to come to emulate in her pious legacy.[60] In chapter 9 we will look at two of
these empresses, Eudocia and Pulcheria, and consider their stories.

---

56. See chap. 6 of part 2 of *Helena Augusta* for Drijvers's reconstruction of the conflict
between Caesarea and Jerusalem and how the legend of the cross most probably originated in
Jerusalem. Drijvers dates the legend to the second half of the fourth century, having developed
in phases with a final version written down by Gelasius of Caesarea (ibid., 139).

57. Ibid., 140.

58. Ibid., 182.

59. Ibid.

60. Drijvers lists some of the laudatory salutes the Augusta receives:
    The commemoration of Aelia Flaccilla, wife of Theodosius the Great, was modeled on
    that of Helena. The wife of Theodosius II (408–450), Aelia Eudocia, made a pilgrim-
    age through the Holy Land and searched for relics in imitation of Helena. In the *vita*
    of Radegunde from ca. 600, the deeds of this Frankish queen are compared to those
    of Helena. Aelia Pulcheria, sister of Theodosius II, was cheered by the bishops at the
    council of Chalcedon (451) as the "New Helena," while her husband Marcianus whom
    she had lately married, was applauded as the "New Constantine." The comparison of
    a ruling couple with Helena and Constantine occurred regularly from Late Antiquity
    on. (*Helena Augusta*, 182–83)
  See also Leslie Brubaker, "Memories of Helena: Patterns in Imperial Female Matronage in
the Fourth and Fifth Centuries," in *Women, Men and Eunuchs: Gender in Byzantium*, ed. Liz
James (London: Routledge, 1997), 52–75.

# 6

# Egeria's *Itinerary*
# and Christian Pilgrimage

"It is a very beautiful shrine. . . . Having arrived there in the name of God, a prayer was said at the shrine [of St. Thecla] and the complete Acts of Saint Thecla was read. I then gave unceasing thanks to Christ our God, who granted to me, an unworthy woman and in no way deserving, the fulfillment of my desires in all things" (*Itinerarium Egeriae* 23).[1] So writes Egeria, a late fourth- or early fifth-century pilgrim from Spain or Gaul, having accomplished her trek to the city of Scleucia of Isauria, a three days' journey southwest along the coast from Tarsus in Asia Minor. This quotation highlights several key themes we explore in this chapter, including the pilgrim's pious desires and conviction that God is guiding her (or him) in the pursuit of enriched worship and understanding. The reality of pilgrimage, of course, is much more layered and complicated, sometimes involving political maneuvering and personal agendas. Wealthy female pilgrims, and perhaps some from religious orders, were in the middle of such discussions and disputes as they promoted shrines and holy places and served as patrons to the male religious and clergy. Through their efforts and influence, the geography of the Holy Lands was reshaped and even in some cases created. After looking at the broad category of Christian

---

1. *Egeria: Diary of a Pilgrimage* (Gingras, 87). See also *Itinerarium Egeriae*, in *Égérie: Journal de voyage*, ed. Pierre Maraval, SC 296 (Paris: Cerf, 1982).

pilgrimage, we will examine Egeria's text closely to discover this woman's insights and experiences of pilgrimage.

## Introduction to Christian Pilgrimage

Egeria's *Itinerary* affords a glimpse into the patterns of life and the personal connections made among Christian women in the fourth and fifth centuries. Her account describes her three years living in Jerusalem and traveling on various pilgrimages to and from that city. Egeria describes the people and places she visits with the fervor of a pilgrim and the clarity of a well-educated observer. Tantalizing tidbits about life at this time among monks and bishops and townspeople are scattered throughout the account. She captures in detail the liturgical life of the Jerusalem churches, revealing the habits and customs among both the average townsfolk and religious orders. Her itinerary gives us categories and concepts, vocabulary and questions about practices and their theological underpinning.

In the fourth and fifth centuries, the church experienced burgeoning building programs and dynamic theological debates. Commentaries were written, letters were exchanged in astonishing numbers, and debates and quarrels fractured communities in the East and West. Pilgrims such as Egeria journeyed from the politically chaotic West to the holy sites in the East. Eager to explore the biblical world, these faithful followed the path of the ancient Israelites from Alexandria, Egypt, southeast to Mount Sinai in the desert, and then northwest to the holy city of Jerusalem. Pilgrims paid special attention to alleged sites of biblical events, such as the rock that Moses struck from which then flowed water, or the place of Melchizedek's grave.[2] The pilgrims then sometimes journeyed further northeast to Edessa, or northwest to Tarsus, or explored western Asia Minor, visiting Ephesus. Pilgrimages multiplied as the stories of miracles and healings at the shrine centers increased. People visited local martyr shrines or holy men in hopes of receiving aid, these places and men being "a channel through which divine grace was able to reach them."[3]

### What Is Christian Pilgrimage?

The question arises as to the distinguishing features of pilgrimage over against other types of travel, such as Helena's *iter principis*, an official imperial

2. The story of Moses striking the rock is told in Num. 20:1–11; see also 1 Cor. 10:4. Melchizedek is introduced in Gen. 14:18–20; see also Ps. 110:4; Heb. 6:20–7:17.
3. Brouria Bitton-Ashkelony, *Encountering the Sacred: The Debate on Christian Pilgrimage in Late Antiquity*, Transformation of the Classical Heritage 39 (Berkeley: University of California Press, 2005), 9.

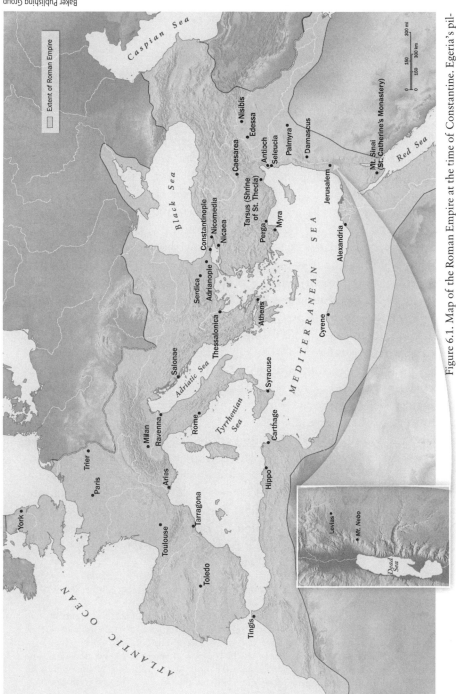

Figure 6.1. Map of the Roman Empire at the time of Constantine. Egeria's pilgrimage occurred perhaps seventy-five years after Constantine united the empire and, with the Edict of Milan, declared Christianity a tolerated religion.

journey. Georgia Frank explains the concept as follows: "Early Christian pilgrimage involved a journey to a place in order to gain access to sacred power, whether manifested in living persons, demarcated spaces, or specific objects."[4] The goals of the journey included discovering the sacred in new ways, whether by viewing a biblical place, listening to a holy monk, or touching a relic. The senses are involved, indeed, and pilgrimage connects mind and body; it is an embodied encounter with the sacred or divine. Each pilgrim desires to "see and touch the sacred."[5] Some sought healing, others sought ecstatic experiences. Pilgrims such as Egeria and Paula, whom we will meet in chapter 8, wanted mainly to experience the land of the Bible, to pray at holy sites, to honor a martyr's shrine.[6] They drew on the expertise of monks and ascetic holy men and women who populated the deserts and clustered in the cities. Ancient pilgrims were not interested in ethnography; they did not wonder at exotic plants or animals they came across. In this they are different from medieval pilgrims, who were quite curious about their world and desired to explore it. Though the early pilgrims might have traveled in groups, they did not write about the relationship between members of the group; they were on a personal quest. Moreover, these early pilgrims did not seem to gain a greater social status upon completing their pilgrimage.[7]

A leading impetus for the Christian pilgrimage was the rise of the cult of the saints and the concomitant rise in the veneration of relics. Another was the enticement of beholding beautiful basilicas often built by the emperors and empresses, starting with Constantine and his mother, Helena, and continued by subsequent rulers. Alongside churches, buildings that catered to pilgrims went up, making the journey feasible. Finally, the growth of the monastic movement in Egypt and Palestine greatly facilitated the pilgrimage movement. It could be seen as a mutually beneficial relationship: some pilgrims stayed and joined the monks/nuns, while others left large donations to their monasteries. The monks taught pilgrims about Christianity, thereby influencing the direction and development of the faith they embraced. And there may have been a very practical reason for Christians to set out on a

---

4. Georgia Frank, "Pilgrimage," in *The Oxford Handbook of Early Christian Studies*, ed. Susan Ashbrook Harvey and David G. Hunter (Oxford: Oxford University Press, 2008), 826.

5. Bitton-Ashkelony, *Encountering the Sacred*, 6.

6. In the middle of the second century, a Christian named Montanus redrew the earthly map from a heavenly viewpoint when he renamed Pepuza (a small town in Phrygia, Asia Minor) as the "new" Jerusalem, the place to which Jesus would return. His decision was based in large part on his teachings about the presence of the Holy Spirit (Paraclete) and his understanding of Christ's second coming. While others chose not to follow Montanus's repositioning of Jerusalem, his boldness in drawing a new religious map took hold at the time of Constantine.

7. Bitton-Ashkelony, *Encountering the Sacred*, 12.

pilgrimage in the fourth and fifth centuries: to flee Rome when it was under attack by the Visigoths and the Vandals. It is possible that Egeria's travel was in part related to fleeing the politically unsettling situation in the West for the relative calm of Constantinople and Palestine, although she makes no mention of such concern and moreover declares her plans to return to her "sisters."

Overall, the relative peace in the East under the new Christian imperial rule facilitated travel; however, it was not simply the Christianization of the Roman Empire that drove pilgrimage. The second- and third-century churches were at best ambivalent about the importance of the earthly Jerusalem and tended to privilege the heavenly Jerusalem to come. But in the fourth century the biblical sites took on an added theological dimension. Julie Ann Smith notes, "The idea of holiness of place was premised on the belief that a place that had witnessed holy events was itself proof of the holy, the historic event ever present at the actual site."[8]

As we look at who went on pilgrimages, the earliest account is by the pilgrim of Bordeaux (ca. 333); interestingly, the gender of the author is unknown. Arius in 335, Gregory of Nyssa in 380, Epiphanius in 393, and Pelagius in 415—all traveled to Jerusalem. Basil of Caesarea in Cappadocia traveled through Palestine, as did Paulinus of Nola.[9] Egeria's pilgrimage fits with this practice, and we will take a closer look after reviewing the influence of Constantine and his mother, Helena, on Christian pilgrimages.

### The Role of Constantine in Pilgrimage

Constantine's influence on Christianity can hardly be overstated—although the relative merits of his agenda continue to be hotly debated. The question we entertain now concerns whether Constantine, and by extension his mother, Helena, paved the way for pilgrimage as we have described it above. Joan Taylor argues that "Constantine brought to Christianity a pagan notion of the sanctity of things and places,"[10] and this was well suited for the recently converted polytheists. Taylor continues: "Suddenly, with Constantine, the Church began to focus on the earth; the divine substance intermixed with certain material sites and resided in things which could be carried about."[11]

8. Julie Ann Smith, "'My Lord's Native Land': Mapping the Christian Holy Land," *CH* 76 (2007): 4.
9. Other men who traveled in the area include John Cassian, Evagrius Ponticus, Palladius, Postumianus, and Peter the Iberian.
10. Joan E. Taylor, *Christians and the Holy Places: The Myth of Jewish-Christian Origins* (Oxford: Clarendon, 1993), 308.
11. Ibid., 314.

While most scholars affirm Taylor's observation that Christians were not copying a Jewish cult of the saints, they hesitate to postulate an abrupt beginning to Christian pilgrimage or to link it solely to a Christianizing of pagan practices.[12] Christian travelers to Palestine before Constantine were few in number (that we are aware of); however, both Origen (*Cels.* 1.51) and Justin Martyr (*Dial.* 78) know of Christians who trekked to the Bethlehem cave believed to be the place of Jesus's birth. Eusebius speaks of Alexander of Cappadocia traveling to Palestine in order that he might pray and study at the historic sites (*Hist. eccl.* 6.11.1–2), and of Melito of Sardis traveling east, likely to Jerusalem, to research and make extracts of Old Testament books (*Hist. eccl.* 4.26.13–14). Eusebius writes of Christians visiting a cave on the Mount of Olives allegedly marking where Jesus ascended to heaven (*Demonstration of the Gospel* [*Demonstratio evangelica*] 6.18.23). Christians from the early fourth century assembled at the location remembered as the site of Pentecost, and nearby at the site of the ascension, and a small community of Christians met at a church on Mount Zion.[13] Thus while "Constantine's recognition and honoring of the holy places ushered in an exciting period of recovery and construction at holy sites in Palestine," the table had already been set for an influx of pilgrims with the end of the age of martyrs and the exponential growth of the Egyptian and Palestinian monastic movements.[14]

The questions related to Constantine's role in pilgrimage serve as a useful example of the much larger problem of researching pilgrimage in the ancient world, indeed of studying the continuity and change that occurred from the Roman Republic through to the Christian Roman Empire. The issues include whether the sacred travel writings of pre-Christian pagan authors should be included in the category, because the Greco-Roman world is filled with stories of travel to mystery cult sanctuaries or healing shrines, or to temples seeking spiritual guidance. The classicist rightly fears that Christian themes or even modern religious ideas will slip into the definition or description of pre-Christian activities. Thus Jaś Elsner and Ian Rutherford warn that denying the existence of pagan pilgrimage "specifically prevents the possibility of comparing phenomena which are not only parallel in terms of location, types of activity and respective social functions, but were also genealogically

---

12. Bitton-Ashkelony, *Encountering the Sacred*, 26. Later Christian authors differentiate the veneration of relics and the practices surrounding the cult of the saints from polytheist practices; thus their silence with regard to Jewish practices most likely means that there were few Jewish analogues to this Christian practice.

13. Smith, "'My Lord's Native Land,'" 9.

14. Ibid., 6, 18.

related in that the pilgrimage practices of antiquity were clearly ancestral to those inherited, borrowed, and adapted in the Christian and Islamic worlds."[15] Their caution is a useful reminder about the complexity of understanding travel for religious purposes in the ancient world, a world that the women we study navigated as they expressed their Christian faith.

### Why Monks and Nuns Should Not Go on Pilgrimages

Not all press concerning pilgrimage was positive. Some debated whether monks and nuns should travel, since they were most suited to a reclusive life; the journey of their soul toward heaven should take precedence over traveling to a physical holy site. Augustine exclaims, "It is not by journeying but by loving that we draw near to God. We approach Him who is everywhere present and present wholly, not by our feet but by our hearts" (*Ep.* 155.672). John Chrysostom expresses a similar sentiment as he speaks positively about pilgrimages overall but declares that prayers done in one's home are as effective (*Stat.* 3.2.49; 4.6.68). Jerome warns away monks because of the urban sin that collects in Jerusalem (*Ep.* 58.4). The Council of Chalcedon (451) placed restrictions on monks and nuns, and in the following century some monks and nuns were forbidden to travel to the Holy Lands out of fear they would meet a heretical Christian.

### Conflicting Views on Pilgrimage in Gregory of Nyssa and Jerome

Gregory of Nyssa presents an interesting case. In his *Life of Macrina*, which he wrote in the early 380s, Gregory speaks highly of his visit to Jerusalem as being one of prayer and devotion. But elsewhere he cautions monks against traveling on pilgrimage, stating that travel might mix the sexes too much (*Ep.* 2).[16] He adds that pilgrimages are not mentioned in the Gospels. Gregory concludes that traveling to find a sacred space implies that God is not in the local place, and Gregory wants to underline to the monks that God desires virtue. They should pursue God, not a location: "For Gregory the sites in Jerusalem associated with the life of Christ are entirely dissociated from the alleged preference of God to dwell there."[17]

---

15. Jaś Elsner and Ian Rutherford, eds., *Pilgrimage in Graeco-Roman and Early Christian Antiquity: Seeing the Gods* (Oxford: Oxford University Press, 2005), 8.

16. Gregory of Nyssa, *Ep.* 2.4, *To Kensitor* on pilgrimages; the recipient of the letter might be a provincial tax collector, or *Censor* is the man's proper name, and thus Gregory is writing to a superior of a monastery. See *Gregory of Nyssa: The Letters, Introduction, Translation and Commentary*, ed. and trans. Anna M. Silvas, VCSup 83 (Leiden: Brill, 2007).

17. Bitton-Ashkelony, *Encountering the Sacred*, 54.

Gregory, however, did not follow his own advice against traveling to Jerusalem. To defend his actions, he explains that he was ordered to travel to Jerusalem, presumably on a diplomatic mission; moreover, he rode in a carriage that kept him from being contaminated by the wretched population and filth.[18] Finally, he declares that seeing the place of Jesus's birth or death did not increase his faith; indeed, "We came to know by comparison that our own places are far holier than those abroad" (*Ep.* 2.15).

The sour attitude toward pilgrimage we find in Gregory's letter is two-pronged. First, he understood that the magnification of local martyrs helped their respective communities find their moorings in the midst of monumental changes within the Roman Empire. As communities mined for Christian roots, they constructed their collective identity in the shape of shrines, local martyr cults, and the appropriation of legends linking their locales to the events of the New Testament.[19] For example, both Gregory and his brother, Basil of Caesarea, promoted the local martyr cults of Cappadocia. These cult shrines held festivals that brought trade to the area; they could be noisy and vulgar affairs.[20] The post-Constantinian church balanced triumphalism with the still poignant need to remain connected to the persecuted past and see itself as the "rightful heirs of the martyrs."[21]

Effectively, the appropriation of legendary Christian heritage and the formation of regional collective identity were a generalization of martyrdom. For the early Christians, these narratives were alive; a community could participate in and add to the great saga that was the story of Christianity. The legend was perceived as inhabiting a new place and time, and each community saw that as an invitation to add a verse to the tale. The physical presence of one who bore witness to the sufferings of Christ in persecution or participated

---

18. In *Ep.* 2 Gregory of Nyssa writes: "Moreover as the inns and caravanserays [*sic*] and cities in the east are so free and indifferent towards vice, how will it be possible for one passing through such fumes to escape without smarting eyes? Where the ear is contaminated and the eye is contaminated, how is the heart not also contaminated by the unsavoury impressions received through eye and ear?" (trans. Silvas, 119).

19. See Raymond Van Dam, *Becoming Christian: The Conversion of Roman Cappadocia* (Philadelphia: University of Pennsylvania Press, 2003), 74–89, for the legendary heritage directly associated with the Cappadocian region.

20. Bitton-Ashkelony, *Encountering the Sacred*, 37–38.

21. R. A. Markus, "How on Earth Could Places Become Holy? Origins of the Christian Idea of Holy Places," *JECS* 2 (1994): 268–70. Markus notes the early Christian reluctance to accord holiness to places and, over the course of the fourth century, how this sentiment shifts concomitantly with the need to preserve Christianity's identity forged in trial and death: "The cult gave place a new significance; it met a felt need to make present in post-Constantinian conditions the past of the persecuted Church. Christianity could not envisage places as intrinsically holy, only derivatively, as the sites of historical events of sacred significance" (257).

in those sufferings as an ascetic was qualification enough to be enshrined. Thus Gregory of Nyssa did not think it necessary to travel all that way to Jerusalem—presumably because one could head to the nearest martyr shrine to see Christ enfleshed (*Ep.* 2).

Second, Gregory's attitude toward pilgrimage was also probably bolstered by his very negative experience with the bishop of Jerusalem, Cyril. Gregory admits that he enjoyed many of the people he met in Jerusalem, believing them to be godly Christians. Yet his views on Christology seem not to have been embraced by Cyril, causing Gregory no little frustration. Brouria Bitton-Ashkelony explains that "for Cyril, history, myth, and geography are intertwined; he is exploiting the memory of the past and the local setting—both the visual and the imaginative—to prove the truth of Christianity, thus he consistently promotes the idea of earthly sacred space on his home ground, in Jerusalem."[22] Gregory wanted none of that. This conflict with Cyril explains what on the surface appears to be his inconsistent view on pilgrimage.

Jerome's letters offer a second example of the complexity of viewpoints on pilgrimage. Not only does he praise his patron Paula's pilgrimage, but he also writes that the tombs of the holy men and martyrs are "heaven's family on earth," urging the faithful to visit such sites in Jerusalem and Bethlehem and other places mentioned in the life of Jesus (*Ep.* 66.14). In his letter to Marcella in 386, written shortly after he and Paula have settled into their monastic life in Bethlehem, he urges Marcella to visit the tomb of Jesus (*Ep.* 46.5). Bitton-Ashkelony suggests that in his plea Jerome offers a unique argument—namely, that pilgrimage to Jerusalem will gain more reward, greater piety, and higher virtue for the pilgrim.[23]

Yet years later, in 394, Jerome changes his tune, urging that one need not venture to Jerusalem to improve one's faith. This about-face could be related to a local argument that led John, the bishop of Jerusalem, to forbid Jerome and his monks from entering the Church of the Holy Sepulchre and churches in Bethlehem. At this time Jerome writes to Paulinus of Nola, who is thinking of traveling to Palestine. Paulinus befriends Melania and Rufinus, and Jerome knows that they could escort Paulinus around Jerusalem and into the churches and holy sites. Jerome's circumstances place him at a disadvantage, and so he discourages Paulinus from making the journey. Jerome writes to Paulinus that it is not so much being in Jerusalem, but living there well, that makes the difference. He adds, "It is just as easy to reach the portals of Heaven from Britain as from Jerusalem" (*Ep.* 58.3). Bitton-Ashkelony concludes that this

---

22. *Encountering the Sacred*, 61.
23. Ibid., 83.

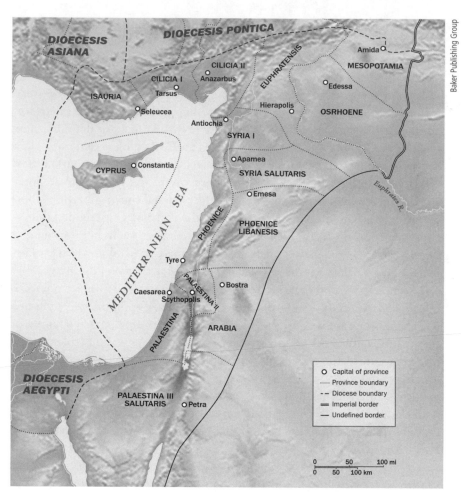

Figure 6.2. The Holy Lands were divided into Roman dioceses or governing provinces. Shown above are the cities of Edessa in the northeast and Tarsus and Seleucea (Seleucia) in the northwest.

letter is not a retraction of Jerome's letter to Marcella, noted above, nor is Jerome discouraging pilgrimage in general, but his advice to Paulinus is based on his competition with Rufinus and Melania for regional and theological influence.[24] In 397 the ban imposed by John was lifted, and Jerome was free to enter the churches; he again extols the benefits of pilgrimage. However, Jerome's relationship with Rufinus and Melania was never repaired and turned into an acrimonious theological controversy, which we will discuss in chapter 8.

24. See ibid., 90, 96–97, citing *Ep.* 68, 71, 76, 122, and 145.

The multifaceted topic of pilgrimage drew much attention in the fourth through sixth centuries. Laity, religious, and clergy alike weighed in on the benefits and drawbacks of traveling to holy sites. Often such evaluations had more to do with personal grievances between leading figures, or political maneuvering between local bishops and clergy. Yet the flow of pilgrims to holy sites, especially in the Holy Lands, continued to grow. Piety fashioned around venerating relics and holy sites captured the imagination of Christians, as Egeria's story testifies.

### Egeria's Landscape and the Jews

Appreciating Egeria's role in shaping our perceptions of the biblical landscape not only helps us today better grasp the dynamics of developing monasticism, veneration of saints, and the codification of liturgical practices; it also reveals an important political and rhetorical move with respect to the Jews in the land and to Judaism. As Patricia Wilson-Kastner notes, Egeria speaks warmly of the Old Testament "saints," but she does not show any awareness of local Jews.[25] Andrew Jacobs concurs and then develops this observation. He argues that the activity of "travel itself could function in the ideological workings of the Roman Empire, and how Christian writing came to participate in this process."[26] Egeria views Jews through the lens of the biblical text, such that actual Jews are cleared from the physical landscape: "The land is totally scriptural; Scripture is entirely Christian."[27] In effect, churches built on sites commemorating Jewish Scripture events or persons commandeered the space as Christian. Monks who inhabited the holy sites served as present representations of the biblical prophets and holy men—overwriting the biblical characters' Jewishness with a Christian identity. And the rituals performed at the sites, including prayer and Eucharist, further stamped the location as Christian.[28] We saw a similar move with respect to the Maccabean martyrs discussed in chapter 2, devoted to the martyrs Perpetua and Felicitas. The church absorbed this Jewish story and appropriated these Jews as their own, labeling them as Christian.

25. Patricia Wilson-Kastner et al., *A Lost Tradition: Women Writers of the Early Church* (Washington, DC: University Press of America, 1981), 74.
26. Andrew Jacobs, "'The Most Beautiful Jewesses in the Land': Imperial Travel in the Early Christian Holy Land," *Religion* 32 (2002): 206. Jacobs suggests that the Christian pilgrimage literature's description of Jews can be categorized in four ways: historicization, textualization, aestheticization, and ritualization. On page 207, he explains textualization as that "by which the Jew and his vestiges are dissolved into the text of Christian Scriptures."
27. Jacobs, "'Most Beautiful Jewesses in the Land,'" 213.
28. Jerome writes in his *Epistle to Dardanus*, "This land, which has now through Christ's passion and resurrection become our Promised Land, is believed by the Jews—so the Jews may contend—to have belonged to the Jewish people after their return from Egypt" (*Ep. to Dardanus*, 129.4).

Jacobs accurately discerns that Egeria sees only "textual" Jews, not the actual Jews living in the places that she visits. Therefore, "the text of Scripture creates landscape" instead of the landscape generating observations that are then linked to Scripture.[29] For example, in an open plain with no visible topographic markers, Egeria reads Deuteronomy, because she believes that space must be the place where Moses wrote it.[30] Additionally, Jacobs argues that Egeria's itinerary suggests that there are no Jews in the Holy Lands, yet we know that in Galilee at least, a growing number of Jews lived there, building beautiful synagogues. Egeria removes Jews from the present and even relabels biblical Jews as Christians. From this recategorization, she is able to reassign ancient biblical spaces as present-day Christian holy sites. This renaming and reclaiming creates a hegemonic landscape that is at once wholly Christian and (in her eyes) holy Christian.[31] Such a vision affirms the wider political aims of the emerging Christian imperial project, whether or not Egeria is conscious of this effect. Egeria's account is shaped by what she sees, and her writing configures the landscape. Her religious focus should not blind us to the cultural and political ramifications of her enterprise.

## Pilgrimage as a Female Act of Piety

Some scholars contrast ancient Christian pilgrimage as an act of female personal piety with travel by religious men for purposes of church business.[32] Perhaps this belief is in part based on the role that Helena, Constantine's mother, played in the story of the discovery of Jesus's True Cross, for this legend "attributed the identification of the most significant of all Christian relics to the archetypal, female pilgrim."[33] Linked to this conclusion that pilgrimage is feminine is the assessment that such activity is nonauthoritative

29. Jacobs, "'Most Beautiful Jewesses in the Land,'" 211.

30. Egeria, *It. Eg.* 10.

31. Jacobs, "'Most Beautiful Jewesses in the Land,'" 211, states, "As a representative of this stream of western piety and eastern *imperium*, Egeria and her textualised representation of the Palestinian Jew create a purely Christian space for the exercise of piety and authority."

32. See, e.g., the contrast between Helena's and Constantine's journeys as described in Lynda L. Coon, *Sacred Fictions: Holy Women and Hagiography in Late Antiquity*, Middle Ages Series (Philadelphia: University of Pennsylvania Press, 1997), 99; see also Ora Limor, "Reading Sacred Space: Egeria, Paula, and the Christian Holy Land," *Revue augustiniennes* 18 (1972): 209–18, repr. as pages 1–15 in vol. 1 of *De Sion exibit lex et verbum domini de Hierusalem: Essays on Medieval Law, Liturgy, and Literature in Honour of Amnon Linder*, ed. Yitzhak Hen, Cultural Encounters in Late Antiquity and the Middle Ages 1 (Turnhout: Brepols, 2001). Limor says Helena made such a journey fashionable for women (1).

33. Smith, "'My Lord's Native Land,'" 10. The transmission of the legend of the True Cross eclipsed Helena's *iter principis* in favor of her journey as the model *peregrinatio religiosa*.

and nondoctrinal, personal rather than intellectual. Countering such ideas, Rebecca Stephens Falcasantos emphasizes that pilgrimage was closely coupled with the patronage system, evidenced clearly in Paula's support of Jerome, for example (see chap. 8).[34] She cautions against creating a picture of the simple, pious pilgrim, instead contending that pilgrims often were the patrons and literate elites of the day, who visited sites and engaged in theological discussions with local monks and bishops. This argument, as we will see below, helps explain the apparently unpolished Latin of Egeria's work as representing an oral presentation of a well-educated woman.

Egeria's *Itinerary* offers a detailed, firsthand account of a woman's reflections on her pilgrimage. Her experiences add to the evidence we have about female Christian pilgrims. Theodoret, bishop of Cyrrhus, writes of two nuns, Marana and Cyra, who traveled to Jerusalem and to the St. Thecla shrine (*Religious History* = *Historia religiosa* [HR] 29).[35] Athanasius writes to a community of female ascetics living in Egypt; his letter can be dated to between 328 and 373, a generation or two before Egeria's journey. These women travel to Jerusalem, along the way visiting Bethlehem and the Cave of the Nativity. In Jerusalem, these women visit Jesus's tomb and Golgotha. And they travel home by way of Mount Sinai, a site described in detail by Egeria. A bit later than Egeria's time, Jerome depicts the pilgrimage of Paula, but he fails to mention that he was with her the entire journey.[36] Jerome minimizes his participation in Paula's pilgrimage most likely because he is writing a eulogy for Paula, contained in a letter to her daughter Eustochium, written in 404. Andrew Cain puts forward the intriguing idea that with this public letter Jerome hoped to promote a cult of St. Paula that would bring pilgrims to her gravesite within the Church of the Nativity, and by extension help his monastery in Bethlehem.[37] If Cain is correct, he provides a further explanation for Jerome's silence about his participation with Paula, and it has nothing to do with the idea that only women went on pilgrimages. Thus, from Athanasius's brief account about the female ascetics, coupled with Eusebius's note about Alexander's journey to Jerusalem, we find that the tradition of women and men traveling to the Holy Lands was an established pattern by Egeria's day.

34. Rebecca Stephens Falcasantos, "Pilgrim or Traveler? Constructions of Ancient Christian Pieties," paper presented at the annual meeting of the North American Patristics Society, Chicago, May 2013.

35. Gregory of Nazianzus also traveled to the Thecla shrine and remained there for quite some time.

36. Jerome, *Ep.* 108; see also *Ep.* 46.

37. Andrew Cain, "Jerome's *Epitaphium Paulae*: Hagiography, Pilgrimage, and the Cult of Saint Paula," *JECS* 18.1 (2010): 117, recognizes Jerome's sincere affection for Paula.

Interestingly, in his letter Athanasius stresses the value of a spiritual journey of the soul to God. With this interpretive move, he downgrades the importance of the physical sites in Jerusalem, Bethlehem, and Mount Sinai; and he puts front and center the concept of the soul's pilgrimage to God. Jerusalem is redefined as a heavenly goal sought through holiness and an ascetic lifestyle. Therefore, one can visit "Jerusalem" without leaving one's monastery. Egeria's text, however, highlights the powerful pull of matching the biblical stories with their physical locations, pilgrimage as exegetical exploration. Doubt in the Bible's historicity did not propel her; to the contrary, it was her conviction of its historical veracity that drove her to link what she read with what she might see. Yet "seeing is believing"; and in telling the story, pilgrims like Egeria create a new conceptual map of the land. Pilgrims helped shape the life of the church as they engaged with monks and participated in the developing liturgy of the churches. In our case, Egeria seems most interested in "systematically confronting the biblical past and the tangible present."[38] She conversed with the monks about biblical questions and expected them to guide and participate in reading Scripture, prayers, and Eucharist. Journeys such as Egeria's have continued into the modern period, and while the reasons for the journeys vary, the allure of the Holy Lands remains to this day.

## The Discovery of Egeria's *Itinerary*

The modern story of Egeria and her pilgrimage begins in 1884, when G. F. Gamurrini, historian and archaeologist, discovered a damaged codex describing a three-year journey in the Holy Land.[39] The manuscript included twenty-two pages of the pilgrimage from Egypt up to Jerusalem, as well as a close description of the liturgical year in Jerusalem's several churches. However, the manuscript was missing the beginning and end, as well as a section of the work's middle. The eleventh-century codex had been produced in the monastery of Monte Cassino, and Gamurrini found it in the library of the Brotherhood of St. Mary in Arezzo, Italy. He identified it as the writings of St. Silvia of Aquitaine.[40]

38. Bitton-Ashkelony, *Encountering the Sacred*, 10.
39. Gamurrini published the work at Rome in 1887. For a discussion, see E. D. Hunt, "The Itinerary of Egeria: Reliving the Bible in Fourth-Century Palestine," in *The Holy Land, Holy Lands, and Christian History*, ed. R. N. Swanson, SCH 36 (Rochester, NY: Boydell, 2000), 34. Also in the codex are works of St. Hilary of Poitiers, including a hymnbook and his work *De mysteriis*.
40. Silvia is the sister-in-law of Rufinus, the minister to Theodosius the Great and Arcadius, as mentioned in Palladius's *Historia Lausiaca*.

By 1903, however, scholars were connecting the pilgrimage account to that referenced in a letter by a seventh-century Spanish monk, Valerius. He explains to fellow monks living in Bierzo, northwestern Spain, that a certain Egeria, a "fragile woman," nevertheless accomplished a heroic feat, scaling Mount Sinai and other mountains in the Holy Land. Valerius calls on these monks to imitate her journey in spirit, practicing self-discipline in climbing the spiritual mountains of their soul toward the pinnacle of godly virtue and piety. Valerius's letter is immensely valuable because it is all we have alongside the *Itinerary* itself to form our understanding of Egeria and her journey. We have three copies of Valerius's letter from the tenth and eleventh centuries, plus two eighteenth-century copies. Frustratingly, the name of the author of the pilgrimage is spelled differently in the Valerius letter copies, including Etheria (Aetheria), Echeria, Eiheria (Aeiheria), and Egeria.[41] Scholars have concluded that "Egeria" is the best-attested option, and the work is currently identified as *Itinerarium Egeriae* (*It. Eg.*).[42]

## Egeria's Journey

Another source of tremendous value is from Peter the Deacon, the twelfth-century librarian of Monte Cassino. In his book *Liber de locis sanctis*, he writes of holy places, depending closely on the Venerable Bede's work describing pilgrimages to the East, as well as on extracts from Egeria's narrative. Drawing on Peter the Deacon's work, we can reconstruct the general contents of the opening nonextant chapters of Egeria's work. Most likely this section included Egeria's description of Clysma, the traditional site of the Israelites crossing the Red Sea in the exodus (near the modern-day port of Suez). From there she would have recorded her journey in the footsteps of the ancient Israelites to Mount Sinai. We glimpse Egeria herself from her account; for that reason, a brief sketch of her pilgrimage is in order. We will say more about her time of visiting churches and participating in the liturgy of the Jerusalem churches later in this chapter.

### Journey to Jerusalem: "I gave unceasing thanks to Christ our God" (It. Eg. 23)

With poetic irony, the broken text begins with the sentence fragment "were shown according to the Scriptures."[43] This announcement is a constant refrain, as well as a neat summary of Egeria's understanding of her journey. She intends to see all that Scripture identifies, linking the words in the text to the geography and topography of the land, and in some cases creating a space in which to place an event (such as the spot where Moses died). As important as following Scripture is to Egeria, we also find her repeatedly praying and at times being taught by, and celebrating the Eucharist with, the holy men or clergy in these places. As she writes in chapter 10, "Whenever we were empowered to reach our destination, it was always our custom first to say a prayer, then to read a passage from the Bible, sing a Psalm fitting the occasion, and finally say a second prayer."[44] These three emphases—reading Scripture, worshiping on site, being instructed by holy men—lend structure to her story.

### Journeys from Jerusalem: "Christ granted me the fulfillment of my desires" (It. Eg. 23)

Egeria travels to Jerusalem but does not remain in that city. Instead, she takes pilgrimages to biblical sites such as Mount Nebo (*It. Eg.* 10–12) and Job's tomb (13–16). To reach Mount Nebo, setting out with a company of holy men, she heads back to the area of Arabia, first crossing the Jordan River and pausing at the town of Livias. This town is on the plain that Egeria believes is the spot where Moses wrote Deuteronomy. She goes to the place commemorating this, prays, reads the relevant passages, and finishes with a second prayer (10). Later she travels from Jerusalem to Job's tomb (an eight-day journey) that she might pray there (13). Her journey takes her past the city of Sedima, which contains the ancient city of Salem, in which Melchizedek lived. In this same journey they pass by the cave of the prophet Elijah, and the place of the holy man Jephthah, who, she notes, is mentioned in the book of Judges. They also pass the cell of a monk who lives in the middle of a valley, commemorating the place where Elijah stayed during the famine when he received food from a crow and drank from a stream.

### Journey of Understanding: "The fulfillment of my desires in all things" (It. Eg. 23)

Throughout her journeys to and from Jerusalem, she places much emphasis on the holy men who educate her at the various sites. For example, she meets a bishop who lives in the town of Arabia, which is in Goshen.[45] She observes that he habitually receives pilgrims, corroborating what we know from other sources—namely, that pilgrims were a rather common sight in her day.

44. Ibid., 66. See also Egeria, *It. Eg.* 11.
45. Gingras, *Egeria*, 62–64; Egeria, *It. Eg.* 8–9.

Additionally, Egeria comments on his deep knowledge of Scripture, linked to the specific holy sites. She remarks that he had been raised in this lifestyle, thus explaining his worthy demeanor and biblical understanding. In chapter 20, Egeria reports an extensive dialogue about the biblical story that she has with the bishop from the city of Haran/Carrhae. Interestingly, when she is in Mesopotamia, she meets three bishops whom she describes as confessors. It may be that these men were connected with the Arian persecution that occurred under Emperor Valens (364–78), or stood against the Monophysite movement.[46]

Beyond biblical knowledge, the priests also inform Egeria of local miracles or physical characteristics of a given site. For example, a priest suggests that she might consider interrupting her trip to Mount Nebo by visiting the rock from which water gushed after Moses struck it. She eagerly follows this monk, and at the site she sees a small church and many holy men who dwell there. They explain that the water is fresh and clear because Moses gave this water to the Israelites. Again, Egeria describes the "saintly priest" of the Melchizedek church who is not only very learned in the Scriptures and highly regarded by other bishops, but is also well versed in the local area. He explains to Egeria that locals who build their homes in the vicinity regularly discover bits of silver and bronze from the foundations of Melchizedek's palace.

Additionally, Egeria received gifts from many of the priests, such as fruit grown at the base of Mount Sinai. She indicates, "They are in the habit of bestowing gifts on those whom they receive hospitably."[47] These gifts do not seem to have special qualities nor function as some sort of tangible piece of holiness, but rather simply reflect the hospitality of the holy men. The priests' actions may also reveal the high status of Egeria, whose honor would be recognized by these gifts.

### Egeria's Jerusalem of Liturgy and Song: "Having arrived there in the Name of God" (It. Eg. 23)

In the second half of the *Itinerary*, Egeria recounts her yearlong stay in Jerusalem, emphasizing the liturgy in the churches within the immediate surroundings of Jerusalem, especially the Holy Sepulchre in the city, and the church of the Nativity a few miles away in Bethlehem, and the church on the Mount of Olives. Her rich details offer great reward to those who study the development of the church's liturgy. She paints a scene of religious orders of men and of women, plus laity joining together at different times

---

46. Gingras, *Egeria*, 204n202.
47. Ibid., 67; Egeria, *It. Eg.* 11; see also chap. 15.

Jean Housen CC BY-SA / Wikimedia Commons

Figure 6.3. This floor mosaic of the Holy Land is from the Church of St. George in Madaba, Jordan, and was created during Justinian's rule (527–65 CE).

of the day at the Holy Sepulchre to sing, chant, and offer prayers (*It. Eg.* 24). Indeed, women's voices singing hymns in congregations and churches resounded across these centuries. As Rebecca T. Rollins explains, "Women participated as singers in the church—from the first century to at least the fifth century, and in localities from Rome to Jerusalem—as an aspect of the spiritual communion and unity of all believers."[48] Thus in the late first century or early second century, 1 Clement (traditionally ascribed to Clement of Rome) speaks of the congregation singing together, bringing unity.[49] Three centuries later, Basil of Caesarea (330–79) praises the congregation who sings psalms together because this creates unity.[50] The Psalms play an important role, for as John Chrysostom (349–407) explains, the words keep away any unholy sexual thoughts. He contrasts this with the bawdy songs women sing at weddings, accompanied by flute and kithara.[51] From Bethle-

48. Rebecca T. Rollins, "The Singing of Women in the Early Christian Church: Why It Occurred, Why It Disappeared" (DMA thesis, Claremont Graduate School, 1988), 39.

49. First Clement 34.5–7; see also Ignatius, *To the Ephesians* 4.2; and Pliny the Younger to Trajan, *Ep.* 10.96, which speaks of Christians gathering at dawn to sing hymns to Christ.

50. Basil, *Homily on Psalm 1* (*Homilia in psalmum 1*) 2. See also Eusebius, *On Psalm 91* (*In psalmum 91*) 4.

51. John Chrysostom, *On Psalm 41* (*In psalmum 41*) 1; and *On No Second Marriage* (*De non iterando coniugio*) 4.

hem, Jerome urges the mother Laeta living in Rome to instruct her young daughter, Paula, to sing psalms. This Paula is named for her grandmother, the patron of Jerome.[52] And as Gregory of Nyssa describes Macrina's funeral, he speaks positively of his beloved sister's services, including singing of psalms, but decries the traditional laments that spontaneously erupted from her fellow virgins. Gregory of Nazianzus (329–90) praises his sister Gorgonia in a eulogy that includes her participation in the all-night vigils where these women sang psalms.[53]

While we might take congregational hymn singing for granted, some in the early church contested women singing for at least three reasons. First, the female voice was linked with lewd singing at pagan banquets. Second, some pointed to the passage in 1 Corinthians 14:34 requiring women to be silent in church as opposing the practice of female singing.[54] Third, many Christians rejected the pagan funerary music as conveying unchristian themes: "The early Christians did not deny the use of music in funerals . . . but assigned to it a different function than did the pagans, namely a consoling one for the living rather than a protective one for the dead."[55]

The churches and martyr shrines, however, were alive with worship, including women's voices singing psalms. Funerals honored the dead by comforting the living with psalms sung by women and men. Women were seen and heard, as Egeria's account confirms. In Thecla's shrine in Seleucia of Isauria, for example, Egeria hears Thecla's story read in much the same way she has heard the biblical text recited at the appropriate geographical site in Egypt and Palestine (*It. Eg.* 23). She experiences this shrine in the company of monks and virgins who live in the many monastic cells in the vicinity. St. Thecla's story and her shrine create a community of stopover pilgrims and permanent monastic residents. Egeria observed much the same thing in Jerusalem, a city brimming with pilgrims visiting sites and monastics remaining within their

52. Jerome, *Ep.* 107. Laeta was the daughter-in-law of Paula, Jerome's patron. The younger Paula is sent by her mother to Bethlehem to be raised by her grandmother and aunt, Eustochium, one of Paula's four daughters. Eventually the younger Paula will serve as head of the nunnery established by her grandmother and namesake.

53. Gregory of Nazianzus, *Or.* 8.14 (*Memorial Panegyric on His Sister Gorgonia* [*In laudem sororis suae Gorgoniae*]).

54. For example, Jerome, *Dialogues against the Pelagians* (*Adversus Pelagianos dialogi*) 1.25. See also Cyril of Jerusalem (315–86), *Procatechesis* 14, who suggests that while women can read and sing and pray in church, they must do so with such a soft voice that no one can hear them.

55. Rollins, "Singing of Women," 54. John Chrysostom admires those who sing psalms at funerals (*On the Holy Bernice and Prosdoce* [*De sanctis Bernice et Prosdoce*] 3) but abhors the practice of employing pagan professional female singers (*Homilies on Matthew* [*Homiliae in Matthaeum*] 31.3; *Homilies on the Epistle to the Hebrews* [*Homiliae in epistulam ad Hebraeos*] 4.5).

walls while praying for those pilgrims and meditating on the biblical sites, literally so near and dear to them. Egeria's itinerary has a soundtrack, if you will, that includes women's singing in these gatherings.

### Journey to Constantinople: "It was a very beautiful shrine" (It. Eg. 23)

In chapter 17, Egeria informs her readers that she is ready to return to her homeland, after being away for three years. Scholars are not agreed as to where her homeland may be, but the majority suggest Spain, with some arguing for Gaul.[56] In any case, this Christian from the West decides to return home, through Constantinople. Before heading north, however, she journeys further east, to Mesopotamia, to the great city of Edessa, and to the shrine of St. Thomas, for as she explains, "There is no Christian who has come as far as the holy places of Jerusalem who does not go to Edessa to pray" (It. Eg. 17).[57] This is a twenty-five-day journey, and she visits churches and martyr shrines along the way, as is her custom.

Egeria returns to Antioch in Syria, and after a week spent resupplying her party, she begins her journey north. Her immediate goal is the shrine of St. Thecla, which is located a three-day journey from Tarsus. At the beginning of her three-year pilgrimage, she had passed through Tarsus on her way to Jerusalem from Constantinople but at that time had not visited Thecla's shrine. Gaining the nearby city of Seleucia, Egeria decides to stay overnight at the church and shrine just beyond the city walls. Here the reunion with a dear friend, Marthana, takes place.[58] This woman oversees the virgins who live in the monastic community at this site. The church contains the shrine of St. Thecla and is encircled by a large wall built as a defense against the locals who frequently rob and seek to deface the monastery. Egeria enters the shrine, a prayer is given, and the entire text of the Acts of Paul and Thecla is read. It may be that Egeria carried a copy of this text with her, or a copy of biblical texts, on her journeys. Forty-seven "miniature codices" containing Christian material that might have been used on pilgrimages have been discovered.[59]

Having satisfied this great desire, she travels directly to Constantinople, making few stops along the way. She concludes the travel section by indicating that she hopes to travel to Ephesus, to offer prayers at the shrine of the

56. Hagith Sivan, "Holy Land Pilgrimage and Western Audiences: Some Reflections on Egeria and Her Circle," ClQ 38 (1988): 534, argues for Gaul.
57. Gingras, Egeria, 76; Egeria, It. Eg. 17.
58. Egeria, It. Eg. 23.
59. Georgia Frank, "Pilgrimage," 833. See Egeria, It. Eg. 23.

apostle John, and then continue westward toward her companions who are the recipients of this itinerary.

## Who Is Egeria?

Several basic questions emerge from Egeria's writing in relation to her background. When did she make her journey? Was she a member of a religious order, and was she a nun? What was her social status, and was she wealthy? What level of education did she have? Solutions to these puzzles provide a clearer image of the enigmatic Egeria.

### When Did Egeria Make Her Pilgrimage?

In answer to the first question, we know that she had to have written after 363, because that was the year when the Sassanian rulers took over Nisibis, thus preventing Egeria from traveling further East (*It. Eg.* 20). And we know she had to have completed her journeys before 540 because that was the year when the Persians conquered and crushed Antioch, the city wherein Egeria spent a week (22). Additionally, she speaks of visiting Ephesus but does not mention the council that happened in that city in 431, and one might expect her to mention that event if it had happened while she was in the city.[60] If we narrow it further, some say she traveled between 381 and 384, arguing from her description of Easter liturgies and timing of other events.[61] Others postulate that her pilgrimage cannot be earlier than 393–96 because in her text she cites Jerome's Latin translation of the *Onomasticon* verbatim, and this was published in 390.[62] Also, we know relics were installed on August 22, 394, at the Basilica of St. Thomas the Apostle in Edessa, and if she implies that she saw them in that location, then we have another firm date from which to judge when she traveled (*It. Eg.* 19). A third option pushes the date ahead to sometime between 404 and 417. Egeria knows the apocryphal correspondence between King Abgar of Edessa and Jesus Christ, and this document, originally

---

60. Gingras, *Egeria*, 15, argues for a date between 404 and 417.

61. Rachel Moriarty, "'Secular Men and Women': Egeria's Lay Congregation in Jerusalem," in *The Holy Land, Holy Lands, and Christian History*, ed. R. N. Swanson, SCH 36 (Rochester, NY: Boydell, 2000), 56. See also Susanna Elm, "Perceptions of Jerusalem Pilgrimage as Reflected in Two Early Sources on Female Pilgrimage (3rd and 4th Centuries A.D.)," in *Critica, Classica, Orientalia, Ascetica, Liturgica: Papers Presented to the Tenth International Conference on Patristic Studies Held in Oxford, 1987*, ed. Elizabeth A. Livingstone, StPatr 20 (Leuven: Peeters, 1989), 219.

62. Eusebius wrote this work about 295–330, a list of proper names of biblical places, in Greek and cross-listed with the new Byzantine names.

written in Syriac, was translated into Greek by Eusebius in his multivolume *Ecclesiastical History* (324), which was then translated into Latin by Rufinus of Aquileia in 403.

### Was Egeria a Member of a Religious Order?

To the question of whether Egeria was in a religious order, some point to her extensive interest in church liturgy as an indication that she is a nun, a member of a religious order, perhaps even an abbess.[63] The monk Valerius speaks of her as *beatissima sanctimonialis uirgo* (most excellent, pious virgin). Again, she has numerous conversations with monks and holy men and is a great friend of Marthana, a deaconess and religious superior at the shrine of St. Thecla. Gingras concludes, "The internal evidence tends to support the affirmation of Valerius that our author was a nun."[64] However, most scholars today agree that she is not a member of a religious order. Reasons for this position include the length of time that she is away from her home. We have no indication that a religious order would permit a member to be gone so long on pilgrimage. Second, Egeria does not embrace an ascetic lifestyle of the sort promoted by Jerome, for example, and expected by the religious orders. Although her travels are arduous, she does not speak of making the journey to mortify her flesh, nor does she embrace hardships such as sleeping in rough accommodations or restricting her diet. Wilson-Kastner notes that "devout ecclesial women of this period did not all follow monastic/ascetic lifestyles."[65] Perhaps a better model for Egeria's situation would be that followed by Macrina or Marcella, whom we will meet in the next two chapters of this book, respectively. The former was Gregory of Nyssa's sister; the latter a friend of Jerome. These women lived on their estates but included monastic practices as part of their daily routine. It may be that Egeria was a member of this sort of social class. Egeria's experiences indicate that laywomen could participate extensively in the daily liturgical life of the church.

### Was Egeria Wealthy?

By all accounts Egeria was a wealthy woman and probably also of high social class. Patricia Wilson-Kastner highlights the length of Egeria's journey—three years—as evidence of disposable income and unlimited time. Both qualities are the possession of the wealthy. Other clues in the text point to

---

63. Gingras, *Egeria*, 8–10.
64. Ibid., 8.
65. Wilson-Kastner, *Lost Tradition*, 76. See also Moriarty, "'Secular Men and Women,'" 60.

her high social status. Hagith Sivan suggests that she is a member of the "urban bourgeoisie," based on what appears to be a series of contacts woven throughout her *Itinerary*. These function "like a commercial network," and Sivan concludes, "Egeria serves as an example of the intensity of urban Christianity as well as of the spread of aristocratic fashions to other classes of society in late antiquity."[66] Other scholars have not picked up Sivan's specific claims regarding Egeria's bourgeois background, but most agree that the text points to Egeria's high status. For example, bishops greet Egeria at almost every site, and even more, Egeria assumes this as natural. Wilson-Kastner points out a parallel between Egeria and Paula, Jerome's patron, in that both women enjoy, as their due, a warm reception from leading clerics in each town they visit.[67] Again, Roman soldiers escort Egeria in part of her journey from Mount Sinai to Egypt, and she is nonchalant about this protocol. Finally, Egeria expresses a desire to travel into Persian territory but is unable to do so, most likely because of her high status within the Roman elite: "The fact that Egeria is blocked from crossing the border makes sense only if she had a higher degree of association with Roman officials than the average pilgrim."[68]

### Was Egeria Educated?

With such wealth and high social status, one assumes that Egeria would be a well-educated woman, and Rachel Moriarty remarks that "this lay woman's account is confident, responsible and equal, and shows no sense of inferiority."[69] Nevertheless, the Latin text lacks the erudition one might expect in an elite Roman woman. Sivan argues that Egeria's education was not up to the quality evidenced by other elite women of her day. Additionally, Egeria shows a "complete ignorance of paganism, literature, and religious practices alike."[70] Yet Egeria knows the Bible very well and makes discerning remarks about the biblical text related to the geography. This puzzle has been addressed with several intriguing arguments, including one that focuses on a possible liturgical backdrop, and another that postulates an oral framework to the text.

Advocating a liturgical tone sounding across the chapters, Leo Spitzer perceives a purpose behind Egeria's numerous vocabulary repetitions: "Such

66. Hagith Sivan, "Who Was Egeria? Piety and Pilgrimage in the Age of Gratian," *HTR* 81 (1988): 72.

67. Wilson-Kastner, *Lost Tradition*, 73.

68. Crystal Dean, "Roman Women Authors: Authorship, Agency and Authority" (PhD diss., University of Calgary, 2012), 158.

69. Moriarty, "'Secular Men and Women,'" 62.

70. Sivan, "Who Was Egeria?," 65.

repetitions as *hic est locus* or *ostenderunt* give the impression of a litany whose aesthetic principle is that of settling on specific words regardless of the monotony thereby engendered, the prolongation of a pious mood being more important than the (also natural) human tendency toward variation."[71] Not only does Egeria's writing style reveal her pious purposes, but also Egeria's Latin reflects her belief "in the significance, inner consistency, and preordained direction of the action, which [she] would have linger in the mind of the reader."[72] Spitzer addresses the perception that Egeria's text lacks a logical flow by arguing that she attends to the dignity of the speaker as more important than a logical description of a site. For example, in a discussion concerning a sycamore tree planted by the patriarchs, Egeria notes twice that the nearby field is the place of the ancient city of Ramesses.[73] The second mention contains the added information given by the bishop—namely, that Pharaoh burned down the city. "She must group the information in an ascending order from anonymous report . . . to the authoritative explanations of the learned bishop—but in doing so she inevitably becomes repetitious."[74] Spitzer concludes that Egeria's text promotes an idealized pilgrimage, and her own authorial voice is a "representative I."[75] This decision allows Egeria to privilege the journey itself and invite each reader/listener to experience it, rather than to present the traveling as her own unique religious experience.

Crystal Dean makes a different argument—namely, that Egeria focuses on her personal perceptions as part of presenting a conventional female public voice. Dean suggests that expressing the personal in public was an acceptable avenue for women, dating back to late first century BCE and Augustus's propaganda program that legitimated imperial rule by embracing codes of private piety.[76] Addressing the relative inferiority of Egeria's Latin, Dean argues that perhaps Egeria *spoke* rather than *wrote* the Latin text.[77] Dean wonders if perhaps Egeria used a scribe who copied her oral presentations and took notes during her conversations with the bishops. As a possible parallel, many of Jerome's sermons were recorded by *notarii*, scribes using

---

71. Leo Spitzer, "The Epic Style of the Pilgrim Aetheria," *Comparative Literature* 1 (1949): 241.

72. Ibid., 234.

73. Egeria, *It. Eg.* 8.

74. Spitzer, "Epic Style," 237.

75. Ibid., 250.

76. See Suetonius, *The Divine Augustus (Divus Augustus)* 73. Dean, "Roman Women Authors," 229, draws on Kristina Milnor's "paradigm for Augustan propaganda" in *Gender, Domesticity, and the Age of Augustus: Inventing Private Life* (Oxford: Oxford University Press, 2005).

77. Dean, "Roman Women Authors," 161. She adds that the work "is suggestive of both oral dictation and scribal note-taking. . . . The text that survives is a record of Egeria's words, but perhaps should not necessarily be viewed as a finished literary text" (167).

shorthand to record an oral presentation.[78] The difference between Egeria's work and Jerome's is that the latter corrected or revised many of these sermons, resulting in a much more polished written document. Interestingly, Jerome's unedited sermons share several characteristics with Egeria's work, including repetition, simple vocabulary, and unsophisticated sentence structure.[79] The poor Latin of Egeria's text, then, is typical of her period's oral presentations.

Dean's picture of Egeria as representative of elite Roman women in terms of their access to education and their public conversations is convincing. Spitzer arrives at a similar portrait, albeit from a different angle. He persuasively concludes that not only is Egeria from a high social rank, but she also reveals "a personality poised in the consciousness that religion entails form and gives form to the person of the believer."[80] Spitzer's point is well taken: Egeria's style of repetition reflects her religious sensibilities as she relies on a sense of liturgical organization to ground and shape her presentation of the pilgrimage. This observation deserves a closer look so as to discover the similarities and differences between Egeria's experiences and other pilgrims' journeys, as well as between her pilgrimage and the wider conversation about the enterprise of pilgrimage. Moreover, Spitzer rightly asks questions about the genre of pilgrimage, for to grasp fully the person of Egeria, we must ask how she understood her task in composing her *Itinerary*. Thus after examining the genre, we will broaden the discussion to include writings in various genres concerning the topic of pilgrimage.

## Genre of the *Itinerary*

Egeria's work broke new ground; as Dean describes it, "Egeria is detailing a spiritual geography, a literary genre that was new."[81] Yet Dean observes that Egeria relied as well on precedents. The descriptions of topography, roads, water sources, town size, and the distance between sites were part of an established Roman political/military genre known as *itinerarium*. Given her comments about military forts and water sources, it is most likely that ancient readers would grasp the official, public tone that Egeria sets.[82] Men and women wrote of their political activities, although scholars often read

78. Ibid., 163.

79. Ibid., 164, drawing on work by A. S. Pease, "Notes on Jerome's Tractates on the Psalms," *JBL* 26 (1907): 107–31.

80. Spitzer, "Epic Style," 249.

81. Dean, "Roman Women Authors," 108.

82. Ibid., 106.

ancient women's records as merely personal reflections on private matters.[83] In a similar vein, we should view Egeria's observations with an awareness of the political and military nuances present in the text: "As a pilgrim, Egeria possessed both the agency and the legitimacy to serve as a collector of information, and her text gives many suggestions that she did precisely this."[84]

Because Egeria mentions the recipients of her text as "sisters" who will benefit from this writing, some scholars speak of this work's genre as a letter. Such a designation seems inadequate since the label "letter" is often associated with interpreting this work as merely an emotional, private, and unreflective missive.[85] If one insists on calling this work a letter, then one must also allow that the work is far longer—over forty chapters—than any general picture of letter we hold today. Moreover, Egeria's personal reflection is not to be understood as a unique or personalized perspective but rather a representative experience, a "didactic I," into which any reader might enter and learn.[86] By insisting that Egeria writes as a representative of every Christian, one gives her pilgrimage account the theological and catechetical respect bestowed by Valerius and likely other readers. Such an approach does not lessen the impact deriving from our text's having been written by a woman, but rather takes account of her genre choice, which is one used by men and women alike.

## Conclusion

Egeria's "sisters" back home read Scripture with her and shared her interest in liturgy and the geography of the Holy Lands. This suggests that at least some women in the third and fourth centuries had a deep knowledge of biblical stories and studied the Bible as a group regularly. While Christians inherited the practice of women studying together from the customs of elite Roman

---

83. Ibid., 25. Dean points to bias in modern scholars' accounts of Agrippina the Younger's *Commentaries* (*Commentarii*) as they minimize her notes as a "diary"—that is, personal and private thoughts. If Nero, her son, had written the work, Dean postulates that scholars would readily admit that it contains notes of political activities. See also Tacitus, *Ann.* 4.53, who explains that Agrippina spoke with politically charged rhetoric and that her notes or memoranda (*Commentarii*) were left for posterity to understand the tribulations and calamities of her family. *Commentarii*, or notes of political officials, were intended for public consumption. The style presented the information as unformed, available for a historian such as Tacitus to shape into a history.

84. Dean, "Roman Women Authors," 227.

85. Limor ("Reading Sacred Space," 3) writes, "Egeria wrote her letter for certain specific women readers and for no one else."

86. Spitzer, "Epic Style," 249–51.

women in the Late Republic and early imperial periods, such specialized study of the Bible might have grown from the church's catechetical instruction. If so, it is possible that the group had a varied social makeup, with slaves and owners, wealthy and poor, studying together. We saw such a group in chapter 2, as Perpetua and Felicitas were trained in the faith through the same catechetical process.[87] In Egeria's era, elite women such as Paula and Marcella, whom we will meet in chapter 8, participate in study circles around a leading theologian such as Jerome. In these latter cases, as well as with Egeria, the groups apparently included only women, most likely with enough education to read the Bible.[88]

Beyond the explicit audience mentioned in the text, we have evidence from Valerius's letter that he found her text instructive and useful for his fellow monks. He transposed the text's key to reflect his own interest in the spiritual journey of the soul, which he read into Egeria's literal discussion of physical spaces. From this evidence, then, we should not assume that Egeria's pilgrimage was of interest only to women. Given the evidence of women's visible presence in the public square and conversation, we think it safe to assume that Egeria imagined a broader audience than simply her immediate circle back home. Others viewed Egeria's expression of her Christian faith as a model for their own behavior, and in this sense her life resembles those of the other women we examined closely in the previous chapters. Thecla, Perpetua, Felicitas, Helena—these women's stories captured the imagination of generations, exerting influence beyond the pages of their texts.[89]

Egeria linked Scripture's text and context and explained the geography as it supported the biblical stories. She constructed a Holy Land that conformed to the church's growing religious and political hegemony in this region. Some scholars have dismissed her work as emotional or simplistic, as letters of merely personal interest to female friends back home.[90] Yet our review of her *Itinerary* indicates another picture. Egeria's text reveals a wealthy, educated woman whose work broke new ground in developing a genre of Christian pilgrimage texts that would influence writings into the medieval period and beyond. Yet Egeria offers more than a new genre; she reminds us that women's voices were heard in church singing and reading Scripture at

87. Dean, "Roman Women Authors," 169–70.

88. Ibid., 173–74, rightly notes that Montanist, gnostic, and other groups labeled "heretical" also included women's study circles and, at times, women instructors for these groups.

89. The questions concerning the historical woman behind the text, if there is one, did not animate ancient conversation; they are modern interests.

90. Some scholars have responded similarly to Eudocia's *Cento*, discussed in chap. 9, suggesting that her work is lowbrow Homeric literature and a novelty of female expression but certainly not to be taken seriously in any kind of literary or theological sense.

Figure 6.4. The Monastery of St. Catherine is a UNESCO World Heritage site. It was founded in the sixth century CE and is the oldest continuously inhabited Christian monastery.

holy sites, women's bodies were present at shrines and religious processions, and women engaged with men in theological discussions. Women were part of the making of the early church.

The extant copy of Egeria's *Itinerary* picks up her story as she approaches Mount Sinai. She meets the monks who live at the foot of the mountain, and some of their number take her to the summit, show her the sites, and present her with gifts. Less than one hundred years earlier, Constantine's mother, Helena, built a church at the traditional site of the burning bush (Exod. 3). The monastery at the church was built by Emperor Justinian around 557, making St. Catherine's the oldest continuously inhabited monastery in the world. St. Catherine's monks continued their work beyond the reaches of the modern world, until in 1844 Constantin von Tischendorf discovered Codex Sinaiticus there. This Bible, written in the mid-fourth century, is a good six hundred years earlier than any extant copy of the Bible available in his day. We can think about the date in another way: this Bible was being copied at about the time of Egeria's visit.

Von Tischendorf's discovery excited many in England, including the twins Agnes Smith Lewis and Catherine Dunlop Gibson, both widowed. In January 1892, they made their way from Cairo to the Sinai. Agnes and Catherine traveled in much the same way as did Egeria. The path to the mountain had changed little in the intervening centuries, for the harsh landscape offers few options. Indeed, the women were aware of Egeria's story since the *Itinerary* had been discovered in 1884. Once at the monastery, Agnes discovered a vellum text (made from animal skin) on which a second text was written over the first text; this is known as a palimpsest. In this case, the second text was written in 697 and contained stories of women saints, including St. Thecla, as well as Eugenia, St. Irene, and St. Barbara, plus the repentant prostitute Pelagia of Antioch.[91] The first text was a Syriac copy of the Gospels (ca. 497). Agnes and Margaret made a second trip to St. Catherine's in the company of Rendel Harris, Francis Burkitt, and Robert Bensly, leading scholars in the field of biblical studies and ancient languages. They examined this palimpsest and made a transcription that was finally published in 1894, *The Four Gospels in the Old Syriac Version Transcribed from the Palimpsest on Mount Sinai*. Agnes wrote the introduction, where she made clear that this manuscript was her discovery, declaring that it "was found by me in the Convent of St. Catherine in Mount Sinai, in the month of February, 1892."[92]

Egeria would have been right at home with these sisters, sharing their interest in the Bible and their boundless curiosity. They also shared similar political histories, because their own people (Roman and British, respectively) led an empire. It was an ancient Syriac palimpsest that propelled the sisters into their life of elevated scholarship. In a perceptive comment, Julie Ann Smith observes that pilgrims, including Egeria, "used a *palimpsest* map upon which pagans, Jews, and Christians had already charted and occupied places—a spiritual cartography [overlaying] the physical realities of existing towns, roads, and natural landscape with Christian markers."[93] The palimpsest is a useful metaphor in connecting these three women.[94] Egeria built her story upon an existing "text," biblical and physical, creating a mental map on top of an existing map and its cultures and people. Agnes and Margaret too were accessing a palimpsest of sorts, as the sisters' text reflects layers of history and Christian landscaping stretching back to Egeria's day.[95]

---

91. Janet Soskice, *The Sisters of Sinai: How Two Lady Adventurers Discovered the Hidden Gospels* (New York: Knopf, 2009), 160.

92. Ibid., 196.

93. Smith, "'My Lord's Native Land,'" 2, emphasis added. She cites a similar use of the image in Jonathan Z. Smith, *To Take Place: Toward Theory in Ritual*, CSHJ (Chicago: University of Chicago Press, 1987), 79.

94. For further discussion, see Haines-Eitzen, *Gendered Palimpsest*.

95. Smith, "'My Lord's Native Land,'" 5, observes that "'landscape' is culturally constructed; it exists through human signification."

# 7

# Macrina the Ascetic Entrepreneur and the "Unlearned" Wisdom of Monica

## Introduction

In this chapter we will look at two women who helped to shape the tradition of the church in the mid-fourth through the early fifth centuries. The first is Macrina, foundress of a monastic community, sister and teacher of bishops, surrogate father, emancipator of slaves, and philosopher who lived her whole life in a small area of Cappadocia in the Greek East. And the second is Monica, devoted woman of prayer, activist for orthodoxy, keen philosophical dialogue partner, and mother who followed her son from Roman North Africa to Italy in the Latin West. Both of these women are known mostly in reference to the famous men in their respective families: Macrina was the sister of two of the most famous architects of Nicene orthodoxy, Basil of Caesarea and Gregory of Nyssa, and Monica was Augustine of Hippo's mother. It was clearly the desire, however, of both Macrina's brother Gregory and Augustine that these women not be, as Gregory puts it, "passed by ineffectually, veiled in silence."[1]

1. Gregory of Nyssa, *Vit. Macr.* 1.5, in *Macrina the Younger* (Silvas, 110).

Gregory wrote his *Life of Macrina* (*Vita s. Macrinae*) soon after her death, and this work shapes her life into a devotional package of sorts for those who would read about her and follow her path. While it is clear that Gregory had a strong connection with his sister, his remembrance of Macrina leans upon their relationship just enough to establish Gregory's suitability for sharing her story. Gregory not only pays beautiful and moving tribute to his sister in *Life of Macrina*; he also casts Macrina in the role of Socrates in a philosophical dialogue with him as her student in *On the Soul and the Resurrection* (*De anima et resurrectione cum sorore sua Macrina dialogus*). Augustine, too, made sure that his mother would be remembered: "But I will not pass over anything that my soul brings forth concerning that servant of yours who brought me forth from her flesh to birth in this temporal light, and from her heart to birth in light eternal."[2] Two of his earliest works (*On the Happy Life* and *On Order*) feature Monica as a wise participant in philosophical discussions because of her stalwart faith, and in his famous *Confessions*, Augustine recognizes Monica's as the voice speaking on behalf of God throughout his troubled youth. It was through their relationship with each other that each came to new understandings of God. Thus Augustine's remembrance of his mother threads throughout his retrospective of his journey back to God in such a way that it would be unthinkable to unlink mother and son. Monica's story is Augustine's story, and vice versa.

Before getting to know Macrina and Monica better, we need to discuss two facets of reading early Christian texts about women. First, while we have talked some about the virginal or ascetic life, it is one of the early Christian ways of life that is generally most foreign to modern readers. Thus it is a good idea to visit the lifelong commitment of Christian renunciation in a little more detail here. Second, since most of the texts about women from Late Antiquity are written by men (with some notable exceptions), it is important to consider what kind of access we have to women like Macrina and Monica, who did not write for themselves but were written about by male authors. This situation raises many questions about whether we are reading about the "real" Macrina and Monica or whether the texts actually serve to obscure these women and their contributions further.

### Like a Virgin: The Blossoming of Christian Asceticism

One of the areas where the Christian ethic had a drastic effect on Roman society was the insistence that lifelong virginity was a valid third category in

2. Augustine, *Conf.* 9.8.17 (Boulding, 222).

addition to the two firmly established Roman categories of married and not yet married. Considering that Roman marriage,
especially that of the aristocracy,
was how power was allotted and
shifted, the idea that a son or a
daughter would not participate
in that structure at all was incon-
ceivable. No sex meant no marriage, and no marriage meant the
uncertain future of fortunes. That
the Christian tradition embraced
not only the renunciation of sex
but also the renunciation of the
social contract of marriage was a
bold move, prioritizing devotion to
God over duty to societal and familial obligations. While men also
renounced sex, it was the more numerous female virgins who became
fixtures of holiness and devotion in
their communities, churches, and
theological and ethical writings.

Michael Bruner

Figure 7.1. At the Museo dell'Opera del
Duomo in Florence, Italy, the placement of the
*Penitent Magdalene* by Donatello in front of
a crucifix attributed to Giovanni di Balduccio
(ca. 1330) is strategic. It illustrates the ascetic
life as fundamentally that of *imitatio Christi*.

The virginal life, though, was not only about renouncing sex and marriage;
it was an understood reality in Greco-Roman society that asceticism—living
a life defined by devotion expressed by renunciation—was necessary for those
who pursued the philosophical life. Therefore, Christians were not the only
ones who understood the renunciation of sex to be somehow special; in fact,
both pagans and Jews in antiquity believed that the virginal state "made the
human body a more appropriate vehicle to receive divine inspiration."[3] Indeed, sexual renunciation was only one aspect of the ascetic life. It was ideal
for the philosophical pursuit for one not to be mastered by anything—sex,
food, one's emotions, and so forth. Asceticism—from the Greek *askēsis*—is
a life ordered for a purpose. The ordered life of asceticism was only possible
if one's internal life was fueling the ordering of the external life. It was not
lost on those who renounced sex and committed to rigorous sleeping and

3. Brown, *Body and Society*, 67.

eating regimens that it was necessary to foster a vibrant inner life. Otherwise it was mere legalism.

The aim of philosophical and Christian asceticism in particular was to bridle one's wild and disordered desires and passions for the sake of cultivating the life of virtue. For Christian women who chose lives of renunciation, their experiences were not monochromatic. Many took vows of extreme poverty and retreated from the world to the desert, others remained at home, and still others helped establish monasteries and took care of the poor. Many of these "holy women" did not totally break from civilization; they were separated from society and yet held an exalted place within it.[4] Women who had only the narrowest of social options in antiquity found themselves presented, by means of virginity, with a new option in Christianity: the ability to choose a life of devotion to Christ.

### Can You Hear Her Now? The Woman's Voice in Patristic Literature

During the patristic period, female voices are largely represented by men writing about women or "quoting" women.[5] This situation brings up the obvious question of whether the women we think we know are in fact represented well. The lives of Macrina and Monica, among others, demonstrate that women were active in their devotion to God during the fourth and fifth centuries. The men who wrote about them were interested not only in giving their accounts of the lives of these exemplary women; they also seemed to "use" them to instruct others or even to expound on their own theological ideas. The reality of the women's lives is indiscriminately mixed together with the theological meanderings of the authors and glowing reports of devotion that served as examples for other religious women (and men). Thus we hear Macrina's voice in Gregory's theologically attuned writings and instructions on the monastic and ascetic ideal.

Are we able to discern the voice of Macrina as distinct from the theological and didactic agendas of her brother? Indeed, Macrina's life, as reported by Gregory, was probably idealized, thereby making it difficult to determine what details are accurate.[6] Certainly the account of Macrina passed down through the centuries includes events to which her brother adds his reflection or whose gaps he has filled in, even though he claims that his narrative is "unstudied and

---

4. Elizabeth A. Clark, "Holy Women, Holy Words: Early Christian Women, Social History, and the 'Linguistic Turn,'" *JECS* 6 (1998): 417.

5. Susan Ashbrook Harvey, "Women and Word: Texts by and about Women," in *The Cambridge History of Early Christian Literature*, ed. Frances Young, Lewis Ayres, and Andrew Louth (Cambridge: Cambridge University Press, 2004), 382.

6. E. Clark, "Holy Women, Holy Words," 416.

simple."[7] At points Gregory includes what might be Macrina's own words, but mostly her voice is translated through her brother's memories and desire to promote his interpretation of her life.

Whether the "real Macrina" (or the real Monica) is discernable in the text is a valid question. Elizabeth A. Clark and Averil Cameron recognize a larger pattern in how the lives of saints, ascetics, martyrs, and bishops make theological subjects more accessible. According to Cameron, second-century accounts of the martyrs and subsequently other ascetics later in antiquity became "the enactment and the symbol of Christian perfection."[8] Early Christian writers were concerned with reaching the uneducated in their preaching, unpacking the nature of Christian knowledge, and exploring how Christian truth can be put into words in the first place.[9] The reality of working with historical texts of any kind, and especially those far distant culturally and chronologically, is that there is no way to access a historical personage in the way we would like. Even with the most thorough of authors, there are always going to be gaps that cannot be filled. According to Clark, these holy men and women still have "lives," but they are forever indiscriminately entangled with "literary interpretation."[10]

Premodern texts and male authorship can be viewed as confines under which holy women are obscured, or, instead, they can be seen as a limited preservation of these women. Of course, it depends on the author's degree of relationship to the woman in the first place as well as his reasons for writing; there is a great deal of variety in the motivations, access, and attitudes of these men. Thus it is important for us not to assume that male authorship means a lack of connection to or exploitation of the women in the texts. For example, Gregory's motivation was likely not to do his sister a disservice by infusing her story and person with his theological ideas. The same would be true of Augustine and many of the other authors. To imply that male biographers used these women merely as mouthpieces imposes a motivation upon the text that is illusory at best. However close Gregory's portrait is to the "real" Macrina, the Macrina of Gregory's remembrance, practically and literarily speaking, is the Macrina we know.[11] She is the

7. Gregory, *Vit. Macr.* 1.5 (Silvas, 111).

8. Averil Cameron, *Christianity and the Rhetoric of Empire: The Development of Christian Discourse*, Sather Classical Lectures 55 (Berkeley: University of California Press, 1991), 51.

9. Ibid., 5.

10. Elizabeth A. Clark, *History, Theory, Text: Historians and the Linguistic Turn* (Cambridge, MA: Harvard University Press, 2004), 181.

11. Francine Cardman observes that in the *Life of Macrina* in particular, the text both distances us from and draws us closer to Macrina; this helps us consider how we might read other texts about early Christian women. See her essay "Whose Life Is It? The *Vita Macrinae*

Macrina whom Gregory wanted to introduce to the world, and she is the Macrina whose legacy has shaped, in no small measure, the ascetic tradition in the East.

Without a doubt, we can know that these women were promoted as examples for others. Authors in antiquity held certain values, like asceticism or orthodox doctrine, that they wished to promote as central to the Christian life. With this background, reading Gregory's memories of his sister or Augustine's remembrance of his mother serves both to illuminate the larger patristic situation by specific examples and to contextualize those examples, thereby decreasing the distance between antiquity and those who study it. Although the texts written by men that feature women tend to follow established literary patterns (e.g., the blatant similarity between Macrina's death and the death of Socrates) and thematically promote chastity, austerity, and wisdom, each woman is unique. Macrina rarely strayed from home, but her faithfulness in that small, albeit important, sphere directly influenced some of the greatest minds of antiquity. Monica, on the other hand, followed Augustine around North Africa and Italy, patiently shepherding him in his search for truth. Stories of women like Macrina and Monica gave others (men *and* women) examples to follow and choices that might not have been available or known to them otherwise.

## Macrina (ca. 327–79)

### Thecla's Namesake and Heir

Gregory of Nyssa wrote two major works that feature his sister: the *Life of Macrina*, a biographical letter of sorts in which he remembers his sister's life, and *On the Soul and the Resurrection*, a Platonic-style dialogue between himself and Macrina on her deathbed.[12] Gregory's portrait offers a wealth of recounted moments of Macrina reconstituting her way of life and orchestrating the same shift for others. Macrina was from no ordinary family. Born to established and wealthy parents in Cappadocia (central Turkey) around 327 as the oldest of ten children, she knew Christianity as her

---

of Gregory of Nyssa," in *Cappadocian Writers, Other Greek Writers: Papers Presented at the Thirteenth International Conference on Patristic Studies Held in Oxford, 1999*, ed. M. F. Wiles and E. J. Yarnold, StPatr 37 (Leuven: Peeters, 2001), 33–50, esp. 34.

12. For a brief introduction to Gregory of Nyssa (331/40–ca. 395), see David L. Balás, "Gregory of Nyssa," in *Encyclopedia of Early Christianity*, ed. Everett Ferguson et al., Garland Reference Library of the Humanities 1839 (New York: Garland, 1997), 495–97; and G. Röwekamp's article "Gregory of Nyssa," in *Dictionary of Early Christian Literature*, ed. Siegmar Döpp and Wilhelm Geerlings (New York: Crossroad, 2000), 263–66.

heritage, and her family had suffered for it in the Great Persecution under Diocletian.[13] When her father died, Macrina's mother, Emmelia, moved the whole family north to their estate at Annisa in Pontus. There we see Macrina overturn the established hierarchical structure, change the functional rhythm, and fundamentally alter the raison d'être of the family estate. In both the *Life of Macrina* and *On the Soul and the Resurrection*, Gregory portrays himself (and his brothers) as beholden to his sister's guidance in matters both personal and philosophical. The biographical letter and the dialogue illustrate his interest in emulating Macrina and humbly offering himself as witness to her legacy.

Written after her death, sometime between 380 and 383, Gregory's *Life of Macrina* introduces us not only to a strong and devout woman but also to a life lived with her brothers who became bishops: Gregory of Nyssa, Basil of Caesarea, and Peter of Sebaste. Gregory, Basil, and Basil's best friend from his schooling in Athens, Gregory of Nazianzus, were the primary architects of the Council of Constantinople in 381. Macrina also had a fourth brother, Naucratius, who, along with Basil, followed in their father's footsteps and received formal rhetorical training. Just as his career was beginning, Naucratius left to embrace a remote life of prayer and poverty. After his sudden death in a hunting accident, the youngest son, Peter, forwent any rhetorical training and was educated at home by Macrina, who had assumed a great amount of responsibility for her family after her father's death. She became the spiritual mentor of the household, educating, comforting, and developing a devoted community. What was it like to live with such brothers? As Gregory of Nyssa informs us, she was their father, mother, teacher, adviser, and guardian, among many other things. The question, then, could be put another way: What was it like to live with such a sister?

From before her birth, Macrina is definitively connected to Thecla. While in labor, Macrina's mother, Emmelia, had a vision of a figure approaching her while she was holding her child after birth; this person addressed the child as "Thecla" three times. Gregory identifies this figure as the same Thecla "whose fame is so great among the virgins." Gregory notes that the figure in Emmelia's dream did not present the name Thecla as a name choice but as a statement of fact. It struck him as having a prophetic ring to it, aligning Macrina and Thecla in life choice and making Macrina a direct recipient of

13. Macrina's paternal grandparents were both confessors, and her maternal grandfather was martyred. Her namesake, Macrina the Elder, passed down her example as well as preserving the traditions of the church brought to her by Gregory Thaumaturgus, a third-century bishop of Caesarea and student of the famous Origen of Alexandria (Silvas, *Gregory of Nyssa: The Letters*, 3).

Thecla's mantle as a matter of holy destiny.[14] Macrina, then, is the reflection of Thecla, the one whom Paul entrusted with the continuation of his apostolic ministry in the apocryphal Acts of Paul and Thecla.[15] Although the events of their lives as reported were not parallel, Macrina's life choices were viewed as a spiritual reflection of Thecla. Macrina has much more in common, at least as described by Gregory, with Methodius's Thecla than with the itinerant preacher and protomartyr found in the Acts of Paul and Thecla.

The *Life of Macrina* culminates in a lengthy deathbed scene in which Macrina is praised for her wisdom and profound intelligence. The scene, which is expanded upon in *On the Soul and the Resurrection*, is artfully constructed to be reminiscent of Socrates's death and even to present Macrina as surpassing the worldly philosopher in wisdom. It is an interesting device for Gregory to choose, considering that he claims Macrina to be educated primarily in the Scriptures and not in the "customary secular curriculum."[16] Whatever the extent of her education, the ideal of philosophy is described as core to Macrina's identity and is woven throughout the *Life of Macrina*.

Gregory's insistence on comparing the figures of Socrates and Thecla to Macrina illustrates his own dependence upon Macrina and the magnitude of her influence in the family. More than once Gregory documents that Macrina's words caused him to pause and humbly to receive correction. For example, Gregory was originally a reluctant bishop. When summoned by his brother, Basil of Caesarea, to the bishopric of Nyssa in 370, he went, but under great protest. Seven years later, an Arian faction had successfully accused Gregory of embezzling church funds, resulting in his banishment by the Arian Emperor Valens.[17] After hearing him complain about the situation, Macrina responds:

> Will you not cease your insensibility to the divine blessings? Will you not remedy the thanklessness of your soul? Will you not compare your lot with that of our fathers? . . . Churches send you as an ally and reformer and churches summon you, and you do not see the grace in it? Do you not recognize the cause of such great blessings, that the prayers of your parents are lifting you on high, since you have nothing in you, or very little, to equip you for this?[18]

Gregory responded to the rebuke with great humility. For Gregory, Macrina is the virgin-philosopher, the wise woman who does not shirk responsibility or mince words. Macrina also held sway over her other family members, often

14. Gregory, *Vit. Macr.* 3.1–3 (Silvas, 112).
15. Gregory, *Vit. Macr.* 3.3 (Silvas, 112).
16. Gregory, *Vit. Macr.* 4.2 (Silvas, 113).
17. Gregory, *Vit. Macr.* 23.1 (Silvas, 131).
18. Gregory, *Vit. Macr.* 23.2–4 (Silvas, 131).

stepping up to set an example of virtue and asceticism. Although Basil does not offer any confirmation of this moment or much of any relationship with his sister, Gregory reports that upon returning from his formal education in Athens, Basil was insufferable in his conceit and opinion of his eloquence: "She [Macrina], however, took him in hand and drew him with such speed toward the goal of philosophy that he withdrew from the worldly show and despised the applause to be gained through eloquence, and went over of his own accord to the life where one toils even with one's own hands, this providing for himself through perfect renunciation."[19] Macrina influenced the lives of her siblings and was the glue that kept the family together.

While on a journey home to visit his sister some years later, Gregory was dismayed to hear that Macrina was very ill. The account of Gregory's final moments with Macrina is particularly illuminating as to the depth of her devotion and her influence over her brother. Three times on his journey to her side, Gregory had a vision of himself holding the relics of martyrs, which emanated a bright gleam of light. It was in her final moments by her bedside that Gregory understood his sister to be the subject of his vision: "The sight that had confronted me was truly the remains of a holy martyr, remains which had *died to sin* but which shone with the indwelling grace of the Spirit."[20] In Gregory's narrative, the inclusion of his vision of holding relics gleaming with light indicates that Macrina should be remembered as a virgin martyr, one who, like Thecla, would be a beacon of Christian devotion. Although the actual events of their lives were not parallel, Macrina's life choices were viewed as a spiritual reflection of Thecla, who was also from Asia Minor. Thus, claiming Macrina's legacy was claiming Thecla's as well. In addition to the legacies of Gregory Thaumaturgus and both sets of grandparents, who suffered imperially sanctioned persecution, Macrina's pedigree included a mark of authority, which not only aided in the kind of transition from martyr to ascetic but also established a local reputation: Pontus and Cappadocia could claim Macrina as their ascetic sage.[21]

### Macrina and Materiality: Living Legacy

When Gregory describes the living circumstances of his mother and sister at their estate in Pontus, he directly associates them with the pinnacle of philosophy. It is clear that the household rearrangement and their "regimen"

19. Gregory, *Vit. Macr.* 8.2–3 (Silvas, 117).
20. Gregory, *Vit. Macr.* 21.3 (Silvas, 129). Gregory draws from Rom. 6:11 and 8:10–11.
21. Raymond Van Dam, *Families and Friends in Late Roman Cappadocia* (Philadelphia: University of Pennsylvania Press, 2003), 16–17. See also Van Dam, *Becoming Christian*, 77.

of daily activities (i.e., *askēsis*) was philosophy as it should be—lived and taught.[22] After the tragic death of their brother Naucratius, Gregory points to the shift when, in her grief, the mother/teacher Emmelia became the daughter/student of Macrina, who now trained her mother's soul to be courageous. This shift in authority led to radical life changes in the household, where the matron became the sister of her maids and had everything in common with those who otherwise would not be her equals. Macrina became a matriarch who would lead the other matriarch through her grief over the loss of her son and into the ascetic life. She would lead several other members of the family and household into monastic retreat as well. Within their family, Gregory assigns her an array of titles that demonstrate flexibility of gender and role, describing Macrina as Peter's father, teacher, guardian, mother, and adviser of every good.[23] These roles bled over into her role in the community as one who created and oversaw the space for devotion to Christ and was sought out as an eminent ascetic leader. Macrina was the spiritual mentor of her household and an ascetic entrepreneur who cultivated a devoted community in her Cappadocian locale.

Macrina repurposed family holdings to mark out the physical space to house her exercise of devotion and for others who would do the same. This action would leave a mark on her community. The Cappadocian region was basically the rural expanse everyone traveled through to get somewhere else. There was nothing particularly remarkable about the region other than its natural resources—grain, wood, marble, precious metals, an abundance of livestock for leather, and horses—until the fourth century, when imperial interest in the region rose both because of its role in the transport and outfitting of the imperial armies and because of the ecclesiastical exploits of several locals (Basil of Caesarea, Gregory of Nyssa, and Gregory of Nazianzus, among others).[24] Even then, Cappadocia would struggle to gain a new reputation.[25] Ordinary people did not generally see much return from the natural spoils of the region. While they had the reputation of being a hardy folk, probably due to the harsh, cold environment and prolonged isolation, poverty was the

22. "Such was the order of their life, so lofty their philosophy and the dignity of their way of life as they lived it day and night, that it surpasses description in words" (Gregory, *Vit. Macr.* 13.3 [Silvas, 121]).

23. Gregory, *Vit. Macr.* 14.2–3 (Silvas, 122).

24. Raymond Van Dam, *Kingdom of Snow: Roman Rule and Greek Culture in Cappadocia* (Philadelphia: University of Pennsylvania Press, 2002), 15.

25. Raymond Van Dam writes: "Cappadocia had long been a marginal region in the ancient world, dismissed as unruly and cold, maligned for its cultural backwardness, hardly registering in historical texts, seemingly little affected by the great political and social changes in the Mediterranean world and the Near East" (*Families and Friends*, 2).

norm for most.[26] The same climate that produced so many resources could also be the
source of extreme danger. Macrina's family
learned all too well the unexpected terror
of a river rushing through the countryside
with the sudden and implacable force of a
flood brought on by melting snowfall when
her brother, the skilled hunter and ascetic
Naucratius, was swept to his death. But
those same rivers could also just as easily
become little more than muddy troughs
when the expected rain did not arrive. Its
lack could plunge the agrarian society into
distress from drought and famine.[27]

Macrina's family owned several estates
in Pontus and Cappadocia. This categorized them as local notables with means,
but they were certainly not in the category of
someone like the Constantinopolitan heiress Olympias.[28] One of the clearest indica-
tors of wealth in an agrarian society was
the ability to partake of and store resources
(owning horses, wearing the clothing that
was produced from the abundance of flocks
and herds, storing grain, and so forth). Un-

Figure 7.2. Statue of St. Macrina on
the colonnade of St. Peter's Square
at the Vatican.

fortunately, it was common for notables to hoard this wealth for themselves in
order to build their power and reputations, even at the expense of the majority
of the population. Systemic exploitation was fundamental to how Cappadocian
society worked.[29] Thus, when Macrina gave away her clothing, emancipated
her slaves, became more like one of those who struggled with hunger and
cold, and established a community of ascetic equality, she did something that
ran counter to the status quo of the other landowners. Her actions would not
have gone unnoticed; ascetic communities were not yet common in the empire.

26. Van Dam, *Kingdom of Snow*, 13–16.
27. Ibid., 42–43.
28. Ibid., 22.
29. Ibid., 20. As in other agrarian economies, "local domination and wealth represented
some sort of exploitation, whether overt or disguised. The most important factor that ensured
the continuing authority of local elites, both kings and aristocrats, was ownership of or control
over land, the people who worked it, and its products."

The Christianization of the Roman Empire was a protracted and colossal shift from old ceremonies, myths, and rituals, not to mention the changes in architecture, artistic expression, law, and the economy. In truth, the fragile experiment could have toppled into historical record as a momentary blip in the otherwise pagan history of dominance in the Roman Empire. In light of the fact that "the success of Christianity was certainly not a foregone conclusion" in the fourth century, what Macrina and her family established was a daring enterprise indeed.[30] They were ahead of the curve with their understanding of Christianity as a societal force for change. We are not suggesting that Macrina singlehandedly shifted the cultural tide of Pontus, but she was on the forefront of the "powerfully disruptive impact" the rise of Christianity had on Cappadocian society.[31]

### Liturgical Legacy: The Life of Macrina

The intimate connection between the virgin and philosophy is clear from the beginning of the Life of Macrina. For Gregory, Macrina is not just another philosopher who can run with the big guys of philosophy—he declares that she certainly can;[32] rather, she is a teacher of the *true* philosophy. She is in a completely different class; her philosophy is grounded in scriptural and lived reality. There is no sophistry to be found here. Philosophy is meant to be a way of life, lived in space and time. The dialectic was not a way to win over your opponent, but a genuine search for truth. However much of Gregory's representation of his sister's philosophical prowess would be owned by her, it is at least clear that Macrina would not have tolerated any way of life that was not centrally about the truth of Christ.

Before Macrina's deathbed scene, Gregory's language displays his sister as the reserved bearer of wisdom and sustainer of the family, but in his account of her final hours, Gregory documents a passionate and emotive Macrina. In her last moments, her love for God is increasingly more apparent. Gregory writes:

> Accordingly it seemed to me that she was then making manifest to those present that divine and pure love of the unseen Bridegroom which she had nourished secretly in the inmost recesses of her soul, and was proclaiming the disposition

30. Van Dam, *Becoming Christian*, 4.
31. Ibid., 70.
32. At one point in *On the Soul and the Resurrection*, Gregory is so impressed by Macrina that he responds in awe: "Your argument . . . has progressed so simply and spontaneously and in such orderly sequence, that to anyone of intelligence it will seem to be correct and to diverge in no way from the truth" (*De anima et resurrectione* 3.51, in *Macrina the Younger* [Silvas, 195]).

of heart by which she hastened towards him for whom she longed, so that, freed from the fetters of the body, she might be with him as quickly as possible. For in truth, her race was towards her Beloved, and no other of the pleasures of this life diverted her eye to itself.[33]

Macrina's philosophy was not fatalistic or without the ability to revel in love. Her mind and body were as restrained as possible in order to pursue her eternal love with all vitality. Gregory observes, "The nearer she approached her exodus, the more clearly she discerned the beauty of the Bridegroom and the more eagerly she hastened to the one for whom she longed."[34] For Macrina, love for Christ is where wisdom and abandon meet.

Faced with her departure from this life, did Macrina flinch in the face of her death? Gregory says no: "Right up to her last breath she philosophized with a lofty mind on the convictions she had formed from the beginning about the life here below. All this seemed to me to be no longer of the human order."[35] In the last moments of her earthly life, Macrina seems to Gregory to be in two states at once, an angelic and a human. Gregory observes this blurred state to be indicative of where her true desires were located—with her Bridegroom—and nothing of earth could keep her from seeing that desire realized.[36] Upon entering into the fulfillment of her true desire, Macrina has achieved a harmonious state, which even her body reflects after her life-giving force departs. Gregory juxtaposes his disquieted and unhinged state against this harmony. He plunges into the depths of despair, grieving the loss of Macrina, the "lamp of our eyes," the "light that guided our souls," the "surety of our life," the "seal of incorruptibility," the "bond of our harmony," "the firmness of the vacillating," and "the cure of the infirm."[37] Gregory then shouts, "Look at her and remember her commands by which she trained you to be orderly and decent in all things!"[38] Death does not hinder her instruction; she is again the lamp, the light, the safety, and the seal of incorruptibility. Macrina's body becomes the shining relic that Gregory had been holding in his dream prior to his arrival.[39]

33. Gregory, *Vit. Macr.* 24.5 (Silvas, 132–33).
34. Gregory, *Vit. Macr.* 25.1 (Silvas, 133).
35. Gregory, *Vit. Macr.* 24.3–5 (Silvas, 132).
36. Gregory, *Vit. Macr.* 24.4–5 (Silvas, 132–33).
37. Gregory, *Vit. Macr.* 28.4 (Silvas, 136–37).
38. Gregory, *Vit. Macr.* 29.2, my translation (cf. Silvas, 137). For the critical edition, see Gregory of Nyssa, *Vita s. Macrinae* 11–13 (GNO VIII.1:401), ed. Virginia Woods Callahan, in *Opera Ascetica*, ed. Werner Jaeger, John Peter Cavarnos, and Virginia Woods Callahan (Leiden: Brill, 1952).
39. Gregory, *Vit. Macr.* 34.2 (Silvas, 142).

This clarion call to remembrance is not only the commissioning of her legacy; it is also a definitive shift in power. Gregory, as her brother and bishop, might have divined some use for Macrina when all was said and done, but according to the narrative, it was Macrina who taught Gregory the true philosophy that would pull him out of despondency. It is clear that he recognized this debt. His shout reveals this power to the rest of the world. Here, in death, lies a true teacher whose pedagogical influence not only remains but also continues to function actively in order to instruct others. Gregory's vision and his realization of its testimony to Macrina's legacy as a martyr provoke him to initiate liturgical memory—that is, a way for others to memorialize and to continue to be instructed by Macrina's Christ-shaped life. It is also a clear moment of recognition of theological authority; Macrina's body in death holds corporeal memory as relic, its power granted by her sharing in the sufferings of Christ. Gregory's declaration is a recognition of Macrina's authority as a physical witness to Christ and as a teacher; this authority is not permitted, granted, or validated by Gregory as the narrator but is beheld, proclaimed, and made sacred in memorial identification with Christ.

It is the theological work of the *Life of Macrina* to integrate Macrina's example into the narrative of the faithful alongside martyrs (Thecla and those from Gregory's own family) and illustrious contributors to the Christian tradition (Basil).[40] Gregory sought to "fill the gaps created by death," but perhaps even more than this, he sought to open Macrina's life for Christians to integrate her pious example to fill in the gaps in their own lives.[41] The christological work of Macrina's living legacy of asceticism sealed in her death, and Gregory's vision of himself handling her bodily and literary remains, link Macrina's story to the martyr cults in which, as Richard M. Price observes, "the veneration of bodily remains, however decayed or fragmentary, cannot be separated either from the celebration of the eucharist, where the consecrated hosts are (in effect) so many fragments of Christ's body, or from the Christian faith in the resurrection of the flesh at the end of time."[42] As we

---

40. The genre of the *Life of Macrina* is difficult to categorize. It has been referred to most often as a hagiography—although this is a rather ill-fitting and anachronistic conclusion—and as a philosophical biography, such as those written about Pythagoras or Plotinus. Silvas offers "mystagogy" as a compelling genre designation that draws attention to the theological work of the *Life of Macrina*. As "mystagogy," the *Life of Macrina* is an exposition of the "mysteries," the "life of Christ as communicated in the liturgical rites, and realized by the virgin mystic in the liturgy of the heart" (Silvas, *Macrina*, 103–5).

41. Derek Krueger, "Writing and the Liturgy of Memory in Gregory of Nyssa's *Life of Macrina*," *JECS* 8 (2000): 484.

42. Richard M. Price, "Martyrdom and the Cult of the Saints," in Harvey and Hunter, *Oxford Handbook of Early Christian Studies*, 814.

are invited through Gregory's account of Macrina to enter into a liturgical remembrance to behold and know Macrina, we find ourselves beholding and knowing Christ in, through, and by her legacy.

### *"My Sister and My Teacher"*: On the Soul and the Resurrection

Gregory of Nyssa imitates Plato in positioning himself as the willing student in his dialogue with the Socratic Macrina on her deathbed in *On the Soul and the Resurrection*, which was written soon after the *Life of Macrina*.[43] With *On the Soul and the Resurrection*, the writer inserts himself into the dialogue and portrays himself as the pupil—sometimes impatient, speaking without thinking beforehand, frustrated, confused, and lacking control of his emotions. This willingness for the master to become or even appear by his own admission as the pupil of another—and that one a woman—is an extraordinary device. Macrina's representation in *On the Soul and the Resurrection* is not relegated to a surprising embrace of inclusion or manipulated insertion; instead, she, like Socrates in the *Phaedo*, is the master philosopher.

Certainly, *On the Soul and the Resurrection* has much to offer by way of theological and philosophical content, but it functions on another level as well. Similar to the *Life of Macrina*, *On the Soul and the Resurrection* reveals the shaping of one ascetic's life for the purpose of shaping the tradition of Christian devotion. *On the Soul and the Resurrection* finds its "functional type in dialogues of Plato, and the expectation of its literary experience in the model of Socrates' gradually teasing out the truth through a series of questions about what constitutes knowledge and how it is acquired."[44] Thus there is little doubt that the content of the dialogue is Gregory's construction and not indicative of an actual conversation he had with his dying sister. However, Gregory's casting of his sister in this dialogue is astounding. A paragon of virginal devotion is remembered by creatively involving her in the timeless philosophical conversation on the soul and the contemporary Christian discussion about the nature of the resurrection.[45] Posing the Macrina remembered in the *Life*

43. Elizabeth A. Clark observes that Macrina is modeled generally after the philosopher Socrates's muse Diotima of the *Symposium*, who instructed him on the nature of true love, but Macrina's dialogue on the soul and the afterlife is patterned after Plato's *Phaedo* ("Holy Women, Holy Words," 424).

44. Susan Wessel, "Memory and Individuality in Gregory of Nyssa's *Dialogus de anima et resurrectione*," *JECS* 18 (2010): 373.

45. The implications for the shaping of what Elizabeth A. Castelli calls the "particular manifestation of ascetic ideal in the East" should not be underestimated ("Virginity and Its Meaning for Women's Sexuality in Early Christianity," in *A Feminist Companion to Patristic Literature*, ed. Amy-Jill Levine, FCNTECW 12 [London: T&T Clark, 2008], 75).

*of Macrina* as participating in such a dialogue has a literary ramification: it assumes that the virginal life is in the arena of constructive and speculative theology. We suggest that Gregory views his sister as an abundant fount of theological wealth coursing through, shaping, and nourishing the Christian tradition that he has received by way of the legendary Thecla and the virgins at Methodius's symposium.

In *On the Soul and the Resurrection*, Macrina draws a direct connection between the virginal and virtuous life and the Christian hope. Gregory's leading question prompts Macrina to engage in dialectic that presumably will lead to truth: "What ground for virtue have they who suppose that their existence is limited to this present life and that beyond it there is nothing more to be hoped for?"[46] Macrina's response ranges widely, from demonstrating the very existence of the soul to pointing to the purpose of human existence as meeting beautiful truth in the face of God.[47] The connector between the desire for beauty, the necessary condition of purity or virtue to pursue that beauty, and beauty itself is hope: "Hope initiates the forward movement, but memory brings up the rear as that movement advances towards the hope. If hope indeed leads the soul to what is beautiful by nature, the trace that this movement of the will imprints upon the memory is a bright one."[48] Hope is a motivator because the human experience of this reality is at present marked by lack but in the future will manifest fulfillment.[49] Virginity—that is, living in the Christian hope—demonstrates that there is more to human life than this version of embodied existence. The fulfillment of the Christian hope is just not yet present.

For Macrina and Gregory (versus Plato), the soul "freed" from the body in death is not in its proper or permanent state. As the soul is the life force of the body and its incorporeality is temporary, in death it experiences a holding pattern of sorts in anticipation of the reality of the resurrected body to come. This is the Christian hope, the bodily resurrection, where the soul no longer argues with the body, where the senses are resurrected, and where the interior and exterior aspects of the person are in harmony. For Macrina, virginity is the practice of this specifically Christian hope. Now in this body, one can and should practice this reality as a Christian, because whoever is a Christian knows the centrality of this hope, and that hope does not give license to think that what is done in the body now does not matter. In fact, because it is the same body, it matters a great deal. Hence the Christian hope necessitates a life of

46. Gregory of Nyssa, *An.* 1.6 (Silvas, 174).
47. Gregory of Nyssa, *An.* 6.13–15 (Silvas, 208–9).
48. Gregory of Nyssa, *An.* 6.18–19 (Silvas, 209).
49. Gregory of Nyssa, *An.* 6.31 (Silvas, 211).

virtue. The soul's incorporeal state is only a rest stop on the great journey of what it means to be human. *On the Soul and the Resurrection* is not about ethereal concepts of the soul, but is a treatise on the reality of what it means to be a Christian in light of Christian hope and what this means for us in the now, as embodied people whose bodies and souls are irrevocably linked.[50] For Macrina, there is no such thing as a homeless soul.

Bolstered by his sister taking on that legendary mantle, Gregory invites his readers to grasp the authority of Thecla through Macrina as the true purveyor of Thecla's legacy and philosophy in the tradition of Socrates. Thecla is literarily grafted in as the hinge upon which the dialogue hangs for historical (in the sense of legacy and tradition) and theological support. Macrina is, similar to the depiction of Socrates by Plato, a once-removed authority as star philosopher. The literary room that Gregory gives to his remembrance of Macrina is striking. The term "remembrance" is more fitting here instead of "representation" since, among the many reasons Gregory chose to spend so much time writing about his sister, one is to create a legacy project that would serve not only as a lengthy epitaph but also as a continuing instructive voice and example for many.

Gregory of Nyssa folds his remembrance of his sister into concerns about the church's ongoing relationship with ascetics (and martyrs) and the construction of the resurrected body, endowing his deeply personal account of touching the dead body of his sister with theological and ecclesiastical importance. His rendering of Macrina's liturgical legacy relies not only upon the manner and meaning of her death, but also upon the choices she made while living. The symbiotic relationship between the material and the christological imbues Macrina's legacy with the necessary liturgical connection for fellow Christians to follow.

Gregory had such a strong understanding of Christian transformation that when he looks at Macrina, he sees two people blurred together: the transforming body of the now and the resurrected one to be. The ascetic life is the angelic life, and in Macrina these two states shift and glimmer, causing a disquieting sense of disjointedness that reminds all that she is living into the reality of the resurrection in her current body. She is, then, what the transformed human looks like. Caroline Walker Bynum writes:

> The body of Macrina—miraculously healed and made immortal and yet marked by its own particular experience—seems to be what Gregory has in

50. This link leads Macrina to deny that souls pass from a female body to the life of a man or vice versa, or even from man to man or woman to woman (Gregory of Nyssa, *An.* 8.31 [Silvas, 222]).

mind when he writes of resurrection as the reassemblage of "the identical atoms" we had on earth "in the same order as before" and yet insists that "there must be change." The resurrected body is both the ascetic who becomes a relic while still alive and the relic that continues after death the changelessness acquired through asceticism.[51]

Macrina was a living example and a herald of the resurrection to come. Her cultivation of an ascetic community, her rebuffing of the social norms, and the mark she made on her region and the people around her as a result—all these matter. In other words, it is not just because she died or even how she died that was of paramount importance; what mattered was that her death was continuous with the Christ-shaped life she lived before death and with the resurrected life to come.

## Monica (November 331 or 332–November 13, 387)

### Being Augustine's Mom: A Case Study in Long-Suffering Parenting

While Augustine mentions several people who either helped him in his journey back to God or journeyed along with him, it is clear from the *Confessions* (begun in 397) that his mother Monica was his mainstay. Augustine compares Monica's long-suffering tenacity and trust for his eventual conversion to Christianity to God's guardianship of his life. Thus Augustine understands the direction of his life to be one of return to its true shape as orchestrated by God and perceived by Monica while he was in the womb. Monica certainly physically travailed to bring him into the world, but Augustine declares with grateful awe: "With far more anxious solicitude did she give birth to me in the spirit than ever she had in the flesh."[52] Augustine's relationship with his mother was not perfect, of course; at times he chafed under the pressure of her sometimes myopic and rigid vision for his life. In remembering Monica, though, Augustine recognizes her voice as God's voice in the silence and as the beacon that helped guide him on his return. As Peter Brown states in his biography of Augustine, "Few mothers can survive being presented to us exclusively in terms of what they have come to mean to their sons, much less to a son as complicated as Augustine."[53]

51. Caroline Walker Bynum, *The Resurrection of the Body in Western Christianity, 200–1336*, Lectures on the History of Religions 15 (New York: Columbia University Press, 1995), 86.
52. Augustine, *Conf.* 5.9.16 (Boulding, 125).
53. Peter Brown, *Augustine of Hippo: A Biography*, new ed. (Berkeley: University of California Press, 2000), 17.

In the *Confessions*, we meet a force of nature in Monica. As with Gregory's remembrance of Macrina, the Monica of whom Augustine wrote is the Monica that we know. Augustine's Monica is surprisingly relatable, not cast as an unassailable saint or seemingly interested in being one. As Gillian Clark notes, "[Monica] was not a martyr or an ascetic. She was a good Christian who showed love of God and love of neighbour."[54] She did have, however, a vivid faith and devotional practice steeped in the colorful idiosyncrasies of the North African church.[55] But Augustine is quick to note that his mother was not wedded to the more eccentric practices, such as getting drunk during meals at cemeteries; when she did participate in such events, it was on a limited and sober basis. When Monica, having followed her son to Italy, discovered that devotional practice took on a different shape there, she adapted and flourished.[56] Thus Augustine succeeds in depicting Monica's Christianity as the right kind: simple, dynamic, nuanced, compelling, and desirable. She drew from the deep well of a cultivated inner life and vigorously clung to her conviction that Augustine would become a man of faith. She was relentless, following him as he moved to new geographical places as well as new ideological places and always seeking advocates or angles to provoke him to faith.

Often, women in more obvious positions of power, such as the empresses we will meet in chapter 9, are tagged with derogatory descriptors such as "domineering" or "bossy," while women like Monica, who seem to exert less-official, relational power, are designated with anachronisms that diminish and distort their roles.[57] Thus, referring (as some have) to Monica as the "queen of helicopter parents," a nag (a common epithet leveled specifically against women in familial relationships), or, even, jokingly, a "stalker" amounts to

54. Gillian Clark, *Monica: An Ordinary Saint*, Women in Antiquity (Oxford: Oxford University Press, 2015).

55. Monica's connection with her North African roots is something of a discussion among scholars. As Gillian Clark notes, in the earliest manuscripts of the *Confessions*, she appears as "Monnica," and some scholars "feel strongly that 'Monnica' links this woman more closely to her African homeland, whereas the traditional 'Monica' claims her for Roman culture and its later reception" (*Monica*, 8). See Rebecca Moore, "Oh Mother, Where Art Thou? In Search of Saint Monnica," in *Feminist Interpretations of Augustine*, ed. Judith Chelius Stark, Re-reading the Canon (University Park: Pennsylvania State University Press, 2007), 147–66. While Monica's Africanness is important and certainly plays into Augustine's portrayal of her, we will be using the Latin version of her name. This is mainly for recognition and not to elide an important aspect of her identity.

56. Augustine, *Conf.* 6.2.2 (Boulding, 135–36). See also Augustine's *Ep.* 54, *To Januarius*, in which Augustine relays Monica's adaptation regarding new fasting practices at Ambrose's church in Milan (*Saint Augustine: Letters*, 1:253–54, trans. Parsons).

57. For an overview of how scholars have read Monica (the positive and the negative), see Anne-Marie Bowrey, "Monica: The Feminine Face of Christ," in Stark, *Feminist Interpretations of Augustine*, 70–73.

a misunderstanding of both Monica and Augustine. Augustine and Monica
certainly had their issues—stubbornness and bouts of drama certainly run in
that family—but to belittle their relationship in such terms does a disservice
to the texts and what Augustine is trying to convey.[58] As Brown observes: "Oc-
casionally, we glimpse a genuinely impressive woman—very much what her
son would have liked himself to be, as a bishop: restrained, dignified, above
gossip, a firm peacemaker among her acquaintances, capable, like her son,
of effective sarcasm."[59] In other words, Monica is the key to envisioning the
landscape of his journey back to God; without her, Augustine would never
have become the Augustine we know. In the *Confessions*, we get the sense that
Monica's pursuit, even when parochially hued, felt, in retrospect, like God's
love and mercy following him all of his days (Ps. 23:6), conscientiously prod-
ding Augustine's "unquiet" heart, which had propelled him to search for a
mentor in Manichaeism, for camaraderie among friends, for sexual fulfillment,
and for answers in Neoplatonism.[60] For Augustine, Monica's relentlessness
was God's relentlessness.

In his moving eulogy for Monica in book 9 of the *Confessions*, Augustine
details her upbringing and her marriage to his father, Patricius.[61] As Brown
observes, Augustine's takeaway from his parents' relationship seems to be the
"subterranean tension" that characterized it.[62] It is not surprising that Augustine's descriptions of his father tend to be oriented in terms of how they fill in
the lines of Monica's personality. Patricius probably died when Augustine was
seventeen (370/371) and, unlike Monica, had very little bearing on his spiritual
journey.[63] Patricius did nothing to hinder his son's conversion to the religion
of his mother, but Monica actively worked to make sure Augustine knew that
his true father was God and not Patricius.[64] His father was a generally gentle

---

58. Monica's pressure on Augustine was fueled by a desire to see him achieve a specific brand
of success. Even when their relationship was strained—such as when she refused to allow him
to live with her because he refused to give up being a Manichaean heretic, or when she forced
him to part with his common-law wife of fifteen years—still he recognized that she was the
beacon that helped guide him on his return to God.

59. Brown, *Augustine*, 17.

60. "You stir us so that praising you may bring us joy, because you have made us and drawn
us to yourself, and our heart is unquiet until it rests in you" (*Conf.* 1.1.1 [Boulding, 39]).

61. Augustine, *Conf.* 9.9.19 (Boulding, 224–25). As for the rest of Augustine's family, he had
one brother, Navigius, although it cannot be known for certain who was the elder, and a sister
who is never named but to whom Augustine refers briefly in a letter as the former head of a
community of religious women (G. Clark, *Monica*, 9).

62. Brown, *Augustine*, 19.

63. John M. Quinn, *A Companion to the* Confessions *of St. Augustine* (New York: Peter
Lang, 2002), 502; Augustine only briefly marks the occasion of Patricius's death in *Conf.* 3.4.7
(Boulding, 79).

64. Augustine, *Conf.* 1.11.17 (Boulding, 50–51).

man who would erupt in "Vesuvius-like outbursts of anger."[65] Unfortunately, for a great many women in antiquity, a husband's wrath often ended in blows.[66] However, Augustine reports that this was never the case for Monica and Patricius. Augustine attributes this surprising element to Monica's discernment and skill in managing her husband. Certainly Monica's approach in dealing with her eruptive and abusive husband is not one to be recommended now, but Augustine applauds Monica's tactics in disarming her husband's violent outbursts and patiently bearing with Patricius's many infidelities until his conversion shortly before he died.[67] Augustine's approval of Monica's tactics reflects his general approach: he was not particularly affronted by, nor did he speak against, violence in marital relationships as he did against infidelity. According to Clark, the picture Augustine gives us is as complex as it is disappointing:

> Augustine's Monica is not a battered wife, weeping because she is a victim of abuse in a culture which prevents her from using her abilities, so that she subordinates her own wishes to the service of others and invests too much hope in her son. She is respected as wife, mother, and neighbour, and though Augustine does not explicitly call her competent and enterprising, he shows that she was. But perhaps Augustine imagined Monica's marriage in accordance with his own views, or perhaps Monica's success contributed to his acceptance of domestic violence.[68]

Monica's marital situation reflects what was probably a common situation in the mid-fourth century as the empire was slowly Christianizing: spouses who came from the same social milieu but were in mixed Christian-pagan relationships.[69]

One thing Monica and Patricius had in common was ambition for their gifted son. This desire on Monica's part, though, was more complicated than it might seem. While Patricius could have possibly been accused of blunt, vain ambition, Monica's reasoning for pushing him into literary studies was, as Augustine points out, a hopeful calculation that his studies would lead him toward God. That Monica could imagine such a thing in the first place is noteworthy since it demonstrates that she had detected a path to be walked into Christian truth through pagan education. Indeed, this is exactly what happened. Reading Cicero's *Hortensius* (no longer extant, but excerpts are preserved) at eighteen was enough to stoke his desire for philosophy as the

---

65. Quinn, *Companion to the* Confessions, 501.
66. G. Clark, *Monica*, 79.
67. Augustine, *Conf.* 9.9.22 (Boulding, 226).
68. G. Clark, *Monica*, 79.
69. Serge Lancel, *Saint Augustine*, trans. Antonia Nevill (London: SCM, 2002), 9.

"love for wisdom" that would eventually lead him to the books of the Platonists and finally to Scripture.[70]

According to Augustine, Monica was possessed of good character, faithful in her devotion to God, full of faith, and, most often noted by Augustine, completely devoted to praying for her son. Augustine spent nine years stuck in the "murky depths" that were Manichaeism, and yet, he observes, "Throughout those years my mother, a chaste, God-fearing, sensible widow of the kind so dear to you, though more eager in her hope was no less assiduous in her weeping and entreaty, never at any time ceasing her plangent prayers to you about me."[71] She wept for him more than mothers weep for their dead children because, for Monica, her son was held captive by death in life.[72] John M. Quinn describes Monica thus: "As the hound of heaven tirelessly hunted for the wandering Augustine, Monica served as a kind of surrogate-hound, a preeminent instrument applied, through never-ceasing prayer, to her son by the Father to bring her prodigal home."[73] Throughout the *Confessions* Augustine builds monuments to Monica's prayers, Ebenezer stones that motivate grateful remembrance (see 1 Sam. 7:12). Prayer and tear-soaked stones of remembrance dot the literary landscape, witnessing to the dialectic Augustine knows is going on between God and Monica on his behalf. It was not an argument with two opposing sides so much as Monica learning through faults of negotiation that her plans for Augustine were too small and tainted with too much worldly-shaped ambition. He praises God upon recollecting the relationship between Monica and God: "O Lord, you heard her and did not scorn those tears of hers which gushed forth and watered the ground beneath her eyes wherever she prayed. Yes, you did indeed hear her."[74] We can celebrate with Monica because she grew and because her prayers and the "sacrifice of her heart's blood" yielded a greater harvest than she thought possible.[75]

Even a militant perseverance like Monica's needed supernatural encouragement and feedback. At a particularly difficult time of estrangement (likely when

---

70. Augustine, *Conf.* 3.4.8–5.9 (Boulding, 79–80).

71. Augustine, *Conf.* 3.11.20 (Boulding, 90). For more on Augustine's Manichaeism, see Brown, *Augustine*, 35–49. It was the Manichaean response to evil that captured Augustine. Manichaeism was a secretive sect that was dualistic: "So convinced were they that evil could not come from a good God, that they believed that it came from an invasion of the good—the 'Kingdom of Light'—by a hostile force of evil, equal in power, eternal, totally separate—the 'Kingdom of Darkness'" (36). Bound to captivity to evil, one could escape only through illumination, the freeing of one's mind or soul (the small spark of divinity that it was) that often required intense bodily austerity.

72. Augustine, *Conf.* 3.11.19 (Boulding, 89–90).

73. Quinn, *Companion to the* Confessions, 499.

74. Augustine, *Conf.* 3.11.19 (Boulding, 89).

75. Augustine, *Conf.* 5.7.13 (Boulding, 122).

he was twenty, in late 374), after she refused to let him live with her, Monica had a dream in which she was standing on a wooden rule (*regula*: the canon; *regula fidei*: the rule of faith and practice) and was approached by a handsome young man who exhibited the cheery opposite of her distraught, tear-stained visage.[76] He asked why she was so downcast because, as Augustine mentions, "as usual his question was intended to teach her, not to elicit information for himself."[77] Monica responded that the source of her grief was Augustine's sinful state. In response, "he then instructed and admonished her to take good heed and see that where she stood, there also stood I. This was to reassure her. She took heed, and saw me standing close beside her on the same rule."[78] The Archimedean strength to stand that was communicated to Monica in this vision was a great comfort to her. Augustine, however, haughtily dismissed her rendering of the dream to excuse his behavior and countered that its true meaning was that she would convert to Manichaeism. Monica gave no ground and replied: "No: I was not told, 'Where he is, you will be too,' but, 'Where you are, he will be.'"[79] The rhetorical thrashing he had just received by his untrained mother stunned Augustine. Augustine eventually gave up on Manichaeism around 382/383 after dedicating nine years of his life to it. Reflecting back on his mother's retort, Augustine was impressed not with the dream but with his mother's staunch, articulate defense that came from a place of certitude.

Augustine's departure from the Manichaeans infused Monica with a renewed energy to provoke her son's conversion. That energy manifested itself via a white-knuckled grip on her idea that marriage would secure her son's baptism.[80] Monica's cheerful insistence that he marry a woman who would qualify statuswise to be his wife wore him down into grudging assent, for he knew that his current situation was not in any way beneficial to his ambitions. Knowing how God communicated with her, he asked if she had received a vision confirming this to be the correct course of action. Augustine relates that she "did have some illusory, fantastic dreams, brought on by the activity of her own human spirit as she busied herself about this matter," but never expressed her usual confidence in a vision from

76. Augustine, *Conf.* 3.11.19 (Boulding, 89–90).
77. Augustine, *Conf.* 3.11.19 (Boulding, 89). Quinn explains that Augustine is referring to how a teacher uses questioning as a way to lead students to access the truth in their interior selves. Thus the dream messenger is not bringing new information to Monica but leading her to the truth she already possessed—that Augustine would embrace the Catholic faith (*Companion to the* Confessions, 173–74).
78. Augustine, *Conf.* 3.11.19 (Boulding, 89).
79. Augustine, *Conf.* 3.11.20 (Boulding, 90).
80. Augustine, *Conf.* 6.13.23 (Boulding, 154).

God.[81] He accepted Monica's lack of visionary confirmation anyway. Grief and misery consumed him when he sent away his common-law wife and mother to his only son, Adeodatus, in the hopes of making a suitable match. Augustine writes: "So deeply was she engrafted into my heart that it was left torn and wounded and trailing blood."[82] His pain at the loss of this relationship drove him to give in to desperate lusts and to run immediately into the arms of another woman in hopes of abating his misery. Monica's mistake here seems to be envisioning a future for her son that was both intractable and too small.

After his eventual baptism and conversion to the ascetic life, Monica never looked back. She let go of her grip on the slippery handholds of a first-rate literary education and a marriage for her son and gladly fell back into the unknown known of God's destiny for her son. Augustine contemplates the source of Monica's joy upon his conversion now that he is standing with her on that rule and no longer captive to worldly ambitions or marital contract: "In so doing you had also converted her grief into joy [Ps. 30:11] far more abundant than she had desired, and much more tender and chaste than she could ever have looked to find in grandchildren from my flesh."[83] The fits and estrangement that had characterized their relationship for so long evolved into an intimate and warm friendship. Augustine came to understand and admire Monica, benefiting from close proximity for those few years before she died. Remarking on their situation during a retreat to a friend's country villa, Augustine reflected on what it was like to have Monica live with him and his small group of newly Christian companions: "My mother kept us company, woman in outward form but endowed with virile faith, uniting the serenity of an elderly person with a mother's love and Christian devotion."[84]

### Girls Are Allowed in This Boys' Club: Monica and Augustine in Dialogue

After finally converting to Christianity and becoming a catechumen at age thirty-two, Augustine decided to quit teaching at his post in Milan. His respiratory health demanded that he take a much-needed break, and he longed for a philosophical retreat with those who would accompany him. In November

81. Augustine, *Conf.* 6.13.23 (Boulding, 154); Augustine says that Monica could tell the difference between God's "revelations to her and the fantasies of her own dreaming soul" with a sense akin to taste.
82. Augustine, *Conf.* 6.15.25 (Boulding, 156).
83. Augustine, *Conf.* 8.12.30 (Boulding, 208).
84. Augustine, *Conf.* 9.4.8 (Boulding, 214). We will address the language of "virile" women in chap. 8.

386, Augustine's friend Verecundus opened up his country villa at Cassiciacum, north of Milan, for the group of intrepid young Christian men and Monica, who not only took care of their living needs but also participated as the mature Christian in the philosophical discussions. For both of these reasons Augustine deems her "our mother." During their eighteen-week stay at Cassiciacum, Augustine produced a series of dialogues, two of which include Monica as a main interlocutor: *On the Happy Life* (*De beata vita*) and *On Order* (*De ordine*).[85] It is clear that Augustine wants her around, not just to take care of them but also because she brings a kind of wisdom to the proceedings that he, with all of his genius and formal training, cannot replicate. So, while Augustine facilitates (and sometimes irritatingly provokes) discussion, he often defers to Monica to help the teenage Licentius, the Roman military veteran Trygetius, his brother Navigius, his teenage son Adeodatus, and his longtime friend Alypius on their respective journeys into true wisdom. *On the Happy Life* and *On Order* offer us the opportunity to witness how Augustine sees the process of growth in wisdom. Fundamental to that project is the face-to-face and humble deference to those who have walked longer in the Christian faith. For Augustine, longevity of relationship with God and stalwart faith qualify Monica as an indispensable authority in their philosophical search for wisdom.

In *On the Happy Life*, Augustine spends three days with his companions at the Cassiciacum villa, discussing such questions as the following: What qualifies as nourishment for the soul? What does it mean to be happy? What kind of person can be said to possess God and therefore be truly happy?

On the question of the soul's nourishment, Monica answers that only understanding and knowledge sustain the soul.[86] Augustine then follows up with a line of questioning about what it takes for someone to be happy since happiness is a universal desire. In answer to his question as to whether possessing what we want makes us happy, Monica responds: "If he wishes and possess good things, he is happy; if he desires evil things—no matter if he possess them—he is wretched."[87] Augustine beams at her in response because in her words he hears an echo of Cicero's *Hortensius*, which first sparked his return to God:

> Mother, you have really gained the mastery of the very stronghold of philosophy. For, undoubtedly you were wanting the words to express yourself like Tullius

---

85. They left in the spring of 387 before March 15. Augustine's other dialogues at Cassiciacum were the *Soliloquies* and *Against the Academics* (Quinn, *Companion to the* Confessions, 485).

86. Augustine, *Beat.* 2.8, in *The Happy Life*, trans. Ludwig Schopp, FC 5 (New York: CIMA, 1948), 53.

87. Augustine, *Beat.* 2.10 (Schopp, 56).

[Cicero], who also has dealt with this matter. In his *Hortentius*, a book written
in the praise and defense of philosophy, he said: "Behold, not the philosophers,
but only people who like to argue, state that all are happy who live according
to their own will. This, of course, is not true, for, to wish what is not fitting is
the worst of wretchedness. But it is not so deplorable to fail of attaining what
we desire as it is to wish to attain what is not proper. For, greater evil is brought
about through one's wicked will than happiness through fortune."[88]

Monica continues on to say that no one can be satisfied with having everything they want even if those possessions are not stripped away as a result
of misfortune; in fact, the person who has everything is miserable in lack.[89]
An exchange follows between mother and son about the link between happiness and possessing the things one desires. Afterward, Augustine appraises
Monica's philosophical ken as fiercely winning a stronghold and holding
it by combat.[90] In fact, her exclamation was so impressive that Augustine
observes that, "entirely forgetting her sex," the young men thought they had
"some great man in [their] midst," even though he knew that her wisdom
flowed from a divine source instead of from the education such great men
had received.[91]

   On the third day everyone makes their way out to a meadow to finish their
dialogue with a discussion on the correlation between misery and want.
To defend Monica's opinion that the miserable person is needy, Augustine
puts forth the hypothetical situation of a man who has everything and who
seemingly is not in want but who is still miserable. That misery, all agree,
is from the fear of losing what he has, not because he is needy. Monica,
though, feels that it was not enough to say this and expresses her thoughts
on the matter thus:

> I do not yet quite understand how misery can be separated from want, and want
> from misery. Although he had great riches and abundance and—according to
> your own statement—desired nothing more, he still was in want of wisdom,
> since he entertained the fear of losing these things. Are we going to consider
> him in want, if he be without silver and money, and not [consider him in want]
> if he should lack wisdom?[92]

88. Augustine, *Beat.* 2.10 (Schopp, 56). In *On the Trinity* (*De Trinitate*) 13.5.8, Augustine
uses this same quote from Cicero's nonextant *Hortensius* (i.e., surviving only in fragments/
quotations).
   89. Augustine, *Beat.* 2.11 (Schopp, 57).
   90. Augustine uses the same terminology in *Soliloquies* (*Soliloquiorum libri*) 1.10.17 (Schopp,
*Happy Life*, 56n8).
   91. Augustine, *Beat.* 2.10 (Schopp, 56).
   92. Augustine, *Beat.* 4.27 (Schopp, 75).

Her doubt raises a point of synthesis that elicits admiration from the other participants and especially from Augustine, who expresses his "joy and delight" because it was Monica who beat him to the punch in offering what he was saving for his "imposing final argument" that he had gleaned from the books of the philosophers.[93] Augustine brings the discussion to its conclusion by stating that true satisfaction for the soul—the happy life—is this: "to recognize piously and completely the One through whom you are led into the truth, the nature of the truth you enjoy, and the bond that connects you with the supreme measure."[94] And this One is the Trinity, the one God, and excludes all imposters and superstitions. The dialogue then swells to its climax when Monica's faith is aroused and prompts her to proclaim joyfully the words of one of Ambrose's hymns (*Deus creator omnium*), "Help, O Trinity, those that pray." She brings the three-day dialogue to a close by affirming Augustine's definition of the happy life: "Indeed, this is undoubtedly the happy life, that is, the perfect life which we must assume that we can attain soon by a well-founded faith, a joyful hope, and an ardent love."[95]

Another dialogue, *On Order*, begins as a middle-of-the-night diversion after the men are awakened by the constant sound of rushing water. As one might expect, not all are terribly interested in being provoked into dialectic as an alternative to insomnia, and thus snippy exchanges and exasperated reactions ensue. That Augustine includes the tangents and the unfiltered reactions of the participants makes this dialogue a particular delight. There is even an amusing section in which they discuss Licentius's new penchant for loudly singing Psalm 79 while using the toilet after Monica complains of hearing the teen singing his new earworm of a hymn yet again and in a rather inappropriate place. Licentius jokingly responds: "So what? If any enemy were to lock me in here, wouldn't God hear my voice?" Augustine offers what amounts to a defense of Licentius's new habit: "When we pray to convert to God and to see His face, don't we ask to be liberated from bodily and other filth and from the darkness of error?"[96] Poor Monica! Apparently she was living in what amounted to a men's college dorm in the fourth century.

The question Augustine puts to the bleary-eyed group that night and over the next couple of days is the relationship between God and the order that "binds and directs this world."[97] Is anything outside of God's control? What

93. Augustine, *Beat.* 4.27 (Schopp, 75).
94. Augustine, *Beat.* 4.35 (Schopp, 83).
95. Augustine, *Beat.* 4.35 (Schopp, 84).
96. Augustine, *Ord.* 1.1.8.22–23; Augustine, *On Order (De Ordine)*, trans. Silvano Borruso (South Bend, IN: St. Augustine's Press, 2007), 29–31.
97. Augustine, *Ord.* 1.1.1.1 (Borruso, 3).

does it mean to be with God and not to be with God? What then is evil and God's responsibility for it? These are some very large questions, and Augustine was not interested in having the discussion without Monica's contribution. She asks why she is to be included in the conversation: "I have never read of women entering into such debates in any of your books." Augustine seems thrilled to say that he did not "give two hoots about the judgment of the proud and the ignorant." Augustine assures her that anyone worth their philosophical salt would not despise engaging with perspectives from more modest sources and would not be troubled by his talking philosophy with her. In fact, he says: "And there will be some, believe me, who will find my talking with you here more pleasing than finding platitudes or high-brow stuff. There are plenty of philosopher-women in ancient times, and I rather like *your* philosophy."[98]

What was Monica's philosophy? Augustine describes Monica as a lover of wisdom. Unlike the philosophers who love only the wisdom of this world, she loved the wisdom of the true philosophy of Christ's kingdom, which is not of this world. Thus what qualifies her for participation in the dialogues is that she loves wisdom more than anything (including her son) and that no setbacks or even death itself gives her fear. This brave love of wisdom, Augustine declares, is core to the inner philosophical life and, according to learned and accomplished philosophers, one of the most difficult states to achieve. Monica's outstanding philosophical quality made her the obvious choice as a skilled mentor.[99] Therefore, Augustine was quite serious about inviting his mother to the dialogue. He had lived with her for a long time and knew her "keen mind and burning love for things divine."[100]

Monica often participates in the lively debates with a confident, mature humility that serves as an example for the others. As Clark explains, women in Late Antiquity did not participate in philosophical discussions because they were not trained to do so.[101] It was expected and hoped that boys would participate in public life, so they were trained by a *grammaticus* who would instruct them in the classical authors and the language and rhetorical skills of Cicero. Of course, this was not the Latin that everyday people spoke but the stylized version found in most literature of the time. Even though she has not had the benefit of the higher learning to which Augustine refers multiple times in the dialogue, he assures her that her lack of liberal arts training in no way disqualifies her because her achievement of character is so impressive. He learns new things from her "great mind" every day, and her freedom from material entanglements

98. Augustine, *Ord.* 1.2.11.31 (Borruso, 43).
99. Augustine, *Ord.* 1.2.11.32 (Borruso, 43–45).
100. Augustine, *Ord.* 2.1.1.1 (Borruso, 47).
101. G. Clark, *Monica*, 88.

and temperance are an inspiration. She might have errors in grammar and not be schooled in how to speak properly and professionally, but even he, as thoroughly trained as he is, cannot claim perfection on those scores.[102] In any case, Monica need not trouble herself with professional grammar and pronunciation because she knows the "divine power and nature of grammar so well, as to possess the grain, as it were, leaving the chaff to the experts."[103] In other words, Monica is the expert on all of the really important stuff. Thus Augustine as the facilitator often defers to her and gives her the last word on many of the topics.

Figure 7.3. The *Saint Augustine Taken to School by Saint Monica* by Nicoló di Pietro (1413–15), tempura on wood panel (Vatican).

Public domain / Wikimedia Commons

## Conclusion

After their retreat at Cassiciacum, Augustine and Monica headed to the port of Ostia on the Tiber to wait to sail back home to Africa.[104] The scene as related in book 9 of the *Confessions* is idyllic; Augustine and Monica gaze out a window overlooking a garden, resting from one journey and preparing for the journey to come. With hearts open to one another and to God, they ponder eternal life and experience a moment of transcendence, a taste of the resurrection to come. This moment is especially poignant since Monica never makes that journey back to North Africa before she dies of a fever at Ostia. One gets the sense that the newly minted bishop who is writing ten years after his mother's death wants and needs to remember this particular moment as significant and precious.

102. Periodically, Monica's lack of formal education shows, and we get a taste of "real" Latin, such as in *Beat.* 2.16 (Schopp, 63–64), when she amuses the other participants with an abrupt and crass remark; see G. Clark, *Monica*, 89.

103. Augustine, *Ord.* 2.2.17.45 (Borruso, 111).

104. Gillian Clark notes that the delay was to wait out a civil war between Magnus Maximus and Valentinian II (*Monica*, 17).

Figure 7.4. Augustine and Monica discussing the kingdom of heaven, from *Confessions* 9 (Ary Scheffer, oil on canvas; The National Gallery, London).

The vision at Ostia is a beautiful example of Christian community. The mature Christian Monica shepherds the new Christian Augustine into a shared experience of the beautiful reality to come. Monica smoothly steps into that role of master teacher with Augustine as her pupil.[105] The contemplative encounter surely would have left a distinct impression on Augustine in any case, but sharing it with Monica made it all the sweeter and more instructive. Augustine certainly did not know that his mother would leave his side so soon, but Monica was ready. Her words are warm and straightforward:

> For my part, my son, I find pleasure no longer in anything this life holds. What I am doing here still, or why I tarry, I do not know, for all worldly hope has withered away for me. One thing only there was for which I desired to linger awhile in this life: to see you a Catholic Christian before I died. And this my God has granted to me more lavishly than I could have hoped, letting me see you even spurning early happiness to be his servant. What now keeps me here?[106]

Nine days later the fifty-five- or fifty-six-year-old Monica died.

When Augustine revisits a loss in the *Confessions*, he views his management of grief as indicating his spiritual health. In book 4, Augustine relays how he responded to the death of an unnamed friend. His grief consumed him, and he was miserable. In trying to stem the tide of his emotions, Augustine tried everything from games to sex, to no avail. What he concludes is that he had not loved his friend well and therefore could not grieve well. Augustine expresses a similar sentiment on being compelled to send away the woman he lived with for fifteen years and with whom he had his son. Augustine did

105. See Bowrey, "Monica," 69–95, for a christological read of Monica as meditator and teacher.
106. Augustine, *Conf.* 9.10.26 (Boulding, 229).

Figure 7.5. Monica was originally buried in Ostia; her remains were later moved to Sant'Agostino in Rome.

not handle the loss well and ended up sleeping with another woman who was neither his common-law wife nor a potential match.

Augustine's remembrance of Monica's death in book 9, however, strikes a different tone. Certainly there are still tears and open expressions of grief, but gone is the weight of death and the retreat into bad habits for consolation. He is compelled to speak about his mother and his last moments with her at the port of Ostia on the Tiber. In her more lucid moments in the midst of her fever, Monica and her sons have a discussion about the burial of her body, specifically the location. Their mother, however, is less concerned with whether she is to be buried in Italy or in Africa than she is with them remembering her before God.[107] Augustine fulfills Monica's desire by remembering her before God near the end of book 9 in the *Confessions*, a heartfelt prayer of thanksgiving and retrospective on her behalf offered before God. He is learning to grieve differently now, experiencing the pain of loss but tempering it with the hope of resurrection.

The bond of family gives us access to two women in this chapter whose family members could not let the world forget them. In his *Life of Macrina*, Gregory lovingly portrays his sister, and he lingers at her deathbed a little longer in *On the Soul and the Resurrection*. And Augustine dedicates his famous *Confessions* to the remembrance of his mother after painting a compelling portrait of her as a relentless beacon of light who, by following him from place

107. Augustine, *Conf.* 9.11.27 (Boulding, 230).

to place, led him into truth.[108] Gregory's remembrance of his sister Macrina offers us the opportunity to think not only of our blood relationships but also of the primary relationships of those who populate the church as sisters and brothers in the faith. Augustine's remembrance of his mother, Monica, is instructive in showing how "mothering" is fundamental to the life of the church. Certainly, as a woman, Monica has the facility to carry a child physically, but the birthing of someone spiritually into the church is a mothering that is open to all Christians, regardless of gender, and it is necessary for the continuance of the church. These relationships and this family are eternal, and so, in reading *Life of Macrina*, *On the Soul and the Resurrection*, the *Confessions*, *On the Happy Life*, and *On Order*, we can flip through the pages like a photo album and remember the family that makes up "so great a cloud of witnesses" (Heb. 12:1) and welcome their instruction.

108. Augustine, *Conf.* 9.13.37 (Boulding, 235–36).

# 8

# Paula, Marcella, and the Melanias: Ascetics, Scholars, and Compatriots in Controversy

### Aristocrats-Turned-Ascetics

In this chapter we meet a cadre of women who negotiated a path of devotion through a sea of changes—widowhood, the death of children, a Gothic invasion, and voluntary impoverishment—to become something new in the Roman Empire: aristocrats-turned-ascetics. We will focus on a few women who called Rome home at some point in their lives. Some stayed (like Marcella), some left by choice (Melania the Elder and Paula), and for others (like Melania the Younger) leaving was a mix of devotional fervor and the desire not just to survive as refugees but also to thrive as monastic entrepreneurs. With the exception of Marcella, the women in this chapter are not easily designated as "western" (that is, from the geographical area of the Latin-speaking, western Roman Empire) or "eastern" (that is, from the Greek East). Thus their lives and respective journeys give us an opportunity to consider the flexibility inherent in the categories of East and West. Even if their ancestry and holdings tied them to the West, their devotion brought them to the East. As will become clear in this chapter, these women represented a Christian impulse to transverse borders—geographically and ideologically, to redefine established modes of displaying virtue, and to invest in a new architecture of piety.

The combination of asceticism and scholarship that characterizes the women of this chapter marks an important shift in the ecclesiastical structure of Christianity. While the bishop remained the official ecclesiastical authority, the rise of the monastic establishment funded by aristocratic money pressed the established structure of the church to contend with new avenues for the wealthy to give to the Christian project. Instead of church building campaigns and large offerings to the poor, the trend was toward building and funding monasteries. Scholars such as Jerome and Rufinus of Aquileia, who enjoyed the support of their wealthy female backers, became prolific writers with the time and space to be among the loudest voices in the acrimonious and long-lasting Origenist controversy. The aristocratic networks of Marcella and Melania the Elder provided pivotal support for their respective factions and generated an amalgamation of doctrinal debate and political rivalry.

The four women we are going to meet in this chapter were all (to varying degrees) part of an elite class in the Roman Empire. Understanding what that means is important because it affects how we read texts about these women and gauge their contributions to early Christianity. Those with means and a desire to imitate Christ and the martyrs channeled that fervor and blended it with aristocratic values and expectations. The result is an ascetic devotion charged with the energy of political connections and the momentum of financial liquidity—that is, large amounts of gold. It is important to remember that, for these women who were aristocrats-turned-ascetics, remaining on their new path was vital. Granting oneself even an inch of one's old life was effectively nostalgia for a life of death without God. Wealth in Late Antiquity was more than mere buying power. Wealth carried with it the responsibility not only to preserve that wealth but also to use it for the security of the empire. But the early Christian fathers viewed the corruption, indulgence, and violence associated with wealthy Romans as fundamentally antithetical to Christianity—that is, as bondage to a false lord and savior. Thus the extreme austerity measures were not understood as ways to accrue merit for the ascetic program but as necessary safeguards against the all-too-easy return back to death that enticed the wealthy with silks and litters and fine foods.

Christian aristocrat-turned-ascetic women had to deal with the problem of their wealth. Of course, no one could deny that money was helpful; it was only thanks to generous gifts that churches were built and that those like Jerome and Rufinus could produce a voluminous amount of work. What happened to all that wealth after a rich widow (or couple, in Melania the Younger and Pinianus's case) chose asceticism was not an easy question to answer, and often the desire to execute a plan for liquidating funds ran into many layers of difficulties. The women in this chapter served as exemplars of a rigorous Christianity made possible by their own lavish funds, and as beacons of devotional purity that lent credibility to the corresponding enterprises and agendas of men such as Jerome and Rufinus. We will begin with the women whom Jerome called friends (Marcella and Paula) and then turn toward Rufinus's comrade Melania the Elder. Her granddaughter, Melania the Younger, and her husband, Pinianus, follow in the Elder's physical footsteps to the Holy Land, but the couple blazes their own distinct ascetic trajectory in other significant ways.

## Marcella and Paula

The Marcella and the Paula that we know are presences mediated through the letters of Jerome. Since the epistolary evidence from these women is lost to us, we have to rely on Jerome's side of the conversation to help us piece their lives and contributions together. This venture is par for the course in reading ancient texts since the vast majority of them are written by men who have varying degrees of familiarity with the women, along with diverse contexts and interests. In Jerome's case, he knows Marcella and Paula personally and has an active epistolary and mentoring relationship with both of them. This results in a certain degree of familiarity in his writing to them and about them that is not found in other Late Antique texts about women. We learn a great deal about these women through how Jerome interacted with them and understood them. However, Jerome was a lethal combination of extraordinary skill, deeply held convictions, and unnerving refusal to back down from a fight. His incendiary pen makes him a particularly entertaining read but can also skew our perception of his circle of aristocratic female friends; thus, attention to Jerome's aims and methods is key.

When the young, ambitious upstart first arrived in Rome from his small hometown of Stridon, Jerome was not immediately granted entry into the presence of the rich and influential. Invitations into those houses and the cultivating of those connections took skill, gumption, and a keen eye for opportunity. Jerome's enthusiastic stubbornness got him into a great deal of trouble on more than one occasion, costing him friendships and his reputation in some circles. He eventually hewed a niche for himself as an eminent ascetic scholar with his hands in a variety of pies. Many of these interests

Public domain / Wikimedia Commons

Figure 8.1. Jerome was known for his relationships with many influential Christian women. Paula and her daughter Eustochium were among his closest compatriots.

and situations ended up being controversial, as we will soon see. A lifestyle of scholarship needed a lot of funding and support; and this is where Marcella, Paula, and others of his Roman circle of aristocratic female friends came into play. Jockeying for power in Rome, however, was a dangerous game, and one's favor and influence could turn sour in a moment. That moment for Jerome was when his ally Damasus, the bishop of Rome, died, and any protection from Jerome's growing list of enemies died with him. Jerome's reputation as a favorite among a circle of aristocratic women did not work in his favor; instead, he became a scandal.[1]

Late in the summer of 385 Jerome was brought before the ecclesiastical court and charged with clerical misconduct—that he used his reputation as a monastic guru to seduce and take advantage of Christian aristocratic women, financially and sexually.[2] For Jerome, however, his best defense was a good offense. He leaned into his relationships with the women as an alternative to distancing himself from the accusation of impropriety and touted what they were building together to be the pinnacle of Christian ascetic practice.[3] Central to this tack was Jerome's publishing of his letters to Marcella and Paula in order to shed some light on the real nature of the relationships and also, presumably, to take advantage of his notoriety to disseminate his particular brand of ascetic

1. Stefan Rebenich rightly points out that Jerome was never uncontroversial and, as a proponent of a particularly rigorous ascetic regime, he was often challenged and had fewer and less-committed fans than his writings would lead us to believe (*Jerome*, ECF [London: Routledge, 2002], 39–40).

2. Jerome, *Jerome's "Epitaph on Paula": A Commentary on the "Epitaphium Sanctae Paulae,"* ed. and trans. Andrew Cain, OECT (Oxford: Oxford University Press, 2013), 5.

3. Peter Brown, *Through the Eye of a Needle: Wealth, the Fall of Rome, and the Making of Christianity in the West, 350–550 AD* (Princeton: Princeton University Press, 2012), 262–63. See *Ep.* 22 for Jerome's detailed advice on how to follow the ascetic regimen.

devotion. All the talk of innuendos and indecorum generated enough heat, though, that even his best offensive strategy still involved his being disgraced and leaving Rome in August of 385. The widow Marcella chose to stay in Rome, which disappointed Jerome and prompted him to nag her continually to join him in the Holy Land. Paula was also a widow, although twenty years younger than the sixty-one-year-old Marcella, and she and her daughter Eustochium chose to follow Jerome.

## Marcella (ca. 325–410)

Marcella's father was already dead when her husband died after only seven months of marriage in the early 360s; neither man's name is mentioned. Thus she was her own woman in many ways, at least as much as a woman could be in Late Antique Rome. Marcella eschewed another marriage by refusing the famous but currently out-of-favor consul named Naeratius (or Neratius) Cerealis, who probably sought to marry downward into a rich family to stabilize his position.[4] In his *Life of Marcella* or *Letter* 127 to Principia (written in 412), Jerome reports that Marcella was not interested and was committed to the life of a pious widow.[5]

As a widow, Marcella was able to check a special box: that of a woman who had lived in a Roman marriage and had left it behind as no longer applicable. Heretofore, Marcella had to submit her wealth and dealings to a father or husband, but their deaths gave her a great deal of financial freedom. Being a widow also exempted Marcella from playing the games and fastidiously caring about the trappings of the aristocratic life. The pressure and the expectation to do so would have been overwhelming. This situation is not so terribly different from what happens every time the Duchess of Cambridge Kate Middleton steps out of her house; every inch of her person is scrutinized and expected to set or reinforce trends. Appearance has long indicated and determined status. Roman society in Late Antiquity is no exception. Marcella, Paula, and the other aristocratic women who disdained the acceptable accoutrements and expectations associated with their class were fracturing cultural architecture. Since the key Roman virtue for women was modesty, we should not be quick to categorize the Christian obsession with a plain appearance as a response to impropriety; it was not so much that as it was a reorientation of what it means for a woman

4. Brown, *Through the Eye of a Needle*, 269.
5. Jerome, *Life of Marcella* (*Ep.* 127) 2, in *Lives of Roman Christian Women*, ed. and trans. Carolinne White, Penguin Classics (London: Penguin, 2010), 60–61.

to exemplify modesty.[6] For the aristocracy in particular, Christian virtue demanded humility. What is going on here certainly does concern modesty, but in the context of a radical departure from the Roman articulation of it.

Jerome weaves a complex discursive web with seemingly apparent contradictions. Women like Marcella achieve freedom from many of the core duties of being Roman aristocratic women by gaining control over finances, a license to travel, and the ability to pursue a particular brand of Christian devotion that melds desire and utility together. At the same time, Jerome clearly does not achieve what we might consider a feminist moment; the intent was not to break patriarchy or attain women's liberation in the modern sense. Early Christian writers (and probably most early Christians, for that matter) understood Christian freedom to be about wholesale bondage to Christ. It was billed as a move with agency so as to give up agency, exchanging one master for another. Thus, when Jerome describes women who market themselves with flashy clothes and perfumes, saying, "Such women end up wishing to rid themselves of male domination, and they go in search of new husbands, not to serve them, as God wills, but to dominate them," he is setting up a dichotomy between masters and outlining the proper sphere for the exercise of feminine virtue.[7] For Jerome, Christian freedom for a woman (married or not) is not about liberation and independence; it is about properly ordered submission to the right master. Marcella, as a woman without father or husband, had two choices: she could go the worldly route and adorn herself to meet another man, which Jerome sees as venturing into the dangerous territory outside of the proper role of a woman (Christian or not); or she could go the route that Jerome touts as the proper Christian way—submit herself to Christ as master and, by extension, to his episcopal representatives (Jerome and bishops). This route was arguably characterized just as much by appearance and modes of behavior as that of typical aristocrats. Here scrutiny was paid to the level of renunciation, marking progress toward humility. Marcella stopped wearing jewelry and began to mediate her contacts with others so that only those who supported her in her ascetic journey spent time in her audience.[8]

Marcella's estate became a monastery, and she set the trend for many women to follow who imitated her and adopted "a way life that [had] turned Rome into Jerusalem" in order to practice asceticism and form monasteries of their own.[9] Any void of industry created by her abdication of the aris-

6. For a discussion on women in early Christianity and the virtue of modesty, see Wilkinson, *Women and Modesty.*
    7. Jerome, *Ep.* 127.3 (White, 62).
    8. Jerome, *Ep.* 127.3 (White, 62).
    9. Jerome, *Ep.* 127.8 (White, 66).

tocratic life was filled with Marcella's energetic and voracious appetite for Scripture. Jerome remembers well her insistence on spending time with him and her sharp refusal to be satisfied with simple answers to her questions on Scripture.[10] Marcella assumed that she would encounter opposition and was therefore assiduous in her preparation for any objection. In addition to all of her other laudable virtues and qualities, Marcella took advantage of everything Jerome had garnered in his study and made it her own—so much so that, after he left Rome, Marcella became the point person to resolve disputes over Scripture. Of course, to observe propriety with regard to a woman teaching, she leaned upon Jerome as her source of the knowledge and utility she had to offer.[11] Her zeal for study and her acuity seem to have surprised and vexed Jerome, who was still nursing his wound caused by her refusal to relocate with him.

*Letter* 46 (*On Visiting Jerusalem by Paula the Elder and Eustochium to Marcella*) to Marcella is traditionally thought to have been written by Jerome in the name of Paula and Eustochium for the purpose of persuading Marcella to visit the sacred sites in Palestine. However, as Carolinne White observes, there is no reason to think that Paula and Eustochium could not have written the letter.[12] *Letter* 46 is a valiant effort, complete with an appeal as Marcella's "pupils" to have the opportunity "to teach our teacher," banking upon Marcella's presumed desire to explore new avenues for study and to witness the success of her influence in their lives: "You were the first to put a spark to our little piece of kindling, you were the first to encourage us, by your words and by your example, to adopt this way of life and like a mother hen you gathered your chicks under your wings. Will you now allow us to fly free without our mother?"[13] *Letter* 46 leans heavily upon intricate interpretation of the biblical text and the redemptive activity of Christ (from Melchizedek as a type of Christ to the crucifixion) to heap significance upon being physically present in Jerusalem, especially since "the whole mystery of our faith is everyday reality in this province and in this city."[14] The author(s) offer(s) corrections to "absurd" interpretations of Jerusalem throughout Scripture, thereby mitigating some of the objections Christians might have to Jerusalem's educational and devotional importance in the Holy Land and at the same time demonstrating a facility with the text that would doubtless

10. Jerome, *Ep.* 127.7 (White, 65).
11. Jerome, *Ep.* 127.7 (White, 65–66).
12. White, *Lives of Roman Christian Women*, 166.
13. Jerome, *Ep.* 46.1 (White, 167).
14. Jerome, *Ep.* 46.3 (White, 169).

make Marcella proud.[15] The epistolary brochure promoting the must-see sites of the Holy Land did not have the desired effect on Marcella, but it does give us some idea of how Christians understood their relationship to the biblical text and physical space made sacred because of God's redemptive activity.

It is easy to forget or pass over the connections and relationships of women, like Marcella, as incidental to the development of the church. However, women were involved in the power networks of the time, heavily involved in the doctrinal discussions, and on the forefront of the construction of Christian identity. Jerome notes that the monastic life was not yet a trend among aristocratic Roman women, but Marcella had met Athanasius and Peter of Alexandria in the 340s during one of the many times the Arians had them on the run.[16] They told her of Antony and the monastic life of the virgins and widows at the monasteries in Egypt founded by Pachomius (ca. 292–348). Jerome portrays Marcella as uninterested in the approval of other nobles and desirous of such a radical life as would be "pleasing to Christ."[17] Marcella became an ascetic trendsetter, though, and many women followed her example, including Paula and her daughter Eustochium. Looking at the fruit of Marcella's example, Jerome quips, "It is easy to judge what the teacher must have been like if this is how her pupils turned out!"[18]

One of those doctrinal discussions became a full-blown "storm of heresy," as Jerome called the publishing of Rufinus of Aquileia's (the friend of Melania the Elder) "scandalous translation" of Origen's *On First Principles*.[19] Marcella had previously worked to avoid becoming partisan in such matters, but Jerome says that the last straw for her was when she observed the faith of many Romans being put in danger and the bishop remaining blissfully unconcerned and trusting. In a bold exercise of doctrinal authority and apologetic defense, she stepped into the public eye to take a stand.[20] Jerome proudly relates that at Marcella's instigation the heretics were roundly condemned

---

15. Jerome, *Ep.* 46.6 (White, 171–78, esp. 173), for instance.

16. Arius of Alexandria (ca. 250 or 256 to 336) had died, but his concern for preserving the transcendence of the Father that led to subordination of the Son raged on until February 27, 380, when Theodosius I issued an edict, *Cunctos populos*, that declared the Nicene trinitarian perspective of Jesus Christ as *homoousios* (same essence) with the Father to be the only legitimate orthodox claim.

17. Jerome, *Ep.* 127.5 (White, 64).

18. Jerome, *Ep.* 127.5 (White, 64).

19. Jerome, *Ep.* 127.9 (White, 66). Jerome, unsurprisingly, had some choice words on the Romans and their embrace of what he considered to be blasphemy: "It is not surprising that in the streets and marketplaces of the city a painted soothsayer can beat the buttocks of the foolish and knock out the teeth of objectors with his gnarled stick, seeing that this poisonous and filthy teaching could find people in Rome to lead astray."

20. Jerome, *Ep.* 127.9 (White, 66–67).

and sent on the run. She was the one who garnered eyewitness testimony of the damage that Origenism had caused and who had helped to dismantle their heretical leanings. She was the one who brought to light just how many were affected and who presented the translation of *On First Principles* as material evidence. She was also the one who began a letter-writing campaign against the "heretics," daring them to reveal and defend themselves. They did not. In Jerome's eyes, Marcella's act of courage served to bolster her orthodoxy and place it in juxtaposition to the display of cowardly reticence. Jerome gives honor to whom he believes it is due: Marcella single-handedly had achieved this victory.[21] For Jerome, the true faith and the lives of those who loved it were in grave danger, and Marcella was on the frontlines winning battles.

Owing to Marcella's understanding of the laudable seamless connection between teaching and action, it makes sense that she would view her obedient actions and diligent study finding their *telos* in the life to come. Jerome mentions that she thought highly of Plato's saying that philosophy was a preparation for death, finding Paul's "I die daily" and taking up the cross to communicate the same sentiment.[22] Yet none of this affords Jerome any comfort upon Marcella's death.

Jerome hears that Rome is under siege in 410 and that many citizens are being robbed and killed. It distresses him even to think about the destruction of the Eternal City and its people: "My voice sticks in my throat and sobs interrupt my dictation of these words. The city which captured the whole world has itself been captured."[23] He retreats into sections of Virgil's *Aeneid* to lament for Rome and for Marcella. Her house was raided, and the virgins with Marcella stayed at her side as she confronted her intruders. He reports that she showed no fear, and in response to their demands for gold, she pointed to her tunic, but they did not believe she had chosen to be poor. Marcella was then beaten with sticks, although Jerome says that she felt no pain. Any begging she did was on behalf of the young women who had stayed with her, that they not be taken away and raped. Jerome reports that Christ worked on their behalf, and the invading party exercised compassion by taking them to the safety of the Basilica of St. Paul. Marcella rejoiced in this intervention and in her asceticism, which had prepared her for such hardship as she and many others would face.[24] A few months later she died and made the poor her heirs through Principia.[25]

21. Jerome, *Ep.* 127.10 (White, 67–68).
22. See 1 Cor. 15:31 and Luke 14:27; Jerome, *Ep.* 127.6 (White, 64).
23. Jerome, *Ep.* 127.12 (White, 68).
24. Jerome, *Ep.* 127.13 (White, 69).
25. Jerome, *Ep.* 127.14 (White, 69).

## Paula (May 5, 347–January 26, 404)

For Jerome, Paula was special. He spares no praise in describing her as the epitome of what his ascetic program can produce. We can assume that this has a great deal to do with her sticking by Jerome when his ideas elicited accusations and punishment from the ecclesiastical establishment in Rome, following him to the Holy Land, and giving herself unreservedly to his particularly rigorous brand of Christian devotion. Several months after her death on January 26, 404, Jerome wrote his *Epitaph on Saint Paula* (*Epitaphium Sanctae Paulae*), or *Letter* 108, an exceptionally skillful text honoring a friend and comrade in the form of a letter to her daughter Eustochium.[26]

Paula and Marcella were related through Pammachius, Jerome's fellow student in the 360s, who was Marcella's cousin and the husband of Paula's second daughter, Paulina. It is possible that it was this school friend who aided a midthirties Jerome in gaining entry into their houses.[27] Paula's wealthy, provincial family was a relatively recent addition to Rome and claimed a legendary heritage.[28] Paula was born on May 5, 347, and grew up in Rome. In the early 360s she married Julius Toxotius and had four daughters (Blaesilla, Paulina, Julia Eustochium, and Rufina) and a son, Toxotius.[29] After her husband died, Paula charted a new course for her life of voluntary poverty and compassion.

Paula connected with Jerome early in her commitment to celibacy. He became Paula's spiritual director and scriptural tutor and monastic mentor to her daughter Eustochium, to whom he dedicated the famous and controversial *Letter* 22 (*Libellus de virginitate servanda*) on the ascetic life. After the Roman Christian establishment accused Jerome of effectively creating an elite class of Christian ascetics, Jerome responded with *Letter* 22, which only served to fan the flames since he intimates that marriage is a necessary evil and only for those who cannot attain to the spiritually elite. The controversy came to a head when Paula's oldest daughter, Blaesilla, named for her grandmother and a recent convert to asceticism, died at age twenty because she undertook a fasting regime that was too extreme. At her funeral, there were calls for the monks who manipulated her to be stoned. Paula seems to have ignored completely any accusations against Jerome and to have gone on

26. English translation in Cain, *Jerome's "Epitaph on Paula."*
27. Brown, *Through the Eye of a Needle*, 268.
28. Her father, Rogatus, was said to have descended from the great Agamemnon, and her mother, Blesilla, from the famous Scipios and the Gracchi (Jerome, *Ep.* 108.1.1–4; 3.1–4 [Cain, 43–47]); see Brown, *Through the Eye of a Needle*, 269.
29. Jerome, *Ep.* 108.4.1–2 (Cain, 47).

planning their joint pilgrimage and permanent relocation to the Holy Land.[30] Notably, in the *Epitaph on Saint Paula*, Jerome adjusts the narrative of Paula's final years in Rome to eradicate the scandal of his being charged and found guilty of clerical misconduct and his disgraced exit. He speaks of tempering her zeal instead of inflaming it, claiming the purest of intentions in all things. Jerome renders the scandal in terms of a manufactured distraction from the good and pure work that they were doing in obedience to God.[31]

The departure scene from Rome is difficult: Paula and Eustochium pulling away from the dock never to return, Paula's other children crying out to their mother not to abandon them, and Paula turning away, determined not to shed tears. Jerome muses on Paula's decision with admiration and tactful deference to Paula's pain: "She disregarded the mother in herself and as a result showed that she was fit to be a maidservant of Christ. She was in emotional agony, and she wrestled with her grief as though she was being torn from her very limbs, proving that she was more worthy of admiration than all others because she was conquering a great love."[32] He aligns his Paula with Paul, stating that she longed to be with the Lord and knew that her true citizenship was not Roman.[33] For Jerome, Paula had chosen the path of true devotion to God, which meant a revocation of all bonds that would distract her from that relationship. As an aristocrat, one had an ontology and function that were irrevocably tied to the Roman economic and family system and all of the requirements therein. It was part and parcel of the ascetic life choice to sever all bonds to the worldly power systems. This meant having to release family connections and all benefits and responsibilities. The noblewoman and mother had to die so that the ascetic paragon could live.

Andrew Cain lays out Paula's time line thus: after Jerome left Rome in August 385, he went to visit Epiphanius at Salamis on the island of Cyprus, where he waited until Paula, Eustochium, and their entourage came several weeks later.[34] After ten days of distributing alms to local monastic establishments, they set sail for Syria, making their way to Antioch and to Paulinus of Nola. Later in 385 they made their way to Jerusalem. They stayed at the

30. Cain, *Jerome's "Epitaph on Paula,"* 4–5. Palladius has a considerably different read on Jerome and Paula's "friendship" in his *Historia Lausiaca*. According to the outspoken Origenist, who was none too keen to afford Jerome any credit for Paula's or her daughter's reputed sanctity, Jerome "stood in her way," "thwarted her with jealousy and prevailed upon her to work to his own end and purpose" (Palladius, *Hist. Laus.* 41.2, in *Palladius: Lausiac History*, trans. Robert T. Meyer, ACW 34 [Westminster, MD: Newman, 1965], 118).

31. Cain, *Jerome's "Epitaph on Paula,"* 21.

32. Jerome, *Ep.* 108.6.3–5 (Cain, 49–51).

33. Jerome, *Ep.* 108.1.3 (Cain, 43).

34. Jerome, *Ep.* 108.7.1–3 (Cain, 51).

Mount of Olives monastery run by Melania the Elder and Rufinus of Aquileia (the same Rufinus whom Jerome later deems "the scorpion") and then went on an extensive pilgrimage of the holy sites through the spring of 386.[35] The end of the tour featured some time spent at the monastic cells at Nitria in northern Egypt, where Paula knelt at the feet of Isidore the Confessor and many others.[36]

Paula took to the pilgrimage with gusto. Jerome describes her as having trouble dragging herself away from one holy site to move on to another, throwing herself on the floor of Christ's tomb and tearfully kissing the stone at the entrance and licking the site where Christ had lain, and experiencing the events of Christ's birth (seeing the swaddled Savior and hearing the Magi worshiping God and the cries of babies being slaughtered by Herod), and prophesying about Bethlehem's significance in redemptive history at the Nativity grotto.[37] Paula's experience in the grotto seems to have designated Bethlehem as her destined home. She therefore began reorganizing the landscape, dotting it with several building projects that she financed from her fortune. These included a monastery for Jerome and a neighboring convent, both of which were erected near the Church of the Nativity.[38]

According to Jerome, Paula is like Abraham because she obeyed God and left her homeland to go where God told her to go. Cain observes that Jerome's comparison of Paula to Abraham is strategic:

> By superimposing the Abrahamic template onto her departure from Rome and subsequent settlement into Bethlehem, he is prompting his readership to conceptualize her life, in typological terms, as something of a biblical story itself. He also is offering Paula to contemporary senatorial Christians as the quintessential pilgrim and, as such, as the embodiment of his own teachings about sacred topography and the Christian's duty to deepen his or her faith by going on pilgrimage.[39]

The text compiles example after example of biblical sites (from both the Old and New Testaments) that Paula visited and a record of her experience at each one. Jerome supplements Paula's experience at the holy places with historical information that the attentive pilgrim would likely find helpful and meaningful in their own encounters at the various sites. Readers are meant

---

35. Jerome, *Ep.* 108.8.1–3 (Cain, 51–53); Lynda L. Coon observes that Paula tours sites in Palestine that are particularly associated with biblical women (*Sacred Fictions*, 104).

36. Jerome, *Ep.* 108.14.1–4 (Cain, 63–65).

37. Jerome, *Ep.* 108.9.1–8 (Cain, 53–57).

38. Jerome, *Ep.* 108.20.1–7 (Cain, 75–79).

39. Cain, *Jerome's "Epitaph on Paula,"* 19.

not only to read about these women but also to draw upon their examples as the wellspring for their own lives of devotion. Assuming a flow of pilgrims on their way to and from Jerusalem, such as the Bordeaux Pilgrim (early 330s) and Egeria (in 381 and 384), Paula likewise funded a nearby hostel to make it convenient for them to spend time at the nativity grotto.[40] Jerome also gives the exact location of her tomb so that the climax of a pilgrim's tour of the biblical sites would lead her to the place where she could mark Paula's life, imitate her devotion, and generally participate in the lives of the saints who have died.[41]

Paula's monastic establishments were viewed as an extension of her shift from the aristocratic economy based on acquisition and maintenance of wealth to a heavenly economy that bucked said values.[42] Thus life in Paula's monastery took on many of the characteristics of its founder. She does make one significant departure from the kind of monastic enterprise of Macrina, however: she divides the women in her monastery according to status and allows dispensations (though perhaps minimal) to those of aristocratic birth.[43] We see here continuity with some of Jerome's tendencies that so worried the church community in Rome; the preservation of social distinction upon taking up the ascetic mantle reeked of a dangerous elitism. Aside from the fact that Jerome's version of asceticism probably influenced this approach to some extent, the structure also reflects Paula's modus operandi of compassion and patience (Jerome takes pains to emphasize both), which allowed for a mitigation of some rigor for the sake of their devotion. Paula's modifications perhaps indicate an awareness of the difficulty inherent in the negotiation of asceticism and wealth.

Paula exhibited the same disgust for heresy (specifically that of Origenism) as her compatriots Marcella, Epiphanius, and Jerome. Naturally, that Jerome highlights this particular quality as staunch refusal to accept a false "orthodoxy" was in itself considered a mark of "orthodoxy." In light of this, it makes sense that Paula hands off dealing with an unnamed Origenist interlocutor to Jerome. He therefore includes the resulting debate dating to the 390s and early 400s on the nature of the resurrected body in the middle of his *Epitaph on Paula.*[44] It was, of course, as demanded by propriety, Paula's habit to avoid heretics as she did all pagans since she did not consider them to be different

40. Ibid., 15–16.
41. Ibid., 26.
42. Jerome, *Ep.* 108.20.1–7 (Cain, 75–79).
43. Jerome, *Ep.* 108.20.1 (Cain, 75).
44. Jerome, *Ep.* 108.23.1–25.4 (Cain, 81–87); the issues raised here are those central to the Origenist controversy: the nature of the resurrected body and the preexistence of souls.

José Luiz Bernardes Ribeiro CC BY-SA 3.0 / Wikimedia Commons

Figure 8.2. This painting by André Reinoso depicts Paula and her nuns in one of her monasteries in Bethlehem.

from pagans.[45] That Jerome got his hands dirty so she did not have to do so demonstrated her orthodoxy and her unassailable and irreproachable purity.[46]

Like Marcella, Paula is presented as exemplary in her extensive memorization of the Scriptures and in her biblical scholarship.[47] Cain observes that almost any time Jerome lends direct speech to Paula in his epitaph, she is quoting a biblical passage from memory, thereby substantiating his claim.[48] Like Marcella, Paula had a gift for languages, with fluency in both Greek and Hebrew, and Jerome marvels at Paula's lack of Latin accent when chanting the Psalms in Hebrew.[49] Not only could Paula read the Bible in the original languages; she also had a studied acuity in biblical exegesis. For example, Paula compiles several passages in order to defend her understanding of Bethlehem as a crucial site in the redemptive economy and decides on proper exegetical readings of passages based on her reading of the original language.[50] Up until Paula's very last moments, Jerome reports that she whispered passages of Scripture, and her death became an occasion for praise: "As soon as she heard her bridegroom summoning her: 'Arise, my love, my fair one, my dove, for the winter is over and the rain is gone,' she joyfully replied: 'Flowers have appeared on the earth, and the time to prune them has come,' and: 'I believe that I [will] see the goodness of the Lord in

45. Jerome, *Ep.* 108.23.1 (Cain, 81).

46. Cain, *Jerome's "Epitaph on Paula,"* 23.

47. According to Jerome, Paula had the Scriptures memorized yet also had a full-fledged and nuanced hermeneutical strategy that went along with her extensive knowledge of the text (*Ep.* 108.26.1–4 [Cain, 87–89]).

48. Cain, *Jerome's "Epitaph on Paula,"* 21.

49. Jerome, *Ep.* 108.26.3 (Cain, 89). Cain notes that facility in Hebrew was practically unheard of even among the most accomplished biblical commentators of the time (*Jerome's "Epitaph on Paula,"* 23).

50. Cain, *Jerome's "Epitaph on Paula,"* 21–22.

the land of the living.'"[51] Paula died when she was fifty-six years old at some point after sundown on January 26, 404.[52]

## Melania the Elder and Melania the Younger

The bitterest feuds happen between friends. What began as a loud argument in 397 between friends over how to read Origen, especially on the nature of the resurrected body, became a widespread controversy among the monastic establishment from Jerusalem to Rome. In the Origenist controversy, Paula, Marcella, and Jerome wrote and advocated against what they saw as dangerous and heretical understandings of Origen's writings. The conflict pitted ascetics against one another, and in Jerome and Rufinus of Aquileia's case, it made former friends into foes.[53] Both men were scholars who depended on the women in their lives for their livelihood and community. While Jerome had some financial support from Paula, Rufinus had the cavernously deep pockets of Melania the Elder.

The Origenist controversy was messy because it was about both doctrine and access to resources—scholarly, saintly, and financial. According to Brown, "In itself, the Origenist Controversy between Jerome and Rufinus was a storm in a teacup."[54] What he means by this is that the Origenist controversy was largely assumed to be an intramonastic debate (at the beginning anyway), one that involved a lot of money and rancor but was isolated to a specific corner of theological thought. Unfortunately, the Origenist controversy did not remain an acrimonious pamphlet war between two men; early on it already had the beginnings of a full-scale offensive on both sides, with the mechanisms in place to wreak havoc on the doctrinal unity of the church. One of those mechanisms was the availability of the scholars on both sides, because of financial backing, to write an enormous amount of material: letters, treatises, biblical commentaries, and so forth. Neither Jerome nor Rufinus was a bishop or under the authority of a bishop, and even though they ran monasteries, both had considerably more freedom and resources than a bishop like Augustine, for instance, to devote to producing so much material over such a long time.[55] Increased funding for monasteries and holy sites in

51. Jerome, *Ep.* 108.28.3 (Cain, 91–93); cf. Song 2:10–12; Ps. 27:13.
52. Jerome, *Ep.* 108.27.2 (Cain, 89–91).
53. For an examination of how social networks propelled the Origenist controversy, see Elizabeth A. Clark, *The Origenist Controversy: The Cultural Construction of an Early Christian Debate* (Princeton: Princeton University Press, 1992).
54. Brown, *Through the Eye of a Needle*, 280.
55. Ibid., 279.

Jerusalem meant that local churches were seeing money from wealthy donors shifting to Palestine, a situation that again put Jerome on the offensive in order to defend his ascetic program and its validity.[56] The church's response to Jerome, especially in Rome, was about the money, but it was also fueled by a suspicion regarding his (arguably) elitist idea of Christian devotion and community.[57] The other mechanism in place was extraordinary support from women such as Paula, Marcella, and Melania the Elder. Not only did they financially support the literary careers of their respective monastic scholars in residence; they also funded building projects, shepherded young women into asceticism, gave their friendship and their skills in languages and scholarship, lent their networks to drum up and buoy support, and allowed their sanctity to be fuel for their causes.

### Melania the Elder (ca. 341–ca. 410)

As a member of the highest echelon of the Roman aristocracy, the Spaniard Melania the Elder used her vast wealth to fund an array of monastic and scholarly endeavors. In scholarship, Melania was rivaled perhaps only by Marcella, and her theological acuity and friendship with Rufinus of Aquileia proved to be a worthy counterpart opposite Jerome, Marcella, and Paula in the Origenist controversy. Melania remained in Spain until after she was widowed at twenty-one years old (ca. 362) and lost two sons; at this point she moved to Rome with her remaining son, Publicola, for ten years.[58] Then she left Rome (causing quite a stir) after situating Publicola in another's charge

56. Ibid., 281–83. As Kate Cooper notes, the habit of the wealthy was to give large, onetime gifts, but this did not necessarily meet the needs of churches ("Poverty, Obligation, and Inheritance: Roman Heiresses and the Varieties of Senatorial Christianity in Fifth-Century Rome," in *Religion, Dynasty, and Patronage in Early Christian Rome, 300–900*, ed. Kate Cooper and Julia Hillner [Cambridge: Cambridge University Press, 2007], 168).

57. The Origenist controversy was not the only controversy in which Jerome became embroiled after his departure from Rome. Backlash to his characterization of virginity as of a higher rank than marriage came a few years after Jerome left Rome in 385 in the form of the monk Jovinian and other ascetics who refused to make such distinctions and compromise Christian unity. See David G. Hunter, *Marriage, Celibacy, and Heresy in Ancient Christianity: The Jovinianist Controversy*, OECS (Oxford: Oxford University Press, 2007).

58. Kevin Wilkinson takes issue with the popular perspective that Palladius either falsified or miscalculated the chronology of Melania's widowhood and her departure from Rome by ten years. He reconstructs a more compelling time line based on the resituating of Melania in her Spanish homeland as her place of residence for the first couple of decades of her life instead of assuming, on the basis of her status and possible family connections, that she lived in Rome. Wilkinson states that we can only speculate as to why Melania would move to Rome; Palladius's plausible answer is that with the death of his father, Publicola would need to secure his future in senatorial society and position among the influential elite ("The Elder Melania's Missing Decade," *JLA* 5 [2012]: 166–84).

and on a secure senatorial path and sailed to Alexandria (ca. 373). There she sold all of her material possessions in exchange for gold to support and spend time with a group of desert fathers for six months. Melania then traveled to Jerusalem in 374 and founded a monastery, where she resided for twenty-seven years with fifty virgins.

Melania's self-exile from Rome was more prolonged than that of Paula or that of her granddaughter Melania the Younger. Paulinus of Nola writes of a woman burdened by grief and left with a son who, instead of alleviating her pain, constantly reminded her of what she lost. According to Paulinus, Publicola was too young to understand or control his own emotions and therefore offered little solace to his mother.[59] The combination of her grief and loneliness did, according to Paulinus, bring her to a realization of the fragility of the world and the need for utter dependence on God. In response she "loved her child by neglecting him and kept him by relinquishing him"—that is, to a guardian until he reached the age of majority, twenty-five years old, and ultimately into the hands of God.[60] While grief prompted her reconsideration of the world, Paulinus does not credit her actions to grief but to a new perspective on life and love: "By commending him to the Lord she was to possess him in absence more firmly than she would have embraced him in person if she had entrusted him to herself."[61] Later, in his *Letter* 45 to Augustine, Paulinus expresses his admiration for Melania the Elder's restrained grief in response to the death of her only remaining son, Publicola (Melania the Younger's father) in 406 or 407. Augustine apparently bore witness to her shift from the pain of natural maternal affection to the

---

59. Paulinus, *Ep.* 29.8 (Paulinus, *Letters* [Walsh, 109]); Kevin Wilkinson points out that Paulinus's use of the term *infans*, indicating that Publicola was five years old or younger or exceptionally slow to develop, might be an exaggeration. If Paulinus is accurate, then this places Publicola's birth between 356 and 361. Regardless of the lack of precision in dating his birth, Wilkinson confidently posits Publicola to have been between twelve and seventeen when Melania left Rome in ca. 373. That Melania timed her departure from Rome to be almost exactly ten years after arriving, when Publicola was a teenager, makes sense, since her leaving occurred during or at the beginning of Publicola's tenure as *praetor urbanus*, as candidates for this office were designated by the Senate ten years in advance ("Elder Melania's Missing Decade," 180–81).

60. Paulinus, *Ep.* 29.9 (Walsh, 109–10). For a discussion on the nature of this guardianship, see Kevin Wilkinson, "Elder Melania's Missing Decade," 181–82. Palladius casts Melania's familial connection as supporting her abundance of hospitality. In effect, she gave so much of herself and her wealth for churches, monasteries, prisons, and others that a space for herself was not prioritized, including the space to love her son in a manner that was separate from her love for Christ. In this way Melania is presented as exemplifying an effective love that involved postponing her full transition from aristocrat to ascetic for ten years, thus allowing for the successful establishment of Publicola in education, character, marriage, and standing (Palladius, *Hist. Laus.* 54.2–3 [Meyer, 134]).

61. Paulinus, *Ep.* 29.9 (Walsh, 110).

pain that accompanied mourning the loss of opportunity for Publicola to relinquish his desire for worldly status and distinction and not to compromise his life after death.[62]

Melania the Elder was the kind of wealthy woman who barely registers as possible. Her wealth could have rivaled that of her younger in-law and governor-turned-bishop Paulinus of Nola, who was what one might term "filthy rich." Unlike Paula, Melania did not renounce her wealth in such a drastic fashion (although her granddaughter Melania the Younger will attempt to do so). The paradigm of the humble pilgrim traveling to visit the Holy Land was not one that fit Melania either, because in 373 she set out for the East on a mission of orthodoxy to lend her financial support to the pro-Nicene Egyptian monks under threat by the pro-Arian emperor Valens, whom Paulinus calls an Arian "lackey." This is a significant difference between Melania and other women in Late Antiquity: Melania came in, doctrinal guns blazing, to deal with a threat against orthodoxy. She was not a pilgrim; she was an enforcer who "stood fast for the faith."[63]

Another author who knew Melania the Elder personally and offers us another glimpse into her life is Palladius, bishop of Helenopolis. Palladius's *Lausiac History* (420), a reflection on his own experiences, including dialogues, speeches, and narratives, serves as a valuable resource with its distinctive account of Melania.[64] Palladius portrays Melania the Elder in the fashion of an ascetic sage, much like the desert fathers she endorsed so fervently.[65] In writing his history, he benefited from Melania's proximity to some ascetics and drew upon her as a source for information and for interviews with an ascetic like Alexandra, who locked herself in a tomb and died after not laying

---

62. Paulinus, *Ep.* 45.2 (Walsh, 246).

63. Paulinus, *Ep.* 29.11 (Walsh, 113).

64. One of the monks with whom Palladius spent many years in the desert was Evagrius of Pontus, who was probably the most famous among Melania the Elder's protégés. Another source for information about the elder Melania is the Evagrian letter collection. As Robin Darling Young observes, even though we only have evidence of Evagrius's side of the epistolary exchanges, they display a warmth of familiarity as well as some information that Palladius and Paulinus do not include. For example, according to Evagrius, Melania the Elder did not just read Origen; she lived a life guided by his work and was considered an ascetic sage. See Young's essay "A Life in Letters," in *Melania: Early Christianity through the Life of One Family*, ed. Catherine M. Chin and Caroline T. Schroeder (Oakland: University of California Press, 2016), 153–70.

65. As Demetrios S. Katos notes, Palladius pays homage to several women in the *Historia Lausiaca*, such as the famous Constantinopolitan heiress Olympias and Melania the Younger, both of whom are portrayed as following in the inspired footsteps of Melania the Elder. According to Katos, this approach was likely a way for Palladius to ingratiate himself with Empress Pulcheria and her sisters, who had taken public vows of chastity and reorganized their lives around ascetic study, works of mercy, and prayer (*Palladius of Helenopolis: The Origenist Advocate*, OECS [Oxford: Oxford University Press, 2011], 105).

eyes on another human in ten years.[66] It was clear to Palladius that the elder Melania had a reputation among the monks of Nitria as one who excelled in virtue and was dubbed a "female man of God."[67]

Melania's biblical and theological knowledge was legendary, and her facility with early Christian texts was of special note. Palladius records that she read three million lines of Origen, two and a half million lines of others such as Basil of Caesarea and Gregory, and enough commentaries on Scripture to dwarf Homer's *Iliad* by three hundred times. Palladius also makes special mention that this was no cursory reading; Melania worked through the texts she read meticulously, sometimes reading them repeatedly, up to seven or eight times.[68] Aside from her own scholarship, Melania and other friends took on the expensive and arduous task of copying and circulating the works of Rufinus.[69] Melania's habits of reading and studying come across as exacting and exhaustive, but Palladius is careful to specify that this was a productive project. He did not see Melania as engaging in drudgery; far from becoming bogged down by these texts, she reckoned them as constituting a path of liberation. Palladius offers a beautiful image of Melania's intensive study: "Thus it was possible for her to be liberated from *knowledge falsely so called* and to mount on wings, thanks to those books—by good hopes she transformed herself into a spiritual bird and so made the journey to Christ."[70]

According to Palladius, Melania was able to come to the aid of thousands of Egyptian monks who had been targeted by the emperor.[71] She provided refuge and food to those on the run and supported those who were arrested. The monks were not allowed servants, and Palladius records that Melania demonstrated the same verve she had in seeking out the desert monks in the first place: she donned a slave's hood to sneak them the necessities of life at night. He reports that when the consul found out that someone was disobeying his order, he threw Melania into prison, not knowing who she was—a mistake he would regret! Palladius records her as saying to the consul: "'I am So-and-so's daughter and So-and-so's wife. I am Christ's slave. Pray do not look down upon my shabby clothes, for I could make more of myself if

---

66. Palladius, *Hist. Laus.* 5.1–2 (Meyer, 36–37).
67. Palladius, *Hist. Laus.* 9 (Meyer, 43).
68. Palladius, *Hist. Laus.* 55.3 (Meyer, 136–37).
69. Brown, *Through the Eye of a Needle*, 279.
70. Palladius, *Hist. Laus.* 55.3 (Meyer, 137).
71. At Nitria, Palladius records that in addition to Pambo, Melania the Elder met Isidore the Confessor, Paphnutius of Scete, and others, spent six months with them, and was seeking out the monks in the Nitrian desert. These monks with whom she had spent so much time and energy were among those banished (*Hist. Laus.* 46.2–3 [Meyer, 123–24]).

I would. I have made this clear to you so that you may not fall under legal charges without knowing the reason'—for one must use the sagacity of a hawk where insensate people are concerned!"[72] When he introduces Melania in the *Lausiac History*, Palladius claims that he forgets which high-ranking man she has married.[73] That he truly forgot is unlikely, but this, in addition to his near flippancy in recording her response to the consul, indicates that Melania's nobility did not merely stem from her ancestry or her familial connections. She seemingly spoke a language of power that the consul understood, and he allowed her to visit the monks unhindered.

Paulinus records a similar stalwart Melania in the face of this adversity. When she was held in contempt by the imperial court for her actions in hiding the pro-Nicene monks from the Arian emperor Valens and was threatened if she did not comply in producing the wanted monks, Paulinus records that Melania fearlessly accepted whatever punishment they might mete out even though arrest was not the outcome she expected. Apparently the judge was so impressed with her that his rage cooled. The result of Melania's fearless advocacy was a remarkable boon for the pro-Nicene cause: "Her funds tipped the balance in favor of the anti-Arian party among the monasteries and heritages of northern Egypt."[74] That gumption for orthodoxy would propel her during the prolonged hostilities of the Origenist controversy to come.

Melania's compatriot Rufinus of Aquileia made the trip to Alexandria in the 370s to protect the pro-Nicene monks with her and accompanied her to Jerusalem, founding monasteries for men and women on the Mount of Olives in 378 or 380.[75] Rufinus stayed by Melania's side for over twenty years and returned to Rome in late 397 (probably settling in one of Melania's villas). After fleeing from the Goths as a refugee along with Melania the Younger and her husband, Pinianus, Rufinus died in Sicily in 412.[76] Melania lived on the Mount of Olives from the establishment of her monastery until her death in 399. That she set up residence in the Holy Land instead of embarking on a pilgrim's *peregrinatio religiosa* represents a major shift in how Christians interacted with the Holy Land. Melania the Elder and Rufinus preceded Paula and Jerome by ten years and during that time brought a stability of funding

72. Palladius, *Hist. Laus.* 46.4 (Meyer, 124).
73. Palladius, *Hist. Laus.* 46.1 (Meyer, 123). On the "plausible hypothesis" that identifies the urban prefect Valerius Maximus as Melania's husband, see Kevin Wilkinson, "Elder Melania's Missing Decade," 178–79.
74. Brown, *Through the Eye of a Needle*, 261.
75. Elizabeth A. Clark, *Ascetic Piety and Women's Faith: Essays on Late Ancient Christianity*, SWR 20 (Lewiston, NY: Edwin Mellen, 1986), 212.
76. Brown, *Through the Eye of a Needle*, 276.

to the monastic projects of Egypt and the Holy Land that had not been previously established.[77]

The "innuendoes" that were exchanged between Jerome (with Paula) and Rufinus (with Melania) had, as Brown quips, "nothing to do with sex and everything to do with money."[78] Rufinus gave as much as he took and fired back at Jerome's biting vitriol, which had a lot to do with his jealousy over the consistent and bountiful access to funds that Rufinus had through Melania the Elder. Instead of selling her estates and thrusting her wealth away from her, Melania the Elder carefully managed her estates to provide consistent income for the monastic establishments in the Holy Land.[79] It allowed Rufinus to live in comfort, working on his scholarship and not having to find other donors to prop up either his scholarly endeavors or monasteries. Melania had no trouble amassing important compatriots through family connections like Paulinus of Nola. It is understandably human of Jerome to chafe and huff in the face of the disparity and the slamming doors of any society connected to Melania the Elder.[80] The "storm in a teacup" that was the Origenist controversy had overflowed, and the ramifications continued into the sixth century; women such as Paula and Melania the Elder played crucial roles on all sides of the debate.

### Melania the Younger (ca. 385–ca. end of December 439)

Melania the Elder's granddaughter made her own path. We read in Gerontius's *Life of Melania the Younger* (*Vita Santae Melaniae Iunioris*) that Melania and Valerius Pinianus were a young couple with a bright future, the highest standing, and a vast fortune.[81] Instead of following in her grandmother's footsteps in order to preserve their family's fortune, Melania the Younger (born ca. 385 to the elder Melania's only surviving son, Valerius Publicola, and Caeonia Albina) could not justify her continued participation in the Roman aristocratic machine, for her "heart burned even more strongly with the divine fire."[82] When their two young children did not live

77. Ibid., 277; Palladius records that Melania built a monastery in Jerusalem and lived there for twenty-seven years and had fifty virgins in her charge (*Hist. Laus.* 46.5 [Meyer, 124]).

78. Brown, *Through the Eye of a Needle*, 277.

79. Ibid.

80. Ibid., 278.

81. Melania and her husband, Valerius Pinianus, were married when they were fourteen and seventeen, respectively (Gerontius, *Vit. Mel.* 1, in *The Life of Melania the Younger*, trans. Elizabeth A. Clark, SWR 14 [New York: Edwin Mellen, 1984], 28).

82. Gerontius, *Vit. Mel.* 2 (Clark, 28). Palladius directly ties the impetus for Melania the Younger's asceticism to the looming example of her grandmother in her life (*Hist. Laus.* 61.2 [Meyer, 142]). Gerontius, on the other hand, will not even mention Melania the Elder by name in his *Life of the Holy Melania the Younger*, perhaps for theologically charged reasons

past infancy, according to Palladius, "finally God took mercy on the young man and implanted in him a desire to leave the world."[83] This transition was anything but easy. In Melania's story we see the difficulty inherent in making the ascetic choice, especially because of the societal entanglement involving extreme wealth in Late Antiquity, as well as an example of the strained relations those of wealth and reputation had with local churches.

In this case, ascetic desire presented a new problem that did not have an immediate solution and had potentially troubling consequences: two vast fortunes without heirs.[84] Melania and Pinianus's renunciation was particularly precarious, not only because they tapped into the growing sense of anxiety associated with the unsettling times in which they lived, but also because they were young and making drastic decisions, a combination that "represented an alliance of vast wealth with eccentricity not usually encountered even in late Roman Rome."[85] As long as her father, Publicola, was alive, he was the guardian of the familial patrimony, and Melania was limited in her actions. According to Gerontius, "Melania and Pinian suffered much pain since they were unable to take up the yoke of Christ freely because of their parents' compulsion."[86] Seven years into their marriage, however, Publicola on his deathbed asked Melania to forgive him for obstructing her desire to live a life of renunciation. Upon his death, Melania and Pinianus left their family palace in Rome and moved to the suburbs to begin their ascetic journey.[87]

---

related to the elder Melania's Origenism. For more on the differences between Palladius's and Gerontius's accounts and the complex matter of negotiating inherited wealth and spiritual legacy in aristocratic families like Melania's, see Christine Luckritz Marquis, "Namesake and Inheritance," in Clark, *Life of Melania*, 34–49.

83. Palladius, *Hist. Laus.* 61.3 (Meyer, 142). Palladius includes a brief biography of Melania the Younger in *Hist. Laus.* 61, but it is the priest Gerontius's Greek *Life of Melania the Younger*—written in 452–53 in Jerusalem, over ten years after Melania the Younger's death in Bethlehem on December 31, 439—that is our main source. The *Life of Melania the Younger* exists in Greek and Latin, and both texts appear to be independent reworkings of a lost original by Gerontius in Greek from before the Council of Chalcedon (451). According to Timothy D. Barnes, the Greek reproduces the original more faithfully (*Early Christian Hagiography and Roman History* [Tübingen: Mohr Siebeck, 2010], 249).

84. In other words, the wealth was not going to be shifted back into the aristocratic establishment by flowing around them to a son (as in Melania the Elder's case) or another family member (Brown, *Through the Eye of a Needle*, 295).

85. Ibid., 296. Elizabeth Clark explains that a young couple like Melania and Pinianus needed a "special dispensation" in order to dispose of their property but, even if that were granted, there were safeguards in place for the family to renege on the venture if the young person demonstrated their unfitness (*Ascetic Piety and Women's Faith*, 69).

86. Gerontius, *Vit. Mel.* 6 (Clark, 30).

87. Gerontius, *Vit. Mel.* 7 (Clark, 31); Roberto Alciati and Mariachiara Giorda, "Possessions and Asceticism: Melania the Younger and Her Slow Way to Jerusalem," *ZAC* 14 (2010): 430–32.

The Roman Empire in 406, some thirty years after Melania the Elder uprooted herself and moved to Palestine, was on a precipice; the aristocracy was weaker than ever, and the Goths were crouched at their front door, ready to pounce. It was under these circumstances that Melania the Younger wanted to dissolve one of the largest and most stable estates in the Roman Empire. Melania and Pinianus upset everyone from their slaves to the imperial family when they abdicated the responsibility of their position in 408, selling or giving away their wealth as quickly as possible. To say that these actions caused a stir would be an understatement. Even with their forceful untangling from their bequest and all that went with the aristocratic life, they still had to contend with how to liquidate and distribute their funds.[88] Considering that Melania is said to have had an income of 120,000 gold solidi per annum (around 1,660 pounds of gold), this was no small feat.[89] Some of their money went to the poor, but the majority of it went toward building and sustaining monastic communities. This shift into asceticism, which happened in fits and starts, also involved reneging their identities as Roman aristocrats and appropriating identities as aristocrats-turned-ascetics. The path Melania and Pinianus took was still very new, and it took the church some time to figure out how to embrace the windfall that accompanied the conversion of the aristocratic conscience and, at the same time, shepherd the eager ascetics-to-be into a new life that was marked by the death of their old lives.

Melania, Pinianus, and Melania's mother, Albina, were among the fortunate refugees who were able to cross the Mediterranean to the safety of North Africa later in 410, "just as Alaric set foot on the property the blessed ones had just sold."[90] Their time spent at their estate just outside of Augustine's hometown of Thagaste proved to be a lesson in cultural and ecclesiological differences. Augustine's longtime friend Alypius was bishop of Thagaste at the time, and upon their arrival the aristocrats-turned-ascetics were eager to get to work in helping the area poor. Word about the potential new benefactors in the area spread quickly.[91] Thus it is no surprise that in the spring of 411, when Melania, Pinianus, and Alypius traveled to meet Augustine in Hippo, his congregation clamored to have Pinianus ordained

88. According to Catherine M. Chin, selling an inherited home such as Melania and Pinianus's estate (traditionally thought to have been on Caelian Hill) was difficult, to say the least. As Chin observes, the house cooperated with Melania and Pinianus's desires only when it was burned by the Goths ("Apostles and Aristocrats," in Chin and Schroeder, *Melania*, 21–22).

89. Gerontius says that this does not even include her real estate holdings or movable goods (*Vit. Mel.* 15 [Clark, 38]; Brown, *Through the Eye of a Needle*, 17).

90. Gerontius, *Vit. Mel.* 19 (Clark, 42).

91. According to Gerontius, other bishops were envious of Alypius as a result of the new ascetics' generous gifts to the church in Thagaste (*Vit. Mel.* 21 [Clark, 44]).

priest. If this wealthy man is determined to give away all of his money, then let it be in Hippo! It was a situation charged with need and opportunity as the congregation demanded Pinianus's ordination in Hippo (thus sealing his benefaction as well).[92] The stakes were high for Pinianus, who would have had to put down roots and commit his wealth to Hippo, but Augustine came up with a solution that allowed Pinianus a way out and would also appease his congregation: get Pinianus to vow that if he ever were to seek ordination, it would be at Hippo.[93]

The plan did not go as expected. Augustine was ready to accept Pinianus's oath when Melania stopped Augustine from adding his name.[94] This charged moment was a tricky negotiation of authority between the aristocrat-turned-ascetic woman and the North African bishop: "In Augustine's recounting, Melania's protest—her 'no'—commands the immediate obedience of the great bishop, so much so that he leaves off signing his full name."[95] The situation indicates that the Roman aristocrats-turned-ascetics had underestimated their value outside of the Roman aristocratic bubble and did not seem to realize just how large the disparity truly was between their kind of wealth and even the wealthiest of provincials.[96] Melania and Pinianus were disappointed by the incident and returned to their estate, leaving Augustine to sort out the mess. Augustine attempts to do so in two letters (our only reference to the incident since Gerontius does not mention it in his *Life of Melania the Younger*): one to a hurt Alypius and another in response to Melania's mother Albina (her letter is not extant), who regarded his congregation as threatening, manipulative, and grabby and who needed convincing that her son-in-law had not given his oath under duress.[97] Augustine had to find some way to soothe the aristocrat-turned-ascetic ego by assuring Albina that Pinianus's character

92. Brown, *Through the Eye of a Needle*, 324.

93. Cooper, "Poverty, Obligation, and Inheritance," 167.

94. Augustine, *Ep.* 126, *To Albina*, in Augustine, *Letters*, vol. 2, *83–130*, trans. Wilfrid Parsons, FC 18 (New York: Catholic University of America Press, 1953), 349.

95. Susanna Drake, "Friends and Heretics," in Chin and Schroeder, *Melania*, 171.

96. Brown, *Through the Eye of a Needle*, 324–25. Brown points out that this was a clash of the entitled wealthy and the overweening mania of a provincial church to acquire a benefactor. He explains how the churches of Africa had not enjoyed much investment, either by senators or wealthy bishops.

97. Augustine, *Ep.* 125, *To Alypius*; and *Ep.* 126, *To Albina*; in Augustine, *Letters* (Parsons, 2:339–56); Kim Power expands on how Augustine navigated this authority structure that was a consequence of the former aristocratic status and the sanctity of the women with Pinianus: "Despite the fact that it was Pinianus' ordination at stake, it is clearly Albina and Melania who wield the power and who must be placated, possibly because much of the wealth at stake also derived from Pinianus' (continent) marriage to the heiress, Melania" (*Veiled Desire: Augustine on Women* [New York: Continuum, 1996], 117–18).

was at the forefront of the minds of those in his congregation and to speak for, as diplomatically as possible, the very poor who would benefit from such a patron.[98] In the end the couple took the advice of Augustine, Alypius, and Aurelius of Carthage and established a monastery for 130 women and another for 24 men.[99] They remained in Thagaste until 417, when they made their way to Palestine.

We again see the difficulty inherent in the renunciations of aristocrats-turned-ascetics illustrated in Melania and Pinianus's eager signing of their names on the church poor registry in Jerusalem.[100] They certainly identified as "poor," but their situation was hardly that of the poor the church had in mind to serve with the registry, especially considering that just a short time later Melania was able to build a new monastery at her own expense.[101] The voluntary poverty of aspiring ascetic aristocrats pushed a discussion of the theological significance of being "poor in spirit" for those who did not reflect the reality of the truly destitute. It was a complex problem because Melania and Pinianus had given up everything and worked diligently to rid themselves of everything of their old lives, but there was no way to eradicate the mark of privilege. As we saw with Jerome's friends, it was a constant refusal of wealth and status over the course of one's life that marked the truly "poor in spirit" among aristocrats-turned-ascetics. Sanctity, then, was marked by relentless philanthropy. One gets the impression that no one was quite sure what it looked like for rich persons to sell everything they had and give the money to the poor (cf. Matt. 19:21; Mark 10:21; Luke 18:22). For Gerontius, they were driven by a Christ-shaped relentlessness: "Thus they became extremely poor for the sake of the Lord, who himself became poor for our sakes and who took the form of a servant."[102]

98. Cooper assesses Augustine's public relations move as unconvincing ("Poverty, Obligation, and Inheritance," 167).

99. Unfortunately, as Alciati and Giorda point out, we do not have much information about the seven years the couple remained in Africa and consequently little on the specifics of how involved Melania and Pinianus were in the administration of these monasteries ("Possessions and Asceticism," 435). For Late Antique sources on Melania's monasteries, see Palladius, *Hist. Laus.* 61.6 (Meyer, 143); and Evagrius Scholasticus, *Historia ecclesiastica* 1.21, 49–51, in *"The Ecclesiastical History" of Evagrius Scholasticus*, trans. Michael Whitby, Translated Texts for Historians 33 (Liverpool: Liverpool University Press, 2000).

100. Gerontius, *Vit. Mel.* 35 (Clark, 51).

101. According to Cooper, "It is likely that, like many an aristocratic black sheep before her, Melania's habit was to spend down her revenues as they came in, and then to wait out the lean periods" ("Poverty, Obligation, and Inheritance," 170). For an exploration of how early Christians thought theologically and practically about wealth and poverty, rich and poor, see Helen Rhee, *Loving the Poor, Saving the Rich: Wealth, Poverty, and Early Christian Formation* (Grand Rapids: Baker Academic, 2012).

102. Gerontius, *Vit. Mel.* 35 (Clark, 51).

A drastic upheaval in the lives of one Roman couple had economic and social ramifications on its own merits, but that decision and the decisions of others to renounce their wealth indicates an increasing anxiety among the aristocracy that also had theological consequences. According to Brown, the infamous Pelagian controversy that is so often characterized as a massive clash between Augustine and Pelagius was just as much about the Gothic invasion and the Roman aristocracy's "crisis of wealth" as it was about theology.[103] In short, Alaric was "unwittingly responsible for the Pelagian Controversy" by forcing so many of Rome's powerful out of Rome into Africa.[104] As we saw with Monica, Augustine's mother, the differences between North African Christianity and that of Italy were significant; in this case, the teachings of the Roman Christian intellectuals were troublingly foreign to the Christianity of Africa.[105]

Aristocrats-turned-ascetics like Melania the Younger used their money not to fund local churches, but to sponsor the intellectual endeavors of their mentors that fueled the theological climate of scholarship and controversy.[106] Rufinus of Aquileia (the elder Melania's ascetic compatriot at the center of the Origenist controversy) was part of the entourage that left Rome with Melania, Pinianus, and Albina. Not only was Rufinus's translation of Origen's *Commentary on Romans* heavily used by Pelagius; the three intrepid aristocrats-turned-ascetics also met with Pelagius in 418 in Palestine after only recently leaving Augustine's company in North Africa.[107] The trio thought their efforts to diffuse the rising tension between Pelagius and Augustine were successful, that Pelagius had clearly affirmed the need for the grace of God through Christ and anathematized those who did not. However, Augustine did not consider their efforts to have succeeded and tells them so in *On the Grace of Christ*, his response in 418 to their letter.[108] It is likely due to the close proximity of Melania, Pinianus, and Albina until 417 in Thagaste that explains Augustine's reluctance to go after Pelagius by name until 415.[109]

103. Brown, *Through the Eye of a Needle*, 291.

104. Ibid., 300.

105. Brown writes: "It was from this growing sense of otherness—as Christian thinkers fostered in one great urban tradition brushed against the accepted wisdom of another—that what we call the Pelagian Controversy exploded" (ibid., 301).

106. Brown explains how the mutually beneficial mentor-protégé relationship accounts for the rise of Pelagius and his connection with the famous Christian Anician family (ibid., 301–3).

107. For the connections between Melania the Younger et al. and Pelagius, see E. Clark, *Ascetic Piety and Women's Faith*, 75–76.

108. Augustine, *On the Grace of Christ, and on Original Sin* 1.2, in NPNF[1] 5:218 (https://www.ccel.org/ccel/schaff/npnf105.xv.iii.html).

109. E. Clark, *Ascetic Piety and Women's Faith*, 76.

In addition to her theological advocacy, Melania the Younger propelled the monastic movement forward in Jerusalem by founding monasteries and having a considerable degree of authority over their oversight. Even though there was already a strong presence of Christian buildings in Jerusalem, such as the Church of the Eleona (between 326 and 333) and the Church of the Ascension (constructed either in the early fourth century by Constantine or later in the fourth century by a woman named Poemenia), Melania the Younger wanted to populate the religious skyline even more specifically with monastic communities. After the death of her mother, Albina, and a few years after her husband died, Melania built the Apostolium (431–32) on the Mount of Olives, where she lived with ninety women until 435–36, and another monastery for women in 432 with a martyrium where she housed relics from Zachariah, Stephen, and the Forty Martyrs of Sebaste. She followed that up by founding a monastery for men in 435–36 and entrusting its construction to Gerontius.[110] Melania's influence did not wane even several years into her time in Palestine and after Pinianus died. When she accepted an invitation from her powerful pagan uncle Rufius Antionius Agrypnius Volusianus in Constantinople, Melania took the opportunity in order to see him convert on his deathbed and to establish a relationship with the Empress Eudocia.[111] A year later Melania accompanied the empress on pilgrimage to the holy sites in Palestine. Melania the Younger's influence upon the ascetic landscape, in theological debate, and on those in power was expansive.

At this point it should be clear that telling the story of the development of Christianity without women is impossible. Women were on the cutting edge of Christianity's search for place and identity. They contributed substantively to scholarship and the development of practice. Women like Paula and Melania the Elder were in the thick of controversy as divergent aristocrats and theological participants. Marcella's and Melania the Younger's stories offer us a window into the societal and economic complexity inherent in the ascetic choice, especially for women of high status and wealth. Choosing the ascetic life was a choice with expansive implications. The erudition of these women allowed them to meet the needs of their respective communities for biblical

110. Gerontius, *Vit. Mel.* 41–48 (Clark, 55–61); Alciati and Giorda, "Possessions and Asceticism," 436.

111. Gerontius, *Vit. Mel.* 50–55 (Clark, 62–68). As was common in the "lives" of saintly people in Late Antiquity and beyond, Gerontius includes miracles performed by Melania the Younger, such as the healing of Empress Eudocia's ankle while she was on pilgrimage and when Melania takes upon herself the pain of her dying, pagan-turned-deathbed-Christian uncle Rufius Antionius Agrypnius Volusianus and, in christological imitation, carries it until he dies on January 6, 437 (Barnes, *Early Christian Hagiography*, 250).

Figure 8.3. The *Menologion* or *Service Book* of Basil II is an illuminated manuscript, compiled ca. 1000 CE, that includes many miniature paintings like this depiction of Melania the Younger.

and theological interpretation and to contribute significantly to the current discussions both in terms of their own theological work and rallying their networks to their respective theological causes.

## Conclusion

The gendered categorization of the Greco-Roman virtues (men are courageous, women are modest, and so forth) caused problems for early Christian writers and in turn raises questions for us readers. The inadequacy of available language and categories to mark an exemplary woman for more than her modesty, industry, and loyalty to her family shows up in the descriptions of men like Gregory of Nyssa, who famously says of his sister Macrina: "It was a woman who prompted our narrative, if, that is, we may call her a woman, for I do not know if it is appropriate to apply a name drawn from nature to one who has risen above nature"; or Paulinus of Nola, who says of Marcella: "What a woman she is, if one can call so virile a Christian a woman!"[112] In

112. Gregory, *Vit. Macr.* 1.5 (Silvas, 110); Paulinus, *Ep.* 29.5–6 (Walsh, 105–6). For a discussion on the virtues of Greco-Roman women, see Hylen, *Modest Apostle*, 23–31.

chapter 2 we looked at Perpetua's fourth vision, wherein she engaged in a gladiatorial bout and declared, "I became a man." How are we to process this language in the texts?

David Brakke helpfully situates this language in the broader scope of the rise and development of the language of monasticism in early Christianity. With regard to a monk's assumption of identity, Brakke writes: "Whether he was fighting demons or his own passions or both, the monk imagined himself as an *agōnistēs*, a 'fighter,' 'contender,' or 'combatant'—a masculine figure. He was a gladiator in the arena facing down demonic beasts or a soldier in the army of Christ arrayed against the demonic army of Satan."[113] Just as Perpetua did not somehow change sex but, as a woman, claimed the masculine quality of courage that fit the gendered constructions available to her, so also desert monks drew upon those same constructions and claimed the same courage as gladiators in the desert arena. We should also remember the "pedagogical pregnancy" of Methodius in chapter 4, that "feminine" experience in which men were also to participate. In other words, the discursive identities of men *and* women were undergoing significant shifts as a result of asceticism. The ascetic ideal brokered a new relationship between the body and spiritual realities in light of the *imitatio Christi* and the resurrection, and the working out of this new relationship involved an interrogation of received understandings about the body (male and female).

The "manliness" attributed to the aristocrat-turned-ascetic women in this chapter certainly echoes the agonistic bent of the desert ascetics. This is not surprising considering how influential the desert way was on women like Melania the Elder and her granddaughter Melania the Younger and on those who wrote about them. But these women and others were also forging a new path, one that Clark calls a "genteel form of asceticism."[114] The ascetic life, then, functionally molded the distinctive experiences of men and women in the empire into a more one-size-fits-all Christian devotion.[115] The messy deliberation on embodiment, virtue, and theology comes out not only in writing as in the above examples by Gregory and Paulinus, but also in the practices described. The negotiations over how much fasting is too much, how much

---

113. David Brakke, *Demons and the Making of the Monk: Spiritual Combat in Early Christianity* (Cambridge, MA: Harvard University Press, 2006), 182.

114. Elizabeth A. Clark, "Ascetic Renunciation and Feminine Advancement: A Paradox of Late Ancient Christianity," *AThR* 63 (1981): 246.

115. According to Katos, Palladius demonstrated an operational ascetic theology in the *Historia Lausiaca* that assumed universality with regard to gender, race, and class. Thus "[Palladius] used the term 'holy fathers' to refer to both men and women, and they could be drawn from the classes of the educated and the illiterate, the nobility and the commonality" (Katos, *Palladius of Helenopolis*, 105).

suppression of one's former identity is necessary, and how much and in what way to regulate the appearance of women ascetics are all examples of forging new foundations for the architecture of the virtuous life. These negotiations are examples of performative theology, the working out of theological ideas and principles through embodied practice.

# 9

## Aelia Pulcheria, "Protectress of the Empire," and Empress Eudocia, a Theological Poet

**Being Empress**

Disney has created an empire based on princesses. The billions of dollars spent every year on princess costumes, movies, and dolls scratch an itch for access to the illusion of royalty and all of the trappings that go with it. Our idea of what it means to be a princess, however, is far removed from the reality of such a position. The same is true with what we think a queen is. A queen might be a cherished public symbol with little governing power or, more likely, a dangerous and even evil woman with great power and serious issues. The idea of empress invokes images of a woman with sweeping power—an image that we cannot seem to separate from a sense of danger. A woman with great power is not an immediately accessible concept; in fact, it tends to cause trepidation and suspicion. So we are faced with two problems here: first, deconstructing the idea that women with true power are dangerous and thus ill-suited for such roles; and second, understanding what it meant to be an empress in the Late Antique Roman Empire.

While the title "empress" has long been out of usage in the Western world, China had queens and empresses as recently as 1946. The fact that we in the West have trouble conceiving of what it would mean to be an empress also says something about whose history we tell and whose we do not. In any case, this title has caused early Christian and Byzantine historians (ancient and modern) no shortage of difficulty in trying to define exactly what the parameters of an empress's position were and how much power she actually wielded. As a result, we have to be careful how we read motivations and actions, especially of those in power. The tendency is to assign official actions to the imperial title (emperor, empress, and so forth) and things that sound Christian to the personal devotion of the subject. For instance, assigning Helena Augusta's trip to the Holy Land as primarily (or merely) a pilgrimage might say something important about the Augusta's Christian devotion, but in the midst of focusing on that at the expense of the official nature of her journey, we might also end up stripping her of the obvious imperial weight that she wielded. It was because she was both Christian and imperial that she effected change in the architecture of piety in the Holy Land.

Why is this caveat so important? Because we are heading into stories of scandal. It should come as no surprise that Christian women did not all have the same experiences in life. It is easy to focus only on the "holy women" of Late Antiquity and leave out some of the other examples. Since we know so little of women at the time, it makes sense to want those whom we do know to be shining exemplars of Christian devotion. In order to protect the little we know, we find it easy to skip over the complexity. This impulse toward selective history is certainly not limited to women in early Christianity; it is a very human impulse to assert control over the narrative that one holds as precious. We explain away questionable actions of our heroes and dismiss problematic ideologies as youthful indiscretions or fringe outliers. While this impulse is understandable, it is antithetical to the project of a historian, who should exercise empathy but also not shrink back from honest appraisal. Complex subjects are more interesting anyway! And early Christian empresses are certainly complex and very interesting.

On the level of Christianity and empire, this engagement is a far messier and imperfect union; but Roman imperials adapted, absorbing and rewriting what it meant for the imperial to include the Christian understanding of power made perfect in weakness as exemplified by Christ's humility (albeit with great difficulty and with varying results).[1] Empresses were swept up in

1. Like the early fourth-century discussions about the divine and human natures of Christ, a central question for the newly Christian empire was how the one obviously more powerful

the evolving situation of women in Christianity and also in its redrawing of imperial authority. Early Christian historians had the difficult job of figuring out how to categorize the confluence of apparent contradictions that were Christian empresses. Thus we find them praised, reviled, or curiously absent. It was difficult enough for early Christian writers (and probably everyone in the Roman Empire) to parse what it meant to be imperial and Christian at the same time, let alone imperial, Christian, and a woman. It will be part of the role of this chapter to explain how empresses possessed and exercised authority and power.

What kind of power did an empress actually wield? A more substantial understanding of the seemingly liquid role of empress is not only possible but also necessary to address her execution of power adequately.[2] The imperial institutional architecture allowed women to hold power, but questions remain as to how consistent, comprehensible, and extensive that power was. Did an empress's power and authority originate from her position, or was it of a more personal nature, such as whether she bore children or because she displayed a certain force of personality? As we are dealing with complex subjects, the answer is likely a combination of factors. One impulse we need to check in our reading of empresses and other women with power is the urge to dismiss their actions as unofficial and slot them into the "maneuvering" or "intrigue" category.[3] In this way we can easily cast women who assert power as not just women with power but also manipulators who grasp at power that is not really theirs, whereas empresses did in fact possess power, authority, and influence.

Unfortunately, it is all too common for women in power today to be slapped with descriptors that separate their femaleness from their power, as though one cannot both be female and have power. The qualities that are praised in a man are often maligned in a woman; instead of "strong" she is "bossy," instead of "ambitious" she is "imperious," instead of "frank" she is "bitchy," instead of displaying "strong leadership" she is "domineering." The idea that

---

authority (imperial/divine) preserves the other obviously weaker counterpart (Christian/human). The solution in both situations is similar: power and authority too narrowly defined as ability and warrant to act over and against another (person, country, discourse, nature) is not a sufficient rendering of power and authority. We assume that power "takes" or "overwhelms" or "lords over," whereas, as the Christian narrative radically states, true power and authority is located with a God who is fully actualized goodness and love perfectly put on display in the ultimate act of humility—the incarnation. In orthodox Christology the divine does not overwhelm the human because God's perfect love preserves it.

2. Liz James, *Empresses and Power in Early Byzantium*, Women, Power, and Politics (New York: Leicester University Press, 2001).

3. James offers some examples in Eudoxia, Pulcheria, and Eirene (ibid., 2).

women are somehow ill suited to or naturally not prone to wielding power is a pervasive and often subconscious notion. Such assumptions are especially problematic with regard to the empresses because it is not immediately obvious what the job description of empress in the predominantly male space of the early Byzantine Empire actually entailed.[4] Thus it is important that we interrogate even the language we use and perhaps expand our understanding of power.

Byzantine historian Liz James helpfully draws on Pauline Stafford's work on medieval queens and defines power and authority as "the ability to act, to take part in events, to have a strategy and to pursue it, without necessarily succeeding, and to be in a position to influence others and to use their labours for one's own prestige. Authority gives one the right to act, gaining obedience without force."[5] To be in power in the early Byzantine Empire included but was not limited to the traditionally male realms of politics, military control, and ecclesiastical authority. A woman's power was circumscribed, but that does not mean that her power was nonexistent or that she did not exercise her power well. These lines of circumscription were more porous than they seem. While casting a Byzantine empress as a Joan of Arc leading an army would be a mistake since, as an imperial woman, she could not command an army, recognizing an empress's authority in administrating the finances of the empire, commissioning public works, and being a key player in ecclesiastical matters is reflective of reality.

This chapter will focus on two contemporary but very different empresses, Aelia Pulcheria and Eudocia. Pulcheria grew up in the imperial family, while Eudocia was elevated from relative obscurity. Pulcheria committed herself to Christianity and virginity from a very young age, and Eudocia converted because of her marriage but became devoted to Christianity. Both women were heavily involved in theological affairs. While Pulcheria became the darling of the orthodox, Eudocia lived out her days far from Constantinople and perhaps even far from orthodoxy. In Pulcheria we have a born leader whose life revolved completely around God and empire. In Eudocia we have a poet and pilgrim who was likely no less devoted to God and made her own way in the world. Their differences allow us to see more shades of imperial life and

4. See James, *Empresses and Power*, 3–4. Averil Cameron notes that at certain points in the Byzantine Empire this structure opens, such as with the behavior of imperial women like Irene and Zoe ("Sacred and Profane Love: Thoughts on Byzantine Gender," in James, *Women, Men and Eunuchs*, 3).

5. Pauline Stafford, "Emma: The Powers of the Queen in the Eleventh Century," *Queens and Queenship in Medieval Europe: Proceedings of a Conference Held at King's College London, April 1995*, ed. Anne J. Duggan (Rochester, NY: Boydell, 1997), 8–13, quoted in James, *Empresses and Power*, 6.

offer us an opportunity to consider the interactions between two women in power at the same time.

## Pulcheria (January 19, 399–ca. August 453)

Aelia Pulcheria was the daughter of Emperor Arcadius and Empress Eudoxia, sister to Theodosius II, Arcadia, and Marina, wife of Marcian, mother to a group of consecrated virgins, and protector of the empire; but for Pulcheria one relationship was primary above all others: virgin of Christ.[6] Named after her grandfather's dead sister, Pulcheria was born January 19, 399, a little over two years before her brother and future emperor Theodosius II (b. April 10, 401). As a daughter of an emperor, Pulcheria was expected to participate in the perpetuation of the Theodosian house. The most obvious way to do so was to be matched advantageously in marriage and continue the family line with children. This was not, however, the only or even the primary way that empresses participated in buoying their respective dynasties.

The acquisition of and access to power in Byzantium depended upon access to the emperor.[7] While one could hold an official position of great power, such as praetorian prefect, one's success in that role depended on the emperor's favor. So in this way, while an empress's position was not obviously official in the sense of holding an office, this did not preclude her from having a great deal of authority since her wielding of power, just like everyone else's ability to do so, was directly connected to the emperor. The Greco-Roman understanding of paterfamilias (the authority of the father/husband over the family unit) that grounded long-term familial relationships for the perpetuation of a family undergirded the reality of the empress having a kind of long-term access to the seat of power that was not generally available to others.

Indeed, the emperor was the empire—its existence and authority rested upon him; but the empire was also more than the emperor in the sense that the office was the umbrella that included the strength of his dynasty. The raison d'être of a member of the imperial family was to protect the empire, and this was accomplished by any means necessary. The emperor was not an infallible leader, but his authority was binding and absolute; and his image

---

6. Holum explains that the name "Aelia" attached to Pulcheria, her mother Eudoxia, and others was not passed on as a family connection to the Empress Aelia Flavia Flaccilla (the first wife of Theodosius I) but must have been regarded and appropriated as a specific "dynastic title of female distinction" (*Theodosian Empresses*, 65).

7. James, *Empresses and Power*, 78.

was, in a way, more important than the man himself. Thus, when an emperor was "weak" like Arcadius or Theodosius II, it fell to another in the imperial family to sustain the power of the emperor. This was expected. An empress, then, was central to the emperor's power because, while the emperor was the sole authority, that authority had to be executed well for the security of the empire—even in spite of the man himself at times.[8] So when an empress took on administration of the empire or became regent or intervened in affairs, this is to be seen not as an acquisitive power grab—women did not have such an option—but as her imperial imperative to facilitate the emperor's power. Thus the empress had a variety of avenues open to her to participate in the implementation of imperial power. In a very real way she was just as important an image of authority in the empire because she was the emperor's "deputy." This role of "deputy" was a very specific arena of authority that shifted with the needs of the emperor and the empire.[9]

### Young and Powerful

Upon the death of Pulcheria and Theodosius's father in 408, the eight-year-old Theodosius II became emperor (408–50). Pulcheria was only ten at the time. The capable praetorian prefect Anthemius (second in power to the emperor) filled the power vacuum until he suddenly disappeared from public life when Pulcheria turned fifteen, was crowned Augusta (July 4, 414), and assumed regency. After a period of time, Pulcheria replaced the long-tenured Anthemius with her choice, Aurelian.[10] The events of this power shift are not clear, but we do know, because the church historian Sozomen does not mention Anthemius, that Pulcheria did not remember him favorably.[11] This

8. As we shall see, Pulcheria is a clear example of this. The Byzantine chronicler Theophanes offers a short anecdote that lodges true imperial power with Pulcheria over her weak brother when she tries to teach Theodosius a lesson to not be so easily deceived: "The emperor Theodosios was easily swayed, carried by every wind, so that he often signed papers unread. Among these even the most wise Pulcheria inserted unread a donation ceding his wife Eudokia to slavery, which he signed and for which he was severely reproached by Pulcheria" (Theophanes AM 5941, in *The Chronicle of Theophanes Confessor: Byzantine and Near Eastern History, AD 284–813*, trans. Cyril Mango and Roger Scott [Oxford: Clarendon, 1997], 157).

9. James, *Empresses and Power*, 40.

10. The order of events and the transference of power were complex affairs. As Alan Cameron and Jacqueline Long note, regency could not pass directly from Anthemius to Pulcheria in a straightforward manner since formal regency did not exist in Roman constitutional law (*Barbarians and Politics at the Court of Arcadius*, Transformation of the Classical Heritage 19 [Berkeley: University of California Press, 1993], 400).

11. Alan Cameron, "The Empress and the Poet: Paganism and Politics at the Court of Theodosius II," in *Later Greek Literature*, ed. John J. Winkler and Gordon Williams, YCS 27 (Cambridge: Cambridge University Press, 1982), 271.

was the first of three significant moves on Pulcheria's part that granted her a substantial amount of power at a young age.

Up until this point the eunuch Antiochus, who had enjoyed the favor of Pulcheria's father and had been promoted to the influential position of grand chamberlain of the palace (*praepositus sacri cubiculi*), had been Theodosius II's tutor. Cognizant of the critical role of education in the shaping of the young emperor and satisfied in her choice of Aurelian as prefect, the Augusta made her second significant move and had Antiochus dismissed as tutor and occupied herself with what she knew was the true business of empire—educating, guiding, and training her younger brother in all things imperial. According to the Byzantine chronicler Theophanes (d. 818), Pulcheria had "gained complete control of affairs" and "managed the empire excellently" and was perfectly suited to educate Theodosius since she had a "great wisdom and a holy mind."[12] In doing so, Pulcheria was effectively running the empire, "directing its affairs with such authority that she became known in society at large as the emperor's 'guardian.'"[13] Sozomen sees Pulcheria as a divine dispensation granted by God to protect the emperor and thus the empire. It is a brave new world in which imperial piety outshines those deeds heretofore expected of mighty men. Sozomen writes:

> It appears to me that it was the design of God to show by the events of this period, that piety alone suffices for the salvation of princes; and that without piety, armies, a powerful empire, and every other resource, are of no avail. The Divine Power which is the guardian of the universe, foresaw that the emperor would be distinguished by his piety, and therefore determined that Pulcheria, his sister, should be the protector of him and of his government.[14]

Pulcheria wrote and spoke in fluent Greek and Latin, and she capably handled the affairs of the empire in the emperor's name while at the same time grooming her brother to be emperor. According to Sozomen, Pulcheria enrolled Theodosius in a comprehensive emperor "charm school." Not only did he have the best instruction in everything; his education also was exhaustive:

> She had him taught by the most skilled men, in horsemanship, and the practice of arms, and in letters. But he was systematically taught by his sister to be orderly

12. Theophanes AM 5905 and 5901 (Mango and Scott, *Chronicle of Theophanes*, 127 and 125). Theophanes's chronology can be a jumbled mess and often not a reliable source for the order of events, such as when Antiochus left and when Pulcheria assumed control.

13. Holum, *Theodosian Empresses*, 91.

14. Sozomen, *Hist. eccl.* 9.1 (Hartranft, 419).

and princely in his manners; she showed him how to gather up his robes, and how to take a seat, and how to walk; she trained him to restrain laughter, to assume a mild or a formidable aspect as the occasion might require, and to inquire with urbanity into the cases of those who came before him with petitions.[15]

Pulcheria spared no expense and left no educational rock unturned, and all things in the imperial household revolved around the emperor's Christian formation. Thus the Augusta's instruction on religious matters was an immersion school; the palace turned into a monastery of sorts so that even the pattern of all things imperial was shaped by piety: "But she strove chiefly, to lead him into piety, and to pray continuously; she taught him to frequent the church regularly, and to honor the houses of prayer with gifts and treasures; and she inspired him with reverence for priests and other good men, and for those who, in accordance with the law of Christianity, had devoted themselves to philosophy."[16] The third significant move by an enterprising teenage Pulcheria was to vow perpetual virginity, which we will discuss more below. Suffice it to say here, we have no reason to think Pulcheria's vow of virginity did not indicate genuine devotion to Christ; yet her public vow also served as a needed stabilizer for the empire and for the strengthening of Theodosian dynastic authority by cutting off any competition.[17]

It seems likely that Pulcheria had a good idea of the precarious position they were in because of the emperor's young age and moved quickly to discourage any question of the dynasty's strength. Not only would the Theodosian house be under threat from without, but also enterprising men from within leaped at the chance to shape the emperor to their own ends. Pulcheria stymied many of these plans by earning her reputation as protector of the empire very early. Those who would vie for influence over the emperor would have to go through his sister first, and she took that job very seriously. Replacing the praetorian prefect Anthemius (who had not necessarily done anything to threaten the dynasty), blocking off access to the emperor's education and imperial training, and vowing virginity, it could be argued, were Pulcheria's means of fulfilling her imperial duty.

Pulcheria was a polarizing figure, praised or reviled depending on which side of official orthodox teaching the historian stood.[18] She is viewed either as

15. Sozomen, *Hist. eccl.* 9.1 (Hartranft, 419–20).
16. Sozomen, *Hist. eccl.* 9.1 (Hartranft, 419). Holum notes that some Christian texts would have replaced some of the traditional classical texts (*Theodosian Empresses*, 92).
17. Holum, *Theodosian Empresses*, 93.
18. See Kathryn Chew, "Virgins and Eunuchs: Pulcheria, Politics and the Death of Emperor Theodosius II," *Historia* 55 (2006): 208; and James, *Empresses and Power*, 18. Socrates Scholasticus and Theodoret barely mention Pulcheria; Evagrius Scholasticus and John Malalas only

Figure 9.1. Left: AEL PVLCHE-RIA AVG diademed, draped bust, with hand of God holding crown overhead. Right: Constantinopolis seated, holding orb and cross and scepter; star to left, shield set on ground to right.

a pious and able deputy who ran the empire and deftly arranged her brother's marriage to Eudocia or as a manipulative, acquisitive woman who was the antithesis of the female imperial exemplar.[19] Part of the complex picture of Pulcheria resulted from some distasteful actions associated with her exercise of imperial authority. For example, Pulcheria's court was silent about her ally bishop Cyril of Alexandria's probable complicity in the murder of Hypatia at the hands of an Alexandrian mob that dragged the famed Neoplatonist philosopher into a church and stoned her to death. There also is evidence that Pulcheria was excessively exclusionist when it came to allowing anyone who had any connection to paganism to serve in the army or the administration. In addition, she relaxed some of the traditional protections for the Jews, thereby opening up synagogues to attacks by Christian fanatics.[20] Of course, we should be appalled at Pulcheria's complicity in such violence, but not any more than we should be appalled by the actions of Theodosius or a bishop like Cyril of Alexandria. People in power often do horrendous things to hold on to their power; women are no exception.

### The Virgin Empress and the Virgin Mary

At fifteen Pulcheria entered into another relationship, that of virgin of Christ, which provided her with another stream of authority and effectively trumped her dynastic relationships and responsibilities but paradoxically also reinforced them. If Pulcheria thought her devotion to Christ and her imperial identity were ever at odds, there is not any evidence of it. Pulcheria receives more attention than some of the other empresses in scholarship, and her virginity is rarely understood in light of the most central component that courses through contemporary descriptions of her—that her virginity was

include her to explain how Eudocia came to be empress; Sozomen and Theophanes praise her, while the seventh-century John of Nikiu accuses her of grasping power and of being immoral and impious.

19. James, *Empresses and Power*, 66–67.
20. Holum, *Theodosian Empresses*, 98–100.

christological discourse. More often than not, because of her involvement in the christological debates in the early fourth century, it is assumed that her virginity owed to a strong devotion to the Virgin Mary and thus fueled the securing of the Theotokos (Mary as the "God-bearer") as orthodox. While Pulcheria certainly was a key player in securing the orthodoxy of the Theotokos, there is almost no evidence to support the assumption that it was because of her involvement in a burgeoning cult of Mary. In fact, from the sources it is clear that she (and her contemporaries) understood her virginity as primarily about her relationship to Christ.

Pulcheria has been credited as directly affecting the rise of the cult of the Virgin; and the three churches she built in Constantinople that became great Marian shrines and her apparent claim to Marian dignity seem to support that conclusion.[21] However, we need to exercise caution rather than automatically credit Pulcheria with being the go-to Marian trendsetter. Indeed, virginity was central to who Pulcheria was, but perhaps the key to understanding what that meant is to read her virginity not as primarily Mary-shaped but as Christ-shaped.[22] Sozomen records that the Augusta inscribes her commitment to virginity on the table used for the Eucharist, the site of christological participation.[23] This carving of her vow into the table communicated to all that the Augusta was Christ's. The Augusta remained committed to her vow, even when she married after age fifty (her husband, Marcian, agreed to a continent marriage) for the sake of the empire.

This emphasis on Pulcheria's devotion as Christ-shaped does not mean that Mary (especially as the Theotokos who grounded Christ in his humanity) was not central to her self-understanding. Underlying the discussions of Christology and salvation is the question of how Christ could represent all people and therefore save all. How can a first-century Jewish man be the firstborn of *all* creation? How can he unlock full humanity for *every* human being, male and female, Jew and gentile? These questions have been variously

21. Liz James, "The Empress and the Virgin in Early Byzantium: Piety, Authority, and Devotion," in *Images of the Mother of God: Perceptions of the Theotokos in Byzantium*, ed. Maria Vassilaki (Aldershot: Ashgate, 2005), 145. James notes that this close connection between the Virgin and Pulcheria had less to do with the events of the time and more with constructing Pulcheria as a pious empress (150–51); cf. Cooper, *Band of Angels*, 263, 256. For a new assessment of Pulcheria's involvement in the building of Marian shrines and other churches, see James, "Empress and the Virgin," 147–49.

22. Many of the conclusions about Pulcheria's virginity as derived from the Virgin Mary are drawn from a few memorable exchanges with Nestorius, the infamous patriarch (and later heretic) of Constantinople (428–31), such as when he removes her portrait from above the altar, removes her robe from the altar itself, and bans her from her custom of taking communion in the sanctuary.

23. Sozomen, *Hist. eccl.* 9.1 (Hartranft, 419).

answered in Christian theology throughout history, but the upshot is that just as all sinned in Adam, all are redeemed in Christ. Even when Christianity has been at its worst in subordinating women and assigning them blame for sin entering the world, there was an understanding that redemption had to be available for all humans regardless of gender. Mary became that touchstone, being a daughter of Eve and bearer of Christ. Mary was the new Eve.[24]

Devotion to Mary was very popular in later Byzantium, and we find the seeds of that popularity in the Constantinopolitan patriarch Proclus and other bishops' sermons and the theological expression of ascetic women like Pulcheria. What we must not miss, however, is that devotion to Mary is grounded in a particular understanding of Christology, one that only works if Christ is fully divine *and* fully human. So, instead of characterizing Pulcheria as one of the first notable converts to Mariology, it is perhaps more appropriate to understand her as espousing an embodied theology, a theology lived and tinged with hope for all, including women and other subordinated groups who were carving out space for their respective voices and the expression of their faith.

Pulcheria was accustomed to a close relationship with the patriarch (archbishop) of Constantinople. For example, Atticus (406–October 10, 425) wrote his treatise *On Faith and Virginity* for Pulcheria and her sisters, and it was a habit for them to dine with either Atticus or his successor Sisinnius (426–27) in his episcopal palace following communion. It was also one of these patriarchs who accepted Pulcheria's robe for use as an altar covering during communion in the Great Church, an honor that was "appropriate to women of distinction and spectacular piety."[25] Prior to Nestorius, all of Pulcheria's engagement with the church revolved around the Eucharist. Her robe and portrait that hung above the altar were reminders of the empress's "special bond with Christ," and taking Eucharist in the sanctuary also facilitated her identity as "Bride of Christ." In a resurrection sermon Proclus, patriarch of Constantinople (ca. 434–446/47), identified Pulcheria's ascetic commitment as christological victory, martyrologically and eschatologically.[26] The particular instantiation that we see here from Pulcheria is not the same as the Christ-shaped imitation of Blandina or Macrina's body in two states at once, but that of literally building the church, making and adorning the physical space where the presence of God is met in the embodied community—both living and dead.

24. Holum explores how the Eve / New Eve paradigm made its way into many of the sermons at the time (*Theodosian Empresses*, 141).
25. Ibid., 143–44.
26. Ibid., 137–38.

On Nestorius's first Easter Sunday (probably April 15, 428) after being consecrated patriarch of Constantinople, Pulcheria arrived to receive communion along with the priests and the emperor in the sanctuary of the Great Church. Once informed of the empress's custom, the newly installed patriarch hastened to the gate to disallow the empress access. The short, heated exchange that followed about giving birth to God or Satan bristled with mutual defiance of each other's presumption of authority—Nestorius barring the way to a layperson and a woman whom he saw as grasping christological authority that was not available to her, and Pulcheria refusing both to cede any territory gained by virgins and to yield to anyone—patriarch or not—her connection with Christ.[27] For Nestorius, "it is Pulcheria's desire to be 'compared to the bride of Christ' that is at the root of the enmity between the two. Further, Nestorius suggests that Pulcheria had cultivated her own clerical entourage independently of the bishop, in order to enact her liturgy."[28] Pulcheria's claim of having "given birth to Christ" says more about her relationship with Christ than it does about her relationship with Mary. For her it was obvious that virginity and Christology go together—that she, like Mary and all other virgins, gives birth to Christ. Pulcheria's entrance into the sanctuary of the Great Church on Easter to take communion with the priests and the emperor makes sense on the level of her enacting the priestly character of an Augustus, but also on the level of her, as a virgin, functioning in the priestly role as Christ did, as both priest and sacrifice.

Pulcheria receives a lot of attention in the sources—as a paragon of orthodoxy or as a Jezebel—because she is the only empress recorded to have played a direct part in imperial councils while the emperor was alive.[29] Pulcheria was right in the middle of the controversy between Cyril of Alexandria and Nestorius over the Theotokos. In his *Bazaar of Heracleides*, Nestorius admits his miscalculation regarding his clash with Pulcheria, and in predictable fashion he implies gross sexual misbehavior on the part of the empress so as to discredit her. However, Nestorius's issues with Pulcheria were less about gender than about the "dangerous encroachment of imperial privilege."[30] For

---

27. Pulcheria did not go quietly and, according to Nestorius, claimed, "Have I not given birth to God?," to which he retorted, "You have given birth to Satan," and expelled her (Nestorius, *Bazaar of Heracleides* 1.3, trans. G. R. Driver and Leonard Hodgson [Oxford: Clarendon, 1925], 96–97), http://www.tertullian.org/fathers/nestorius_bazaar_0_intro.htm.

28. Kate Cooper, "Contesting the Nativity: Wives, Virgins, and Pulcheria's *imitatio Mariae*," *SJRS* 19 (1998): 34.

29. James, *Empresses and Power*, 66. See John Anthony McGuckin, *St. Cyril of Alexandria: The Christological Controversy; Its History, Theology, and Texts* (Crestwood, NY: St. Vladimir's Seminary Press, 2004).

30. Cooper, "Contesting the Nativity," 42.

Nestorius, the iconography of the empress over the altar meant the imperial commandeering of christological and intercessory power. This objection on the part of Nestorius is understandable in the context of the continuing negotiation between the civic and ecclesiastical spheres.

Imperial images represented "the divinely chosen imperial dignity," and they continued to be used unabated in Theodosius's celebrations in the Hippodrome that blurred the line between civic ceremony and church worship with him as bishop.[31] This blurring of the public and ecclesiastical arenas had to make many bishops very uncomfortable. It was one thing to have an emperor creating a quasi-ecclesiastical space outside of the basilica, but it was quite another for an imperial image to enter the ecclesiastical space itself, to be honored with full imperial dignity in association with Christ's mediation on behalf of humanity. Virginity itself had been established previously as a performing Christology,[32] so it was not the virgin-Christ link or even the Theotokos-virgin-Christ link that was so problematic; the problem for Nestorius was the invasion of the imperial into the ecclesiastical space—the Augusta-Theotokos-virgin-Christ link. Nestorius's trepidation was perhaps warranted, as both the ecclesiastical space and the imperial space were swiftly morphing into almost unrecognizable versions of themselves.

## Material Devotion: Relics, Churches, and Shrines, Oh My!

The post-Constantinian church balanced triumphalism with the still poignant need to remain connected to the persecuted past and see themselves as the "rightful heirs of the martyrs."[33] As material remains or personal objects of a holy person, relics pointed to the incarnational reality of Christ and how Christians could connect with that reality in the bodies of those who had followed him in imitation. Hence, a martyr's relics received a welcoming into their shrine (*adventus*) similar to the one that Jesus experienced when he entered Jerusalem, or to that of an emperor or empress when they returned to their city from battle or official visits or pilgrimages. Relics also served, especially among those in power, to increase the piety of the one who discovered a relic. Empresses were especially keen to be in close proximity to the relics at all stages: the discovery, retrieval, and building of shrines as close as possible to the empress herself. For empresses, piety was imperial capital.

31. Limberis, *Divine Heiress*, 47.

32. See Amy Brown Hughes, "'Chastely, I Live for Thee': Virginity as Bondage and Freedom in Origen of Alexandria, Methodius of Olympus, and Gregory of Nyssa" (PhD diss., Wheaton College, 2013).

33. Markus, "How on Earth Could Places Become Holy?," 268–70.

Figure 9.2. Ivory tablet possibly depicting the reception of a relic of Stephen the Protomartyr by Pulcheria in 421 CE.

Thus the *adventus* of St. Stephen's relics into Constantinople brought them directly to Pulcheria's palace complex so she could, quite literally, live with the relics. Welcoming a relic (and therefore the martyr) into one's space allowed for proximity to that martyr's imitation of Christ.

The *adventus* of relics into the capital had many of the same trappings and weight that an emperor's return from battle did. One of the central features of both the *adventus* ceremony for an emperor and that for relics was the rhetorical art form of the panegyric, originally intended to praise the emperor's virtues and deeds.[34] The *adventus* of relics was not a rare site in Constantinople.[35] Panegyrics were written for these arrivals and became part of the liturgical cycle of the church.[36] For Pulcheria specifically, she as a virgin also understood herself to share in the imitation of Christ and therefore experienced a sense of continuity and solidarity with the martyrs as a living martyr. Pulcheria's role in these ceremonies grew over time. Sometimes this led to rivalries, like that between Pulcheria and Eudocia over the relics of St. Stephen and later those of the Forty Martyrs of Sebaste.[37]

34. Limberis, *Divine Heiress*, 51.

35. Limberis lists some of the arrivals that Theodosius, Pulcheria, and their sisters presided over: "the arrivals of Sts Samuel, Joseph, and Zechariah, and the building of the martyrium of St. Anthimius" (ibid., 52).

36. Limberis, *Divine Heiress*, 62.

37. Regarding Eudocia and Pulcheria's respective (and contradictory) claims on the discovery and possession of the relics of St. Stephen, see Elizabeth A. Clark, "Claims on the Bones of Saint Stephen: The Partisans of Melania and Eudocia," *CH* 51 (1982): 141–56; and, for the back-and-forth about the Forty Martyrs, see James, "The Empress and the Virgin," 150; Michael Whitby and Mary Whitby, trans., Paschal Chronicle (Chronicon Paschale) O.306 (81),

Pulcheria spent a considerable amount of money on housing relics and creating intimacy with the martyrs and other revered saints. She built the palatine Church of St. Stephen yet erected other structures that were accessible to the people of the city. Examples of this include her construction of the Church of St. Lawrence, memorializing the Roman deacon who was martyred in the third century, and another church to house relics of the prophet Isaiah, both built after 421 in the Pulcherianai (Pulcheria's section of the city).[38] Both of these churches housed relics, and their situation in Pulcheria's neighborhood afforded the empress the derivative honor that comes with proximity to material holiness on display. It was a reciprocal relationship for the empresses. Church and shrine building, as well as other projects for the populace such as baths, both reinforced the empress's standing and gained her "symbolic capital."[39]

Aside from building churches for relics, the Augusta possessed numerous properties, and many people relied on the patronage of Pulcheria and her younger sisters, Arcadia and Marina, for their livelihood. Pulcheria's philanthropy was not exercised purely for the imperial domain as benefiting the city, but was mixed to include patronage of the monastic communities in the area. As we will see with Eudocia, Pulcheria also had personal connections with specific monks. These monks linked the empresses to a manifestation of popular monastic zeal that was different from the establishment piety that bishops offered.

## Ephesus and Chalcedon

### *"Many years to the orthodox one!" The Council of Ephesus (431)*

Once Cyril of Alexandria (ca. 376–444) realized that Emperor Theodosius II was standing with Nestorius against his stern recommendations, the Egyptian patriarch mounted a letter-writing campaign. He wrote to all the members of the imperial family, but Pulcheria was singled out, probably because she was not only interested in orthodoxy but also the most likely candidate to succeed in swaying (her brother) the emperor to Cyril's side against Nestorius. Pulcheria, though, was in a difficult position because while she was passionately on the side of the Theotokos and what would become orthodoxy on the person of Christ, the emperor was not. As the one who

---

in *Chronicon Paschale, 284–628 AD*, Translated Texts for Historians 7 (Liverpool: Liverpool University Press, 1989), 451; and Sozomen *Eccl. hist.* 9.2 (Hartranft, 420).

38. Holum, *Theodosian Empresses*, 136–37.

39. James, "Empress and the Virgin," 152.

brought the promising and intense Nestorius to Constantinople, Theodosius was inclined to support him.[40] Pulcheria was not only (or even primarily) concerned with right doctrine but also with the unity of the church at large for the sake of the empire's stability. For etiquette purposes Cyril addressed his letters to the empresses as a unit, but it was clear that Pulcheria was the intended addressee.[41] Pulcheria was no mere go-between. Even though the empress pushed back against Cyril to moderate his doctrinal views so as not to offend those who were inclined to support Nestorius, Cyril seems to have taken it in stride, most likely because she was probably his best chance to influence the emperor.[42] Much hung in the balance in these epistolary exchanges.

The Council of Ephesus (431) was not short on drama. The protracted feud between the sees of Alexandria and Constantinople for supremacy emerged in the form of Cyril's assertion of his right to open the council. He summarily deposed and excommunicated Nestorius before the latter and his Antiochene supporters even arrived in Ephesus. By the time Nestorius and company arrived, it was too little, too late; tempers, already running hot on account of the doctrinal debate, now boiled over. Add in a populace primed for a fight and Cyril's sponsored mob of rabble-rousers who brutally suppressed any Nestorian sympathizers in the city, and the result is a council that was more farcical than fair.

It is unclear just how much of a hand Pulcheria had in the arrangement of the council, such as the shift in location to one city that could truly be called a stronghold for the Theotokos.[43] But her influence over the council's outcome was keenly felt by those in Constantinople, as indicated by the large crowd that descended on the Great Church on July 4, chanting, "Many years to Pulcheria! She it is who has strengthened the faith! . . . Many years to Pulcheria! Many years to the empress! Many years to Pulcheria! She has strengthened the faith! . . . Many years to Pulcheria! Many years to the orthodox one!"[44] After the Council of Ephesus in 431, the penalties for those who had compromised the unity of the church were meted out with unmistakable harshness. For this show of decisive punishment, Nestorius blamed Pulcheria, which was probably

40. Holum, *Theodosian Empresses*, 148.

41. In letters addressed to or intended for Pulcheria specifically, such as the *Address to the Most Pious Empresses on the Correct Faith*, Cyril offered content that functioned as "ammunition" for the empress in the form of biblical passages about the Theotokos, as his defense of his christological position and as a summary of how Nestorius's view is therefore erroneous. See Holum, *Theodosian Empresses*, 159–61.

42. Holum, *Theodosian Empresses*, 181.

43. See ibid., 164, about the implications of choosing Ephesus for the council.

44. Ibid., 170. The chant for Pulcheria is found in Eduard Schwartz, ed., *Acta Conciliorum Oecumenicorum* (ACO) 1.1.3.14 (Berlin: de Gruyter, 1927).

not far from the truth. Pulcheria was certainly concerned with coming to an orthodox decision on the Theotokos, but right belief was not the only thing in play; she needed unity as well. Pulcheria was probably behind the campaign to impose unity on the church and to bring the events of Ephesus to a swift and decisive conclusion, which probably included orchestrating a solidly "orthodox" new patriarch of Constantinople at the earliest opportunity.[45] Nestorius's successor as patriarch of Constantinople, Maximian, died after only a few years on April 12, 434. To prevent any Nestorian sympathizers from seizing the important position there, Proclus was selected, a man who was not only an obvious supporter of the Theotokos but who would also be a champion for Pulcheria's virginity.[46]

### "The Augusta believes thus! Thus we all believe!" The Council of Chalcedon (451)

While Pulcheria was not living in the palace in the 440s because of the powerful eunuch Chysaphius's machinations,[47] she was still very much involved in the debate that led to the definitive statement on Christ's person at the Council of Chalcedon in 451. The empress joined forces with the archimandrite (supervisor of a monastic community) Manuel and other monks to protest the imperial shift toward support of another archimandrite and priest, Eutyches, who had emerged with a glow from many years of ascetic confinement and became the leader of the monastic communities in and near Constantinople. Eutyches's vehement distaste for anything that sounded even remotely like a Nestorian separation of natures in Christ caused him to swing the pendulum wildly in the other direction, even to a complete fusing of the divine and human natures in Christ, a position that will be definitively ruled as heretical at the Council of Chalcedon in 451. Eutyches had the support of the emperor and had baptized the infamous eunuch Chrysaphius, whom he now advised. In addition he found a natural ally in Cyril of Alexandria's less-than-civil successor Dioscorus, who was no supporter of reconciliation with

---

45. Holum, *Theodosian Empresses*, 182.

46. Limberis, *Divine Heiress*, 51. Holum notes that a late source designates Pulcheria as responsible for Proclus's becoming patriarch of Constantinople (*Theodosian Empresses*, 182).

47. John Malalas describes Chrysaphius thus: "The emperor Theodosius was passionately in love with the *cubicularius* Chrysaphios, known as Ztoummas, since he was extremely handsome. He gave him many gifts, whatever he asked for, and Chrysaphios had free access to the emperor. He had control over all affairs and plundered everything. He was the patron and protector of the Greens" (*Chronicon* [*Chronicle*] 14.19, in *The Chronicle of John Malalas*, trans. Elizabeth Jeffreys et al., Byzantina Australiensia 4 (Melbourne: Australian Association for Byzantine Studies, 1986), 198.

the powerful Antiochene see.[48] This alliance was problematic for Pulcheria, who with Cyril and many others supported the Formula of Reunion in 433, which helped to bring the skittish Antiochenes back into a rapprochement with the Alexandrians after the outcome of the Council of Ephesus and the ousting of Nestorius in 431. The reunion was a hard-won reconciliation, and reconciliation was the way to a stable empire. Therefore, when Theodosius sided with Eutyches and Dioscorus against the Formula of Reunion, Pulcheria was all the more determined to stay the course of unity.

Pulcheria's new ally of convenience was Pope Leo I (440–61). On June 13, 449, the Roman bishop sent to Flavian—now patriarch of Constantinople— his famous *Tome*, which would become core to Chalcedonian orthodoxy.[49] Leo also sent letters to garner support for Flavian from the archimandrites of Constantinople and to the imperial household, specifically Pulcheria (*Ep.* 31), who he knew was key in dealing with the emperor. Unfortunately, this letter never reached Pulcheria, and the campaign to drum up support for the patriarch Flavian had been supplanted by what later would be called the Robber Synod in 449. Leo sent another letter to Pulcheria, a bit more frantic this time, pleading with her to intervene and persuade the emperor to call another council, this time in Italy. However, Leo received no response from the East, perhaps because his letters, again, did not reach their intended addressee. In this charged atmosphere leading up to Chalcedon in 451, Pulcheria was not in a position to affect affairs directly. Chrysaphius still had the ear of the emperor, and he was a supporter of Eutyches.

Pulcheria might have conceived of the inevitability of Chrysaphius overextending himself and falling out of favor, but she probably did not predict that it would happen as soon as it actually did.[50] In 450, Chrysaphius's schemes failed, and Theodosius unceremoniously confiscated his wealth and exiled him. Pulcheria wasted no time and quickly returned to her brother's side sometime between March and early July 450. This reset of access to imperial power did not bring about an immediate change in the ecclesiastical situation, but it did get Pulcheria back in the game. Within weeks, though, her ability to hold the empire together was put to the test when Theodosius died on July 26, 450, while on a hunting trip.[51] While we do not have any records

48. Holum, *Theodosian Empresses*, 199.
49. Ibid., 202.
50. Theophanes AM 5942 (Mango and Scott, *Chronicle of Theophanes*, 158–59).
51. John Malalas records that before Theodosius died he talked to his sister and told her about Marcian and how Marcian was to succeed him as emperor (*Chron.* 14.27 [Jeffreys et al., 201]); Theophanes records that it was Pulcheria who summoned the ex-tribune and declared that he was her choice (AM 5942 [Mango and Scott, *Chronicle of Theophanes*, 159]). The Chronicon Paschale follows Malalas and adds the detail that Theodosius announced Marcian

of what happened in the immediate aftermath, we can assume that Pulcheria stepped forward to arrange an imperial funeral and, just to make sure that the past several years being hamstrung by a presumptuous eunuch were put to bed once and for all, the empress handed Chrysaphius over to the son of a victim for execution.[52]

Pulcheria could not fully embrace the role of sole protector in the absence of the emperor, but she was deeply committed to the empire. Instead of seeing her vow to Christ and her imperial commitment to be in conflict, she quickly moved to broker a marriage with a man who could live with the requirement of abstinence. Pulcheria found the perfect match in the tribune Marcian, who was "tall, with straight grey hair and enflamed feet"[53] and not into making waves. He was not of imperial or even aristocratic blood, but he was Roman. They married on November 25, 450, and some sources state that Pulcheria proclaimed him emperor herself before the patriarch of Constantinople and the senate after he swore to protect her virginity.[54] Pulcheria and Marcian's arrangement seems to have worked out well, not only because Marcian kept his pledge to her to preserve her virginity but also because they mounted a strong offensive at the outset, moving quickly to address the ecclesiastical melee.

No doubt Pulcheria was the force behind the new policy for enforcing the unity of the church that was issued in the autumn of 450.[55] Pulcheria wrote to Leo to expound on the progress that had been made to remedy the problematic dissolution of the Formula of Reunion. She also requested that Leo summon other bishops for a council in a location that the emperor would choose. This could be construed as quite the presumption on Pulcheria's part since calling a council and summoning bishops was the exclusive purview of the emperor. Pulcheria and Marcian were ready for big-picture work—revisiting the Formula of Reunion and piecing the East back together again. In May 451 the emperor called for a general council in Nicaea for the beginning of September but, because Marcian was needed on the warfront with the Huns, Leo later

---

as his choice in the presence of the general Aspar and the rest of the senators (Chron. Pasch. O.306 (80) [Whitby and Whitby, 450]).

52. Theophanes AM 5943 (Mango and Scott, *Chronicle of Theophanes*, 160).

53. Malalas, *Chron.* 14.28 (Jeffreys et al., 201). Malalas records this bit here to foreshadow Marcian's anger at a riot started by members of the Green faction (Marcian favored the Blues). His stress level was such that it enflamed his sensitive feet, which led to a five-month battle with gangrene before he died at age sixty-five. He outlived Pulcheria by two years (*Chron.* 14.34 [Jeffreys et al., 202]).

54. Theophanes AM 5942 (Mango and Scott, *Chronicle of Theophanes*, 159). As Holum notes, this was not unprecedented, but it was highly unusual (*Theodosian Empresses*, 208–9).

55. Holum notes that Pope Leo I certainly thought so in his *Ep.* 95, *To Pulcheria*, on July 20, 451 (*Theodosian Empresses*, 211).

moved the council to Chalcedon. Pulcheria chose the Basilica of St. Euphemia (a local martyr from the Diocletianic persecution) in Chalcedon, and about 520 bishops arrived on October 8, 451.

The combination of bishops and Roman administrators helped the council to be productive, and between October 8 and November 1, 451, sixteen sessions brought confirmation of orthodoxy and resolution to a number of lingering questions. Owing to imperial pressure, the bishops also formulated not another creed but a "definition" that expanded on the Formula of Reunion. Also, Constantinople was elevated to the first rank of the episcopacy, with the authority to consecrate metropolitans for Pontus, Asia, and Thrace as the "New Rome."[56] While the Augusti were not yet present at this point, those who recorded the council proceedings made sure to include the acclamations of the assembled bishops: "The Augusta believes thus! Thus we all believe!" "The Augusta cast out Nestorius! Many years to the orthodox one!"[57] On October 25, 451, the council formally adopted what became known as the Chalcedonian Definition, and Marcian and Pulcheria arrived in person to appear before the bishops. It was unusual for a woman to come before such a group, but she and Marcian were extolled as the "New Helena" and the "New Constantine," and Pulcheria specifically as "the light of orthodoxy" and the "protectress of the faith."[58]

The chanting bishops and supposedly decisive victory at Chalcedon did not indicate a smooth acceptance across the empire, however. Because Juvenal, bishop of Jerusalem, had supported Dioscorus of Alexandria at what was later known as the Robber Synod, he was required to embrace Chalcedonian orthodoxy or lose his position. Unfortunately, his assent to those conditions did not sit well with the monastic community in Palestine, and a revolt ensued. Juvenal fled for his life, and a group of looting, burning, and murderous monks replaced him with their own Theodosius, a monk.[59] Eudocia, whom we will meet shortly, was firmly on the side of these insurgent monks—whether this was because she was angry about Pulcheria's victory, because she was truly convinced that Chalcedon had been a victory for heretics, or a little of both is not clear.[60] It was not until late 455 or so that some ecclesiastical heavyweights (Simeon Stylites and Pope Leo among others) finally persuaded Eudocia to

56. Holum, *Theodosian Empresses*, 214.
57. Ibid., 214–15. These acclamations are found in the official *Acta Conciliorum Oecumenicorum* (e.g., ACO 2.1.1.69)
58. Holum, *Theodosian Empresses*, 215–16.
59. Evagrius, *Hist. eccl.* 2.5 (Whitby, 78–81). See also Gerontius, *Vit. Mel.* 19–20 (Clark, 24).
60. Theophanes places the blame on the radical archimandrite Theodosius for convincing Eudocia and the monks in Jerusalem (AM 5945 and 5947 [Mango and Scott, *Chronicle of Theophanes*, 164–65 and 167]).

submit to Chalcedon. She died five years later, on October 20, 460, and in communion with the Chalcedonian faith.[61]

## Eudocia (ca. 400–October 20, 460)

As the story goes, her father, the famous Athenian sophist Leontius, died and favored his sons but left his daughter, Athenais, impoverished. He justified his abandonment by portentously alluding to her "good fortune, which exceeds that of all other women."[62] Understandably, Athenais was not consoled by such cryptic comfort. She pleaded with her brothers to help her, but they coldly rebuffed her, giving her no choice but to seek aid elsewhere. Athenais made her way to Constantinople to live with her father's aunt, who orchestrated the opportunity for her to plead her case before Empress Pulcheria and receive relief. Little did she know that her arrival was propitious; it was high time for the twenty-year-old Theodosius II to find a wife.

Theodosius was not impressed with the patrician selection at his disposal, and the imperial matchmaking duo of Pulcheria and the emperor's childhood friend Paulinus were put on the case. In the narratives Theodosius comes across as a romantic and hormonal young man, assuring his sister that as long as the girl was beautiful and he loved her, it did not matter to him if she was of low birth! The chronicler John Malalas records Theodosius telling Pulcheria:

> I want you to find me a really lovely young girl, so that no other woman in Constantinople—whether she be of imperial blood or of the highest senatorial family—may possess such beauty. If she is not superlatively beautiful, I am not interested, neither in high rank or imperial blood or wealth. But whoever's daughter she is, providing she is a virgin and exceedingly beautiful, her I shall marry.[63]

When the beautiful, educated, and eloquent Athenais came before her, Pulcheria embraced serendipity. Athenais was led into Pulcheria's quarters so that Theodosius and Paulinus could observe her from behind a curtain, and Theodosius fell fast in love with her. Athenais was subsequently baptized a Christian, renamed Eudocia by Theodosius, and they married in 421. What of her negligent brothers? Upon learning about their sister's drastic change

---

61. Holum, *Theodosian Empresses*, 224.
62. Malalas, *Chron.* 14.4 (Jeffreys et al., 192).
63. Malalas, *Chron.* 14.3 (Jeffreys et al., 191–92). See also Chron. Pasch. O.300 (66–69) (Whitby and Whitby, 420). The sixth-century historian Evagrius Scholasticus includes only the comment that Pulcheria was the intermediary for Eudocia's marriage to Theodosius (*Hist. eccl.* 1.20 [Whitby, 47]).

in fortune, they fled. Eudocia, however, did not visit revenge upon them but instead had them brought back and rewarded with positions in the Theodosian court.[64] At its end the story brings the brothers back in, with the abandoned sister taking care of them out of her abundance. The text leads us to the conclusion that her father Leontius was right: Athenais did have "good fortune"!

It is quite a Cinderella story—a virtuous and admirable heroine who has been dealt a surprising and undeservingly harsh hand. Pulcheria plays a matchmaking fairy godmother, and her brother the prince sweeps the young maiden off her feet and out of obscurity. These kinds of stories, romanticizing imperial relationships or, on the other end of the spectrum, sensationalizing the failure of those relationships (as we will see shortly), were common in Late Antiquity. It is difficult to know where the facts end and the legend begins.[65] The earliest information we have on Eudocia's origins comes from the fifth-century church historian Socrates (who wrote before she leaves court permanently): that she was very well educated by her father Leontius the sophist and was baptized as a Christian by the patriarch Atticus before marrying Theodosius.[66] Later sources like John Malalas tend to elaborate on her education and on her father's position.[67] Theodosius is depicted as a "moonstruck lover," and Athenais's father as a clairvoyant and therefore defensibly negligent father. While this narrative could serve as a taste of hostilities to come, the text does not foreshadow enmity. Therefore, it is plausible that there is some truth to the serendipity of it all, even if some of the trappings about her brothers and Paulinus are more narratival color than reality.[68] In other words, the legend is a calculated one, but the case for its authenticity, at least for the framework of the story, is there.

Eudocia's career as empress was mixed. She had only one child who survived into adulthood, a daughter named Licinia Eudoxia (b. 422) after Theodosius's mother. Eudocia was proclaimed Augusta shortly afterward, in 423. After her daughter was married to Valentinian III (to whom she was engaged since

64. Malalas, *Chron.* 14.5 (Jeffreys et al., 193): Gessius was appointed to be praetorian prefect of Illyricum and Valerius to be *magister* (master/chief).

65. Holum observes that the Byzantine chronicles (John Malalas, Evagrius Scholasticus, the anonymous Chronicon Paschale, John of Nikiu, and Theophanes) for the most part adopted John Malalas's account of Eudocia's marriage with some enhancements. The ecclesiastical historians are much more varied in their treatment of Eudocia. Some, like Socrates Scholasticus, praise her; others, like Sozomen and Theodoret, barely mention her at all, probably due their having written after her scandalous exit from the Theodosian court in 443. See Holum, *Theodosian Empresses*, 114–16.

66. Socrates, *Hist. eccl.* 7.21 (trans. A. C. Zenos, NPNF² 2:164).

67. Alan Cameron, "Empress and the Poet," 273. See Malalas, *Chron.* 14.4 (Jeffreys et al., 192–93); Chron. Pasch. O.300 (67–68) (Whitby and Whitby, 420).

68. Alan Cameron, "Empress and the Poet," 276–77.

Figure 9.3. Left: AEL EVDOCIA AVG, diademed, draped bust, hand of God holding nimbus above. Right: Constantinopolis seated, foot on prow, holding orb and cross and scepter; shield at side to right, star in left field.

infancy) on October 29, 437, Eudocia embarked on a pilgrimage to the Holy Land that brought honor to her and the empire. She also butted heads with Pulcheria, found herself on the wrong side of many alliances, and for reasons that are potentially scandalous lived out the rest of her days in Palestine instead of by her husband's side. Aside from these events, one thing that sets Eudocia apart is her having a career of sorts in addition to her imperial duty as "deputy"—although Pulcheria had this job very much in hand for most of Theodosius's life. Eudocia is one of the very few women speakers and writers in antiquity who produced a selection of works that are still extant.[69] We know Eudocia was very well educated and specifically trained in the rhetorical arts. She was a poet and gave speeches on her official visits to appreciative audiences. Because of the combination of her being educated and growing up as a pagan, one might expect her work to be Homeric. However, Eudocia was also a Christian.

### Eudocia in the Holy Land

Travel in antiquity was risky, and for women especially it often proved perilous. But travel, especially to the Holy Land, could also offer a boon to those who took the journey. Sometimes, as Noel Lenski posits, travel to the Holy Land could mitigate the dangers: "In the Holy Land . . . these empresses found the space, both literal and metaphorical, to fashion an ideal place, a place like no other, where imaginary worlds were made real and the real world was re-imagined with consequences that persist even to the present."[70]

69. Nothing survives of empresses' voices except a selection from Eudocia's writings. She wrote verses celebrating the Roman victories over Persia in 421/22, a verse paraphrase of part of the Old Testament, a hexametric poem on the martyrdom of St. Cyprian, and a compilation of *Homerocentones*. Only the last two of these survive, with only the *Homerocentones* in full (James, *Empresses and Power*, 11).

70. Noel Lenski, "Empresses in the Holy Land: The Creation of a Christian Utopia in Late Antique Palestine," in *Travel, Communication and Geography in Late Antiquity: Sacred and Profane*, ed. Linda Ellis and Frank L. Kidner (Aldershot: Ashgate, 2004), 114.

Augusta Eudocia took two trips to the Holy Land. The first was a pilgrimage /
official trip like Helena's, and the second was after her marriage had failed.
It can be argued that both times Eudocia needed a new start: the first time to
invigorate herself and the second time to reinvent herself.

At the end of chapter 8 we briefly mentioned Melania the Younger's
uncle Volusian, the prominent figure sent from the western court to Constantinople to complete the marital arrangement of Eudocia's daughter
Licinia Eudoxia to the emperor Valentinian III. Though Volusian was a
pagan, his niece was also in Constantinople, visiting from her convent in
Jerusalem so as to convert her uncle at the end of his life. Gerontius records
that Melania stayed in Constantinople to mourn her uncle after he died in
January 437, and while there she struck up a relationship with the Empress
Eudocia and even begged the emperor to let the empress go and worship at
the Holy Places.[71] Thus, over a century after Helena, Eudocia became the
first Augusta since then to follow in the mother of Constantine's footsteps
to the Holy Land in 438.[72]

Like Helena's sojourn to the Holy Land, Eudocia's was not only a *peregrinatio religiosa* but also an *iter principis*, an official imperial journey. Like
Helena, Eudocia also visited other places on her journeys to the Holy Land.
In Eudocia's case, the stop that garners the most attention is Antioch, where
she gave a speech that delighted her audience. The Augusta drew upon her
education and apparently stunning oratorical skills, presenting herself as a
Christian empress with a knack for drawing upon Homer in clever and skillful ways. The only thing we know about the content of this famous speech
is that Eudocia ends with an adaptation of a verse from Homer.[73] We do,
however, know more about the context of the speech. The presence of an
imperial personage meant tangible help for the city, and this aid typically
came in the form of overseeing building (a basilica) and restoration projects
(the city walls and a bath complex), as well as humanitarian care.[74] To host
an imperial visit meant that there was proximity to lobby for patronage on
behalf of that city. Her speech was a response that linked imperial custom

71. Gerontius, *Vit. Mel.* 68 (Clark, 56).
72. Brubaker, "Memories of Helena," 62.
73. Evagrius writes: "Some time later [after her daughter Licinia Eudoxia was betrothed
to Valentinian III], when Eudocia was travelling towards the holy city of Christ our God,
she came here and in a public speech to the populace here she concluded her speech with
this line, 'Of your race and blood I am proud to be,' alluding to the colonies that were sent
here from Greece" (*Hist. eccl.* 1.20 [Whitby, 47–48]). This passage is adapted from Homer's
*Iliad* 6.211; 20.241.
74. Brian Patrick Sowers, "Eudocia: The Making of a Homeric Christian" (PhD diss., University of Cincinnati, 2008), 17–18.

with a Homeric-shaped nod to her origin and prestige, associating herself with the Antiochenes in a show of friendship.[75] Even the most skilled speaker would probably not garner both gold and bronze statues made in their image, but Augusta Eudocia did.

After her visit to Antioch, Eudocia continued on to Jerusalem (about a two-month journey in total) and was met by Melania in Sidon (about fifty miles outside Jerusalem) just after Easter in 437.[76] Gerontius describes the reunion of the two women and the establishment of a small martyr shrine and monastic community. When she heard that the empress was coming, Melania deliberated about whether to go out to meet her or stay: "If I go out to meet her, I fear lest I bring reproach by traveling through the cities in this humble attire. But if I remain here, I must beware that this behavior not be thought arrogant on my part." She decided to go because she wanted to support "such a faithful empress." When she arrived, Melania observed that the Augusta was "zealous to please the Lord even in the matter of a dwelling, as well as in conversation and every other activity." As for their meeting, Gerontius records it as follows:

> When the God-loving empress saw her, she fittingly received her with every honor, as Melania was a true spiritual mother. It was a glory for her to honor the woman who had so purely glorified the heavenly King. The saint, acknowledging her faith and the burden of her journey, exhorted her to proceed still further in good works. The pious empress answered her with this speech, worthy of remembrance: "I am fulfilling a double vow to the Lord, to worship at the Holy Places and to see my mother, for I have wished to be worthy of Your Holiness while you still serve the Lord in the flesh."[77]

Augusta Eudocia then eagerly joined Melania at her monastery and "regarded the virgins as if they were her own sisters." The reported interaction here communicates a rich combination of warmth and deference on the part of both women and an example of the negotiation between Christian imperial and ascetic authority. Gerontius presents Eudocia as a woman who gains a new

75. Ibid., 21.
76. Elizabeth Clark argues for a 437 date over the 438 date that Holum holds, arguing that there is no way that Melania could have made the journey in time in 438 (Easter was on March 27 as opposed to April 11 the previous year). Even though Melania set for herself a punishing pace in the midst of treacherous wintery conditions and made the 1,200-mile trip in only six weeks (Gerontius, *Vit. Mel.* 68 [Clark, 56]), it is still not enough time after her mourning period had ended for her to arrive by Easter in 438 (Clark, *Life of Melania*, 134).
77. Gerontius, *Vit. Mel.* 70–71 (Clark, 58).

family that is not imperial but ascetic—her "true spiritual mother" Melania and her sisters the virgins.[78]

When the time came for the Augusta's return to Constantinople, Melania traveled with her as far as Caesarea. Gerontius emphasizes that the holy woman and the empress came alongside one another in the deepest bond of friendship: "They were scarcely able to be separated from one another, for they were strongly bonded together in spiritual love. And when she returned, the saint gave herself anew to ascetic discipline, praying thus up to the end that the pious empress would be returned to her husband in good health, which the God of all things granted to her."[79] Thus Eudocia returned to Theodosius, buoyed by her time with Melania; and Melania returned to her monastery, newly fueled for her ascetic life.[80]

An exultant Eudocia returned from the Holy Land in early 439 and enjoyed an increase of status in the imperial palace upon her return. It was not lost on the resourceful and ambitious in the palace that her shift in status might afford an opportunity for access to power. As the imperial sword-bearer and perhaps *praepositus sacri cubiculi* (grand chamberlain of the palace) as well, the powerful eunuch Chrysaphius was in the position to take advantage of the situation in order to deal with Pulcheria. The eunuch's plans against Pulcheria involved another empress high on her own power after returning from the Holy Land. Chrysaphius tapped Eudocia's invigorated power and the jealousy of Pulcheria to remove the rival for access to the emperor. Basically, as we see in Theophanes, Chrysaphius played Eudocia.[81] He suggested Eudocia make a power play and ask Theodosius to give her Pulcheria's *praepositus* and court.[82] When Theodosius declined, Chrysaphius changed tactics. He had Eudocia

78. The portrayal of the empress in the Greek version is more flattering than that of the Latin version of the *Life of Melania the Younger*. These differences have a lot to do with the theological concerns of the author. See Christine Shepardson, "Posthumous Orthodoxy," in Chin and Schroeder, *Melania*, 186–201.

79. Gerontius, *Vit. Mel.* 71–72 (Clark, 59).

80. Eudocia spent time with other monastics as well, in particular the Syrian archimandrite Barsauma, who had an affinity for burning down synagogues and pagan temples, wielding cudgels to intimidate Jews and pagans, and practicing extreme asceticism. Apparently she left his presence persuaded to give more of her wealth to the poor. See Evagrius, *Hist. eccl.* 1.21–22 (Whitby, 49–52).

81. Theophanes AM 5940 (Mango and Scott, *Chronicle of Theophanes*, 154).

82. Pulcheria owned significant properties with private palaces and her quarters at the suburban palaces of the Hebdomon and the Rufinianae, an estate also called "the Oak" formerly owned by the prefect Rufinus but that had become imperial property since his death. Once her brother married and there was another empress in town, Theodosius probably provided his sister with her own *praepositus* (a eunuch that managed her affairs akin to the one the emperor had), an imperial staff, a security detail, and a court consisting of many *cubiculariae*, the imperial version of ladies in waiting (Holum, *Theodosian Empresses*, 131–32).

suggest to Theodosius that his pious and capable sister needed to live fully the ascetic life she had chosen and be ordained as a deaconess and not mess around in politics anymore. It was a brilliant power move, and Theodosius agreed. The emperor then instructed Proclus, patriarch of Constantinople, and friend and ally of Pulcheria, to ordain her. Even though Proclus warned Pulcheria and thus averted the removal of her power via ordination, Pulcheria had still been outflanked and bested. She dismissed her *praepositus* and staff and withdrew from Constantinople to the Hebdomon palace for a more private life.[83] Her withdrawal ultimately worked in her favor, and Chrysaphius eventually tumbled from power, but none of this was yet on the horizon. Unfortunately for Eudocia, the tide of Chrysaphius's lust for power would shift against her sooner rather than later.

### The Big Apple Scandal

Following the sixth-century Byzantine chronicler John Malalas in transmitting the rather bizarre tale of a piece of fruit causing a grand scandal, tradition has it that Theodosius II received an impressive apple of unusual size from a poor man.[84] He presented it as a token of love (a common practice) to his wife. Eudocia gave the apple to the handsome Paulinus, Theodosius's childhood friend and master of offices. Paulinus then unwittingly regifted the apple to the emperor. Theodosius, understandably, was quite upset to receive back his token of love. When confronted, Eudocia denied that it was the same apple and claimed that she ate the one the emperor had given to her. This confirmed Theodosius's suspicions that his wife was cheating on him with his friend. Theodosius had Paulinus executed, and his wife demanded she be allowed to go and pray in the Holy Land rather than stay with him. Eudocia permanently resettled in Palestine.

This tale is almost certainly fiction, but Augusta Eudocia did leave Constantinople, and Paulinus was executed; this combination and proximity of events presents a large target upon which to pin scandal. Did Eudocia commit adultery? We have no idea. But the accusation and her leaving Constantinople permanently (which may or may not have been linked to the charge) place her in the expansive category of women who are judged by their sexual reputations.[85] It should not surprise us that Chrysaphius, who so roundly defeated

83. Ibid., 191–92.

84. Malalas, *Chron.* 14.8 (Jeffreys et al., 194–95). See Theophanes AM 5940 (Mango and Scott, *Chronicle of Theophanes*, 155); Chron. Pasch. O.306 (73–75) (Whitby and Whitby, 444).

85. Pulcheria was as "above reproach" as one could be, but her sexuality was still used against her. According to James, "Sexual intrigue and adultery were always a good and very popular

Figure 9.4. Depiction of "Hagia Eudokia" (Holy Eudocia).

Pulcheria, was instrumental in Eudocia's downfall as well; apparently he is the one who charged her with adultery in 443.[86] Unfortunately, Paulinus was an easy target because he was handsome, was a longtime intimate of the family, and had been linked to adultery before by Nestorius (spuriously, and with Pulcheria).

This story does not end here, though. Marcellinus reports in his *Chronicle* (written in 518) that in 444 Theodosius still considered Eudocia a threat and sent Saturninus, his *comes domesticorum* (the head of the emperor's bodyguard), to deal with her.[87] Two of her clerical companions, a priest and a deacon, were assassinated, and the evidence indicates that it was quite possibly Eudocia herself who killed Saturninus in response.[88] At this point Theodosius deprived her of her imperial entourage, and Eudocia's ties with the imperial palace were all but completely severed. Yet Theodosius still did not withdraw her imperial distinction, and she retained her wealth and holdings.

Eudocia does not seem to have been cowed by her fall from the emperor's good graces; instead, the empress went about the business of empire in the Holy Land. Instead of fading into obscurity, Eudocia threw herself into building projects, such as restoring the wall of Jerusalem, rebuilding a more expansive

weapon to use against overambitious empresses who needed to be put in their place" (*Empresses and Power*, 16).

86. Eudocia also gave birth to a son, Arcadius, who was erased from the historical record probably because Chrysaphius discredited not only the Augusta's fidelity but also the paternity of her son (Sowers, "Eudocia," 25).

87. It is unclear exactly what Theodosius had in mind for Eudocia by sending his *comes domesticorum*. Brute force was obviously intended, but we know little more than that violence against her entourage was met with her retribution in kind. See Marcellinus, *Chronicle* 444.4, in *Count Marcellinus and His Chronicle*, by Brian Croke (Oxford: Oxford University Press, 2001), 45; Holum, *Theodosian Empresses*, 194.

88. Alan Cameron, "Empress and the Poet," 271. Cameron also includes an extended discussion about the difficultly in nailing down a chronology for the apple scandal, Eudocia's second and final departure from Constantinople, and the incident with Saturninus (259–71).

version of the Church of St. Stephen that Cyril had consecrated in 438 on her last visit, and constructing an episcopal palace and many centers for public works, such as shelters for the poor.[89] Eudocia never adopted the ascetic lifestyle of Pulcheria or those whom she admired. However, the empress did surround herself with men of some ecclesiastical and monastic reputation to whom she granted favors and who became her confidants.[90]

### Eudocia the Scholar

Empresses tended to be well-educated women, but Eudocia was especially notable in this regard. Eudocia in particular was associated with the "so-called university of Constantinople" and the Christianization of classical education in the academic centers of the empire, such as Antioch and Alexandria.[91] Education was core to the Roman identity, and those skilled in the art of rhetoric and poetry and philosophy were not just well regarded but also considered vital for the survival of the Roman ideal. It is easy to see this as an area where Theodosius and Eudocia might have shared a common interest. Theodosius issued three constitutions on education that benefited those who excelled in their literary craft, even those who were not Christians.[92]

It seems that a part of Eudocia's self-understanding was that of a Christian scholar. During her permanent exile, the empress's longtime love of scholarship blossomed. Most, if not all, of Eudocia's works were written after her relocation to the Holy Land, between around 440 and 460. She attended the lectures of the famous *grammaticus* Orion and interacted with him enough that he dedicated a collection of wise sayings to her. Those around her mastered languages, wrote, and philosophized. The empress wrote biblical hexameter paraphrases of Zechariah and Daniel (not extant), an eight-book sequence on the Octateuch (the first eight books of the Old Testament, also not extant), the *Homerocentones* (a cento using Homer's *Odyssey* and *Iliad*, extant), and a hagiographical paraphrase in three books on the martyrdom of Cyprian of Antioch (martyred during the Diocletianic persecution, extant in part).[93] Both of Eudocia's extant works, the *Martyrdom of St. Cyprian*

89. Holum, *Theodosian Empresses*, 219.

90. According to Holum, these included men like Anastasius (the local bishop), Cosmas (one tasked with guarding the True Cross), and Gabriel and Chrysippus, brothers of Cosmas (monks whom she had ordained priests of the Resurrection Church) (*Theodosian Empresses*, 219).

91. Ibid., 125–26. See also Alan Cameron, "Empress and the Poet," 285–86.

92. Holum, *Theodosian Empresses*, 127.

93. Alan Cameron, "Empress and the Poet," 282. In the *Martyrdom of St. Cyprian*, Eudocia collects the stories that have been circulating since the fourth century about the previously unknown bishop and martyr Cyprian of Antioch and forms them into a dramatic conversion

and her *Homerocentones*, are fascinating and unlike most of the works we have from early Christianity. Here we will focus on her cento, with which Eudocia joins the ranks of those poets who raid the epics for the materials to tell another story entirely.

### What Is a Cento?

Karl Olav Sandnes offers this definition: "A cento is . . . a poem or a poetic sequence made up of *recognizable* lines from one or more existing poems, usually highly valued literature. The literary name for this genre is taken from Latin *cento*, meaning a patchwork garment. The genre is an extreme form of paraphrase whereby the composition brings forth a new story consisting of familiar building-blocks."[94] One of the best ways to understand the genre is to see Eudocia as a quilter of poetry, searching the *Odyssey* and the *Iliad* for scraps of text and stitching them together to make a new whole. Centoists imitated the style of Homer or Virgil, borrowing their lines and retaining the hexametric form. Eudocia was not the only woman to write a cento; the West has its representative in Faltonia Betitia Proba (ca. 320–ca. 370), who stitched together lines from Virgil's *Aeneid* to tell the Christian story.[95] A skilled centoist will not only preserve the integrity of the source text as much as possible but also allow Homer (or Virgil, for Proba) to contribute to the story at hand, which, in this case, is a 2,400-line poem that tells the redemptive story of the Bible from the creation of the world to the ascension of Christ.[96]

---

narrative in hexameter. Sowers's is the first complete English translation available of the 801 extant lines. The *Martyrdom* could have been part of an annual celebration of the life and death of a martyr (Sowers, "Eudocia," 280).

94. Karl Olav Sandnes, *The Gospel "According to Homer and Virgil": Cento and Canon*, NovTSup 138 (Leiden: Brill, 2011), 107.

95. See Elizabeth A. Clark, Diane F. Hatch, and James A. Massey, eds., *The Golden Bough, the Oaken Cross: The Virgilian Cento of Faltonia Betitia Proba*, AARTTS 5 (Chico, CA: Scholars Press, 1981). See also Scott McGill, "Virgil, Christianity, and the *Cento Probae*," in *Texts and Culture in Late Antiquity: Inheritance, Authority, and Change*, ed. J. H. D. Scourfield (Swansea: Classical Press of Wales, 2007), 173–93; McGill, *Virgil Recomposed: The Mythological and Secular Centos in Antiquity*, American Classical Studies 48 (Oxford: Oxford University Press, 2005); and David Vincent Meconi, "The Christian Cento and the Evangelization of Christian Culture," *Logos* 7 (2004): 109–32.

96. Eudocia did not compose this cento from scratch; she credits Patricius, a Christian cleric, with originating the text in the fourth century CE, and she significantly edited and expanded the text (M. D. Usher, *Homeric Stitchings: The Homeric Centos of the Empress Eudocia*, Greek Studies: Interdisciplinary Approaches [Lanham, MD: Rowman & Littlefield, 1998], 3). Usher posits, though, that nearly three-quarters of the 2,400 lines are Eudocia's additions since Patricius had not rendered Homer accurately enough to do justice to the beauty and harmony of his poems (22–23). Most of the Homeric lines in Eudocia's cento are intact, but for the sake of grammatical form and sometimes subject matter (if the text would compromise the integrity

A copy of Proba's *Cento Virgilianus* made its way east to the Theodosian court as a gift to Theodosius II's father. It is possible, especially considering her facility with languages, that Eudocia read it, but Proba's influence on the empress remains unknown.[97] Eudocia composed her cento sometime after 443, while in exile in Jerusalem.

One of the problems particularly erudite Christians faced was the fact that the biblical narrative was no match literarily for these bastions of classical poetry. What the Christians had to offer as their central text for everything from ethics to theology in the Septuagint (the Greek translation of the Old Testament) and the Greek of the New Testament was embarrassingly unsophisticated compared to the classical legacy. However, for Christians, this lack of sophistication and embarrassing style was also exactly what pointed to its divine inspiration.[98] Centos occupied the middling place: an attempt to fold the classical literary legacy into the Christian sacred text tradition and use that same classical legacy for a completely different endeavor. The staying power rests in the didactic nature of the cento and its use of classical content to retell a biblical narrative, both of which put it right in the middle of discussing the reception of the classical legacy and coming to terms with it, a process occurring at this time in Christian history. There was really no way to be an educated person in antiquity without Homer and Virgil as one's "true companions" in that endeavor.[99]

Centos are often viewed, however, as an inherently lowbrow genre—perhaps good for a laugh, but parasitic at the core and therefore not serious literature.[100] As a result Eudocia's cento, marked as it is by its more serious and pious content, has received very little attention. It would be easy to dismiss Eudocia's poem as some kind of compromise—that Eudocia thought very little of the Bible and needed to translate it into the words of her beloved pagan heritage for it to be palatable. The evidence, however, does not indicate that Eudocia prioritized her pagan sensibilities in this way. In fact, the composition indicates both that Eudocia was highly trained and adept at working with the Homeric texts and that she possessed a rich understanding of the whole story

---

of the biblical narrative in some way), she does make accommodations. See Usher, *Homeric Stitchings*, 37–44.

97. M. Eleanor Irwin, "Eudocia Augusta, Aelia," in *Handbook of Women Biblical Interpreters: A Historical and Biographical Guide*, ed. Marion Ann Taylor and Agnes Choi (Grand Rapids: Baker Academic, 2012), 194.

98. Sandnes, *Gospel "According to Homer and Virgil,"* 83.

99. Ibid., 6.

100. There are more examples of Latin Virgilian centos than their Greek cousins. Centos come from all corners of the empire, with widely varying approaches; some feature pious Christian content, while others are erotic or absurd (Sowers, "Eudocia," 54–55).

of redemption found in the Bible. The act of composing a cento like this is profoundly theological. Eudocia exercises a specific hermeneutic in choosing which texts from the *Odyssey* and the *Iliad* will be able to carry the weight of the story of Christianity. She presupposed an audience that was familiar not only with Homer but also with the story found in the biblical text.[101] Since centos (like most writing in antiquity) were likely read aloud, one can imagine what it would have been like to hear this cento, to revel in the beautiful words of Homer while at the same time hearing the precious story of Christ.

### Eudocia's Cento

Because the content is essentially the redemptive story of the Bible, there is a sacredness to centos like Eudocia's and Proba's. Therefore, examining these creative interpretations of the biblical story raises interesting hermeneutical and theological questions. At their best, centos can be products of thoughtful theological and cultural engagement. The audacious assumption of a centoist is that the Christian story of redemption in Christ is *the* story, and therefore that using the best words available to tell it demonstrates its timeless truth.

Both Proba and Eudocia cover the Old Testament through the Synoptic Gospels. Eudocia spends less time in the Old Testament (only 201 lines out of 2,400) than Proba (694 lines almost equally divided between Old and New Testaments), possibly because her focus, in keeping with the theological debates of the day, is primarily christological.[102] In order to stay true to the cento form, Eudocia cannot use any biblical names or terms; her only palate is Homer. As a result, she has to make very specific decisions about what the core themes of the biblical text are in order to retain them once they are conveyed in Homeric form. There is a certain amount of "poetic license" that Eudocia employs, in part to transpose the biblical narrative into a key more pleasing and familiar to pagan ears. In her reception of the Samaritan woman text, for example, Eudocia imports the discussion with its radical implications for questions of ethnicity and gender, renders it in roughly the same length, and decides on the themes of Jesus's identity and how others see him.[103]

Eudocia's cento hinges upon humanity's need for redemption because of the fall and Christ's role in fulfilling that redemption. Indeed, her retelling of the

101. Usher, *Homeric Stitchings*, 85.
102. A notable example from Eudocia's cento that indicates how she approached the biblical text and what her theological contributions were, specifically in christological reflection, is Jesus's encounter with the Samaritan woman found in the biblical text of John 4:4–42. The Greek text and an English translation can be found in Sowers, "Eudocia," 126–32.
103. Ibid., 98.

core of salvation history in Homeric hexameter could be counted as a serious contribution to the contemporary debates on Christology. The christological debates were certainly born out of biblical interpretation, but Eudocia's Christ is storied, albeit packaged in Homeric hexameter, and Eudocia's Christology is also storied, linked irrevocably with the life of the Jesus in the Gospels. This has the effect of grounding her Christology in the text and also presenting it definitively as about a storied person. Her Christology is practical—dealing with the question, via the genre change, of whether Jesus's incarnational power extends to the text—the "good news" for the Greco-Roman legacy. Eudocia certainly thought so. For her, this was an obvious and appropriate utilization of Homer's texts because their beauty and order was properly the purview of the Christian God. Thus it is fitting that the most beautiful words tell the most beautiful story of the salvation of humanity in Christ.

## Conclusion

It is easy to assign more doctrinal and therefore ecclesiological significance to the doctrinal debates in letters and at councils than to other more "unofficial" avenues for grinding out orthodoxy. This is problematic, however, because so much of the continuing working out of the self-identity of the church happened outside of these channels. Because of Pulcheria's more obvious engagement in these more "official" channels and because of her vow of virginity, she had a significant impact on the church. There is no doubt about this. Eudocia, on the other hand, tends to reside in Pulcheria's shadow as her contemporary. She may not have been involved in the same ways that Pulcheria was, but Eudocia's contribution and ecclesial identity were significant in their own right.

When we read of women like Pulcheria and Eudocia, about whom we know much but not nearly enough, we need to be aware of a few important things. First, historians and chroniclers need to be read in their own context since their allegiances vary; sometimes, dulling the sheen of a specific imperial figure so as to tend carefully to another was central to their approach—a shaping of remembrance that serves to buoy a particular understanding of Christianity and empire. Second, we need to resist the temptation to draw big conclusions about a historical figure's relationship to their faith based on one or a few poignant episodes. While our sources have their own drawbacks, they can give us context for these famous moments and help us ground our subjects. Sozomen, for example, is determined to present a Pulcheria who all but has a halo around her head at all times, but his descriptions also push us to think of Pulcheria as more than merely an empress or a virgin or her brother's minder. For Sozomen, her love for Christ is what drove her and made her the force against heresy that she truly was.[104] As she had throughout her career, Pulcheria spent the last years of her life as devoted as ever to the holy men and women who shared with her the ascetic life.

Eudocia might not be the poster woman for the kind of character we want to hear from in Late Antiquity. We might wish that we had more straight-forwardly theological or biblical writings from a "more laudable" example like Macrina or Melania the Elder. Instead, we have a strange compilation of Homeric texts that radically alters the biblical text and an imperial author who was marked by potential scandal, spent her last years in exile after rumors of infidelity and tension with the lauded Pulcheria, and very likely killed a man. But we must remember that the saintliest of women were not the only ones who engaged the biblical narrative and lived as Christians; so did a daughter of a pagan philosopher who became an empress and talented writer. We should responsibly remember Christian women like Pulcheria and Eudocia by recognizing their multiple contributions to the literary, theological, political, and conciliar history of Christianity instead of passing them over in our hunt for those we consider to be more pious champions.

104. Sozomen, *Hist. eccl.* 9.1 (Hartranft, 419–20).

# Conclusion:
# Responsibly Remembering

We might well ask whether a female ascetic in second-century Asia Minor could have imagined the changes in her Christian community three hundred years hence. Standing in the streets of Ephesus, could she fathom a church council being held there in the theater, with imperial women engaged in the wider doctrinal debates? Could a third-century female slave entering an arena to be martyred imagine that she would be remembered and honored by generations of Christians? Such thoughts would have been beyond their imagination. We, too, face a struggle to imagine women active in all areas of the early church; we strive to connect with these ancient women who inhabited a Mediterranean and Middle Eastern world vastly different from our own. We have trouble envisioning the ascetic life or the newly formed Christendom, with political and spiritual power united in a Christian emperor and his imperial family.

Moreover, the names sound strange to our ears: Thecla, Perpetua, Egeria, Macrina; yet their stories link to our own in significant ways and shape our sense of what is possible. For centuries afterward, Thecla's story of ascetic faithfulness in the face of threatening death shaped the ideals of discipleship for men and women. Perpetua's visions comforted generations of sufferers even as her teachings shaped the church's understanding of God's faithfulness. Felicitas's public humiliation only served to embolden others' confidence in God's good purposes, as her martyrdom was retold yearly in the church's festival cycle. Women's voices joined with those of men in singing psalms, and Christians gathered to honor the passing of their loved ones—images preserved in Rome's catacombs. Women such as Egeria journeyed to the Holy Lands, reshaping geography to fit theological understanding. Wealthy women fortunate enough to have education, such as Melania the Elder and Melania the Younger, along with Macrina, read the Bible deeply and communicated their interpretations and theological ideas to leading male theologians such as Gregory of Nyssa and Augustine. Their patronage to the church in building monasteries benefited and shaped the Latin West and Greek East for centuries. Imperial women such as Helena, Pulcheria, and Eudocia shaped ecclesial decisions by wielding their authority.

Our exploration of Christian women ends as the Roman Empire shifts its center of gravity to the East, to Constantinople (modern Istanbul). In 396 the Visigoths, led by Alaric, swept down from the northeast and took the Balkan Peninsula, and in 410 they sacked Rome. In 443 Attila the Hun threatened the Eastern empire, and Theodosius II sued for peace. Skirmishes continued across the empire, now divided into East and West, until in 476 Rome fell, and with that fall the Western empire unraveled toward the Middle Ages. Constantinople continued as the capital of the Byzantine Empire and reached its zenith in 527–65 with Justinian's rule. Just a few years later, in 569/70, Muhammad was born, and the landscape of the Middle East and the Mediterranean changed again.

Jerusalem remained a focal point for Christians in the midst of Rome's demise and the Byzantine Empire's consistently fragile borders. The churches established by Helena in the Holy Land grew and flourished, and pilgrims beat a steady path to their doors. The Persians took Constantinople in 614, and then were subsequently defeated by the Muslims in 637. Within about thirty years, Constantinople faced its first of many sieges as various Muslim dynasties (Turks, Egyptians, and Arabs) swept across the Middle East, North Africa, Spain, and Asia Minor. Then in 1099 the first Crusaders from Western Europe reached Jerusalem, ending Muslim rule. Within a year, Baldwin, count of Edessa, was declared king of Jerusalem. His cousin, Baldwin II, became king after him. Baldwin II's daughter, Melisende, rose to become queen at his death and ruled Jerusalem for two decades (1143–61). She corresponded with Bernard of Clairvaux, the famous Cistercian abbot, who said, "The eyes of all will be upon you, and on you alone the whole burden of the kingdom will rest. You must set your hand to great things and, though a woman, you must act as a man . . . so that all may judge you from your actions to be a king rather than a queen."[1]

She acted on that advice, and later historians do not forgive her for it. As we saw above concerning previous imperial women such as Pulcheria, his-

---

1. Sharan Newman, *Defending the City of God: A Medieval Queen, the First Crusades, and the Quest for Peace in Jerusalem* (New York: Palgrave Macmillan, 2014), 176.

torians challenge, excoriate, and question a woman's use of authority and political power. Regarding Melisende, modern historians take a familiar tack and have labeled her authoritarian, vindictive, and a "power-hungry Queen Dowager."[2] In a brief biography, Peter Lock states, "Melisende was a forceful character with a thirst for political power" who "refused to hand over power on his [her son's] coming of age."[3] Sharan Newman argues, however, that Queen Melisende ruled because her son was not yet ready to take up the reins. As she points out, none of Melisende's contemporary historians saw her as a power-hungry queen, and some believed she made a better ruler than her son.[4]

Indeed, one contemporary chronicler, William of Tyre, praises her: "For thirty years and more, during the lifetime of her husband, as well as afterwards, in the reign of her son, Melisende had governed the kingdom with strength surpassing that of most women. Her rule had been wise and judicious."[5] He further notes her patronage of the arts, and as evidence one can point to the beautiful psalter she sponsored, now on display in the British Museum. Melisende also founded a nunnery in Bethany, outside Jerusalem, where her sister served as abbess and where Melisende spent her final months of life after she suffered a stroke.

Newman suggests that "Melisende's legacy was in setting an example for another generation."[6] Her grandson became king, while her two granddaughters each were queen. Within twenty years after her death, however, Jerusalem again fell to the Muslims, led by Saladin. Newman's lament that "the histories of the Latin States have too often ignored the contribution made by women" rings true as well for the time period studied in our book,[7] and her exploration of Melisende's life reminds us that the examples of imperial women of the Late Antique period continued to be influential down through the centuries within Christian history.

This book introduced the different ways Christian women lived and shaped the story of Christianity. For the most part, however, the women we examined did not wield authority and power in the traditional sense of governance or public ideological discourse (e.g., Emperor Constantine; Augustine, bishop of Hippo). On the one hand, what authority and power they did have was

2. Ibid., 214. She cites René Grousset, *Histoire des croisades et du royaume franc de Jérusalem* (Paris: Librarie Plon, 1935), 2:314.
3. Peter Lock, *The Routledge Companion to the Crusades* (New York: Routledge, 2006), 246.
4. Newman, *Defending the City*, 216.
5. Ibid., 218, citing William of Tyre, *A History of Deeds Done beyond the Seas*, trans. Emily Atwater Babcock and A. C. Krey (New York: Octagon, 1976), 2:283.
6. Newman, *Defending the City*, 218.
7. Ibid., 220.

generally limited, either by choice—such as Melania the Elder, who untangled her wealth from any semblance of temporal power and funneled it to the poor and to monastic enterprises—or because of another delimiting factor. Among those factors are: (1) unpredictable spates of persecution (prior to 313), sometimes resulting in a premature death; (2) regional isolation (e.g., Macrina in Cappadocia); and (3) the various forms of circumscription of women in Greco-Roman culture. On the other hand, the empresses were products of a culture that had very particular understandings about what it meant to be a Roman woman as opposed to a Roman man. Yet empresses often seem breezily unaware of such limitations, in part because they enjoyed the wealth and status given to imperial family members.

No one could deny that the women described in this book and countless other holy women had power; but it was a circumscribed power as Christianity was coming to grips with martyr-ascetic influence (excepting perhaps the empresses). This kind of authority is drawn from the core of Christianity's self-understanding. The renunciation, retreat, devotion, and commitment to a new philosophy are all grounded in the *imitatio Christi*; power in submission, vulnerability, and weakness.[8] This narrative of power in weakness was familiar to Christians for whom persecution was still a fresh reality and who, through letters and at councils, had spent the better part of 150 years discussing and arguing about the identity of Jesus Christ. The dialectic between imperial Rome and this Christian antipower power of humility was not an easy or obvious conversation.

### Where Do We Go from Here?

In reading these texts by women and about women, we seek to connect with their context even across great distance and difference. John Donne's famous "Meditation 17" reverberates well past its seventeenth-century publication with its familiar refrain:

> No man is an island, entire of itself; every man is a piece of the continent, a part of the main. If a clod be washed away by the sea, Europe is the less, as well as if a promontory were, as well as if a manor of thy friend's or of thine own were: any man's death diminishes me, because I am involved in mankind, and therefore never send to know for whom the bell tolls; it tolls for thee.[9]

8. See Sarah Coakley, *Powers and Submissions: Spirituality, Philosophy and Gender*, Challenges in Contemporary Theology (Oxford: Blackwell, 2002).

9. See http://www.online-literature.com/donne/409/.

Every human life is stitched into the fabric of society; its thread touches others and plays its particular part in the tapestry. The women featured in this volume hail from different regions and time periods, but they all embraced Christian devotion and are remembered for their roles in constructing the narrative of Christianity that comes down to us.

Of course, ancient Christian women did not have a corner on effecting change. Attending to the stories and contributions of women from other cultures and religious traditions adds needed complexity to narratives based on assumptions and encourages a thicker engagement with our own tradition. For example, learning about the resolve of Malala Yousafzai, a Pakistani Muslim who at age sixteen survived an assassin's bullet for the sake of educational access for girls in Pakistan, may help enrich our reading of Thecla's steadfastness in facing death rather than backing down from her convictions. And, as I (Lynn) researched the ancient female martyrs' stories, I remembered my own shock and horror at learning of the murdered/martyred nuns in El Salvador in 1980. I was entering my freshman year in college when the terrible violence began destroying that country; moreover, I had just been baptized and made a profession of faith. Jean Donovan (lay missionary) and Ita Ford, Maura Clarke, Dorothy Kazel (Catholic nuns)—these women's example of service at any cost stood as a sobering reminder of the possible price of serving others in defiance of those in power, much as did Perpetua and Felicitas's courage expose the impotence of Roman authority to silence them. Indeed, the last three decades have exposed the US government's role in covering up the crime, a work of the El Salvador National Guard, indicating the continuing need to remember and emulate these brave women.[10]

When I (Amy) was researching Macrina, I remembered my delight in learning who Marie Wilkinson was. The civil rights leader and devout Catholic began to make her mark on the second-largest city in Illinois just after she moved to Aurora from New Orleans shortly after 1930. Her home was simply known as "Marie's house," and it was opened to all—the unemployed, the homeless, the sick, and the mistreated. She became an advocate for Hispanic factory workers in the area who were being subjected to squalid living and working conditions; she challenged City Hall to provide them educational opportunities and housing. In the late 1940s, when she was refused seating at a local restaurant because she was African American, she won her case before the State Appellate Court. Before she died in 2010 at 101, Marie helped

10. Raymond Bonner, "Bringing El Salvador Nun Killers to Justice," *The Daily Beast*, November 9, 2014, http://www.thedailybeast.com/articles/2014/11/09/bringing-el-salvador-nun-killers-to-justice.html.

This bronze sculpture depicts Marie Wilkinson holding the whip used on her father-in-law, an escaped slave, and warmly inviting anyone to sit with her on the bench.

launch more than sixty charitable organizations and established college funds for underprivileged children, and she is credited with the first Fair Housing Ordinance in Illinois.[11] In Aurora, where I lived for over a decade, one will find Marie's name on a child care center, on a food pantry, and on a street; outside the Aurora Public Library is a bronze statue of her sitting on a bench and welcoming all to sit next to her. After Marie was awarded the Catholic Church's highest honor for a missionary, the Lumen Christi Award, in 2002, Carrie Swearingen interviewed her: "'You can get angry at the things people do, but you can't hate any person,' says Marie Wilkinson while grasping the torture whip she inherited from her father-in-law, an escaped slave. 'I take this whip and I teach a lot of people not to hate.'"[12] Marie Wilkinson's legacy spurs the people of Aurora to go and do likewise, reaching across racial, religious, and socioeconomic lines and advocating for those in need. I like

11. See Joan Giangrasse Kates, "Marie Wilkinson, Civil Rights Activist, Dies at Age 101," *Chicago Tribune*, August 17, 2010, http://articles.chicagotribune.com/2010-08-17/features /ct-met-wilkinson-obit-0818-20100817_1_aurora-alderman-aurora-mayor-tom-weisner-quad -county-urban-league.

12. Carrie Swearingen, "She Opens Doors: Marie Wilkinson," *St. Anthony Messenger*, May 2002, https://www.franciscanmedia.org/she-opens-doors-marie-wilkinson/.

to think Marie would have gotten along very well with Macrina—a woman who radically pushed social norms for the sake of her faith and the oppressed.

In the introduction I (Amy) mentioned how the impetus for writing this book finds purchase in the question asked by my friend Sarah about how she can contribute to the church. I think the answer to her question includes telling the stories of women in Christianity and recognizing their contributions so that there is a context for women contributing to the Christian story in fundamental and not merely peripheral ways. Modern scholarship has done us a great service by translating many texts that were not heretofore available and by working through the thorny methodological issues that come from reading ancient texts about women, thereby helping readers fruitfully access the legacies of women. We have sought to build upon that work and focus on how these women were fundamental to the development of Christianity. Thus we offer a fuller picture of the construction of the Christian story.

Our responsible remembrance of women like Perpetua, Helena, Monica, Paula, and Eudocia broadens our understanding of Christian history and theology and gives us a foundation for advocacy of representation of women in various ways. As we recall their contributions and legacy, we cannot imagine Christianity without them. By extension we cannot imagine Christianity now without Jean Donovan, Ita Ford, Maura Clarke, Dorothy Kazel, Marie Wilkinson, and the "Sarahs" that are in every congregation. Justo González tells us that responsible remembrance leads to "responsible action."[13] Michael Gorman, in his book on Revelation, stresses how important it is to remember our Christian history, especially the history of the martyrs.[14] He observes that when we forget these ancient martyrs and ignore the contemporary ones, we often fill the void with national heroes and martyrs, creating a civil religion of the state that ultimately undermines the church's call of sacrificial love and service to the world. Recalling the witness of ancient women martyrs and ascetics helps us today locate ourselves in this great tradition of service to others and resistance to oppression that characterized these women's lives. These women made stunning sacrifices for others, worked through difficult questions, made mistakes and even destructive decisions. Their story is part of the bigger human and Christian narrative. Responsibly remembering the women who helped construct Christianity at such an influential time allows us today to build on their legacy, influencing toward the good, and using what authority we may have to bless our neighbors.

13. González, *Mañana*, 79.
14. Michael J. Gorman, *Reading Revelation Responsibly: Uncivil Worship and Witness; Following the Lamb into the New Creation* (Eugene, OR: Cascade, 2011), 135.

# Bibliography

**Primary Sources**

*The Acts of Paul and Thecla*. Translated by Jeremy W. Barrier with commentary. WUNT 2/270. Tübingen: Mohr Siebeck, 2009.

Ambrose. *De obitu Theodosii*. Pages 174–202 in *Ambrose of Milan: Political Letters and Speeches*. Translated by J. H. W. G. Liebeschuetz and Carole Hill. Translated Texts for Historians 43. Liverpool: Liverpool University Press, 2010.

Augustine. *The Confessions*. The Works of Saint Augustine: A Translation for the 21st Century. Vol. I/1. Edited by John E. Rotelle. Translated by Maria Boulding. Hyde Park, NY: New City, 1997.

———. *The Happy Life*. Translated by Ludwig Schopp. FC 5. New York: CIMA, 1948.

———. *Letters*. Vol. 1. Translated by Wilfrid Parsons. FC 12. New York: Catholic University of America Press, 1951.

———. *Letters*. Vol. 2. Translated by Wilfrid Parsons. FC 18. New York: Catholic University of America Press, 1953.

———. *On the Grace of Christ and on Original Sin*. NPNF[1] 5:214–55.

———. *On Order (De Ordine)*. Translated by Silvano Borruso. South Bend, IN: St. Augustine's Press, 2007.

———. *Sermons III/8 (273–305A) on the Saints*. The Works of Saint Augustine: A Translation for the 21st Century. Edited by John E. Rotelle. Translated by Edmund Hill. Hyde Park, NY: New City, 1994.

Egeria. *Egeria: Diary of a Pilgrimage*. Translated and annotated by George E. Gingras. ACW 38. Westminster, MD: Newman, 1970.

———. *Itinerarium Egeriae*. Pages 121–319 in *Égérie: Journal de voyage*. Edited by Pierre Maraval. SC 296. Paris: Cerf, 1982.

Eusebius. *Eusebius: Ecclesiastical History, Books 1–5*. Translated by Kirsopp Lake. LCL 153. Cambridge, MA: Harvard University Press, 1926.

———. *Eusebius: Ecclesiastical History, Books 6–10*. Translated by J. E. L. Oulton. LCL 265. Cambridge, MA: Harvard University Press, 1932.

———. *Eusebius: Life of Constantine*. Translated by Averil Cameron and Stuart G. Hall. Clarendon Ancient History Series. Oxford: Clarendon, 1999.

Evagrius Scholasticus. *"The Ecclesiastical History" of Evagrius Scholasticus*. Translated by Michael Whitby. Translated Texts for Historians 33. Liverpool: Liverpool University Press, 2000.

Gerontius. *The Life of Melania the Younger*. Translated by Elizabeth A. Clark. SWR 14. New York: Edwin Mellen, 1984.

Gregory of Nyssa. *Gregory of Nyssa: The Letters, Introduction, Translation and Commentary*. Edited and translated by Anna M. Silvas. VCSup 83. Leiden: Brill, 2007.

———. *The Life of Macrina*. Translated by Anna M. Silvas. Pages 93–148 in *Macrina the Younger, Philosopher of God*. Medieval Women: Texts and Contexts 22. Turnhout: Brepols, 2008.

———. *On the Soul and the Resurrection*. Translated by Anna M. Silvas. Pages 149–246 in *Macrina the Younger, Philosopher of God*. Medieval Women: Texts and Contexts 22. Turnhout: Brepols, 2008.

———. *Vita s. Macrinae*. Edited by Virginia Woods Callahan. GNO VIII.1. Pages 370–414 in *Opera Ascetica*. Edited by Werner Jaeger, John Peter Cavarnos, and Virginia Woods Callahan. Leiden: Brill, 1952.

James of Edessa. *James of Edessa: The Hymns of Severus of Antioch and Others*. Translated by E. W. Brooks. PO 6–7. Paris: Firmin-Didot, 1911.

Jerome. *Jerome's "Epitaph on Paula": A Commentary on the "Epitaphium Sanctae Paulae."* Edited and translated by Andrew Cain. OECT. Oxford: Oxford University Press, 2013.

———. *Life of Marcella* (Jerome, *Letter* 127, to Principia). Pages 57–70 in *Lives of Roman Christian Women*. Edited and translated by Carolinne White. Penguin Classics. London: Penguin, 2010.

———. *On Visiting Jerusalem*, by Paula the Elder and Eustochium to Marcella (Jerome, *Letter* 46). Pages 165–78 in *Lives of Roman Christian Women*. Edited and translated by Carolinne White. Penguin Classics. London: Penguin, 2010.

Malalas, John. *The Chronicle of John Malalas*. Translated by Elizabeth Jeffreys, Michael Jeffreys, Roger Scott, and Brian Croke. Byzantina Australiensia 4. Melbourne: Australian Association for Byzantine Studies, 1986.

Methodius of Olympus. *Convivium decem virginum*. Edited by J.-P. Migne. In *Methodii Opera omnia*. PG 18:28–220. Paris: Migne, 1857.

———. *St. Methodius: The Symposium; A Treatise on Chastity*. Translated by Herbert Musurillo. ACW 27. Westminster, MD: Newman, 1958.

———. *Symposion.* Edited by G. N. Bonwetsch. Pages 1–141 in *Methodius.* GCS 27. Leipzig: Hinrichs, 1917.

———. *Symposium sive Convivium decem virginum.* In *Méthode D'Olympe: Le Banquet.* Edited by Herbert Musurillo. Translated by Victor-Henry Debidour. SC 95. Paris: Cerf, 1963.

Nestorius. *Bazaar of Heracleides.* Translated by G. R. Driver and Leonard Hodgson. Oxford: Clarendon, 1925. http://www.tertullian.org/fathers/nestorius_bazaar_0 _intro.htm.

Origen. *Contra Celsum.* Edited and Translated by Henry Chadwick. Cambridge: Cambridge University Press, 1953.

Palladius. *Palladius: Lausiac History.* Translated by Robert T. Meyer. ACW 34. Westminster, MD: Newman, 1965.

*Passion de Perpétue et de Félicité suivi des Actes.* Edited with French translation by Jacqueline Amat. SC 417. Paris: Cerf, 1996.

*Passio sanctarum Perpetuae et Felicitatis.* Vol. 1, *Textum Graecum et Latinum ad fidem codicum mss.* Edited by Cornelius I. M. I. van Beek. Nijmegen: Dekker & Van de Vegt, 1936.

Paulinus of Nola. *Letters of St. Paulinus of Nola.* Vol. 2. Translated by P. G. Walsh. ACW 36. New York: Newman, 1967.

Plato. *Republic.* Pages 971–1223 in *Plato: The Complete Works.* Edited by John M. Cooper. Translated by G. M. A Grube. Revised by C. D. C. Reeve. Indianapolis: Hackett, 1997.

———. *Theaetetus.* Pages 157–234 in *Plato: The Complete Works.* Edited by John M. Cooper. Translated by M. J. Levett. Revised by Myles Burnyeat. Indianapolis: Hackett, 1997.

Polycarp. *To the Philippians.* Pages 130–41 in *The Apostolic Fathers in English.* Translated and edited by Michael W. Holmes. 3rd ed. Grand Rapids: Baker Academic, 2006.

Reardon, Bryan P., ed. *Collected Ancient Greek Novels.* Berkeley: University of California Press, 1989. New ed., 2008.

Rufinus of Aquileia. *Historia ecclesiastica.* In *The Church History of Rufinus of Aquileia, Books 10 and 11.* Translated by Philip R. Amidon. Oxford: Oxford University Press, 1997.

Schneemelcher, Wilhelm, ed. *New Testament Apocrypha.* 2 vols. Translated by R. McL. Wilson. Rev. ed. Louisville: Westminster John Knox, 1992.

Schwartz, Eduard, ed. *Acta Conciliorum Oecumenicorum: Tomus primus, Concilium universale Ephesenum.* Vol. 1, *Acta graeca: Pars tertia.* Berlin: de Gruyter, 1927.

Socrates Scholasticus. *Socrates: Church History from AD 305–439.* Translated by A. C. Zenos. *NPNF*[2] 2:1–178.

Sozomen. *Sozomenus: Church History from AD 323–425.* Translated by Chester D. Hartranft. *NPNF*[2] 2:179–427.

Theodoret of Cyrrhus. *Theodoret, Jerome, Gennadius, Rufinus: Historical Writings.* Translated by Blomfield Jackson. *NPNF*² 3:1–348.

Theophanes. *The Chronicle of Theophanes Confessor: Byzantine and Near Eastern History, AD 284–813.* Translated by Cyril Mango and Roger Scott. Oxford: Clarendon, 1997.

Whitby, Michael, and Mary Whitby, trans. *Chronicon Paschale, 284–628 AD.* Translated Texts for Historians 7. Liverpool: Liverpool University Press, 1989.

William of Tyre. *A History of Deeds Done beyond the Seas.* Translated by Emily Atwater Babcock and A. C. Krey. Vol. 2. New York: Octagon, 1976.


## Secondary Sources

Alciati, Roberto, and Mariachiara Giorda. "Possessions and Asceticism: Melania the Younger and Her Slow Way to Jerusalem." *ZAC* 14 (2010): 425–44.

Ameling, Walter. "*Femina Liberaliter Instituta*—Some Thoughts on a Martyr's Liberal Education." Pages 78–102 in Bremmer and Formisano, *Perpetua's Passions.*

Balás, David L. "Gregory of Nyssa." Pages 495–97 in *Encyclopedia of Early Christianity.* Edited by Everett Ferguson, Michael P. McHugh, Frederick W. Norris, and John McRay. Garland Reference Library of the Humanities 1839. New York: Garland, 1997.

Barnes, Timothy D. *Constantine and Eusebius.* Cambridge, MA: Harvard University Press, 2006.

———. *Constantine: Dynasty, Religion and Power in the Later Roman Empire.* Blackwell Ancient Lives. Oxford: Wiley-Blackwell, 2011.

———. *Early Christian Hagiography and Roman History.* Tübingen: Mohr Siebeck, 2010.

Barrier, Jeremy W. *The Acts of Paul and Thecla.* WUNT 2/270. Tübingen: Mohr Siebeck, 2009.

Benko, Stephen. *The Virgin Goddess: Studies in the Pagan and Christian Roots of Mariology.* SHR 59. Leiden: Brill, 2004.

Bitton-Ashkelony, Brouria. *Encountering the Sacred: The Debate on Christian Pilgrimage in Late Antiquity.* Transformation of the Classical Heritage 39. Berkeley: University of California Press, 2005.

Bonner, Raymond. "Bringing El Salvador Nun Killers to Justice." *The Daily Beast,* November 9, 2014. http://www.thedailybeast.com/articles/2014/11/09/bringing-el-salvador-nun-killers-to-justice.html.

Bowersock, G. W. *Martyrdom and Rome.* Cambridge: Cambridge University Press, 1995.

Bowrey, Anne-Marie. "Monica: The Feminine Face of Christ." Pages 69–96 in J. Stark, *Feminist Interpretations of Augustine.*

Boyarin, Daniel. *Dying for God: Martyrdom and the Making of Christianity and Judaism*. Stanford, CA: Stanford University Press, 1999.

Bracht, Katharina. *Vollkommenheit und Vollendung: Zur Anthropologie des Methodius von Olympus*. Studien und Texte zu Antike und Christentum 2. Tübingen: Mohr Siebeck, 1999.

Bradley, Keith. "Sacrificing the Family: Christian Martyrs and Their Kin." Pages 104–25 in *Apuleius and Antonine Rome: Historical Essays*. Toronto: University of Toronto Press, 2012.

Bradshaw, Paul F., and Maxwell E. Johnson. *The Origins of Feasts, Fasts, and Seasons in Early Christianity*. Alcuin Club Collections 86. Collegeville, MN: Liturgical Press, 2011.

Brakke, David. *Demons and the Making of the Monk: Spiritual Combat in Early Christianity*. Cambridge, MA: Harvard University Press, 2006.

Bremmer, Jan N. "Felicitas: The Martyrdom of a Young African Woman." Pages 35–53 in Bremmer and Formisano, *Perpetua's Passions*.

Bremmer, Jan N., and Marco Formisano. *Perpetua's Passions: Multidisciplinary Approaches to the "Passio Perpetuae et Felicitatis."* Oxford: Oxford University Press, 2012.

Brock, Sebastian P., and Susan Ashbrook Harvey. *Holy Women of the Syrian Orient*. Transformation of the Classical Heritage 13. Berkeley: University of California Press, 1998.

Brown, Peter. *Augustine of Hippo: A Biography*. New ed. Berkeley: University of California Press, 2000.

———. *The Body and Society: Men, Women, and Sexual Renunciation in Early Christianity*. Lectures in the History of Religions 13. New York: Columbia University Press, 1988. New ed. CCR. New York: Columbia University Press, 2008.

———. *Through the Eye of a Needle: Wealth, the Fall of Rome, and the Making of Christianity in the West, 350–550 AD*. Princeton: Princeton University Press, 2012.

Brubaker, Leslie. "Memories of Helena: Patterns in Imperial Female Matronage in the Fourth and Fifth Centuries." Pages 52–75 in *Women, Men and Eunuchs: Gender in Byzantium*. Edited by Liz James. London: Routledge, 1997.

Brubaker, Leslie, and Mary B. Cunningham, eds. *The Cult of the Mother of God in Byzantium: Texts and Images*. Birmingham Byzantine and Ottoman Studies. Farnham: Ashgate, 2011.

Burris, Catherine, and Lucas van Rompay. "Some Further Notes on Thecla in Syriac Christianity." *Hug* 6.2 (2009): 337–42. http://www.bethmardutho.org/index.php/hugoye/volume-index/155.html.

Bynum, Caroline Walker. *The Resurrection of the Body in Western Christianity, 200–1336*. Lectures on the History of Religions 15. New York: Columbia University Press, 1995.

Cain, Andrew. "Jerome's *Epitaphium Paulae*: Hagiography, Pilgrimage, and the Cult of Saint Paula." *JECS* 18.1 (2010): 105–39.

———, ed. and trans. *Jerome's "Epitaph on Paula": A Commentary on the "Epitaphium Sanctae Paulae."* OECT. Oxford: Oxford University Press, 2013.

Calef, Susan A. "Thecla 'Tried and True' and the Inversion of Romance." Pages 163–85 in *A Feminist Companion to the New Testament Apocrypha*. Edited by Amy-Jill Levine with Maria Mayo Robbins. FCNTECW 11. London: T&T Clark, 2006.

Cameron, Alan. "The Empress and the Poet: Paganism and Politics at the Court of Theodosius II." Pages 217–89 in *Later Greek Literature*. Edited by John J. Winkler and Gordon Williams. YCS 27. Cambridge: Cambridge University Press, 1982.

Cameron, Alan, and Jacqueline Long. *Barbarians and Politics at the Court of Arcadius*. Transformation of the Classical Heritage 19. Berkeley: University of California Press, 1993.

Cameron, Averil. *Christianity and the Rhetoric of Empire: The Development of Christian Discourse*. Sather Classical Lectures 55. Berkeley: University of California Press, 1991.

———. "Sacred and Profane Love: Thoughts on Byzantine Gender." Pages 1–23 in *Women, Men and Eunuchs: Gender in Byzantium*. Edited by Liz James. London: Routledge, 1997.

Cardman, Francine. "Whose Life Is It? The *Vita Macrinae* of Gregory of Nyssa." Pages 33–50 in *Cappadocian Writers, Other Greek Writers: Papers Presented at the Thirteenth International Conference on Patristic Studies Held in Oxford, 1999*. Edited by M. F. Wiles and E. J. Yarnold. StPatr 37. Leuven: Peeters, 2001.

Carlsen, Jesper. "Exemplary Deaths in the Arena: Gladiatorial Fights and the Execution of Criminals." Pages 75–91 in *Contextualising Early Christian Martyrdom*. Edited by Jacob Engberg, Uffe Homsgaard Eriksen, and Anders Klostergaard Petersen. Frankfurt: Peter Lang, 2011.

Castelli, Elizabeth A. *Martyrdom and Memory: Early Christian Culture Making*. GTR. New York: Columbia University Press, 2004.

———. "Pseudo-Athanasius: *The Life and Activity of the Holy and Blessed Teacher Syncletica*." Pages 265–311 in *Ascetic Behavior in Greco-Roman Antiquity: A Sourcebook*. Edited by Vincent Wimbush. Minneapolis: Fortress, 1990.

———. "Virginity and Its Meaning for Women's Sexuality in Early Christianity." Pages 72–100 in *A Feminist Companion to Patristic Literature*. Edited by Amy-Jill Levine. FCNTECW 12. London: T&T Clark, 2008.

Chew, Kathryn. "Virgins and Eunuchs: Pulcheria, Politics and the Death of Emperor Theodosius II." *Historia* 55 (2006): 207–27.

Chin, Catherine M. "Apostles and Aristocrats." Pages 19–33 in Chin and Schroeder, *Melania*.

Chin, Catherine M., and Caroline T. Schroeder, eds. *Melania: Early Christianity through the Life of One Family*. Oakland: University of California Press, 2016.

Clark, Elizabeth A. *Ascetic Piety and Women's Faith: Essays on Late Ancient Christianity*. SWR 20. Lewiston, NY: Edwin Mellen, 1986.

———. "Ascetic Renunciation and Feminine Advancement: A Paradox of Late Ancient Christianity." *AThR* 63 (1981): 240–57.

———. "Claims on the Bones of Saint Stephen: The Partisans of Melania and Eudocia." *CH* 51 (1982): 141–56.

———. *History, Theory, Text: Historians and the Linguistic Turn*. Cambridge, MA: Harvard University Press, 2004.

———. "Holy Women, Holy Words: Early Christian Women, Social History, and the 'Linguistic Turn.'" *JECS* 6 (1998): 413–30.

———. *Jerome, Chrysostom, and Friends: Essays and Translations*. SWR 2. New York: Edwin Mellen, 1979.

———, trans. *The Life of Melania the Younger*. SWR 14. New York: Edwin Mellen, 1984.

———. *The Origenist Controversy: The Cultural Construction of an Early Christian Debate*. Princeton: Princeton University Press, 1992.

Clark, Elizabeth A., Diane F. Hatch, and James Massey, eds. *The Golden Bough, the Oaken Cross: The Virgilian Cento of Faltonia Betitia Proba*. AARTTS 5. Chico, CA: Scholars Press, 1981.

Clark, Gillian. "Bodies and Blood: Late Antique Debate on Martyrdom, Virginity and Resurrection." Pages 99–115 in *Changing Bodies, Changing Meanings: Studies on the Human Body in Antiquity*. Edited by Dominic Montserrat. London: Routledge, 1998.

———. *Monica: An Ordinary Saint*. Women in Antiquity. Oxford: Oxford University Press, 2015.

Coakley, Sarah. *Powers and Submissions: Spirituality, Philosophy, and Gender*. Challenges in Contemporary Theology. Oxford: Blackwell, 2002.

———. *Re-thinking Gregory of Nyssa*. Oxford: Blackwell, 2003.

Cohick, Lynn H. *Women in the World of the Earliest Christians: Illuminating Ancient Ways of Life*. Grand Rapids: Baker Academic, 2009.

Constas, Nicholas. *Proclus of Constantinople and the Cult of the Virgin in Late Antiquity: Homilies 1–5, Texts and Translations*. VCSup 66. Leiden: Brill, 2003.

Coon, Lynda L. *Sacred Fictions: Holy Women and Hagiography in Late Antiquity*. Middle Ages Series. Philadelphia: University of Pennsylvania Press, 1997.

Cooper, Kate. *Band of Angels: The Forgotten World of Early Christian Women*. New York: Overlook, 2013.

———. "Contesting the Nativity: Wives, Virgins, and Pulcheria's *imitatio Mariae*." *SJRS* 19 (1998): 31–44.

———. "Poverty, Obligation, and Inheritance: Roman Heiresses and the Varieties of Senatorial Christianity in Fifth-Century Rome." Pages 165–89 in Cooper and Hillner, *Religion, Dynasty, and Patronage in Early Christian Rome.*

———. *The Virgin and the Bride: Idealized Womanhood in Late Antiquity.* Cambridge, MA: Harvard University Press, 1996.

Cooper, Kate, and Julia Hillner. *Religion, Dynasty, and Patronage in Early Christian Rome, 300–900.* Cambridge: Cambridge University Press, 2007.

Croke, Brian. *Count Marcellinus and His Chronicle.* Oxford: Oxford University Press, 2001.

Davis, Stephen J. *The Cult of Saint Thecla: A Tradition of Women's Piety in Late Antiquity.* OECS. Oxford: Oxford University Press, 2001.

Dean, Crystal. "Roman Women Authors: Authorship, Agency and Authority." PhD diss., University of Calgary, 2012.

Denzey, Nicola. *The Bone Gatherers: The Lost Worlds of Early Christian Women.* Boston: Beacon, 2007.

Drake, Susanna. "Friends and Heretics." Pages 171–85 in Chin and Schroeder, *Melania.*

Drijvers, Jan Willem. "Helena Augusta, the Cross and the Myth: Some New Reflections." *Millennium-Jahrbuch* 8 (2011): 125–74.

———. *Helena Augusta: The Mother of Constantine the Great and the Legend of Her Finding of the True Cross.* Brill's Studies in Intellectual History 27. Leiden: Brill, 1992.

Droge, Arthur J. "The Apologetic Dimensions of the *Ecclesiastical History.*" Pages 492–509 in *Eusebius, Christianity, and Judaism.* Edited by Harold W. Attridge and Gohei Hata. Detroit: Wayne State University Press, 1992.

Elkins, Kathleen Gallagher. "Mother, Martyr: Reading Self-Sacrifice and Family in Early Christianity." PhD diss., Drew University, 2013.

Elm, Susanna. "Perceptions of Jerusalem Pilgrimage as Reflected in Two Early Sources on Female Pilgrimage (3rd and 4th Centuries A.D.)." Pages 219–23 in *Critica, Classica, Orientalia, Ascetica, Liturgica: Papers Presented to the Tenth International Conference on Patristic Studies Held in Oxford, 1987.* Edited by Elizabeth A. Livingstone. StPatr 20. Leuven: Peeters, 1989.

Elsner, Jaś. "Archaeologies and Agendas: Reflections on Late Ancient Jewish Art and Early Christian Art." *JRS* 93 (2003): 114–28.

Elsner, Jaś, and Ian Rutherford. *Pilgrimage in Graeco-Roman and Early Christian Antiquity: Seeing the Gods.* Oxford: Oxford University Press, 2005.

Emanuel, Madeleine. "The Utility of the Fractio Panis as Evidence in the Case for Women's Ordination." MA thesis, Claremont Graduate University, 2014.

Engberg, Jakob. "Martyrdom and Persecution: Pagan Perspectives on the Prosecution and Execution of Christians, c. 110–210 AD." Pages 93–117 in *Contextualising Early Christian Martyrdom.* Edited by Jacob Engberg, Uffe Homsgaard Eriksen, and Anders Klostergaard Petersen. Frankfurt: Peter Lang, 2011.

Falcasantos, Rebecca Stephens. "Pilgrim or Traveler? Constructions of Ancient Christian Pieties." Paper presented at the annual meeting of the North American Patristics Society, Chicago, May 2013.

Farrell, Joseph. "The Canonization of Perpetua." Pages 300–320 in Bremmer and Formisano, *Perpetua's Passions*.

Fiorenza, Elisabeth Schüssler. *In Memory of Her: A Feminist Theological Reconstruction of Christian Origins*. New York: Crossroad, 1983.

Frank, Georgia. "Pilgrimage." Pages 826–41 in *The Oxford Handbook of Early Christian Studies*. Edited by Susan Ashbrook Harvey and David G. Hunter. Oxford: Oxford University Press, 2008.

Frend, W. H. C. *Martyrdom and Persecution in the Early Church: A Study of a Conflict from the Maccabees to Donatus*. New York: New York University Press, 1965.

Gaventa, Beverly Roberts, and Cynthia L. Rigby, eds. *Blessed One: Protestant Perspectives on Mary*. Louisville: Westminster John Knox, 2002.

Gingras, George E., trans. *Egeria: Diary of a Pilgrimage*. ACW 38. New York: Newman, 1970.

Glancy, Jennifer A. *Slavery in Early Christianity*. Oxford: Oxford University Press, 2002.

Gold, Barbara K. "Gender Fluidity and Closure in Perpetua's Prison Diary." *Eugesta* 1 (2011): 237–51.

González, Justo L. *Mañana: Christian Theology from a Hispanic Perspective*. Nashville: Abingdon, 1990.

Goodine, Elizabeth A., and Matthew W. Mitchell. "The Persuasiveness of a Woman: The Mistranslation and Misinterpretation of Eusebius' *Historia Ecclesiastica* 5.1.41." *JECS* 13 (2005): 1–19.

Gorman, Michael J. *Reading Revelation Responsibly: Uncivil Worship and Witness; Following the Lamb into the New Creation*. Eugene, OR: Cascade, 2011.

Grafton, Anthony, and Megan Williams. *Christianity and the Transformation of the Book: Origen, Eusebius, and the Library of Caesarea*. Cambridge, MA: Harvard University Press, 2006.

Grant, Robert M. *Eusebius as Church Historian*. Eugene, OR: Wipf & Stock, 2006.

Grousset, René. *Histoire des croisades et du royaume franc de Jérusalem*. Vol. 2. Paris: Librarie Plon, 1935.

Hachlili, Rachel. *Ancient Synagogues—Archaeology and Art: New Discoveries and Current Research*. Handbuch der Orientalistik 105. Leiden: Brill, 2013.

Haines-Eitzen, Kim. *The Gendered Palimpsest: Women, Writing, and Representation in Early Christianity*. Oxford: Oxford University Press, 2012.

Harvey, Susan Ashbrook. "Women and Word: Texts by and about Women." Pages 382–90 in *The Cambridge History of Early Christian Literature*. Edited by Frances Young, Lewis Ayres, and Andrew Louth. Cambridge: Cambridge University Press, 2004.

Heffernan, Thomas J. *The Passion of Perpetua and Felicity*. Oxford: Oxford University Press, 2012.

Heine, Susanne. *Women and Early Christianity: Are the Feminist Scholars Right?* Translated by John Bowden. London: SCM, 1987.

Henten, Jan Willem van. "Jewish and Christian Martyrs." Pages 163–81 in *Saints and Role Models in Judaism and Christianity*. Edited by Marcel Poorthuis and Joshua Schwartz. Leiden: Brill, 2004.

Herzfeld, Ernst, and Samuel Guyer. *Meriamlik und Korykos: Zwei christliche Ruinenstätten des rauhen Kilikiens*. MAMA 2. Manchester: Manchester University Press, 1930.

Hoffman, Daniel L. *The Status of Women and Gnosticism in Irenaeus and Tertullian*. SWR 36. Lewiston, NY: Edwin Mellen, 1995.

Holum, Kenneth G. *Theodosian Empresses: Women and Imperial Dominion in Late Antiquity*. Transformation of the Classical Heritage 3. Berkeley: University of California Press, 1982.

Hughes, Amy Brown. "'Chastely, I Live for Thee': Virginity as Bondage and Freedom in Origen of Alexandria, Methodius of Olympus, and Gregory of Nyssa." PhD diss., Wheaton College, 2013.

———. "The Legacy of the Feminine in the Christology of Origen of Alexandria, Methodius of Olympus, and Gregory of Nyssa." *VC* 69 (2015): 1–26.

———. "Responsible Remembrance: Rethinking Persecution and Martyrdom in the Early Church." *Books & Culture* (November/December 2014): 8–9. http://www.books andculture.com/articles/2014/novdec/responsible-remembrance.html?paging=off.

Humphrey, Edith M. *Joseph and Aseneth*. Sheffield: Sheffield Academic, 2000.

Hunt, E. D. "The Itinerary of Egeria: Reliving the Bible in Fourth-Century Palestine." Pages 34–54 in *The Holy Land, Holy Lands, and Christian History*. Edited by R. N. Swanson. SCH 36. Rochester, NY: Boydell, 2000.

Hunter, David G. *Marriage, Celibacy, and Heresy in Ancient Christianity: The Jovinianist Controversy*. OECS. Oxford: Oxford University Press, 2007.

Huskinson, Janet. "Women and Learning: Gender and Identity in Scenes of Intellectual Life on Late Roman Sarcophagi." Pages 190–213 in Miles, *Constructing Identities in Late Antiquity*.

Hylen, Susan E. *A Modest Apostle: Thecla and the History of Women in the Early Church*. Oxford: Oxford University Press, 2015.

Irwin, M. Eleanor. "Eudocia Augusta, Aelia." Pages 193–95 in Taylor and Choi, *Handbook of Women Biblical Interpreters*.

Jacobs, Andrew S. "'Her Own Proper Kinship': Marriage, Class and Women in the Apocryphal Acts of the Apostles." Pages 18–46 in *A Feminist Companion to the New Testament Apocrypha*. Edited by Amy-Jill Levine with Maria Mayo Robbins. FCNTECW 11. New York: T&T Clark, 2006.

————. "'The Most Beautiful Jewesses in the Land': Imperial Travel in the Early Christian Holy Land." *Religion* 32 (2002): 205–25.

James, Liz. "The Empress and the Virgin in Early Byzantium: Piety, Authority, and Devotion." Pages 145–52 in *Images of the Mother of God: Perceptions of the Theotokos in Byzantium*. Edited by Maria Vassilaki. Aldershot: Ashgate, 2005.

————. *Empresses and Power in Early Byzantium*. Women, Power, and Politics. New York: Leicester University Press, 2001.

Jensen, Robin M. "Compiling Narratives: The Visual Strategies of Early Christian Visual Art." *JECS* 23.1 (2015): 1–26.

————. "Dining in Heaven: The Earliest Christian Visions of Paradise." *BRev* 14.5 (1998): 32–39.

————. "Early Christian Art and Divine Epiphany." *TJT* 28 (2012): 125–44.

————. *Understanding Early Christian Art*. New York: Routledge, 2000. Repr., 2007.

Kates, Joan Giangrasse. "Marie Wilkinson, Civil Rights Activist, Dies at Age 101." *Chicago Tribune*, August 17, 2010. http://articles.chicagotribune.com/2010-08-17/features/ct-met-wilkinson-obit-0818-20100817_1_aurora-alderman-aurora-mayor-tom-weisner-quad-county-urban-league.

Katos, Demetrios S. *Palladius of Helenopolis: The Origenist Advocate*. OECS. Oxford: Oxford University Press, 2011.

Kenaan, Vered Lev. *Pandora's Senses: The Feminine Character of the Ancient Text*. Wisconsin Studies in Classics. Madison: University of Wisconsin Press, 2008.

Kienzle, Beverly Mayne, and Pamela J. Walker. *Women Preachers and Prophets through Two Millennia of Christianity*. Berkeley: University of California Press, 1998.

König, Jason. *Saints and Symposiasts: The Literature of Food and the Symposium in Greco-Roman and Early Christian Culture*. Greek Culture in the Roman World. Cambridge: Cambridge University Press, 2012.

Kraemer, Ross Shepard. *Unreliable Witnesses: Religion, Gender, and History in the Greco-Roman Mediterranean*. Oxford: Oxford University Press, 2011.

————, ed. *Women's Religions in the Greco-Roman World: A Sourcebook*. Oxford: Oxford University Press, 2004.

Kraemer, Ross S., and Shira L. Lander. "Perpetua and Felicitas." Pages 1048–68 in vol. 2 of *The Early Christian World*. Edited by Philip F. Esler. London: Routledge, 2000.

Krueger, Derek. "Writing and the Liturgy of Memory in Gregory of Nyssa's *Life of Macrina*." *JECS* 8 (2000): 483–510.

Lancel, Serge. *Saint Augustine*. Translated by Antonia Nevill. London: SCM, 2002.

Lander, Shira L. "Ritual Power in Society: Ritualizing Late Antique North African Martyr Cult Activities and Social Changes in Gender and Status." PhD diss., University of Pennsylvania, 2002.

Layton, Bentley. *The Gnostic Scriptures: A New Translation with Annotations and Introductions*. Garden City, NY: Doubleday, 1987.

Lefkowitz, Mary R., and Maureen B. Fant. *Women's Life in Greece and Rome: A Source Book in Translation*. Baltimore: Johns Hopkins University Press, 1982.

Lenski, Noel. "Empresses in the Holy Land: The Creation of a Christian Utopia in Late Antique Palestine." Pages 113–24 in *Travel, Communication and Geography in Late Antiquity: Sacred and Profane*. Edited by Linda Ellis and Frank L. Kidner. Aldershot: Ashgate, 2004.

Levine, Amy-Jill, and Maria Mayo Robbins, eds. *A Feminist Companion to Mariology*. FCNTECW 10. London: T&T Clark, 2005.

Limberis, Vasiliki. *Architects of Piety: The Cappadocian Fathers and the Cult of the Martyrs*. New York: Oxford University Press, 2011.

———. *Divine Heiress: The Virgin Mary and the Creation of Christian Constantinople*. London: Routledge, 1994.

Limor, Ora. "Reading Sacred Space: Egeria, Paula, and the Christian Holy Land." *Revue augustiniennes* 18 (1972): 209–18. Reprinted as pages 1–15 in vol. 1 of *De Sion exibit lex et verbum domini de Hierusalem: Essays on Medieval Law, Liturgy, and Literature in Honour of Amnon Linder*. Edited by Yitzhak Hen. Cultural Encounters in Late Antiquity and the Middle Ages 1. Turnhout: Brepols, 2001.

Lock, Peter. *The Routledge Companion to the Crusades*. New York: Routledge, 2006.

Ludlow, Morwenna. *Gregory of Nyssa: Ancient and (Post)modern*. Oxford: Oxford University Press, 2007.

Madigan, Kevin, and Carolyn Osiek, eds. and trans. *Ordained Women in the Early Church: A Documentary History*. Baltimore: Johns Hopkins University Press, 2005.

Marjanen, Antti. "Male Women Martyrs: The Function of Gender-Transformation Language in Early Christian Martyrdom Accounts." Pages 231–47 in *Metamorphoses: Resurrection, Body and Transformative Practices in Early Christianity*. Edited by Turid Karlsen Seim and Jorunn Økland. Ekstasis 1. Berlin: de Gruyter, 2009.

Markus, R. A. "How on Earth Could Places Become Holy? Origins of the Christian Idea of Holy Places." *JECS* 2 (1994): 257–71.

Matthews, Shelly. "Thinking of Thecla: Issues in Feminist Historiography." *JFSR* 17 (2001): 39–55.

McGill, Scott. "Virgil, Christianity, and the *Cento Probae*. Pages 173–93 in *Texts and Culture in Late Antiquity: Inheritance, Authority, and Change*. Edited by J. H. D. Scourfield. Swansea: Classical Press of Wales, 2007.

———. *Virgil Recomposed: The Mythological and Secular Centos in Antiquity*. American Classical Studies 48. Oxford: Oxford University Press, 2005.

McGuckin, John Anthony. *St. Cyril of Alexandria: The Christological Controversy; Its History, Theology, and Texts*. Crestwood, NY: St. Vladimir's Seminary Press, 2004.

McGuire, Anne. "Gnosis and Nag Hammadi." Pages 204–26 in *The Routledge Companion to Early Christian Thought*. Edited by D. Jeffrey Bingham. New York: Routledge, 2010.

————. "Women, Gender, and Gnosis in Gnostic Texts and Traditions. Pages 257–99 in *Women and Christian Origins*. Edited by Ross S. Kraemer and Mary Rose D'Angelo. Oxford: Oxford University Press, 1999.

McKnight, Scot. *The Real Mary: Why Evangelical Christians Can Embrace the Mother of Jesus*. Brewster, MA: Paraclete, 2007.

Meconi, David Vincent. "The Christian Cento and the Evangelization of Christian Culture." *Logos* 7 (2004): 109–32.

Miles, Richard, ed. *Constructing Identities in Late Antiquity*. Routledge Classical Monographs. New York: Routledge, 1999.

Miller, Patricia Cox. *Women in Early Christianity: Translations from Greek Texts*. Washington, DC: Catholic University of America Press, 2005.

Milnor, Kristina. *Gender, Domesticity, and the Age of Augustus: Inventing Private Life*. Oxford: Oxford University Press, 2005.

Moore, Rebecca. "Oh Mother, Where Art Thou? In Search of Saint Monnica." Pages 147–66 in J. Stark, *Feminist Interpretations of Augustine*.

Moriarty, Rachel. "'Secular Men and Women': Egeria's Lay Congregation in Jerusalem." Pages 55–66 in *The Holy Land, Holy Lands, and Christian History*. Edited by R. N Swanson. SCH 36. Rochester, NY: Boydell, 2000.

Moss, Candida R. *Ancient Christian Martyrdom: Diverse Practices, Theologies, and Traditions*. AYBRL. New Haven: Yale University Press, 2012.

————. "The Discourse of Voluntary Martyrdom: Ancient and Modern." *CH* 81.3 (2012): 531–51.

————. *The Myth of Persecution: How Early Christians Invented a Story of Martyrdom*. New York: HarperOne, 2013.

Musurillo, Herbert, trans. *St. Methodius: The Symposium; A Treatise on Chastity*. ACW 27. Westminster, MD: Newman, 1958.

Nestori, Aldo. *Repertorio topografico delle pitture delle catacombe romane*. 2nd ed. Rome: Pontificio Istituto di Archeologia Cristiana, 1993.

Newman, Sharan. *Defending the City of God: A Medieval Queen, the First Crusades, and the Quest for Peace in Jerusalem*. New York: Palgrave Macmillan, 2014.

Ng, Esther Yue L. "*Acts of Paul and Thecla*: Women's Stories and Precedent?" *JTS* 55 (2004): 1–29.

Osiek, Carolyn. "Perpetua's Husband." *JECS* 10 (2002): 287–90.

Pagels, Elaine H. *The Gnostic Gospels*. New York: Random House, 1979.

Parvis, Sara. "Perpetua." *ExpTim* 120.8 (2009): 365–72.

Patterson, Lloyd George. *Methodius of Olympus: Divine Sovereignty, Human Freedom, and Life in Christ*. Washington, DC: Catholic University of America Press, 1997.

Pease, A. S. "Notes on Jerome's Tractates on the Psalms." *JBL* 26 (1907): 107–31.

Perkins, Judith. *The Suffering Self: Pain and Narrative Representation in the Early Christian Era*. New York: Routledge, 1995.

Perry, Tim S. *Mary for Evangelicals: Toward an Understanding of the Mother of Our Lord*. Downers Grove, IL: IVP Academic, 2006.

Power, Kim. *Veiled Desire: Augustine on Women*. New York: Continuum, 1996.

Price, Richard M. "Martyrdom and the Cult of the Saints." Pages 808–25 in *The Oxford Handbook of Early Christian Studies*. Edited by Susan Ashbrook Harvey and David G. Hunter. Oxford: Oxford University Press, 2008.

Quinn, John M. *A Companion to the* Confessions *of St. Augustine*. New York: Peter Lang, 2002.

Rajak, Tessa. "Dying for the Law: The Martyr's Portrait in Jewish-Greek Literature." Pages 39–67 in *Portraits: Biographical Representation in the Greek and Latin Literature of the Roman Empire*. Edited by M. J. Edwards and Simon Swain. Oxford: Clarendon, 1997.

———. *The Jewish Dialogue with Greece and Rome: Studies in Cultural and Social Interaction*. Leiden: Brill, 2002.

Ramsey, William M. *The Church in the Roman Empire before A.D. 170*. New York: Putnam's Sons, 1892.

Rapp, Claudia. *Holy Bishops in Late Antiquity: The Nature of Christian Leadership in an Age of Transition*. Berkeley: University of California Press, 2005.

Rebenich, Stefan. *Jerome*. ECF. London: Routledge, 2002.

Rhee, Helen. *Early Christian Literature: Christ and Culture in the Second and Third Centuries*. New York: Routledge, 2005.

———. *Loving the Poor, Saving the Rich: Wealth, Poverty, and Early Christian Formation*. Grand Rapids: Baker Academic, 2012.

Rollins, Rebecca T. "The Singing of Women in the Early Christian Church: Why It Occurred, Why It Disappeared." DMA thesis, Claremont Graduate School, 1988.

Ronsse, Erin. "Rhetoric of Martyrs: Listening to Saints Perpetua and Felicitas." *JECS* 14 (2006): 283–327.

Röwekamp, G. "Gregory of Nyssa." Pages 263–66 in *Dictionary of Early Christian Literature*. Edited by Siegmar Döpp and Wilhelm Geerlings. New York: Crossroad, 2000.

Rubery, Eileen. "From Catacomb to Sanctuary: The Orant Figure and the Cults of the Mother of God and S. Agnes in Early Christian Rome, with Special Reference to Gold Glass." Pages 129–74 in *Papers Presented at the Conference on Early Christian Iconography, Held in Pècs, Hungary*. Edited by Allen Brent and Markus Vinzent. StPatr 73. Leuven: Peeters, 2014.

Rutgers, Leonard V. *The Jews in Late Ancient Rome: Evidence of Cultural Interaction in the Roman Diaspora*. Leiden: Brill, 2000.

Salisbury, Joyce E. *Perpetua's Passion: The Death and Memory of a Young Roman Woman*. New York: Routledge, 1997.

Salvadori, Sharon Marie. "*Per Feminam Mors, Per Feminam Vita*: Images of Women in the Early Christian Funerary Art of Rome." PhD diss., New York University, 2002.

Sandnes, Karl Olav. *The Gospel "According to Homer and Virgil": Cento and Canon.* NovTSup 138. Leiden: Brill, 2011.

Scott, Joan Wallach. *Gender and the Politics of History.* Rev. ed. New York: Columbia University Press, 1999.

Shaw, Brent D. "The Passion of Perpetua." *Past and Present* 139 (1993): 3–45.

Shepardson, Christine. "Posthumous Orthodoxy." Pages 186–201 in Chin and Schroeder, *Melania.*

Sigismund-Nielsen, Hanne. "Vibia Perpetua—an Indecent Woman." Pages 103–17 in Bremmer and Formisano, *Perpetua's Passions.*

Silvas, Anna M., trans. *The Life of Macrina.* In *Macrina the Younger, Philosopher of God.* Medieval Women: Texts and Contexts 22. Turnhout: Brepols, 2008.

Sivan, Hagith. "Holy Land Pilgrimage and Western Audiences: Some Reflections on Egeria and Her Circle." *ClQ* 38 (1988): 528–35.

———. "Who Was Egeria? Piety and Pilgrimage in the Age of Gratian." *HTR* 81 (1988): 59–72.

Smith, Eric C. "Mimicry, Mirroring, Subversion, and Critique: Reading Heterotopia in the Cubicula of the Sacraments." PhD diss., University of Denver and the Iliff School of Theology, 2013.

Smith, Jonathan Z. *To Take Place: Toward Theory in Ritual.* CSHJ. Chicago: University of Chicago Press, 1987.

Smith, Julie Ann. "'My Lord's Native Land': Mapping the Christian Holy Land." *CH* 76 (2007): 1–31.

Snyder, Glenn E. *Acts of Paul: The Formation of a Pauline Corpus.* WUNT 2/352. Tübingen: Mohr Siebeck, 2013.

Solevåg, Anna Rebecca. *Birthing Salvation: Gender and Class in Early Christian Childbearing Discourse.* BibInt 121. Leiden: Brill, 2013.

Soskice, Janet. *The Sisters of Sinai: How Two Lady Adventurers Discovered the Hidden Gospels.* New York: Knopf, 2009.

Sowers, Brian Patrick. "Eudocia: The Making of a Homeric Christian." PhD diss., University of Cincinnati, 2008.

Spitzer, Leo. "The Epic Style of the Pilgrim Aetheria." *Comparative Literature* 1 (1949): 225–58.

Stafford, Pauline. "Emma: The Powers of the Queen in the Eleventh Century." Pages 3–26 in *Queens and Queenship in Medieval Europe: Proceedings of a Conference Held at King's College London, April 1995.* Edited by Anne J. Duggan. Rochester, NY: Boydell, 1997.

Stark, Judith Chelius, ed. *Feminist Interpretations of Augustine.* Re-reading the Canon. University Park: Pennsylvania State University Press, 2007.

Stark, Rodney. *The Rise of Christianity: A Sociologist Reconsiders History.* Princeton: Princeton University Press, 1996.

Sutherland, Reita J. "Prayer and Piety: The *Orans*-Figure in the Christian Catacombs of Rome." MA thesis, University of Ottawa, 2013.

Swearingen, Carrie. "She Opens Doors: Marie Wilkinson." *St. Anthony Messenger*, May 2002. https://www.franciscanmedia.org/she-opens-doors-marie-wilkinson/.

Taylor, Joan E. *Christians and the Holy Places: The Myth of Jewish-Christian Origins.* Oxford: Clarendon, 1993.

Taylor, Marion Ann, and Agnes Choi, eds. *Handbook of Women Biblical Interpreters: A Historical and Biographical Guide.* Grand Rapids: Baker Academic, 2012.

Tilley, M. A. "One Woman's Body: Repression and Expression in the *Passio Perpetuae*." Pages 57–72 in *Ethnicity, Nationality and Religious Experience*. Edited by P. C. Phan. The Annual Publication of the College Theology Society 37. Lanham, MD: University Press of America, 1995.

Tolbert, Mary Ann. "Defining the Problem: The Bible and Feminist Hermeneutics." Pages 113–26 in *The Bible and Feminist Hermeneutics*. Edited by Mary Ann Tolbert. Semeia 28. Chico, CA: Scholars Press, 1983.

Torjesen, Karen Jo. "The Early Christian *Orans*: An Artistic Representation of Women's Liturgical Prayer and Prophecy." Pages 42–56 in Kienzle and Valker, *Women Preachers and Prophets through Two Millennia of Christianity*.

———. *When Women Were Priests: Women's Leadership in the Early Church and the Scandal of Their Subordination in the Rise of Christianity*. San Francisco: HarperSanFrancisco, 1993.

Toynbee, J. M. C. *Death and Burial in the Roman World*. Baltimore: Johns Hopkins University Press, 1971.

Tulloch, Janet H. "Art and Archaeology as an Historical Resource for the Study of Women in Early Christianity: An Approach for Analyzing Visual Data." *Feminist Theology* 12 (2004): 277–304.

———. "Image as Artifact: A Social-Historical Analysis of Female Figures with Cups in the Banquet Scenes from the Catacomb of SS. Marcellino e Pietro, Rome." PhD diss., University of Ottawa, 2001.

Usher, M. D. *Homeric Stitchings: The Homeric Centos of the Empress Eudocia*. Greek Studies: Interdisciplinary Approaches. Lanham, MD: Rowman & Littlefield, 1998.

Van Dam, Raymond. *Becoming Christian: The Conversion of Roman Cappadocia*. Philadelphia: University of Pennsylvania Press, 2003.

———. *Families and Friends in Late Roman Cappadocia*. Philadelphia: University of Pennsylvania Press, 2003.

———. *Kingdom of Snow: Roman Rule and Greek Culture in Cappadocia*. Philadelphia: University of Pennsylvania Press, 2002.

Van Sleet, Susan. *Mary and Me beyond the Canvas: An Extraordinary Story of Adoption, Loss, and Reunion*. Denver: Outskirts Press, 2013.

Vogt, Kari. "'Becoming Male': One Aspect of an Early Christian Anthropology." *Concilium: International Journal for Theology* 182 (1985): 72–83.

Waugh, Evelyn. *Helena*. New York: Penguin, 1963.

Wessel, Susan. "Memory and Individuality in Gregory of Nyssa's *Dialogus de anima et resurrectione*." *JECS* 18 (2010): 369–92.

Wijngaards, John. *No Women in Holy Orders? The Women Deacons of the Early Church*. Norwich: Canterbury, 2002.

Wilkinson, Kate. *Women and Modesty in Late Antiquity*. Cambridge: Cambridge University Press, 2015.

Wilkinson, Kevin. "The Elder Melania's Missing Decade." *JLA* 5 (2012): 166–84.

Wilson-Kastner, Patricia, G. Ronald Kastner, Ann Millin, Rosemary Rader, and Jeremiah Reedy. *A Lost Tradition: Women Writers of the Early Church*. Washington, DC: University Press of America, 1981.

Young, Robin Darling. *In Procession before the World: Martyrdom as Public Liturgy in Early Christianity*. Milwaukee: Marquette University Press, 2001.

———. "A Life in Letters." Pages 153–70 in Chin and Schroeder, *Melania*.

# Index of Ancient Sources

# Index of Subjects

Abraham, 20n38, 73, 78–79, 200
Adam, 73, 229
Adeodatus (son of Augustine), 180–81
Aelia Flaccilla, 125n60, 223n6
Africa, 34n28, 57n91, 77n41, 185, 187, 212n96, 213n99, 214. *See also* North Africa
agency, xxii–xxiii, xxv, 9–10, 14, 29, 97n12, 149n68, 152, 194
Agnes, Saint, xxxv n32, 87
Agrippina the Younger, 152n83
Albina (mother of Melania the Younger), 209, 211–12, 214–15
Alexander (bishop of Alexandria), 92
Alexander of Antioch, 5, 11, 15
Alexander of Cappadocia, 132, 139
Alexandria, 23, 54, 128–29, 205, 208, 227, 234, 236, 247
Alypius (bishop of Thagaste), 181, 211–13
Ambrose (bishop of Milan), 83, 87, 111–13, 119–20, 123–24, 175n56, 183
Anthemius, 224, 226
Antioch
  Pisidian, 8
  Syrian, xxxvi, 5–6, 11–12, 14, 114n21, 129, 136, 146–47, 199, 242–43, 247
Antiochus (Theodosius II's tutor), 225
Antiochus IV Epiphanes, 30, 34
*aphtharsia*, 98n18
apostolic succession, 93–95, 98, 102
Arcadia (daughter of Emperor Arcadius and Empress Eudoxia), 223, 233
Arcadius (emperor), 140n40, 223–24
"Archvirgin," Christ as, 102

Arete, 101–2
Arian controversy, 87, 100. *See also* Arius
Arianism, 117n30, 124
  and Constantius II (emperor), 87
  and Valens (emperor), 143, 164, 206, 208
  *See also* Arius
aristocracy
  female/woman, 190–94, 196, 201
  Roman, 111, 113, 149, 159, 167n29, 190, 194, 199, 204, 209, 210n82, 210n84, 211–12, 213n101, 214, 237
aristocrats-turned-ascetics, xx, xxxi, xxxvi, xxxviii, 189, 205n60, 211–15, 217
Arius, 89, 92, 131, 196n16
  and Arian faction, 181, 196
  *See also* Arian controversy; Arianism
art
  burial, xxix, 69–70, 74, 77–79, 87
  Christian imperial, 75, 77, 231
  funerary, 70, 76–78, 84–86, 145
asceticism, xix, xx, xxvii, xxix, xxxv, 1–3, 7, 36n39, 158–60, 162, 165, 170, 174, 190–91, 194, 197–98, 201, 204, 209n82, 211, 217, 244n80
  ethic of, 32, 201, 204n57
  ideal of, 160, 171n45, 199, 217, 253
  life of, xxix–xxxi, 3, 11, 21, 23–24, 78, 99, 140, 148, 158–59, 166, 171, 173, 180, 198–99, 210, 215, 217, 244–45, 247, 252–53
  message of, 3
  as movement, 90
  philosophical, 160
  practice of, 190–92, 194, 198, 204, 206n65, 244

285